FRANK MILLER'S

SIN CITY ®

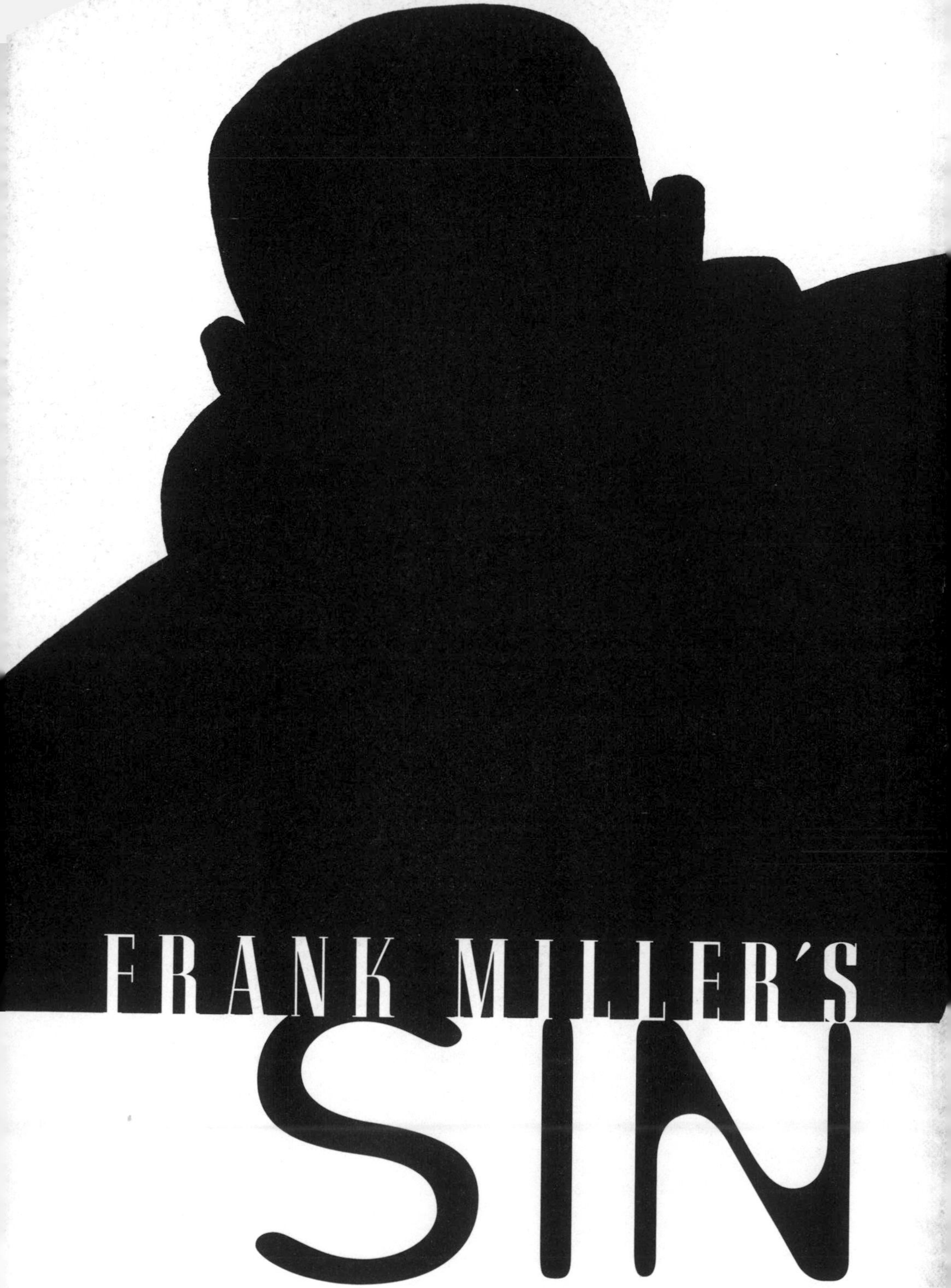

FRANK MILLER'S SIN

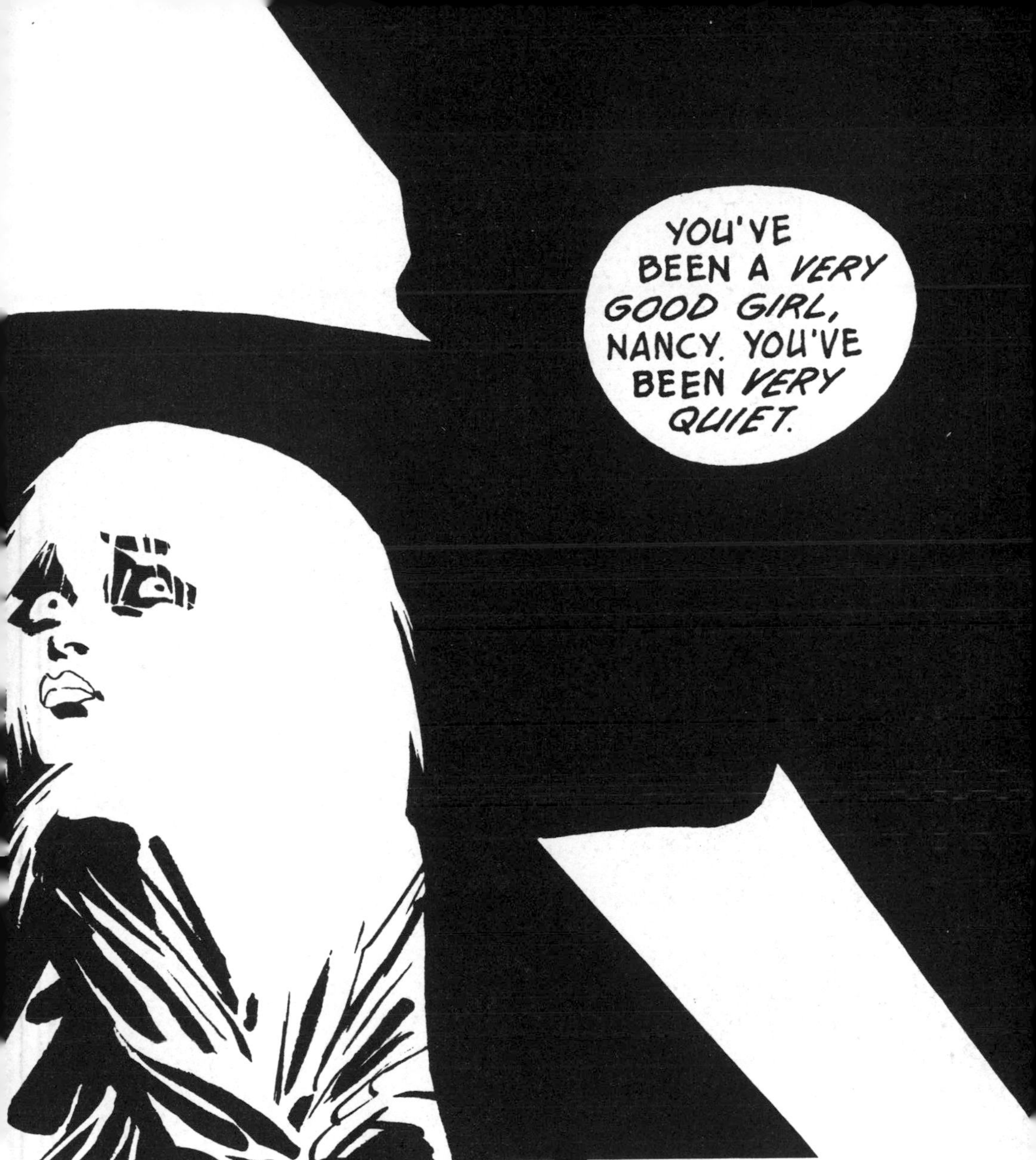
YOU'VE BEEN A *VERY* GOOD GIRL, NANCY. YOU'VE BEEN *VERY* QUIET.

CITY®

THAT YELLOW BASTARD

DARK HORSE BOOKS™

publisher
MIKE RICHARDSON

editor
BOB SCHRECK

cover gallery color
LYNN VARLEY

sin city classic logo design
STEVE MILLER

cover design
CHIP KIDD

book design
MARK COX
CHIP KIDD
LIA RIBACCHI

FRANK MILLER'S SIN CITY® VOLUME 4: THAT YELLOW BASTARD

This volume collects issues one through six of the Dark Horse comic book series *Sin City: That Yellow Bastard*.

Published by
Dark Horse Books
A division of Dark Horse Comics, Inc.
10956 SE Main Street
Milwaukie, Oregon 97222

darkhorse.com

Second Edition: February 2005
ISBN 1-59307-296-1

2 3 4 5 6 7 8 9 10

Printed in Canada

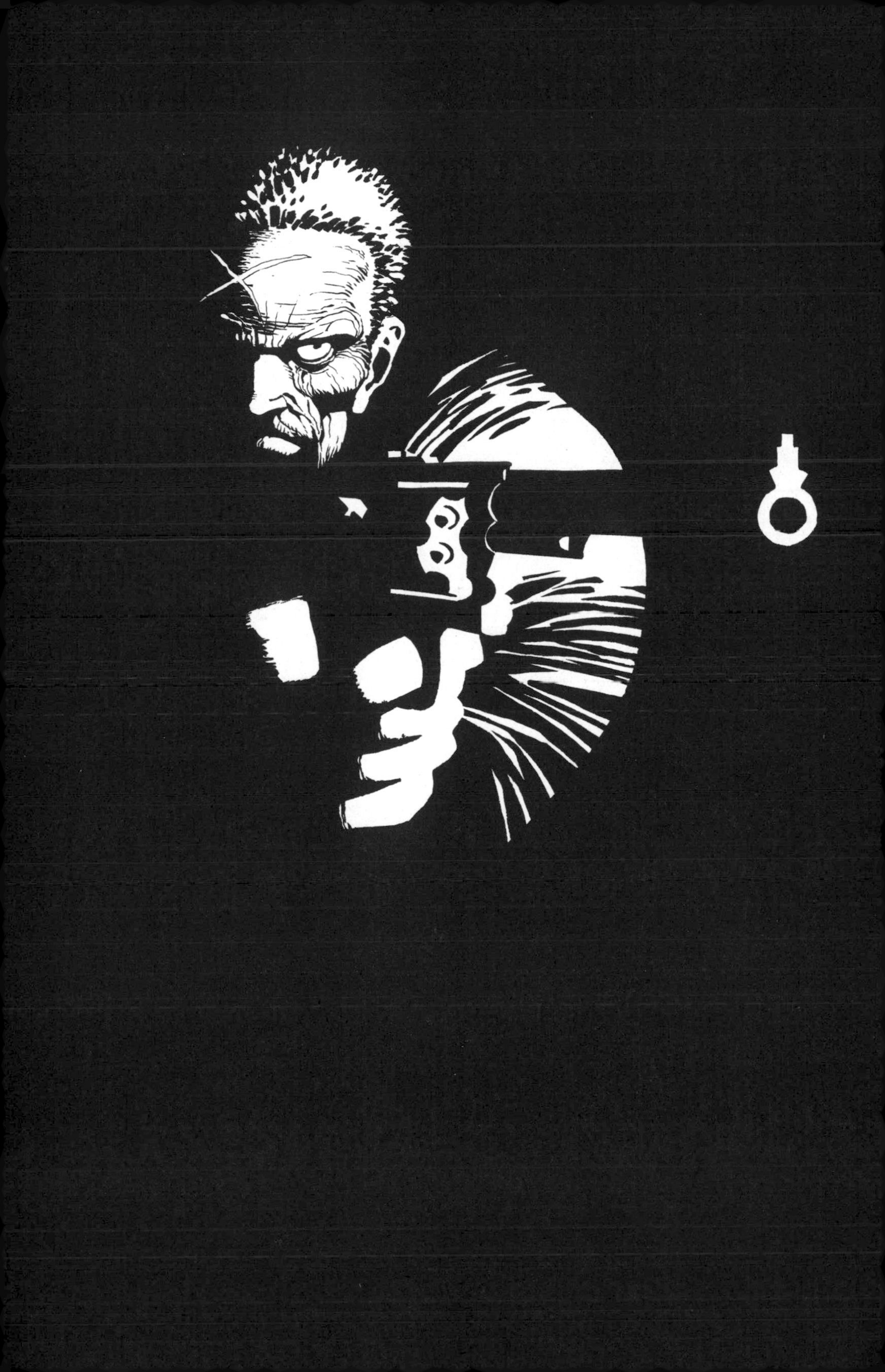

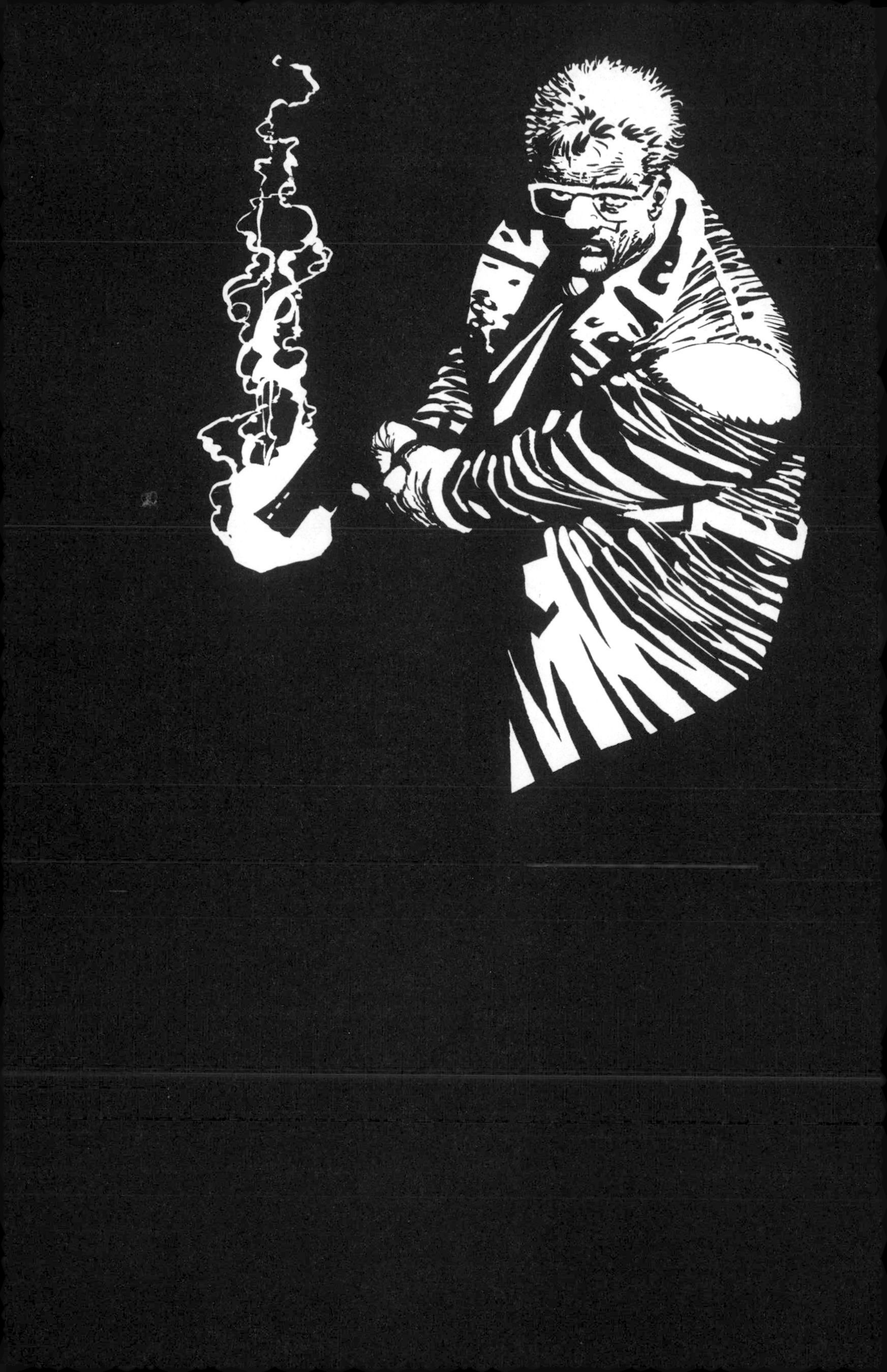

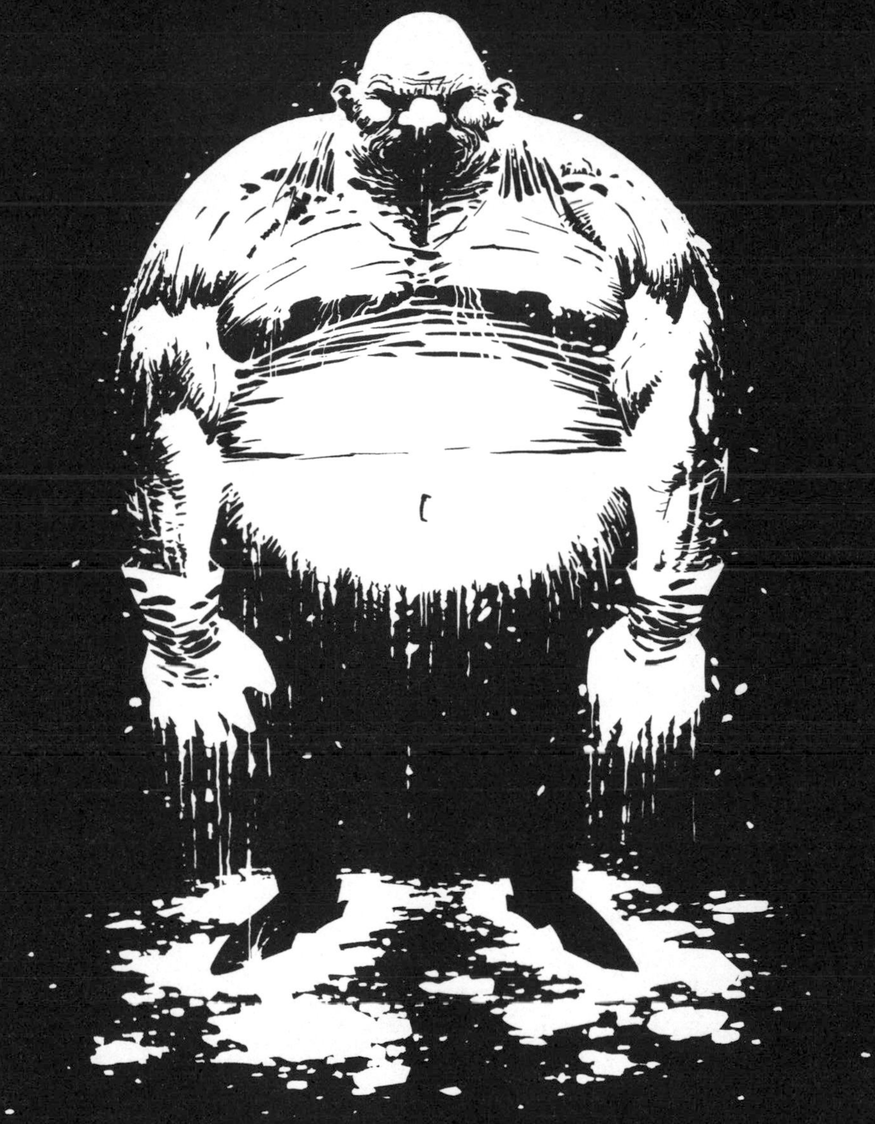

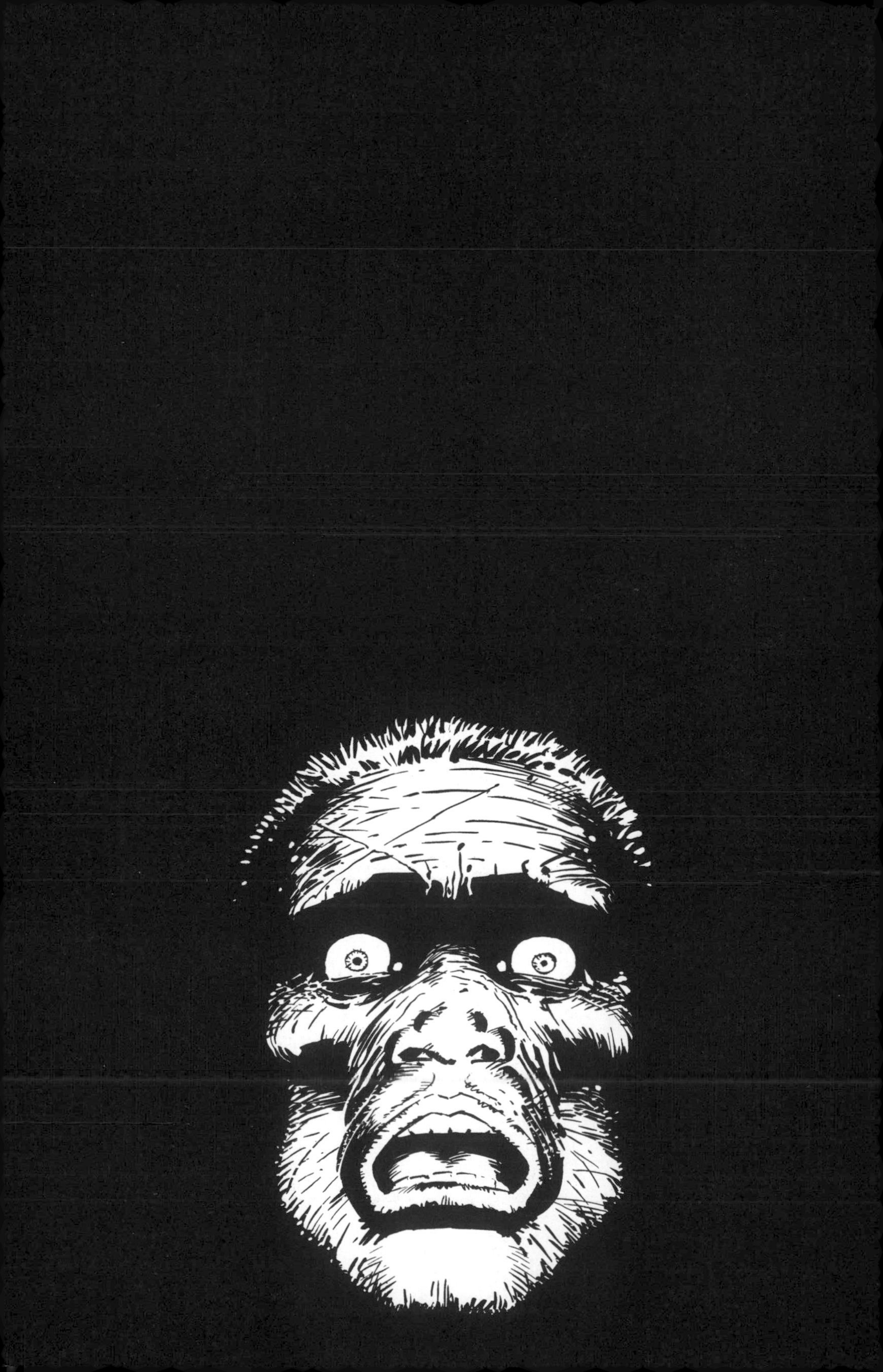

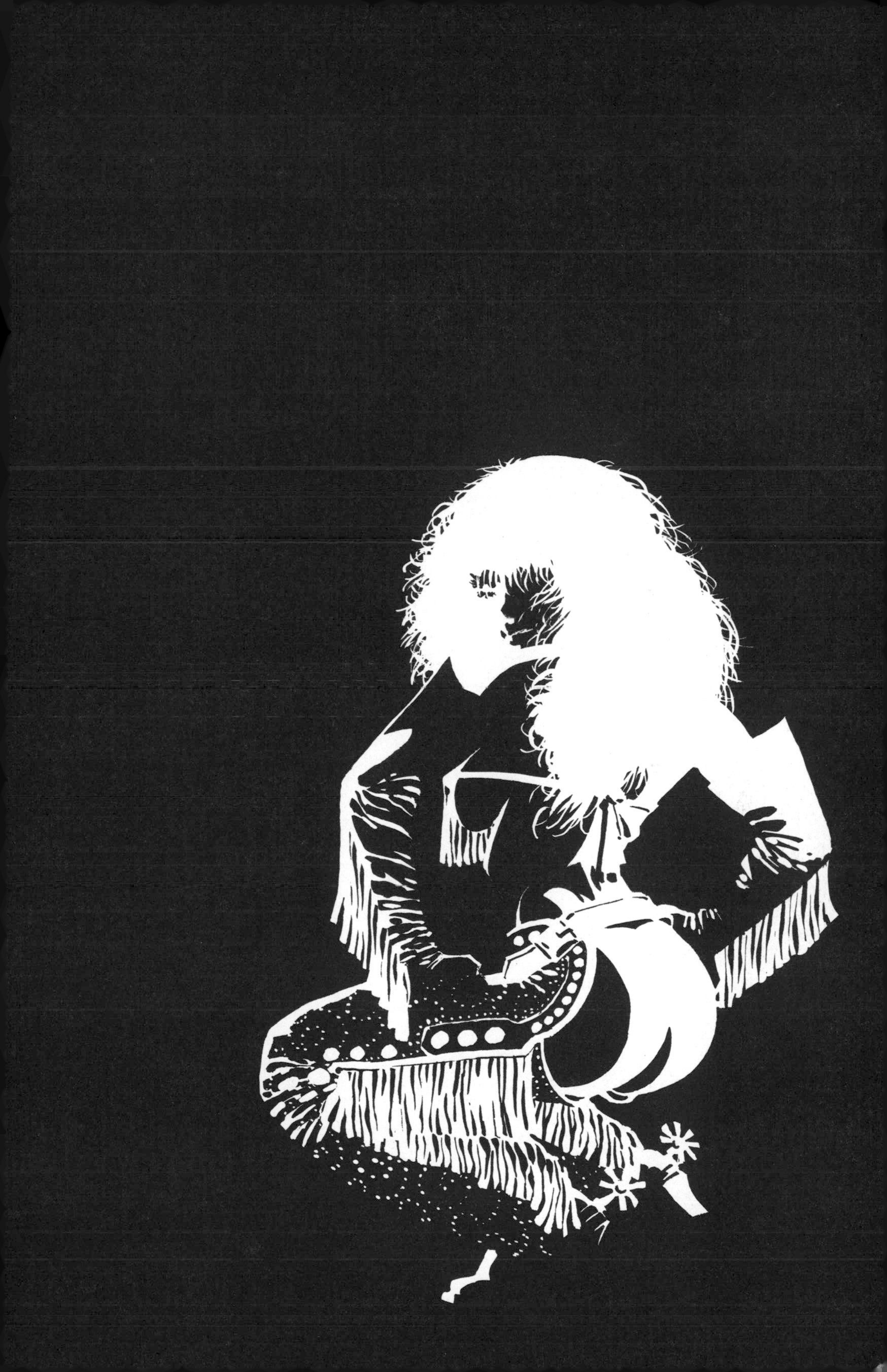

CHAPTER ONE

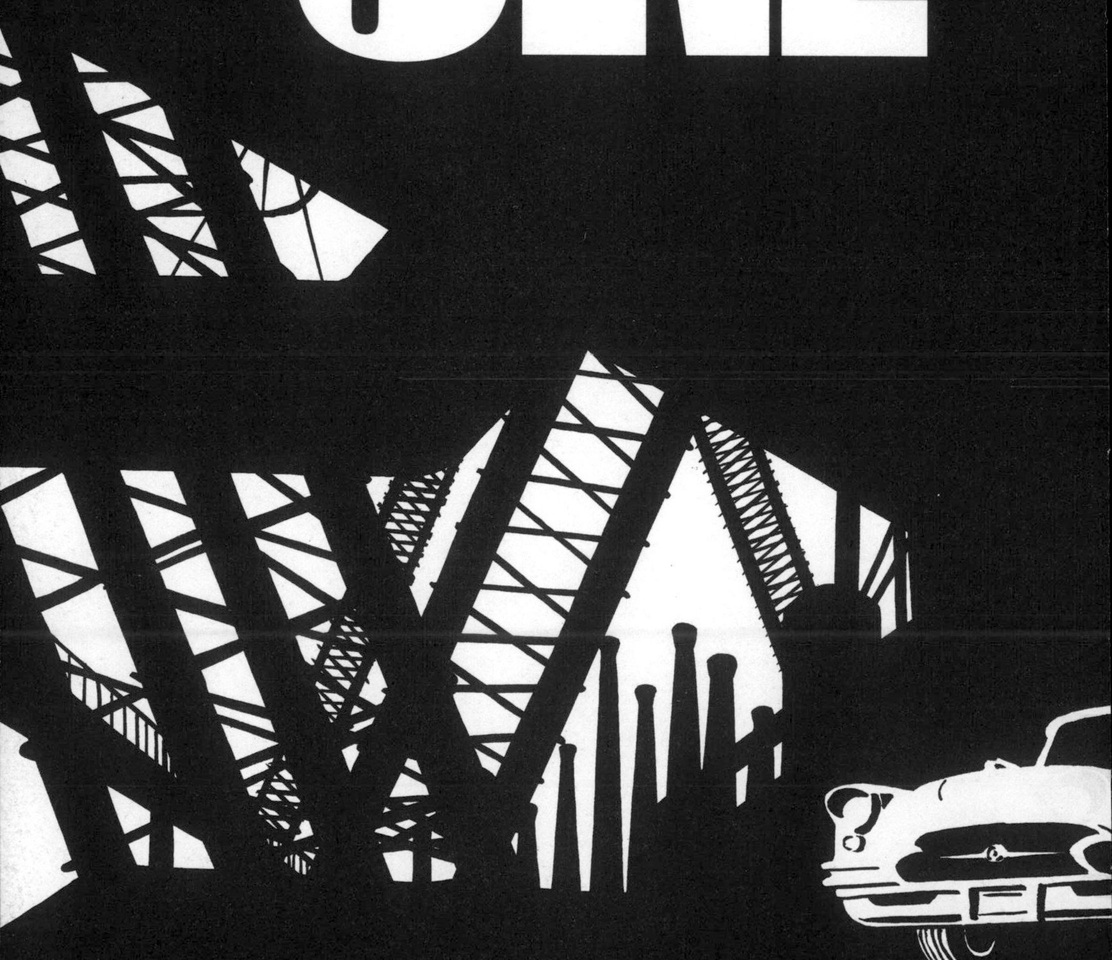

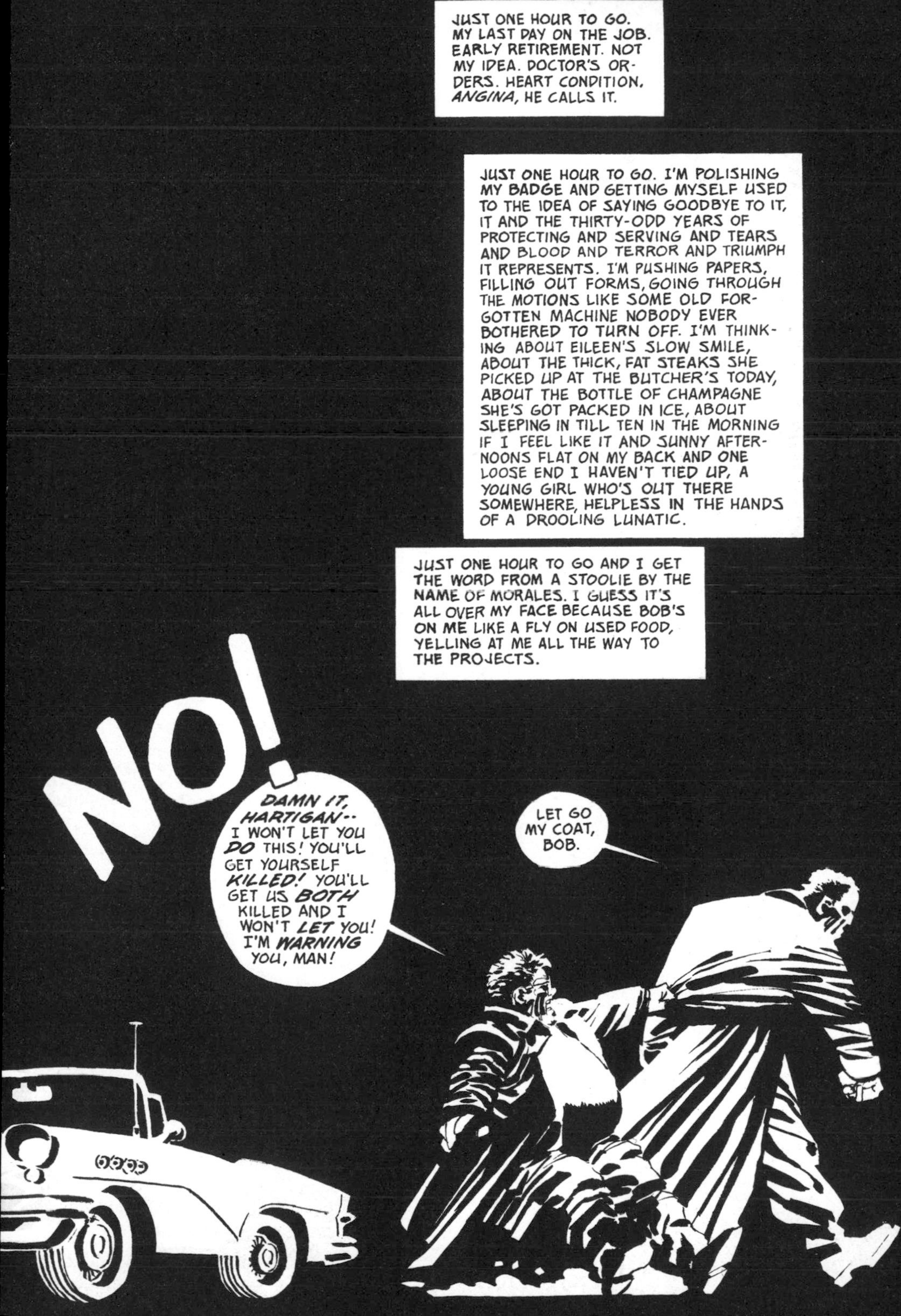

JUST ONE HOUR TO GO. MY LAST DAY ON THE JOB. EARLY RETIREMENT. NOT MY IDEA. DOCTOR'S ORDERS. HEART CONDITION. *ANGINA*, HE CALLS IT.
JUST ONE HOUR TO GO. I'M POLISHING MY BADGE AND GETTING MYSELF USED TO THE IDEA OF SAYING GOODBYE TO IT, IT AND THE THIRTY-ODD YEARS OF PROTECTING AND SERVING AND TEARS AND BLOOD AND TERROR AND TRIUMPH IT REPRESENTS. I'M PUSHING PAPERS, FILLING OUT FORMS, GOING THROUGH THE MOTIONS LIKE SOME OLD FORGOTTEN MACHINE NOBODY EVER BOTHERED TO TURN OFF. I'M THINKING ABOUT EILEEN'S SLOW SMILE, ABOUT THE THICK, FAT STEAKS SHE PICKED UP AT THE BUTCHER'S TODAY, ABOUT THE BOTTLE OF CHAMPAGNE SHE'S GOT PACKED IN ICE, ABOUT SLEEPING IN TILL TEN IN THE MORNING IF I FEEL LIKE IT AND SUNNY AFTERNOONS FLAT ON MY BACK AND ONE LOOSE END I HAVEN'T TIED UP, A YOUNG GIRL WHO'S OUT THERE SOMEWHERE, HELPLESS IN THE HANDS OF A DROOLING LUNATIC.
JUST ONE HOUR TO GO AND I GET THE WORD FROM A STOOLIE BY THE NAME OF MORALES. I GUESS IT'S ALL OVER MY FACE BECAUSE BOB'S ON ME LIKE A FLY ON USED FOOD, YELLING AT ME ALL THE WAY TO THE PROJECTS.
NO!
DAMN IT, HARTIGAN-- I WON'T LET YOU *DO* THIS! YOU'LL GET YOURSELF *KILLED!* YOU'LL GET US *BOTH* KILLED AND I WON'T *LET* YOU! I'M *WARNING* YOU, MAN!
LET GO MY COAT, BOB.

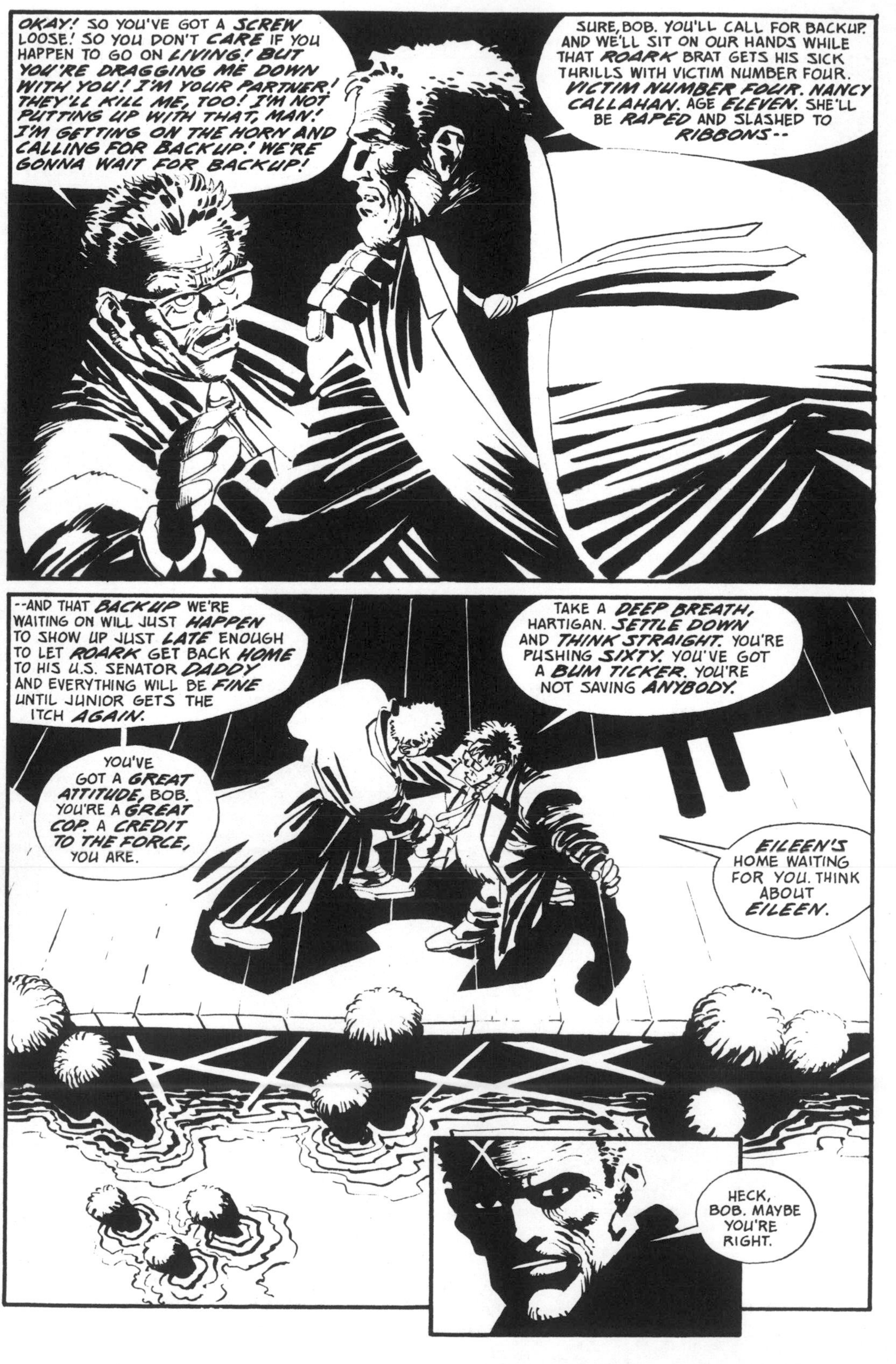
OKAY! SO YOU'VE GOT A SCREW LOOSE! SO YOU DON'T CARE IF YOU HAPPEN TO GO ON LIVING! BUT YOU'RE DRAGGING ME DOWN WITH YOU! I'M YOUR PARTNER! THEY'LL KILL ME, TOO! I'M NOT PUTTING UP WITH THAT, MAN! I'M GETTING ON THE HORN AND CALLING FOR BACKUP! WE'RE GONNA WAIT FOR BACKUP!
SURE, BOB. YOU'LL CALL FOR BACKUP. AND WE'LL SIT ON OUR HANDS WHILE THAT ROARK BRAT GETS HIS SICK THRILLS WITH VICTIM NUMBER FOUR. VICTIM NUMBER FOUR. NANCY CALLAHAN. AGE ELEVEN. SHE'LL BE RAPED AND SLASHED TO RIBBONS--
--AND THAT BACKUP WE'RE WAITING ON WILL JUST HAPPEN TO SHOW UP JUST LATE ENOUGH TO LET ROARK GET BACK HOME TO HIS U.S. SENATOR DADDY AND EVERYTHING WILL BE FINE UNTIL JUNIOR GETS THE ITCH AGAIN.
TAKE A DEEP BREATH, HARTIGAN. SETTLE DOWN AND THINK STRAIGHT. YOU'RE PUSHING SIXTY. YOU'VE GOT A BUM TICKER. YOU'RE NOT SAVING ANYBODY.
YOU'VE GOT A GREAT ATTITUDE, BOB. YOU'RE A GREAT COP. A CREDIT TO THE FORCE, YOU ARE.
EILEEN'S HOME WAITING FOR YOU. THINK ABOUT EILEEN.
HECK, BOB. MAYBE YOU'RE RIGHT.

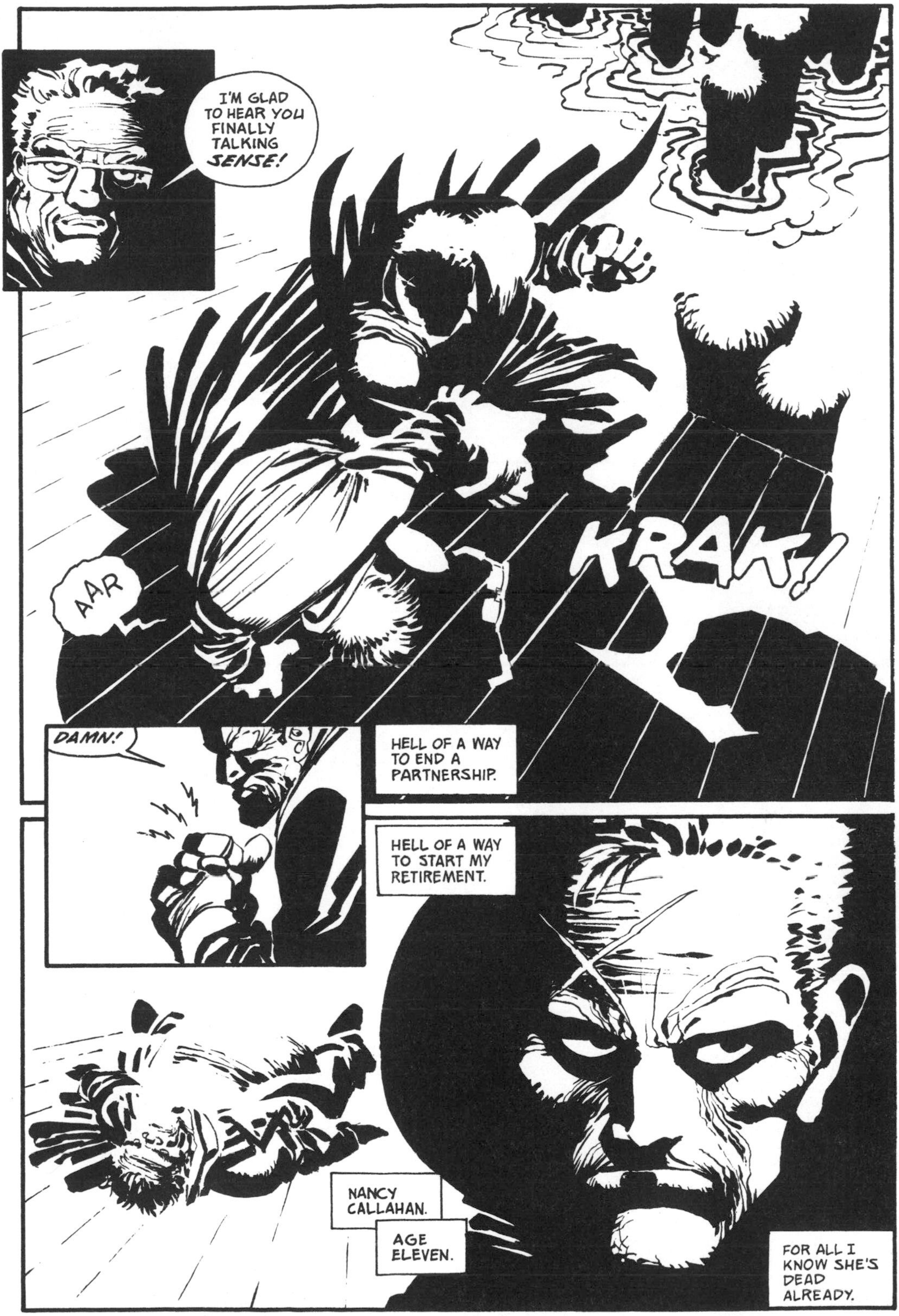
I'M GLAD TO HEAR YOU FINALLY TALKING SENSE!
KRAK!
AAR
DAMN!
HELL OF A WAY TO END A PARTNERSHIP.
HELL OF A WAY TO START MY RETIREMENT.
NANCY CALLAHAN.
AGE ELEVEN.
FOR ALL I KNOW SHE'S DEAD ALREADY.

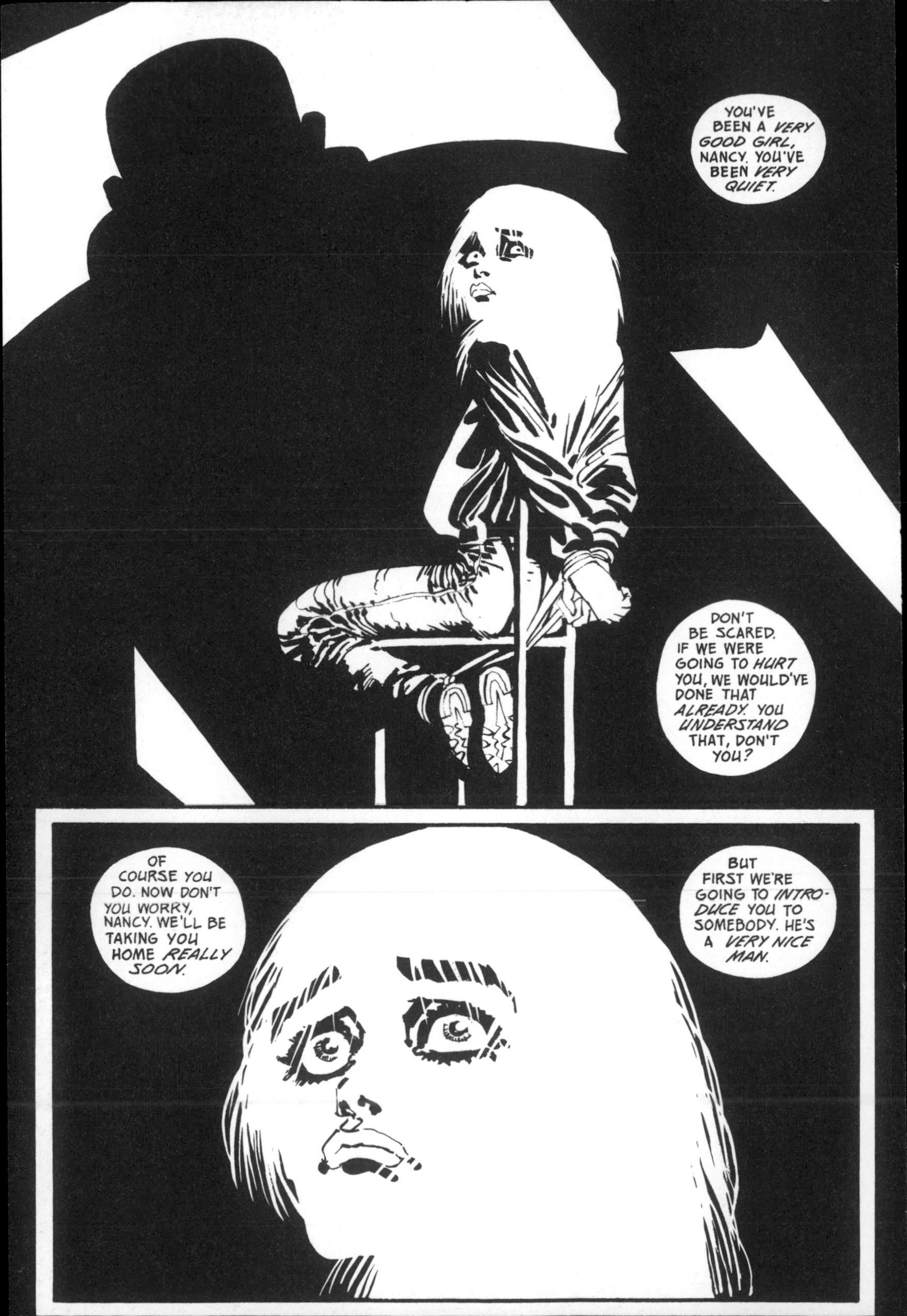
YOU'VE BEEN A *VERY GOOD GIRL*, NANCY. YOU'VE BEEN *VERY QUIET*.
DON'T BE SCARED. IF WE WERE GOING TO *HURT* YOU, WE WOULD'VE DONE THAT *ALREADY*. YOU *UNDERSTAND* THAT, DON'T YOU?
OF COURSE *YOU* DO. NOW DON'T YOU WORRY, NANCY. WE'LL BE TAKING *YOU* HOME *REALLY SOON*.
BUT FIRST WE'RE GOING TO *INTRODUCE* YOU TO SOMEBODY. HE'S A *VERY NICE MAN*.

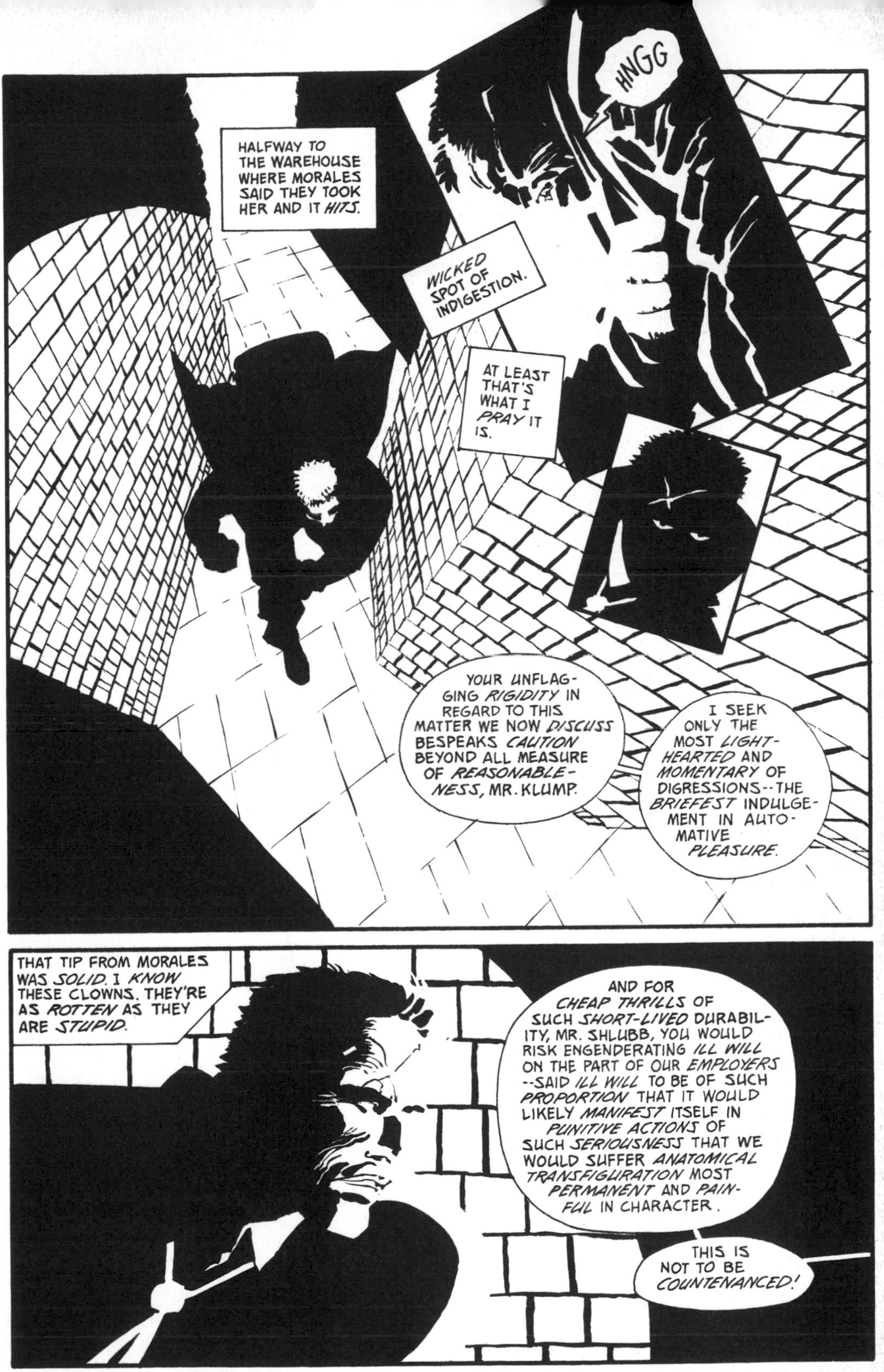
HALFWAY TO THE WAREHOUSE WHERE MORALES SAID THEY TOOK HER AND IT *HITS*.
HNGG
WICKED SPOT OF INDIGESTION.
AT LEAST THAT'S WHAT I *PRAY* IT IS.
YOUR UNFLAG-GING *RIGIDITY* IN REGARD TO THIS MATTER WE NOW *DISCUSS* BESPEAKS *CAUTION* BEYOND ALL MEASURE OF *REASONABLE-NESS*, MR. KLUMP.
I SEEK ONLY THE MOST *LIGHT-HEARTED* AND *MOMENTARY* OF DIGRESSIONS--THE *BRIEFEST* INDULGE-MENT IN AUTO-MATIVE *PLEASURE*.
THAT TIP FROM MORALES WAS *SOLID*. I *KNOW* THESE CLOWNS. THEY'RE AS *ROTTEN* AS THEY ARE *STUPID*.
AND FOR *CHEAP THRILLS* OF SUCH *SHORT-LIVED* DURABIL-ITY, MR. SHLUBB, YOU WOULD RISK ENGENDERATING *ILL WILL* ON THE PART OF OUR *EMPLOYERS* --SAID *ILL WILL* TO BE OF SUCH *PROPORTION* THAT IT WOULD LIKELY *MANIFEST* ITSELF IN *PUNITIVE ACTIONS* OF SUCH *SERIOUSNESS* THAT WE WOULD SUFFER *ANATOMICAL TRANSFIGURATION* MOST *PERMANENT* AND *PAIN-FUL* IN CHARACTER.
THIS IS NOT TO BE *COUNTENANCED*!

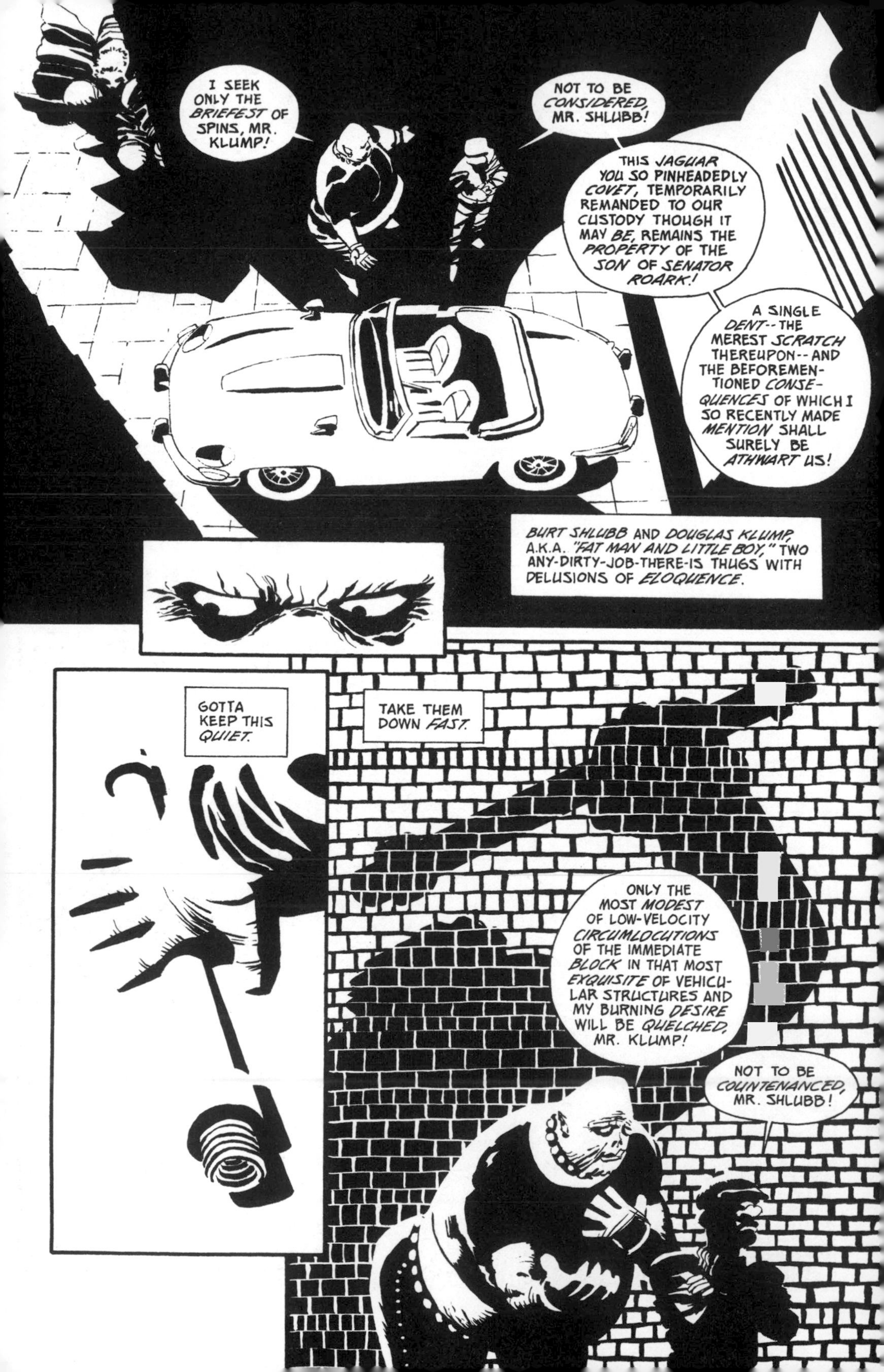
I SEEK ONLY THE BRIEFEST OF SPINS, MR. KLUMP!
NOT TO BE CONSIDERED, MR. SHLUBB!
THIS JAGUAR YOU SO PINHEADEDLY COVET, TEMPORARILY REMANDED TO OUR CUSTODY THOUGH IT MAY BE, REMAINS THE PROPERTY OF THE SON OF SENATOR ROARK!
A SINGLE DENT-- THE MEREST SCRATCH THEREUPON-- AND THE BEFOREMENTIONED CONSEQUENCES OF WHICH I SO RECENTLY MADE MENTION SHALL SURELY BE ATHWART US!
BURT SHLUBB AND DOUGLAS KLUMP, A.K.A. "FAT MAN AND LITTLE BOY," TWO ANY-DIRTY-JOB-THERE-IS THUGS WITH DELUSIONS OF ELOQUENCE.
GOTTA KEEP THIS QUIET.
TAKE THEM DOWN FAST.
ONLY THE MOST MODEST OF LOW-VELOCITY CIRCUMLOCUTIONS OF THE IMMEDIATE BLOCK IN THAT MOST EXQUISITE OF VEHICULAR STRUCTURES AND MY BURNING DESIRE WILL BE QUELCHED, MR. KLUMP!
NOT TO BE COUNTENANCED, MR. SHLUBB!

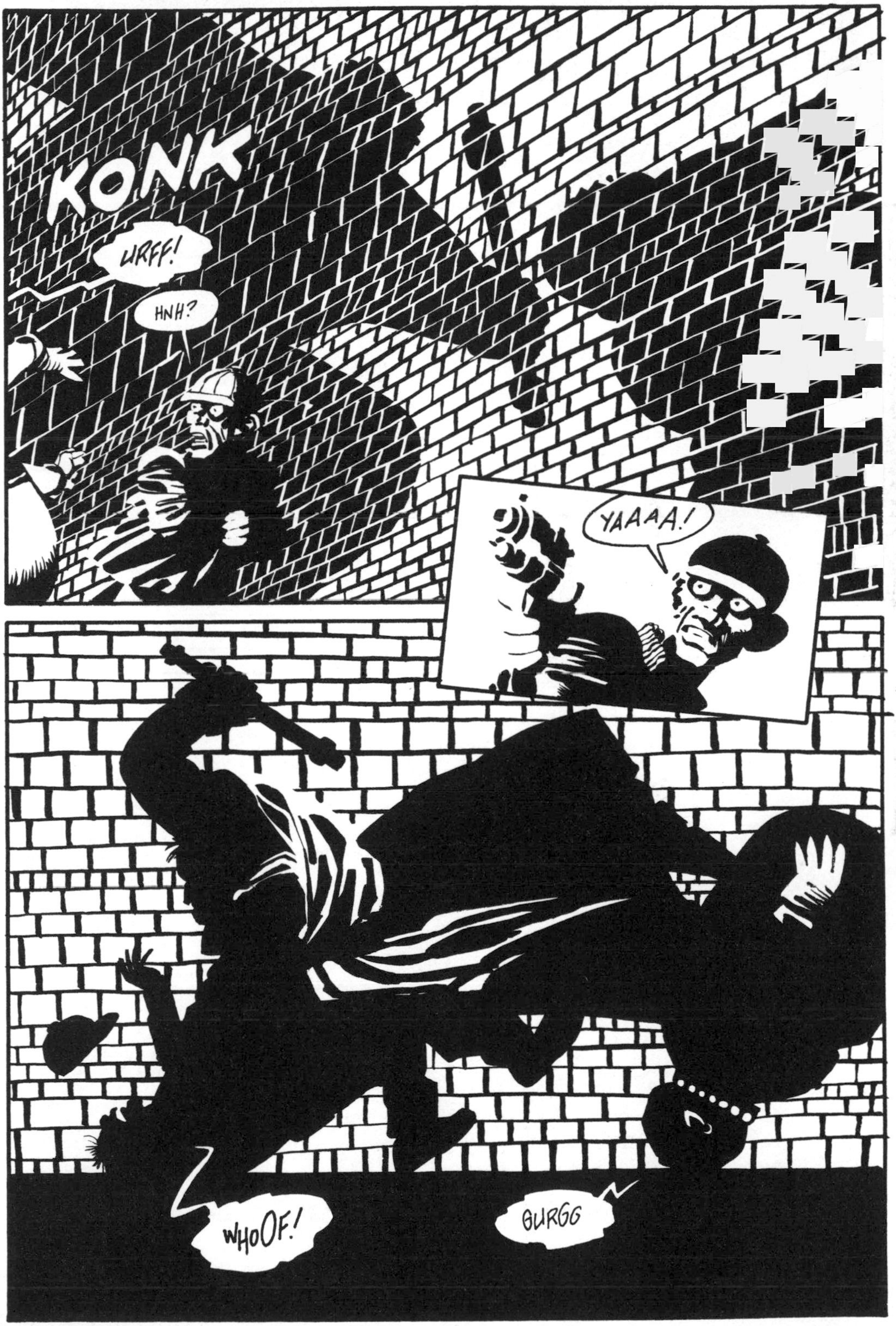
KONK
URFF!
HNH?
YAAAA!
WHOOF!
GURGG

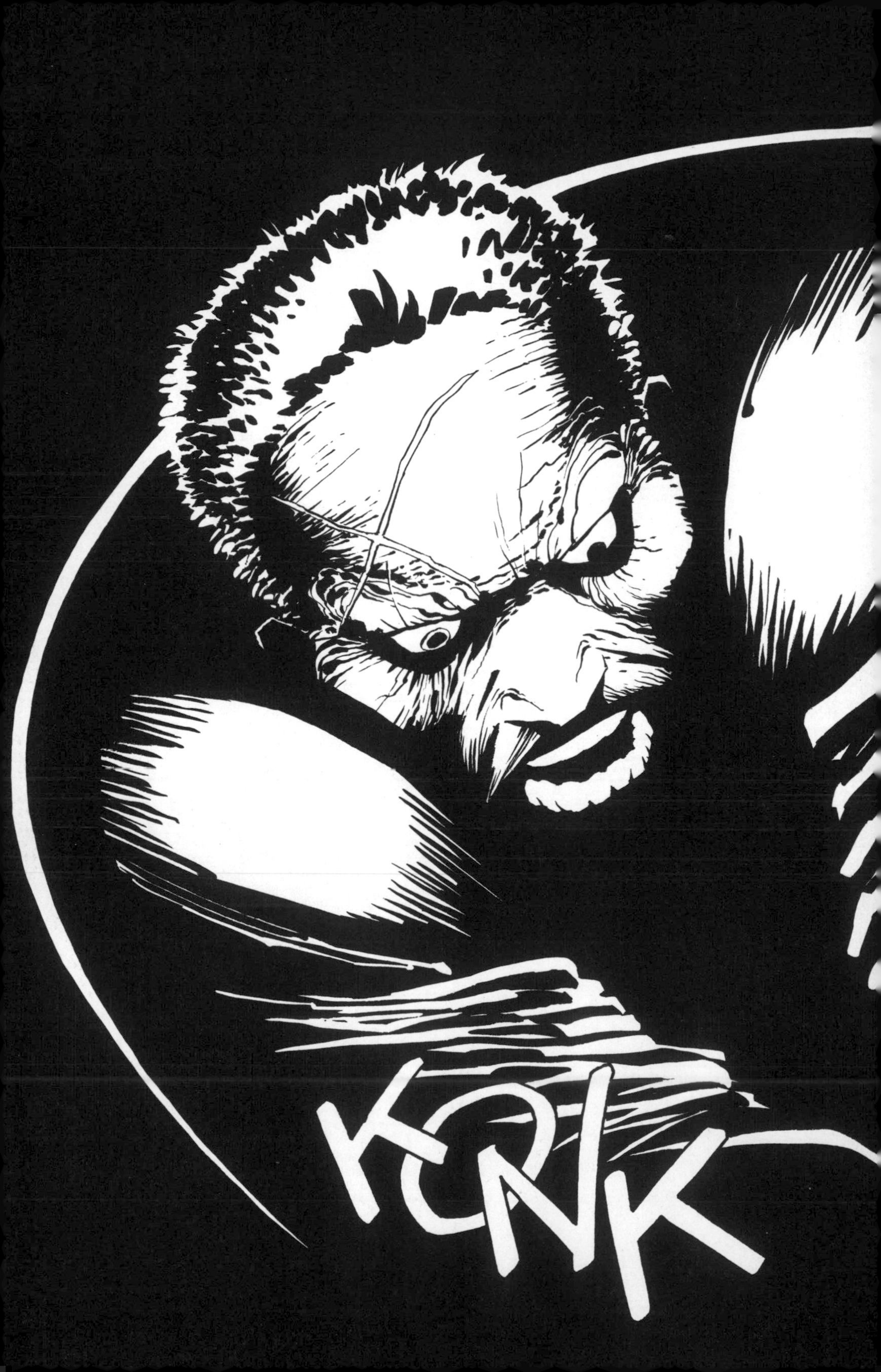
KONK

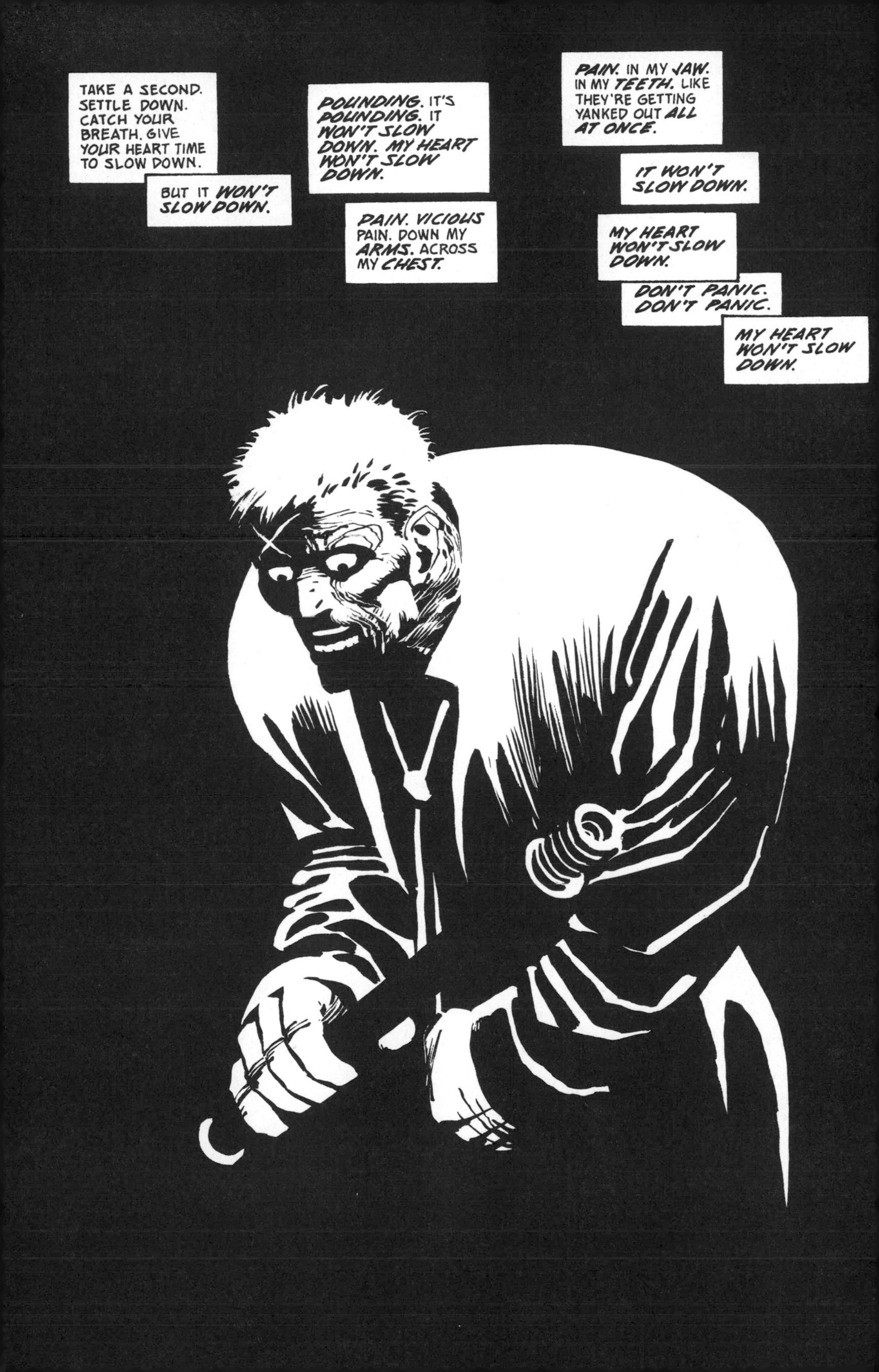
TAKE A SECOND. SETTLE DOWN. CATCH YOUR BREATH. GIVE YOUR HEART TIME TO SLOW DOWN.
BUT IT WON'T SLOW DOWN.
POUNDING. IT'S POUNDING. IT WON'T SLOW DOWN. MY HEART WON'T SLOW DOWN.
PAIN. VICIOUS PAIN. DOWN MY ARMS. ACROSS MY CHEST.
PAIN. IN MY JAW. IN MY TEETH. LIKE THEY'RE GETTING YANKED OUT ALL AT ONCE.
IT WON'T SLOW DOWN.
MY HEART WON'T SLOW DOWN.
DON'T PANIC. DON'T PANIC.
MY HEART WON'T SLOW DOWN.

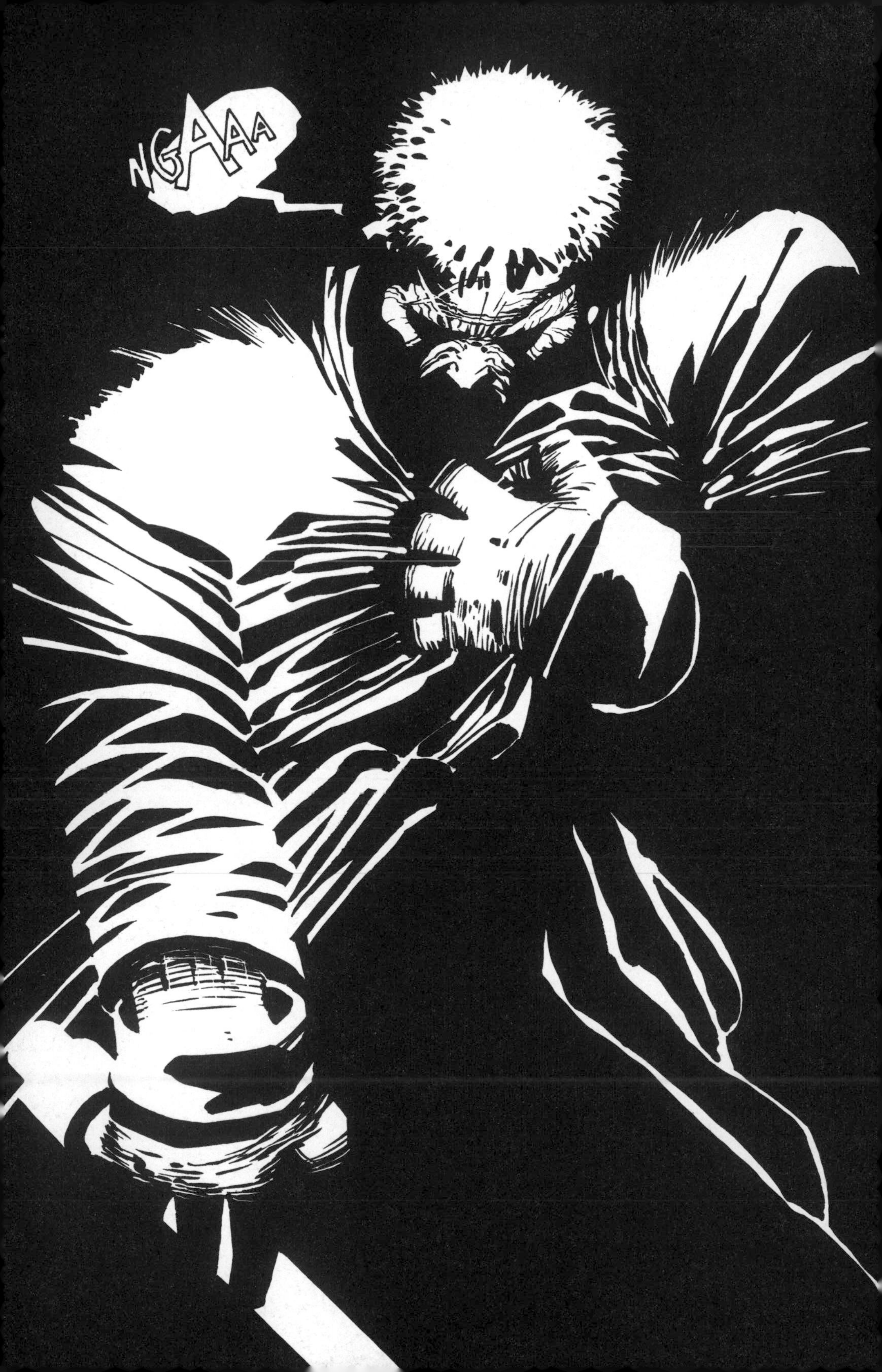
NGAAA

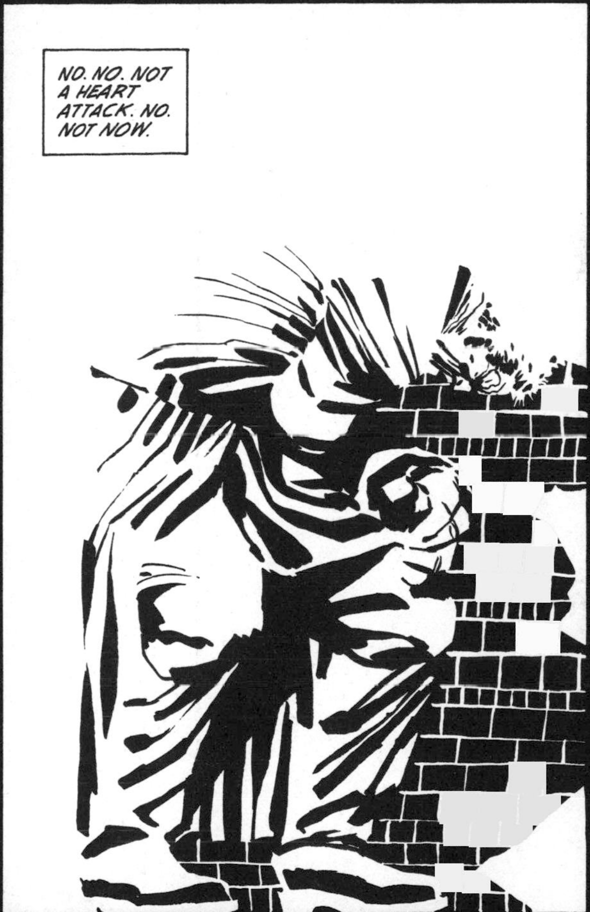
NO. NO. NOT A HEART ATTACK. NO. NOT NOW.

NOT NOW.

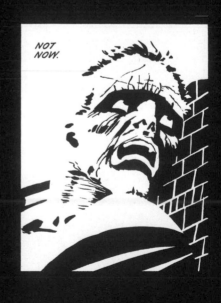

NOT
NOW.

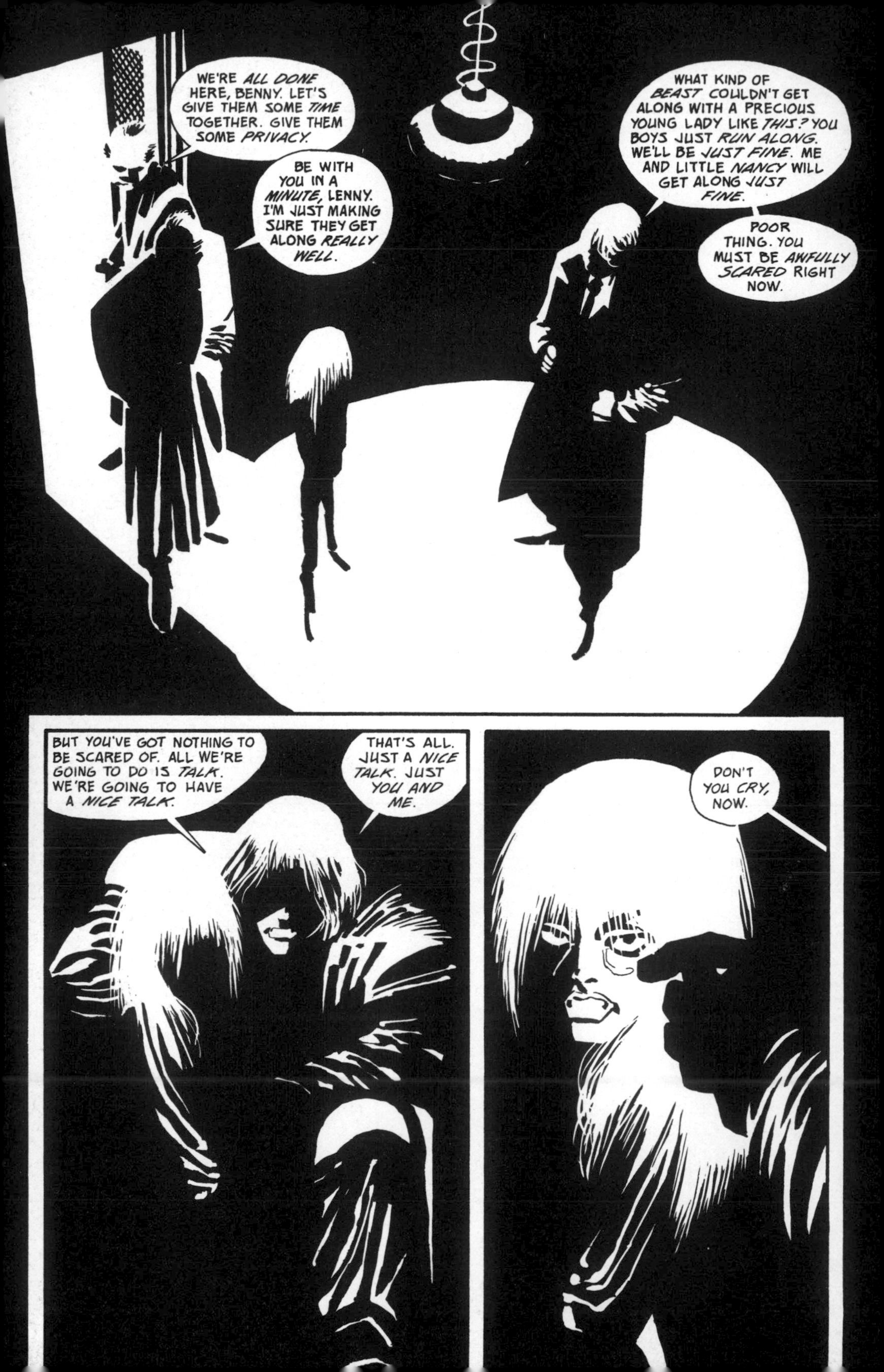
WE'RE ALL DONE HERE, BENNY. LET'S GIVE THEM SOME TIME TOGETHER. GIVE THEM SOME PRIVACY.
BE WITH YOU IN A MINUTE, LENNY. I'M JUST MAKING SURE THEY GET ALONG REALLY WELL.
WHAT KIND OF BEAST COULDN'T GET ALONG WITH A PRECIOUS YOUNG LADY LIKE THIS? YOU BOYS JUST RUN ALONG. WE'LL BE JUST FINE. ME AND LITTLE NANCY WILL GET ALONG JUST FINE.
POOR THING. YOU MUST BE AWFULLY SCARED RIGHT NOW.
BUT YOU'VE GOT NOTHING TO BE SCARED OF. ALL WE'RE GOING TO DO IS TALK. WE'RE GOING TO HAVE A NICE TALK.
THAT'S ALL. JUST A NICE TALK. JUST YOU AND ME.
DON'T YOU CRY, NOW.

NO.

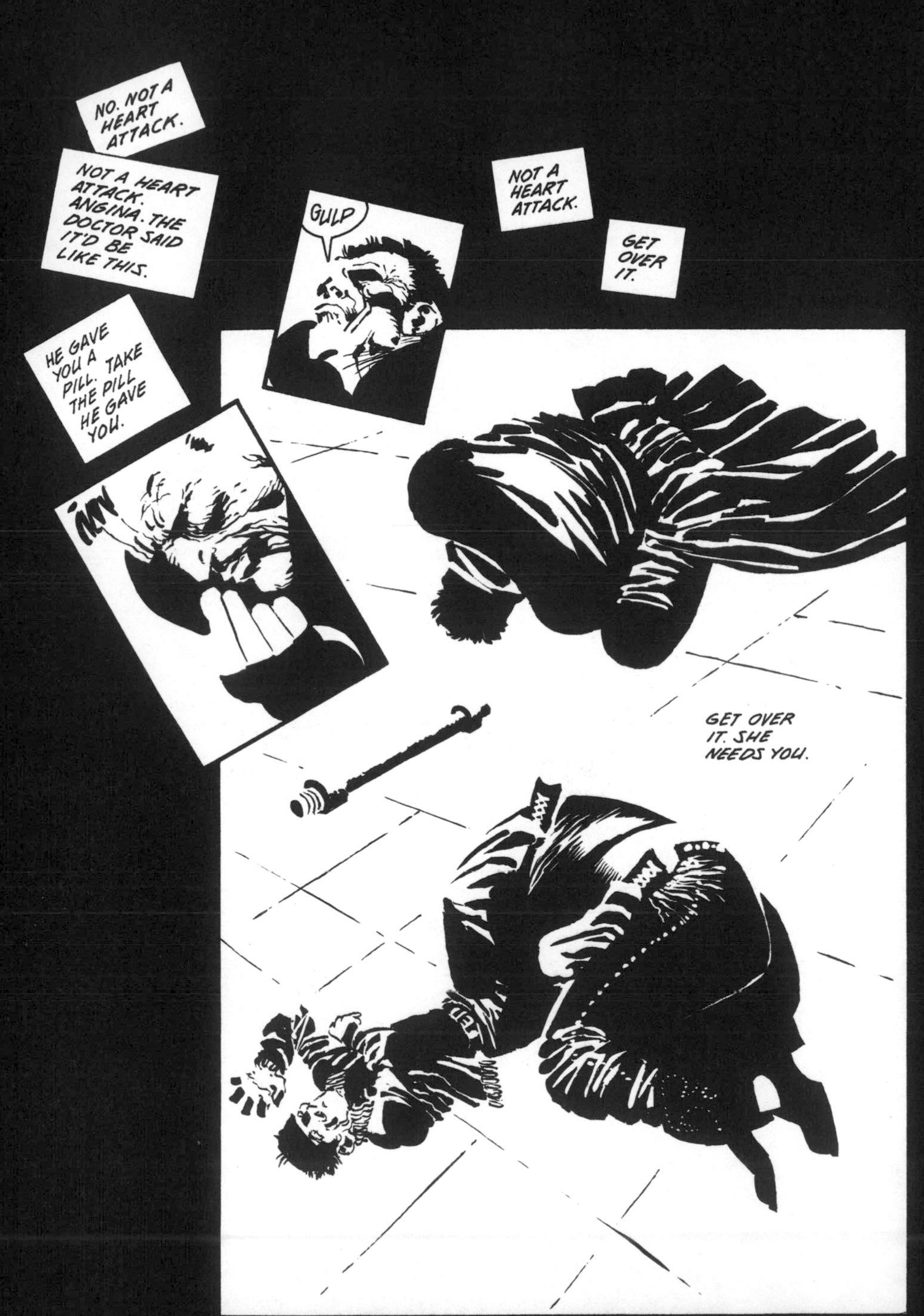
NO. NOT A HEART ATTACK.
NOT A HEART ATTACK. ANGINA. THE DOCTOR SAID IT'D BE LIKE THIS.
GULP
NOT A HEART ATTACK.
GET OVER IT.
HE GAVE YOU A PILL. TAKE THE PILL HE GAVE YOU.
GET OVER IT. SHE NEEDS YOU.

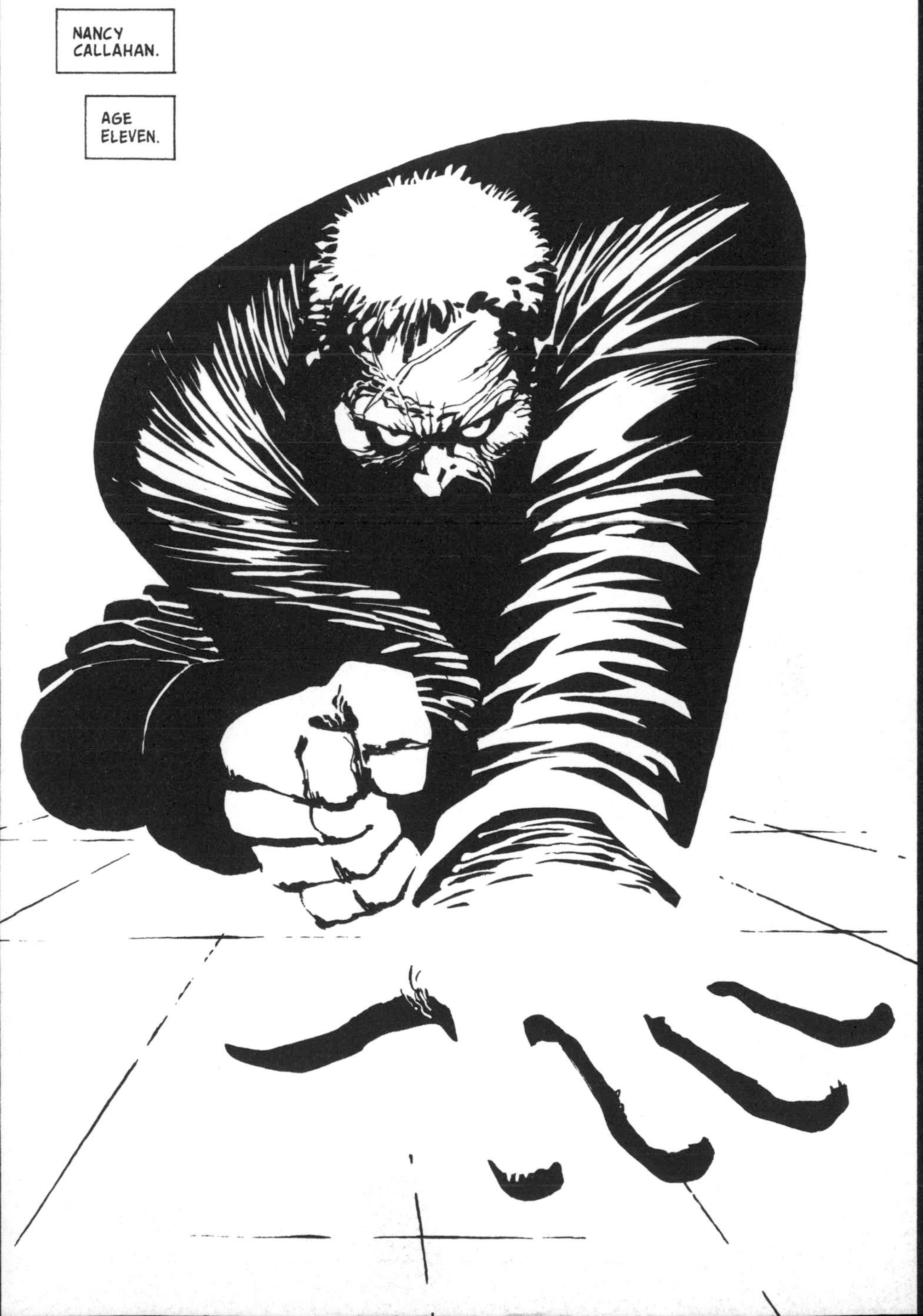
NANCY CALLAHAN.
AGE ELEVEN.

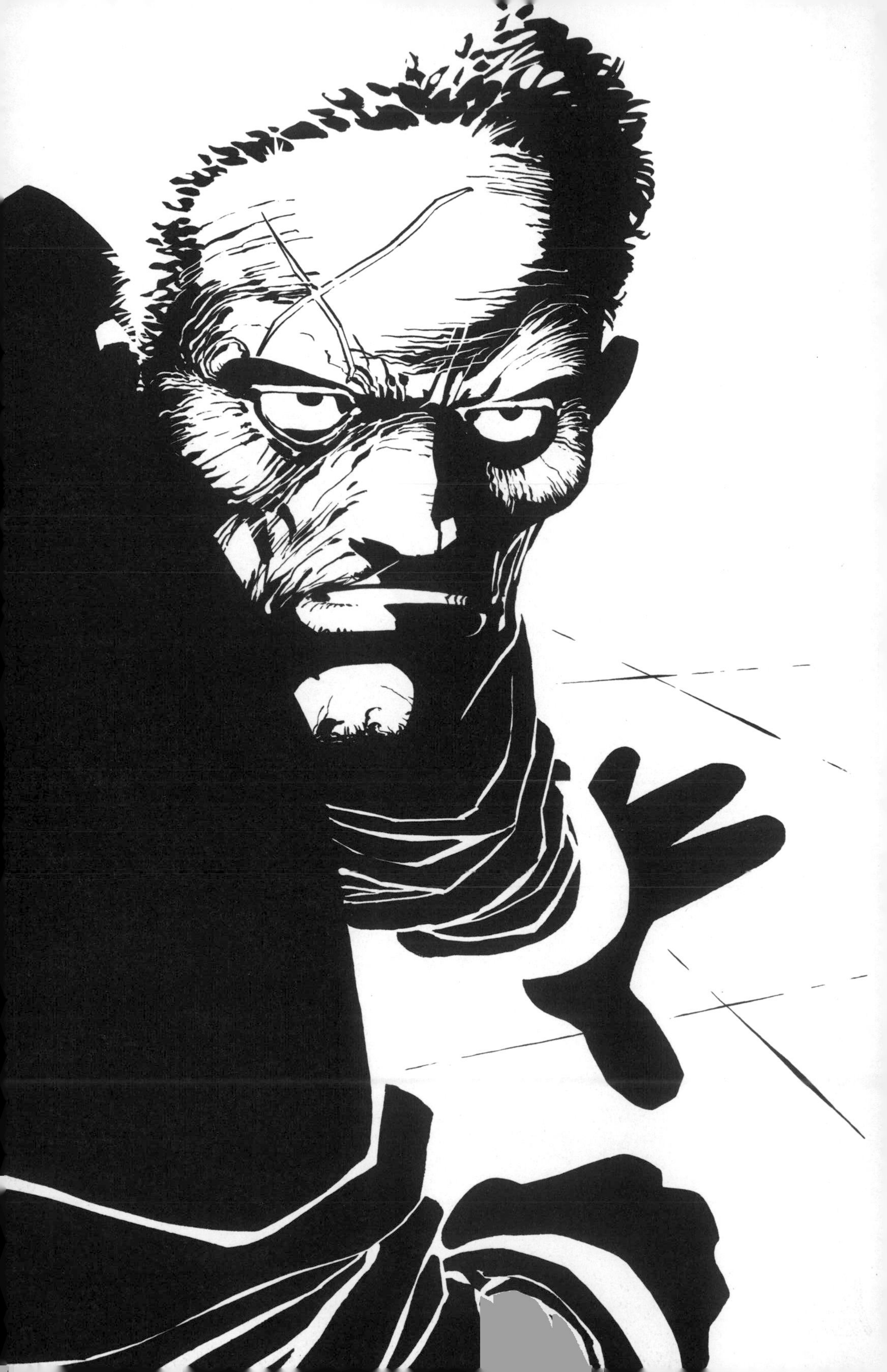

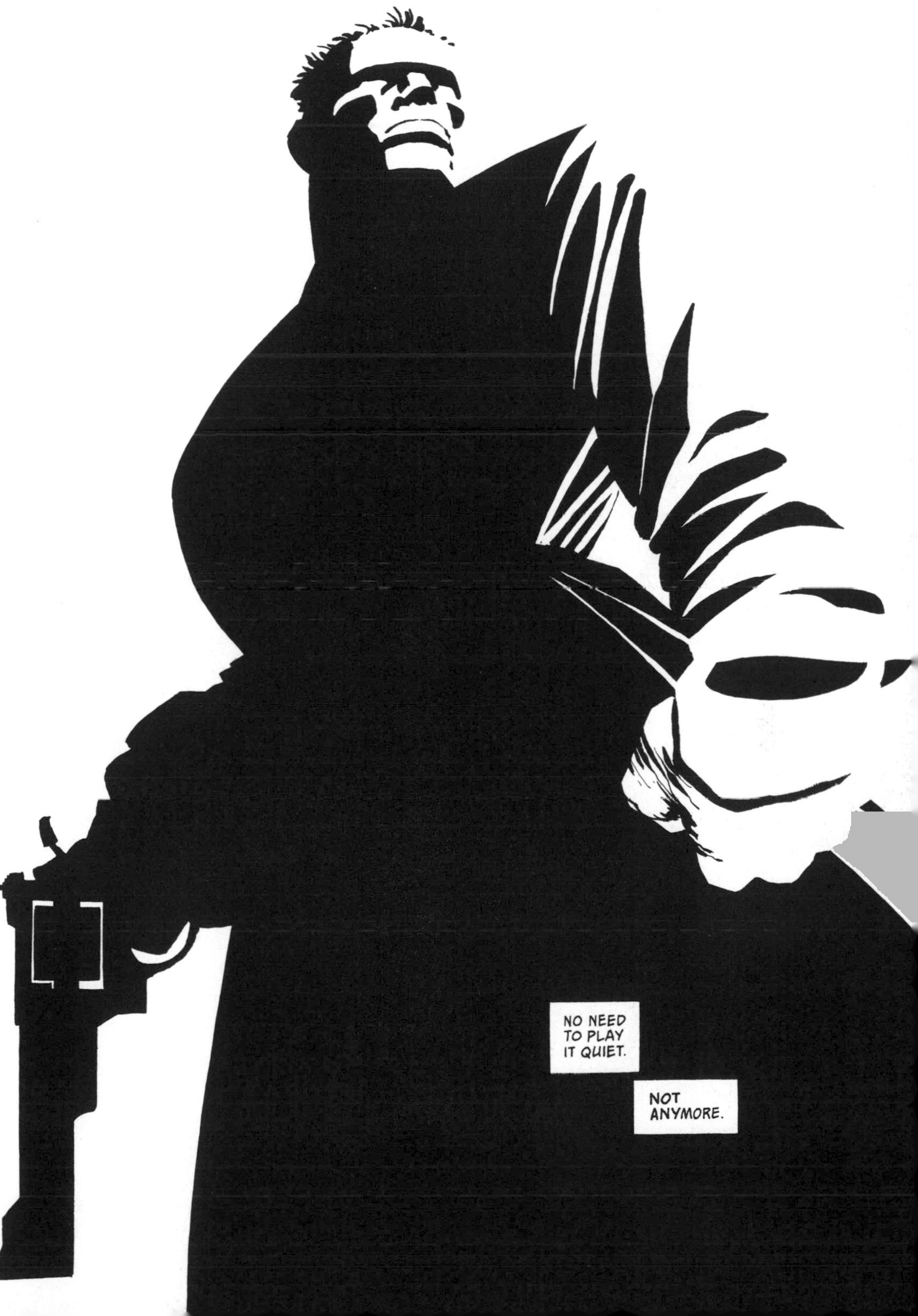
NO NEED TO PLAY IT QUIET.
NOT ANYMORE.

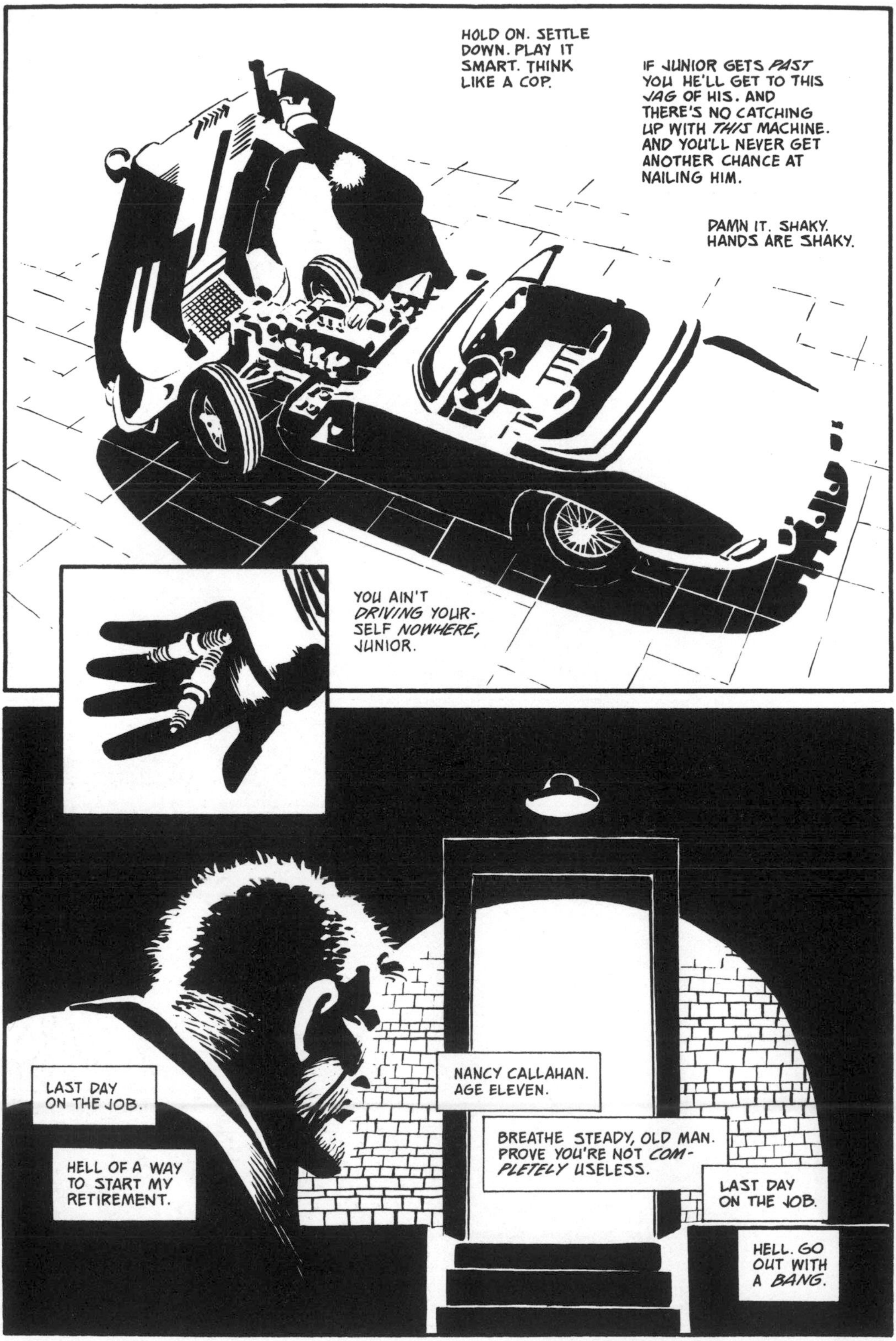
HOLD ON. SETTLE DOWN. PLAY IT SMART. THINK LIKE A COP.
IF JUNIOR GETS *PAST* YOU HE'LL GET TO THIS *JAG* OF HIS. AND THERE'S NO CATCHING UP WITH *THIS* MACHINE. AND YOU'LL NEVER GET ANOTHER CHANCE AT NAILING HIM.
DAMN IT. SHAKY. HANDS ARE SHAKY.
YOU AIN'T *DRIVING* YOURSELF *NOWHERE*, JUNIOR.
LAST DAY ON THE JOB.
HELL OF A WAY TO START MY RETIREMENT.
NANCY CALLAHAN. AGE ELEVEN.
BREATHE STEADY, OLD MAN. PROVE YOU'RE NOT *COMPLETELY* USELESS.
LAST DAY ON THE JOB.
HELL. GO OUT WITH A *BANG*.

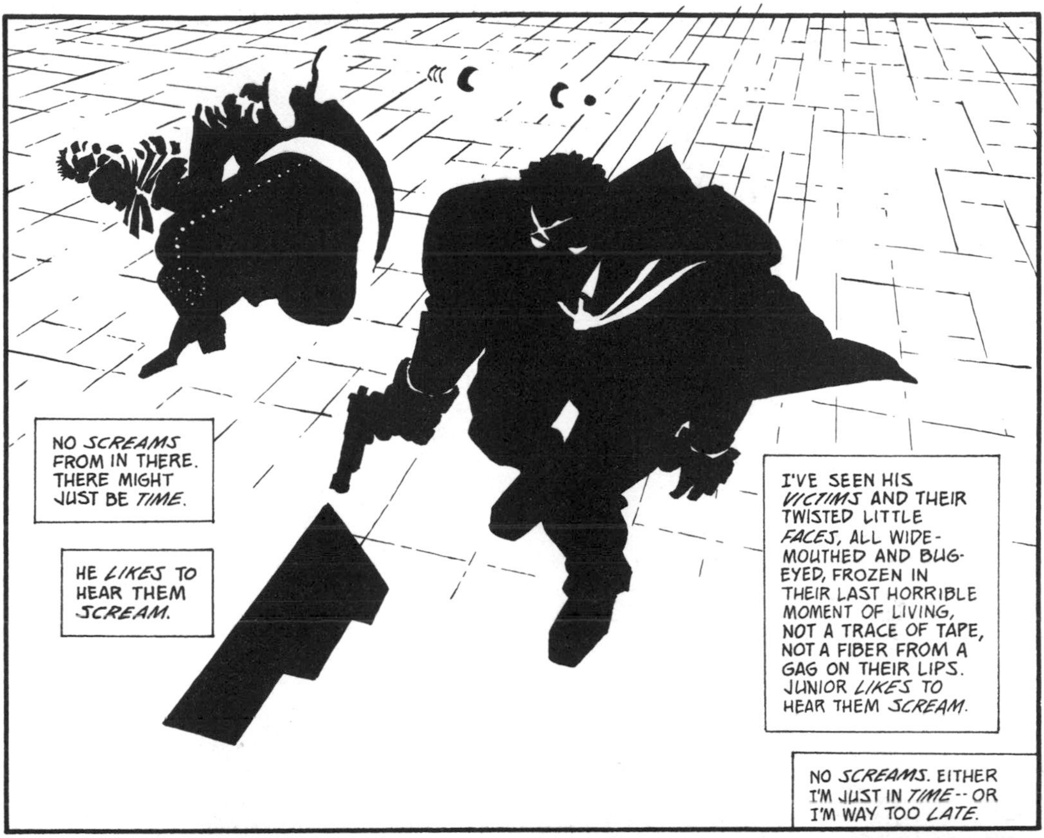
NO *SCREAMS* FROM IN THERE. THERE MIGHT JUST BE *TIME*.
HE *LIKES* TO HEAR THEM *SCREAM*.
I'VE SEEN HIS *VICTIMS* AND THEIR TWISTED LITTLE *FACES*, ALL WIDE-MOUTHED AND BUG-EYED, FROZEN IN THEIR LAST HORRIBLE MOMENT OF LIVING, NOT A TRACE OF TAPE, NOT A FIBER FROM A GAG ON THEIR LIPS. JUNIOR *LIKES* TO HEAR THEM *SCREAM*.
NO *SCREAMS*. EITHER I'M JUST IN *TIME*-- OR I'M WAY TOO *LATE*.

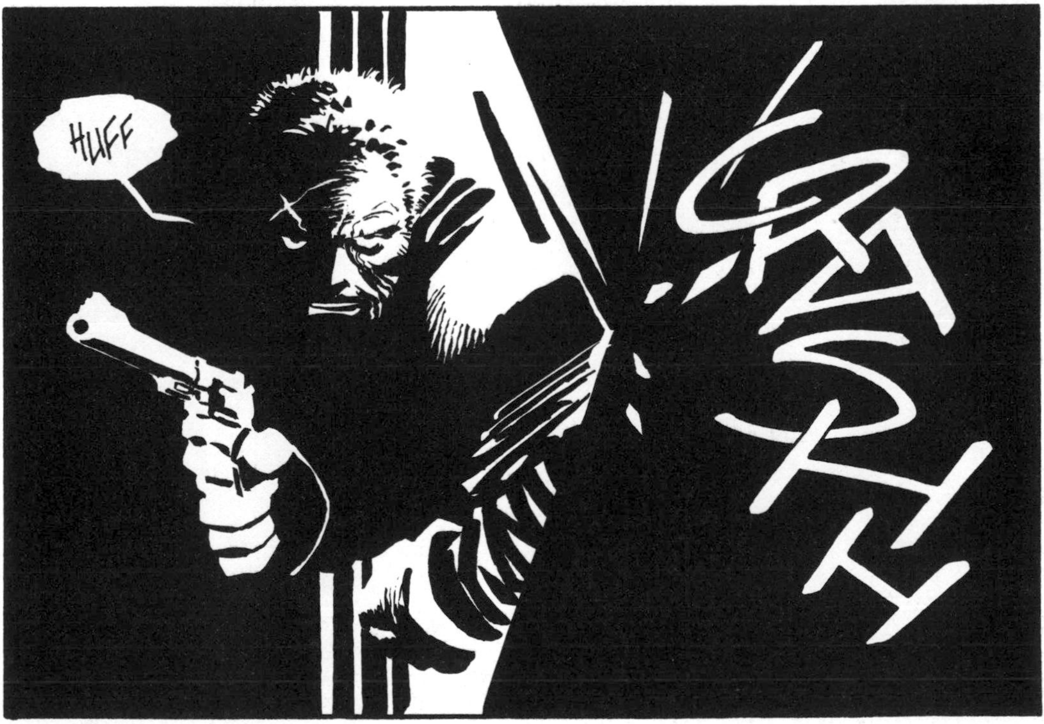
HUFF
CRASHH

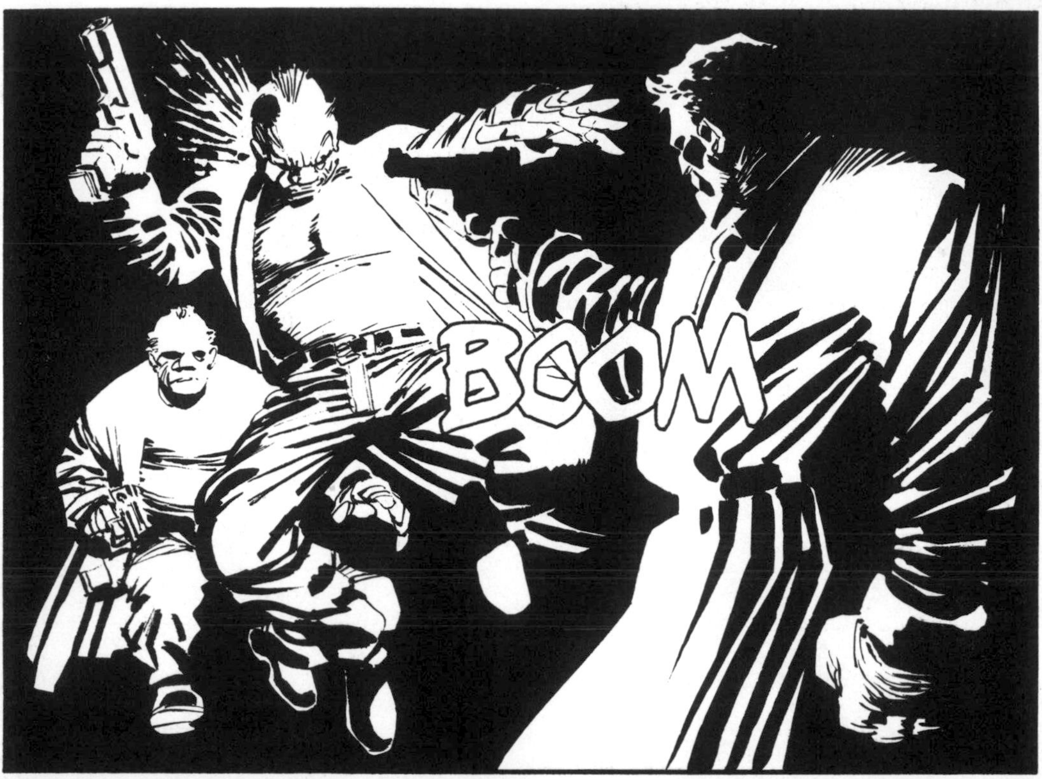
BOOM

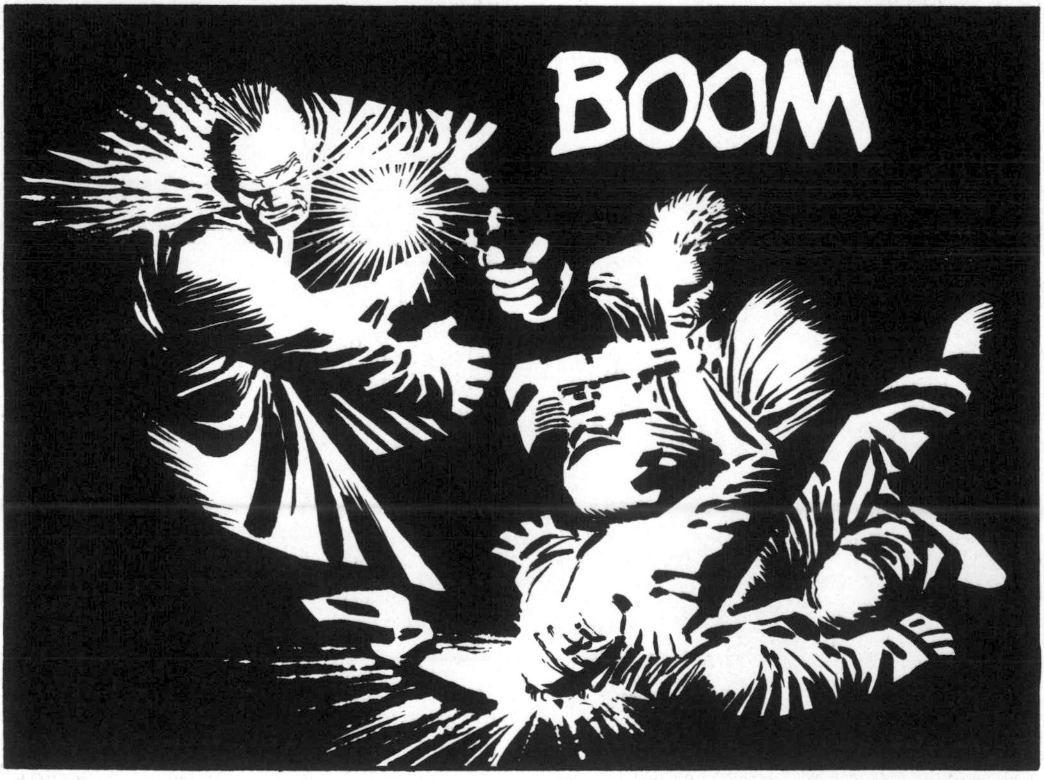
BOOM

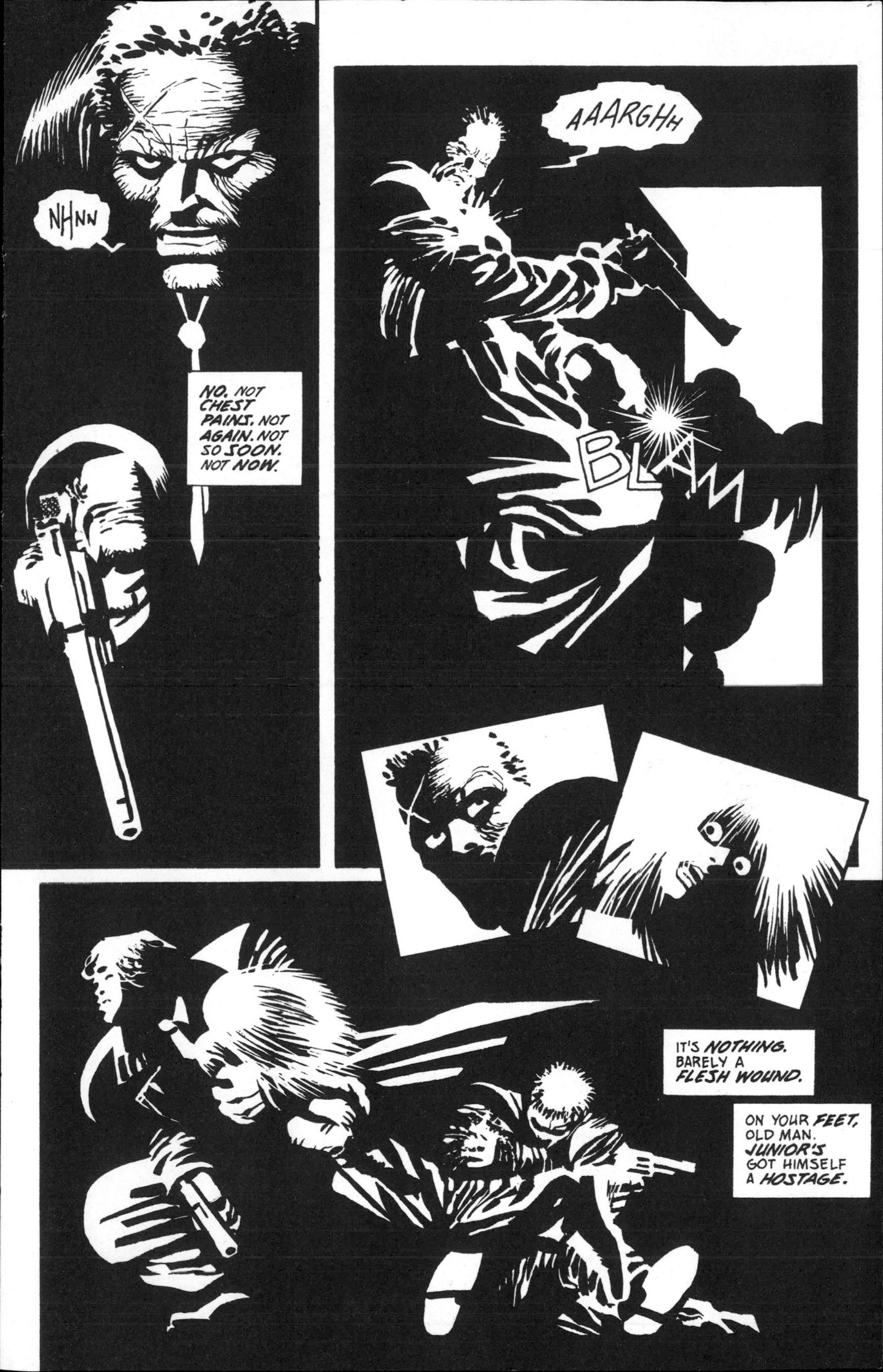
NHNN
NO. NOT CHEST PAINS. NOT AGAIN. NOT SO SOON. NOT NOW.
AAARGHH
BLAM
IT'S NOTHING. BARELY A FLESH WOUND.
ON YOUR FEET, OLD MAN. JUNIOR'S GOT HIMSELF A HOSTAGE.

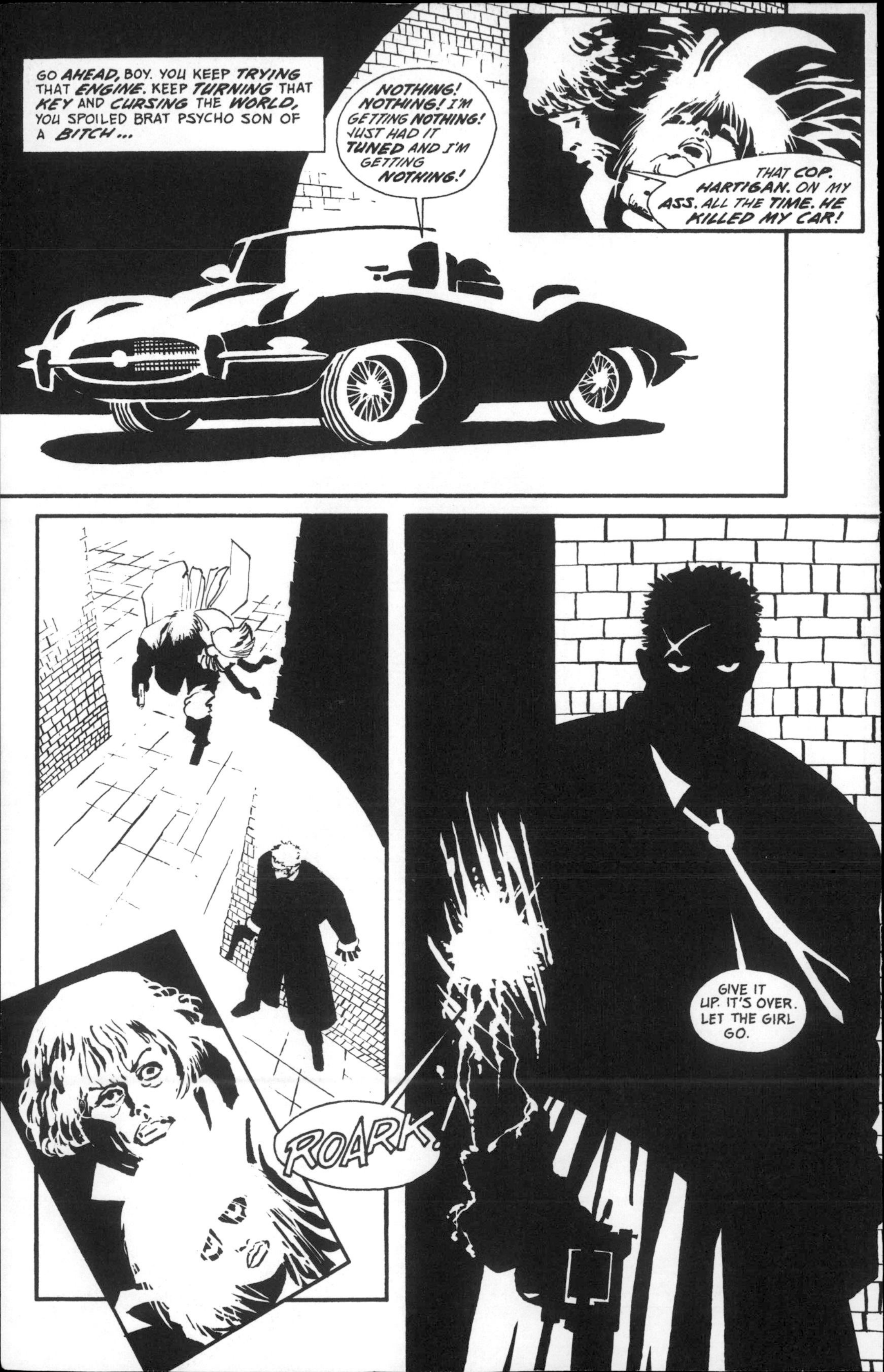
GO AHEAD, BOY. YOU KEEP TRYING THAT ENGINE. KEEP TURNING THAT KEY AND CURSING THE WORLD, YOU SPOILED BRAT PSYCHO SON OF A BITCH...
NOTHING! NOTHING! I'M GETTING NOTHING! JUST HAD IT TUNED AND I'M GETTING NOTHING!
THAT COP. HARTIGAN. ON MY ASS. ALL THE TIME. HE KILLED MY CAR!
ROARK!
GIVE IT UP. IT'S OVER. LET THE GIRL GO.

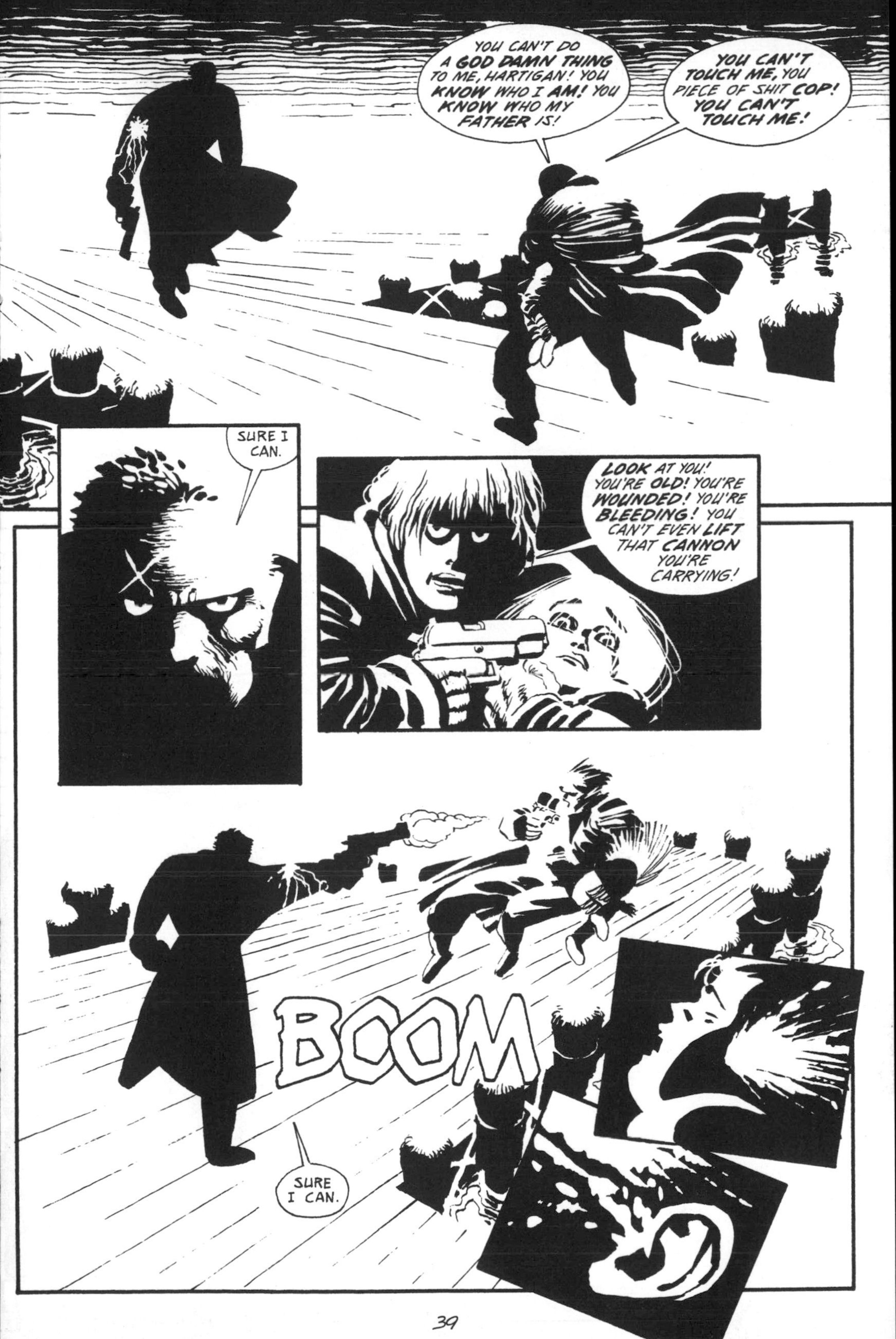
YOU CAN'T DO A GOD DAMN THING TO ME, HARTIGAN! YOU KNOW WHO I AM! YOU KNOW WHO MY FATHER IS!
YOU CAN'T TOUCH ME, YOU PIECE OF SHIT COP! YOU CAN'T TOUCH ME!
SURE I CAN.
LOOK AT YOU! YOU'RE OLD! YOU'RE WOUNDED! YOU'RE BLEEDING! YOU CAN'T EVEN LIFT THAT CANNON YOU'RE CARRYING!
BOOM
SURE I CAN.

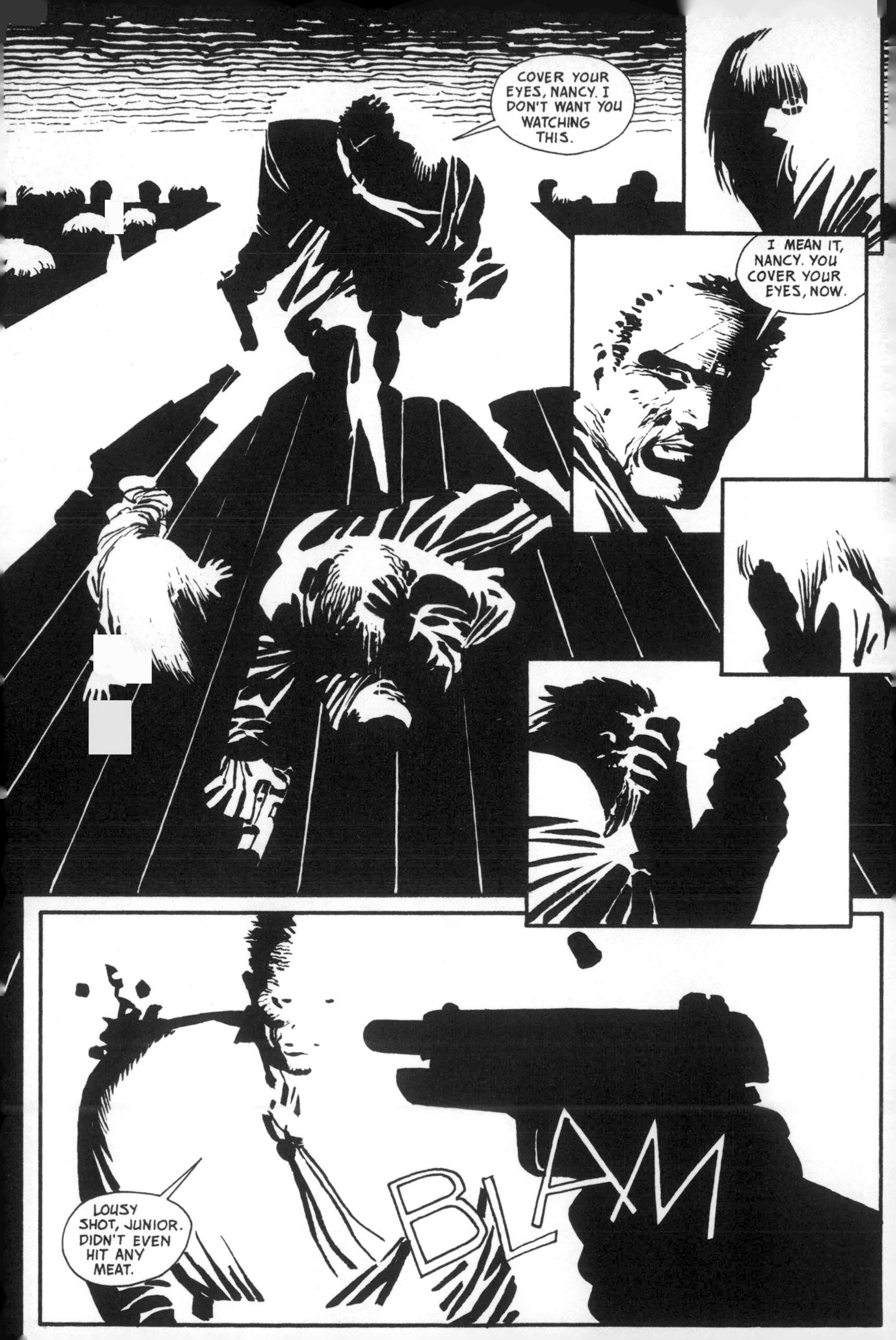
COVER YOUR EYES, NANCY. I DON'T WANT YOU WATCHING THIS.
I MEAN IT, NANCY. YOU COVER YOUR EYES, NOW.
BLAM
LOUSY SHOT, JUNIOR. DIDN'T EVEN HIT ANY MEAT.

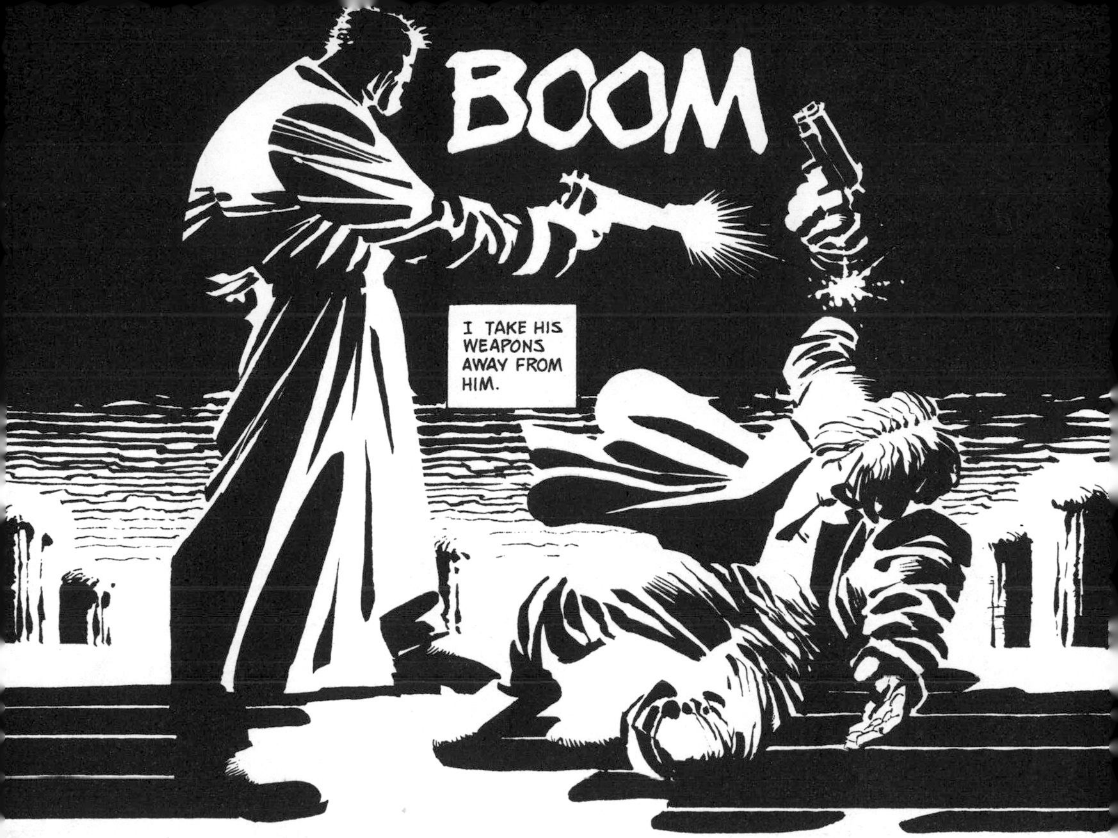
BOOM
I TAKE HIS WEAPONS AWAY FROM HIM.

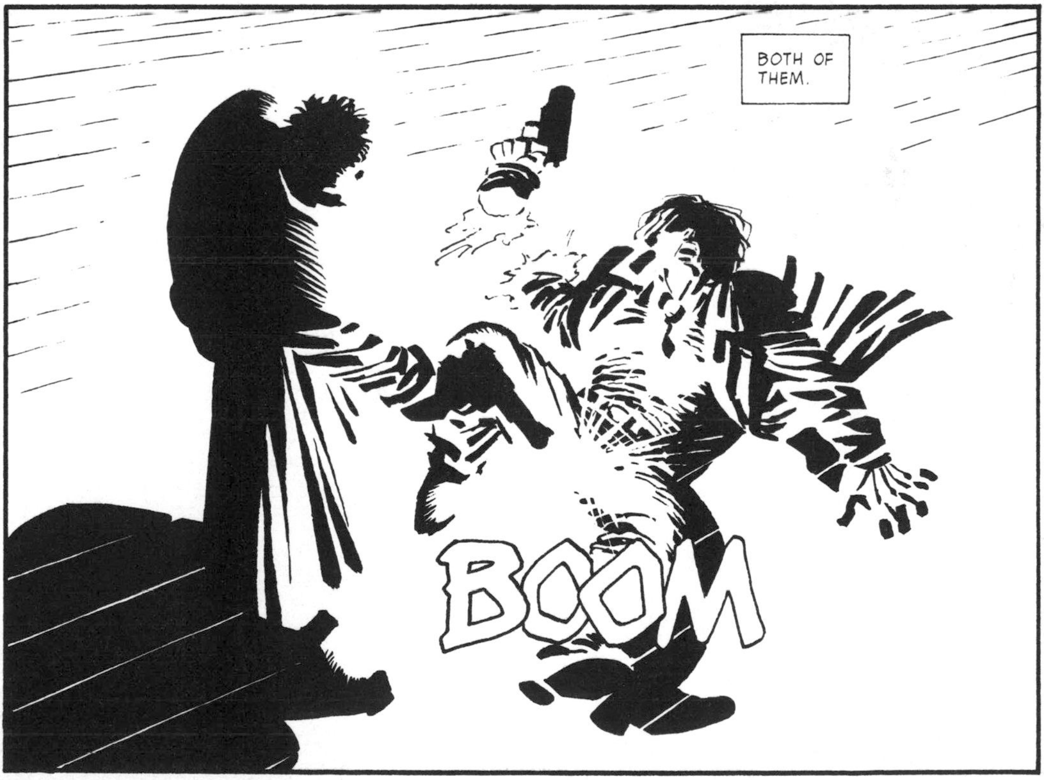
BOTH OF THEM.
BOOM

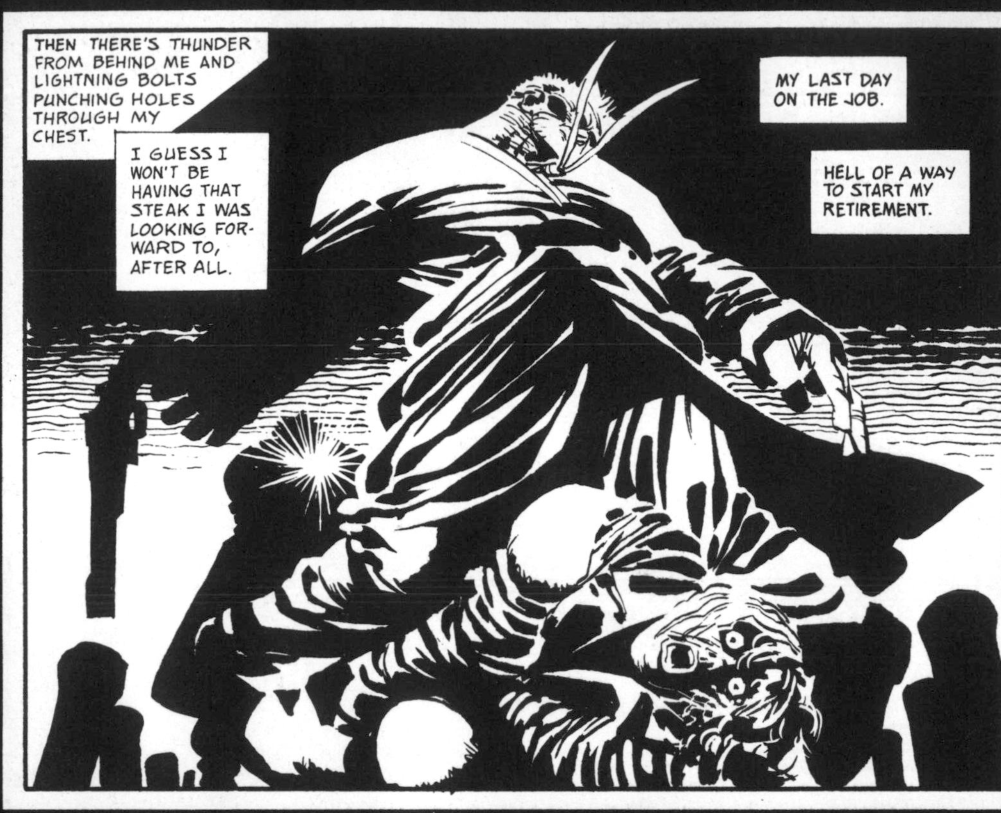
THEN THERE'S THUNDER FROM BEHIND ME AND LIGHTNING BOLTS PUNCHING HOLES THROUGH MY CHEST.
I GUESS I WON'T BE HAVING THAT STEAK I WAS LOOKING FOR-WARD TO, AFTER ALL.
MY LAST DAY ON THE JOB.
HELL OF A WAY TO START MY RETIREMENT.

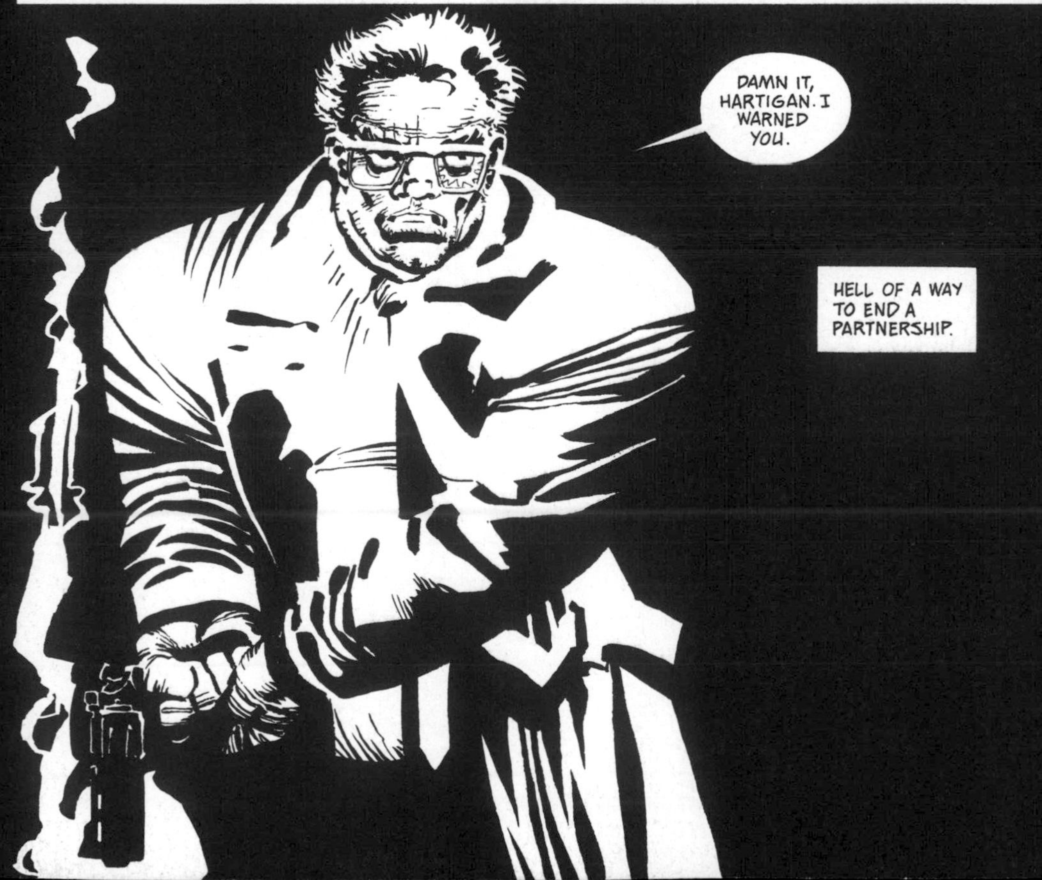
DAMN IT, HARTIGAN. I WARNED YOU.
HELL OF A WAY TO END A PARTNERSHIP.

CHAPTER TWO

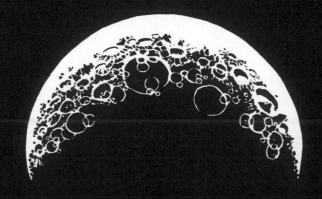

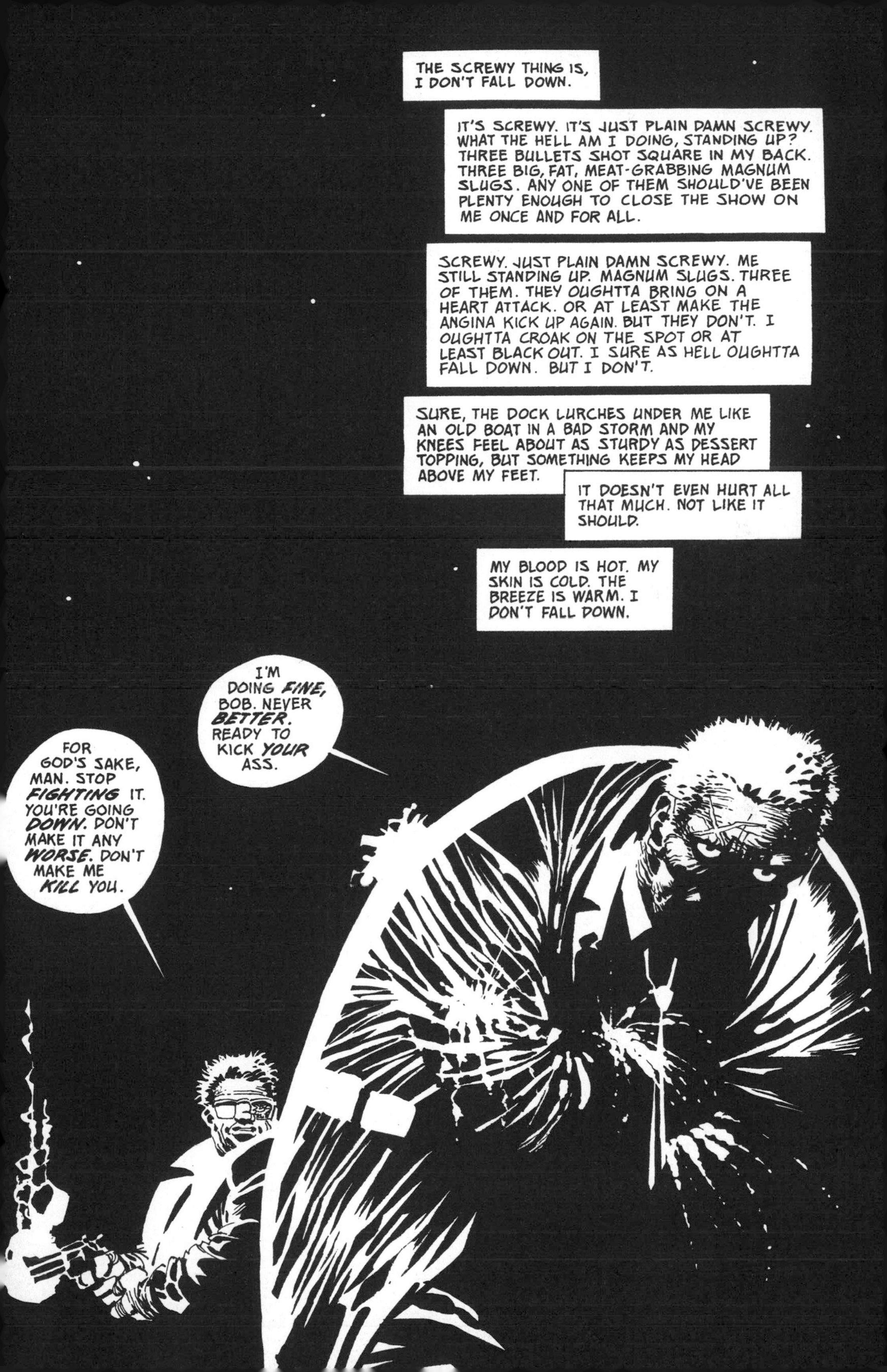
THE SCREWY THING IS, I DON'T FALL DOWN.
IT'S SCREWY. IT'S JUST PLAIN DAMN SCREWY. WHAT THE HELL AM I DOING, STANDING UP? THREE BULLETS SHOT SQUARE IN MY BACK. THREE BIG, FAT, MEAT-GRABBING MAGNUM SLUGS. ANY ONE OF THEM SHOULD'VE BEEN PLENTY ENOUGH TO CLOSE THE SHOW ON ME ONCE AND FOR ALL.
SCREWY. JUST PLAIN DAMN SCREWY. ME STILL STANDING UP. MAGNUM SLUGS. THREE OF THEM. THEY OUGHTTA BRING ON A HEART ATTACK. OR AT LEAST MAKE THE ANGINA KICK UP AGAIN. BUT THEY DON'T. I OUGHTTA CROAK ON THE SPOT OR AT LEAST BLACK OUT. I SURE AS HELL OUGHTTA FALL DOWN. BUT I DON'T.
SURE, THE DOCK LURCHES UNDER ME LIKE AN OLD BOAT IN A BAD STORM AND MY KNEES FEEL ABOUT AS STURDY AS DESSERT TOPPING, BUT SOMETHING KEEPS MY HEAD ABOVE MY FEET.
IT DOESN'T EVEN HURT ALL THAT MUCH. NOT LIKE IT SHOULD.
MY BLOOD IS HOT. MY SKIN IS COLD. THE BREEZE IS WARM. I DON'T FALL DOWN.
FOR GOD'S SAKE, MAN. STOP FIGHTING IT. YOU'RE GOING DOWN. DON'T MAKE IT ANY WORSE. DON'T MAKE ME KILL YOU.
I'M DOING FINE, BOB. NEVER BETTER. READY TO KICK YOUR ASS.

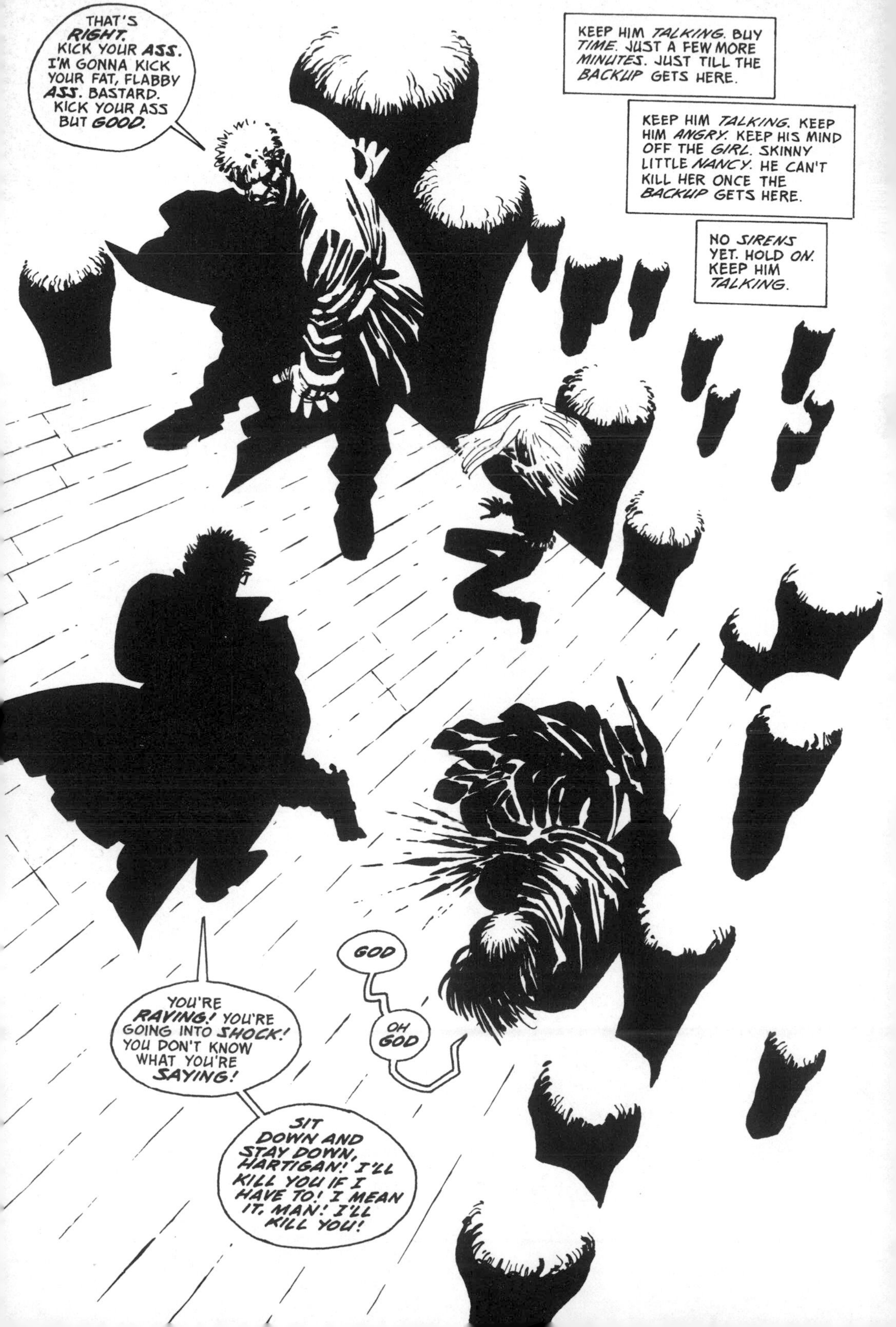
THAT'S RIGHT. KICK YOUR ASS. I'M GONNA KICK YOUR FAT, FLABBY ASS. BASTARD. KICK YOUR ASS BUT GOOD.
KEEP HIM TALKING. BUY TIME. JUST A FEW MORE MINUTES. JUST TILL THE BACKUP GETS HERE.
KEEP HIM TALKING. KEEP HIM ANGRY. KEEP HIS MIND OFF THE GIRL. SKINNY LITTLE NANCY. HE CAN'T KILL HER ONCE THE BACKUP GETS HERE.
NO SIRENS YET. HOLD ON. KEEP HIM TALKING.
GOD
OH GOD
YOU'RE RAVING! YOU'RE GOING INTO SHOCK! YOU DON'T KNOW WHAT YOU'RE SAYING!
SIT DOWN AND STAY DOWN, HARTIGAN! I'LL KILL YOU IF I HAVE TO! I MEAN IT, MAN! I'LL KILL YOU!

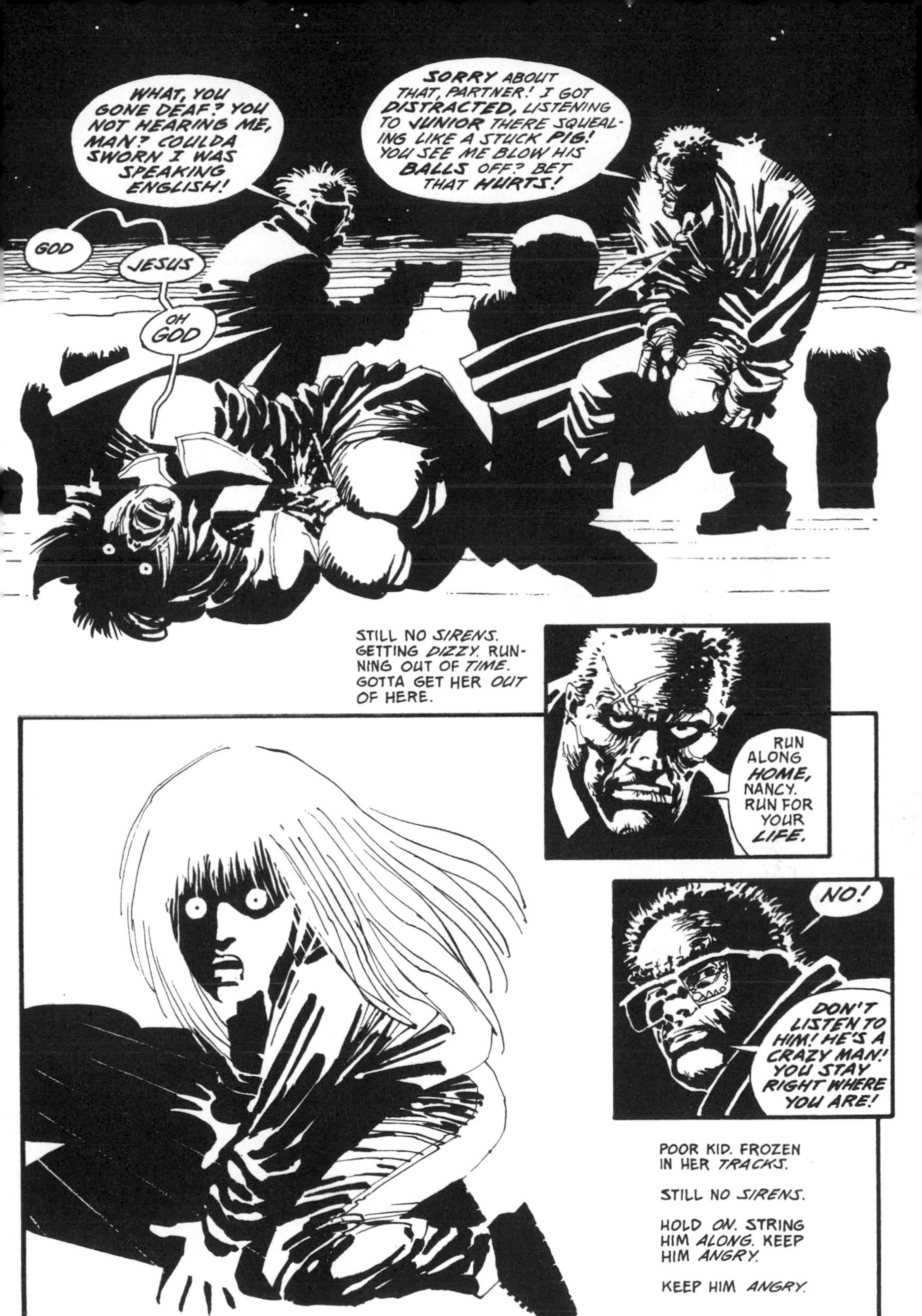

WHAT, YOU GONE DEAF? YOU NOT HEARING ME, MAN? COULDA SWORN I WAS SPEAKING ENGLISH!
SORRY ABOUT THAT, PARTNER! I GOT DISTRACTED, LISTENING TO JUNIOR THERE SQUEALING LIKE A STUCK PIG! YOU SEE ME BLOW HIS BALLS OFF? BET THAT HURTS!
GOD
JESUS
OH GOD
STILL NO SIRENS. GETTING DIZZY. RUNNING OUT OF TIME. GOTTA GET HER OUT OF HERE.
RUN ALONG HOME, NANCY. RUN FOR YOUR LIFE.
NO!
DON'T LISTEN TO HIM! HE'S A CRAZY MAN! YOU STAY RIGHT WHERE YOU ARE!
POOR KID. FROZEN IN HER TRACKS.
STILL NO SIRENS.
HOLD ON. STRING HIM ALONG. KEEP HIM ANGRY.
KEEP HIM ANGRY.

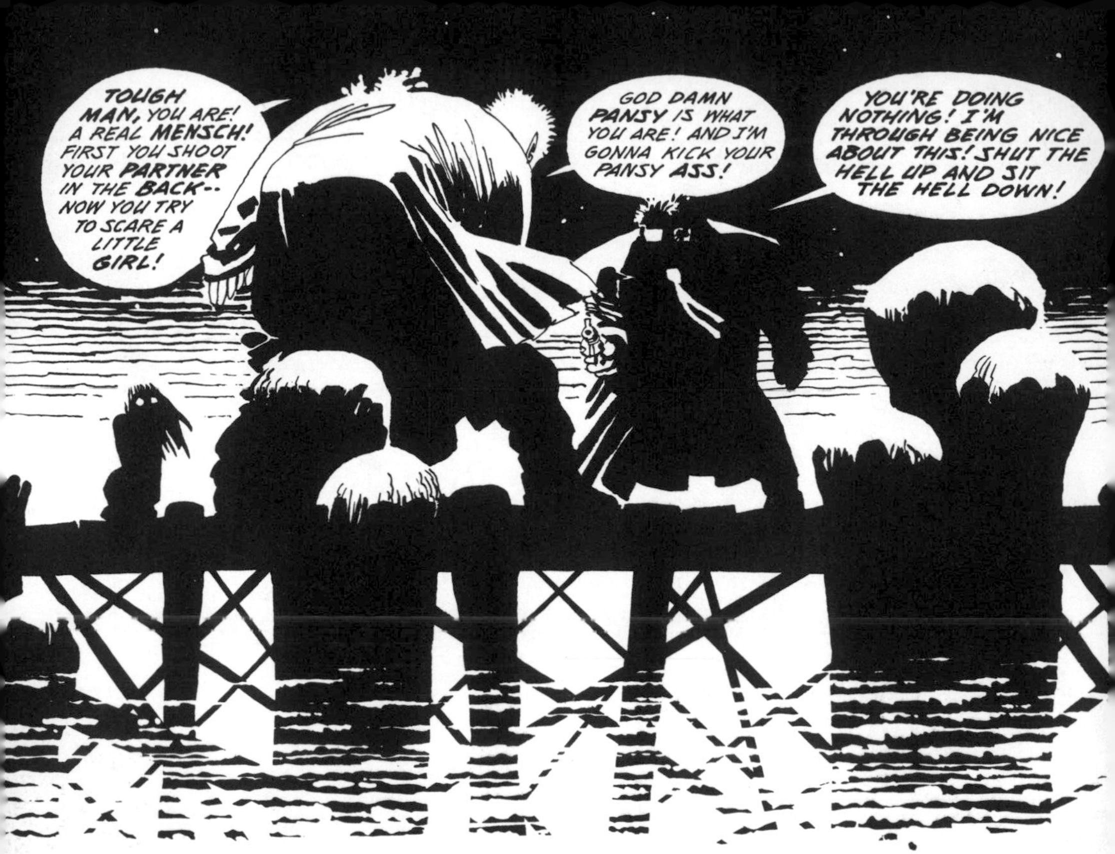
TOUGH MAN, YOU ARE! A REAL MENSCH! FIRST YOU SHOOT YOUR PARTNER IN THE BACK-- NOW YOU TRY TO SCARE A LITTLE GIRL!
GOD DAMN PANSY IS WHAT YOU ARE! AND I'M GONNA KICK YOUR PANSY ASS!
YOU'RE DOING NOTHING! I'M THROUGH BEING NICE ABOUT THIS! SHUT THE HELL UP AND SIT THE HELL DOWN!

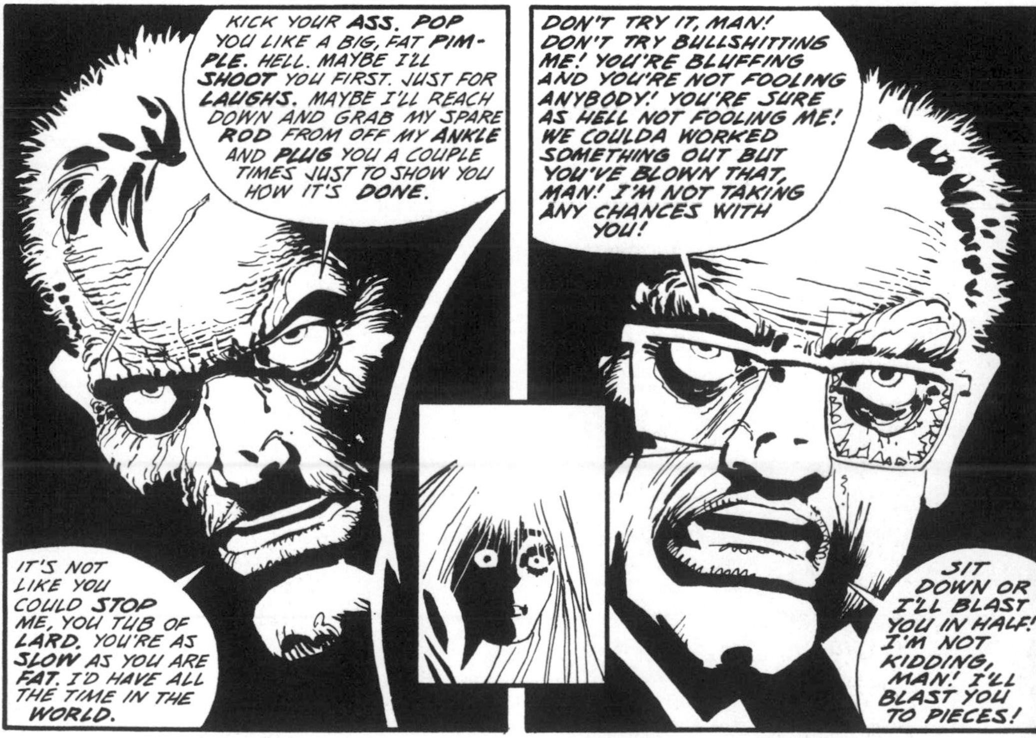
KICK YOUR ASS. POP YOU LIKE A BIG, FAT PIMPLE. HELL. MAYBE I'LL SHOOT YOU FIRST. JUST FOR LAUGHS. MAYBE I'LL REACH DOWN AND GRAB MY SPARE ROD FROM OFF MY ANKLE AND PLUG YOU A COUPLE TIMES JUST TO SHOW YOU HOW IT'S DONE.
IT'S NOT LIKE YOU COULD STOP ME, YOU TUB OF LARD. YOU'RE AS SLOW AS YOU ARE FAT. I'D HAVE ALL THE TIME IN THE WORLD.
DON'T TRY IT, MAN! DON'T TRY BULLSHITTING ME! YOU'RE BLUFFING AND YOU'RE NOT FOOLING ANYBODY! YOU'RE SURE AS HELL NOT FOOLING ME! WE COULDA WORKED SOMETHING OUT BUT YOU'VE BLOWN THAT, MAN! I'M NOT TAKING ANY CHANCES WITH YOU!
SIT DOWN OR I'LL BLAST YOU IN HALF! I'M NOT KIDDING, MAN! I'LL BLAST YOU TO PIECES!

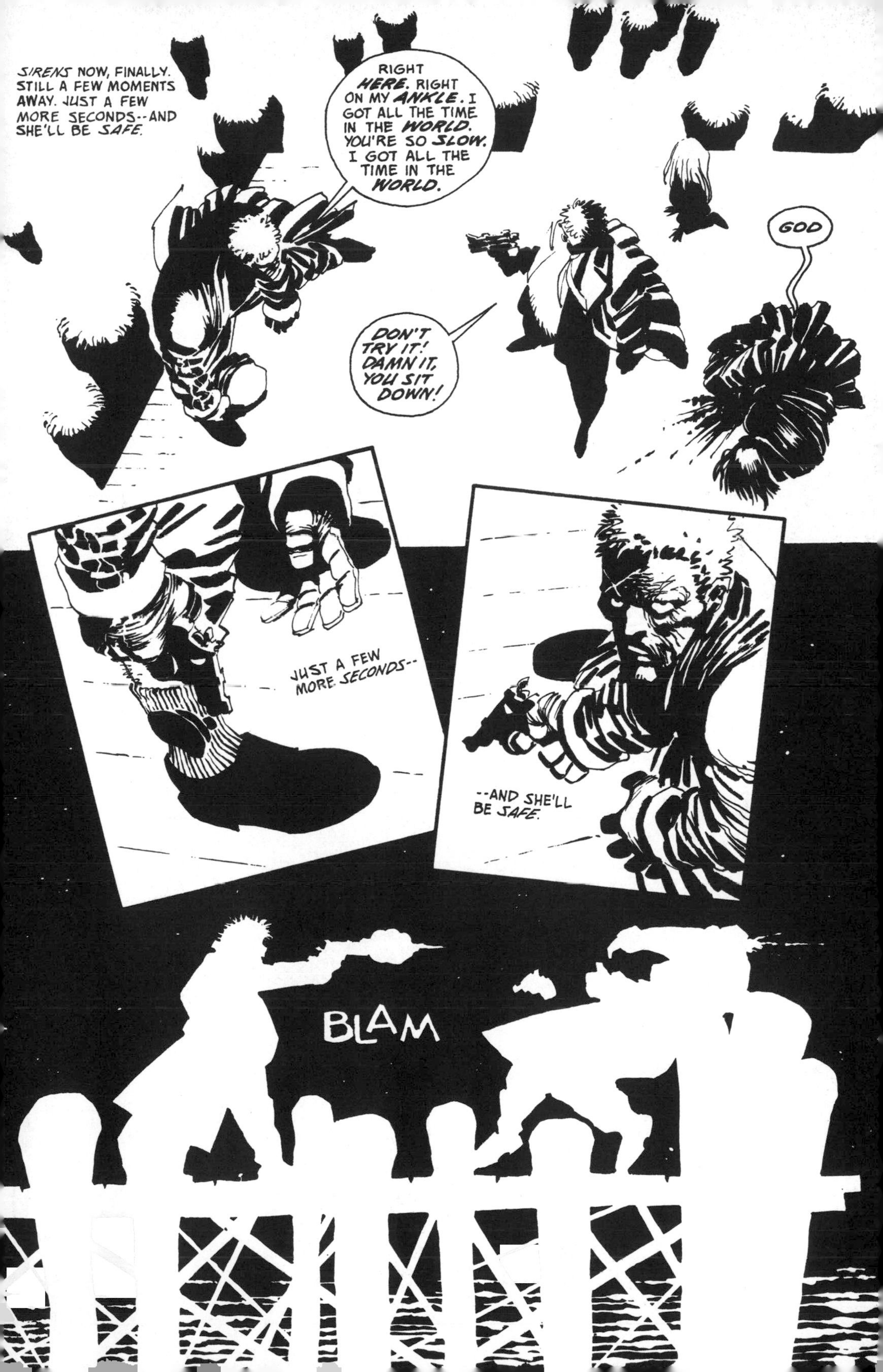
SIRENS NOW, FINALLY. STILL A FEW MOMENTS AWAY. JUST A FEW MORE SECONDS--AND SHE'LL BE SAFE.
RIGHT HERE. RIGHT ON MY ANKLE. I GOT ALL THE TIME IN THE WORLD. YOU'RE SO SLOW. I GOT ALL THE TIME IN THE WORLD.
GOD
DON'T TRY IT! DAMN IT, YOU SIT DOWN!
JUST A FEW MORE SECONDS--
--AND SHE'LL BE SAFE.
BLAM

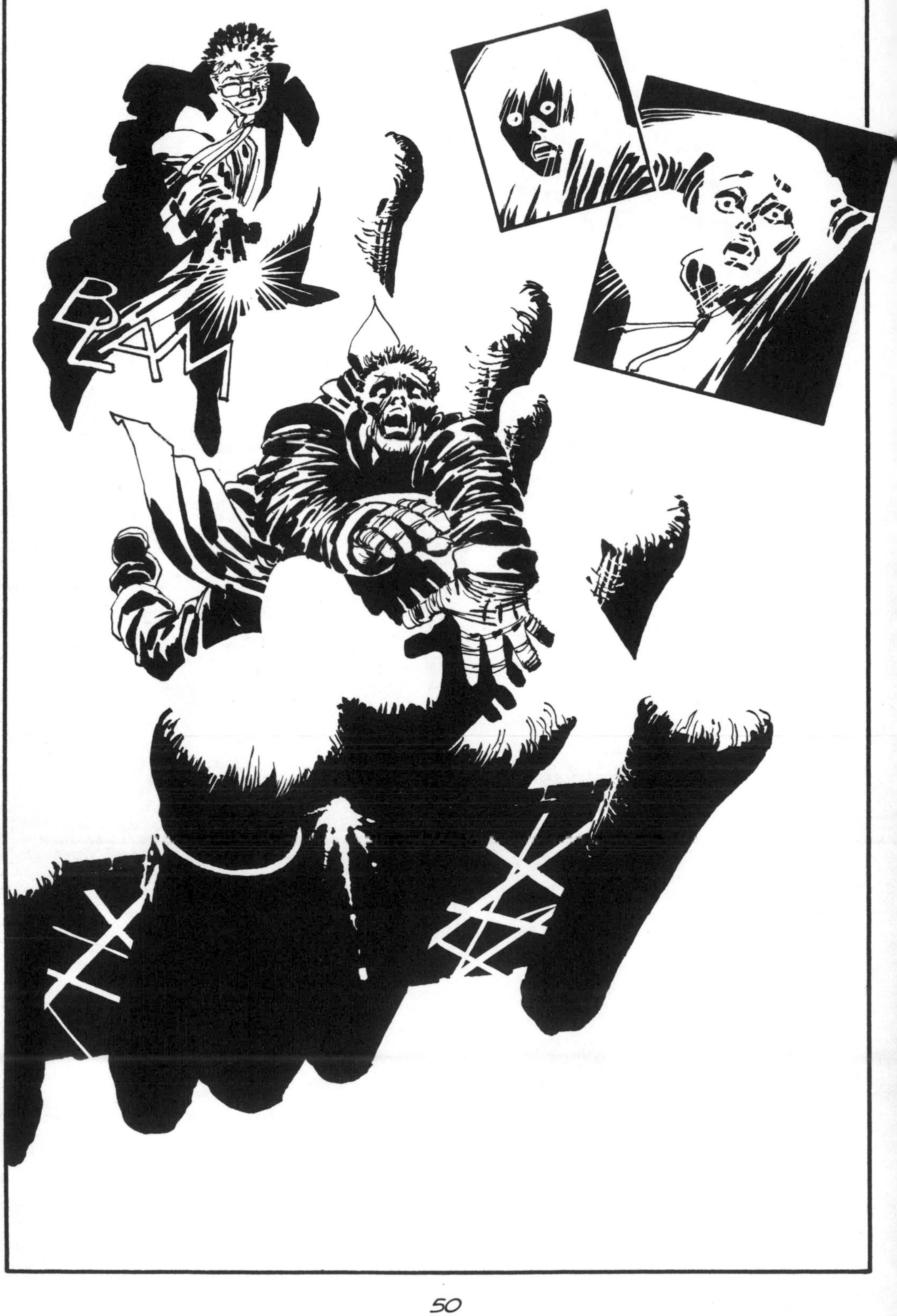
BLAM

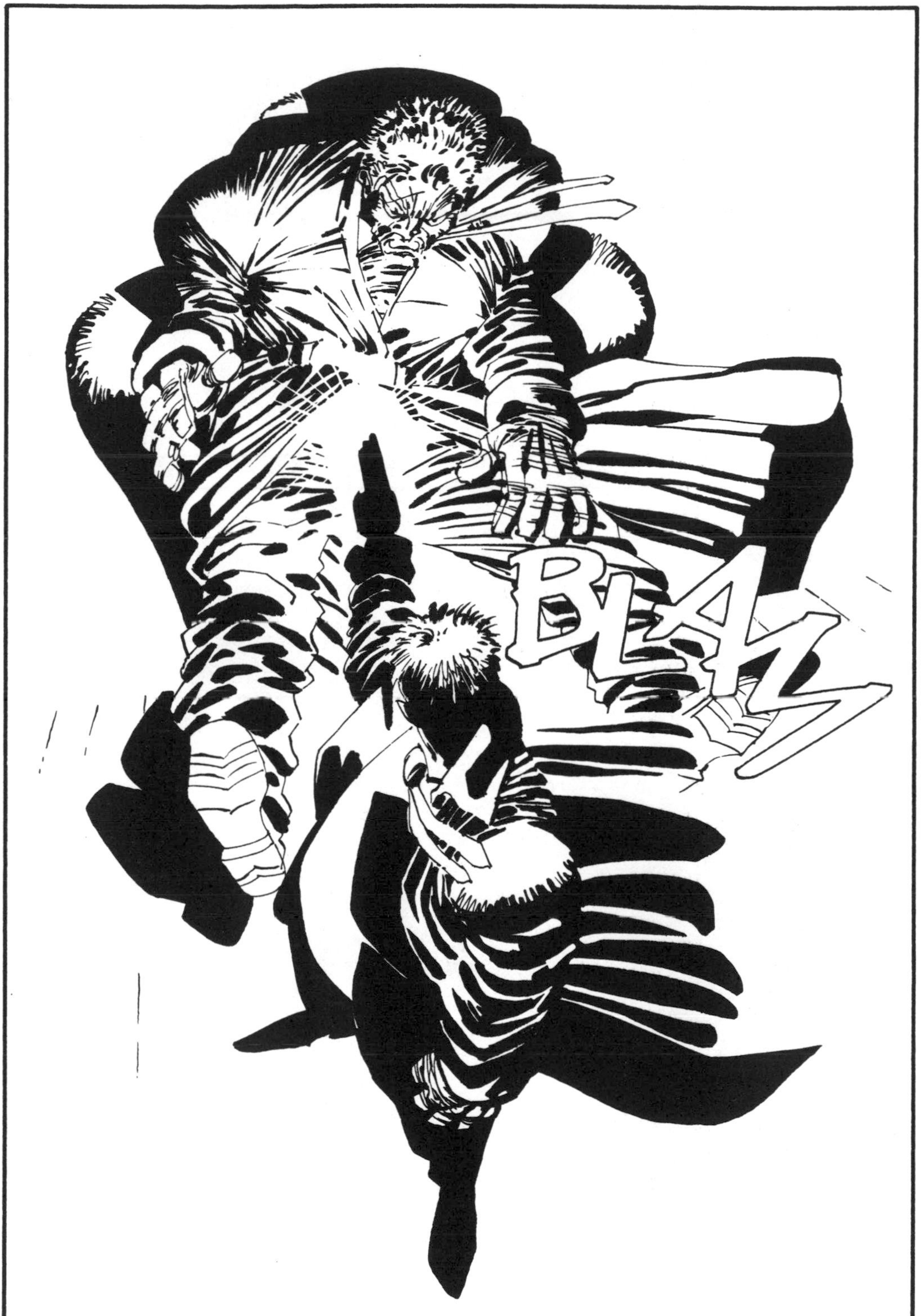
BLAM

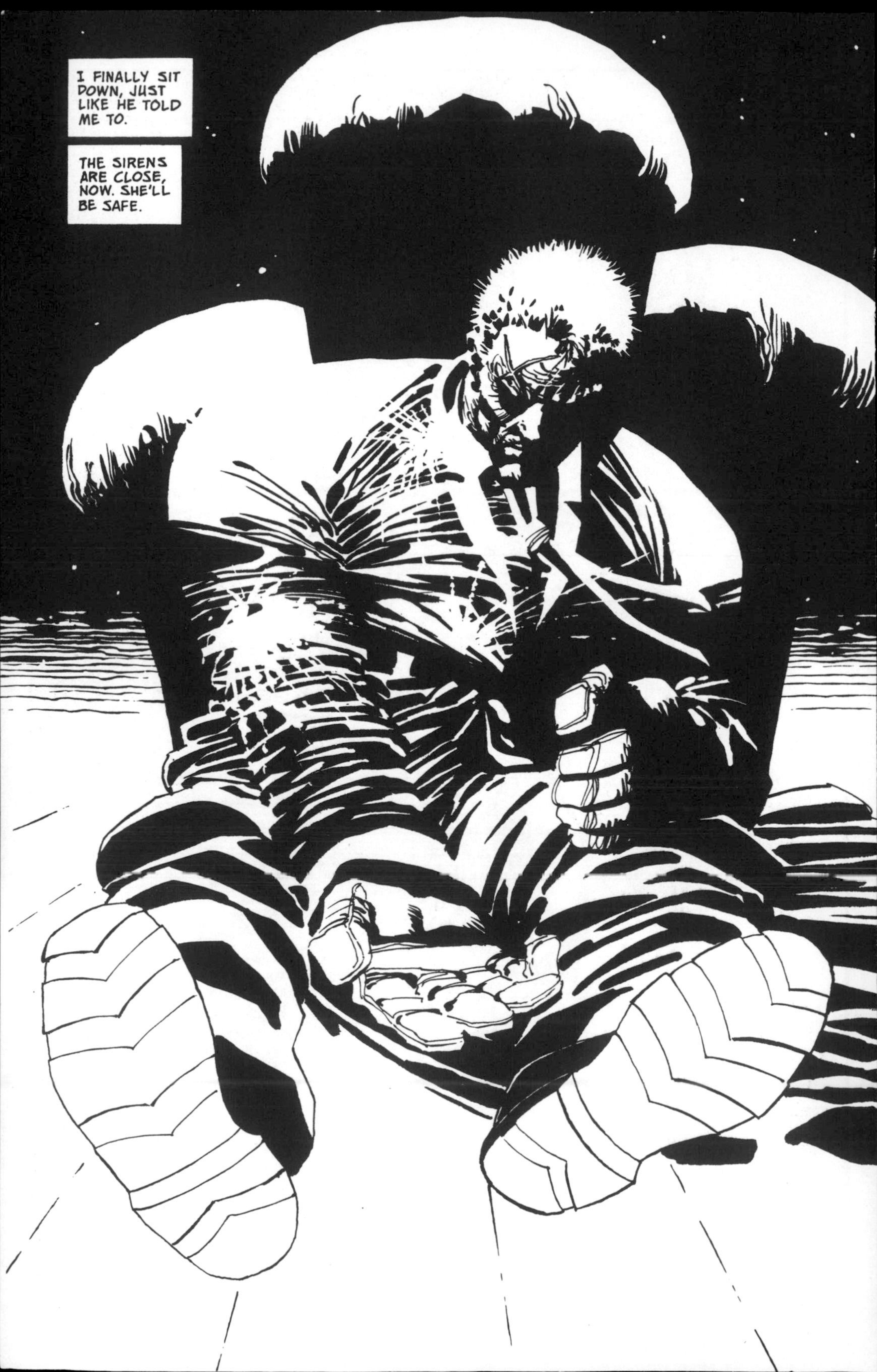
I FINALLY SIT DOWN, JUST LIKE HE TOLD ME TO.
THE SIRENS ARE CLOSE, NOW. SHE'LL BE SAFE.

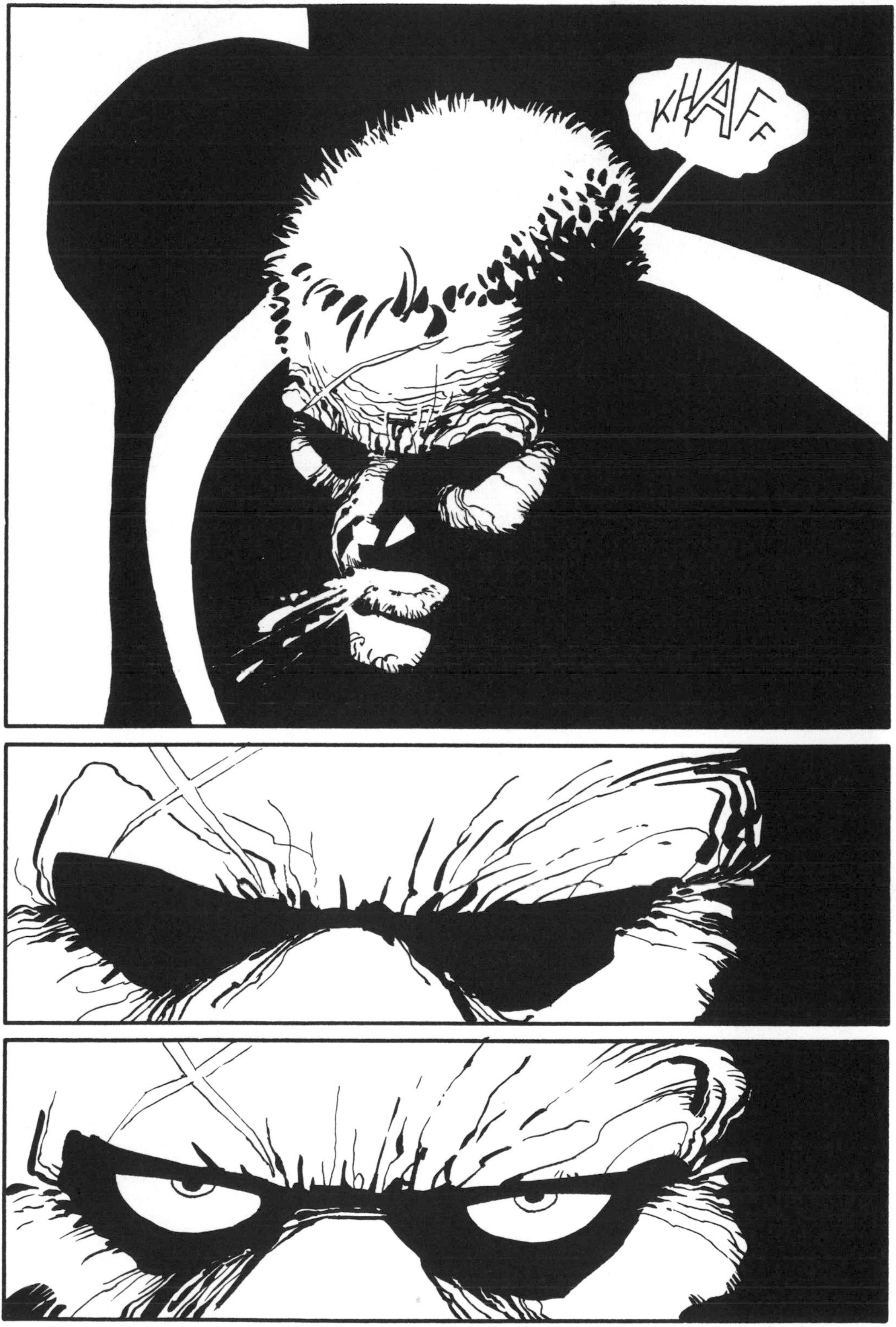
KHAFF

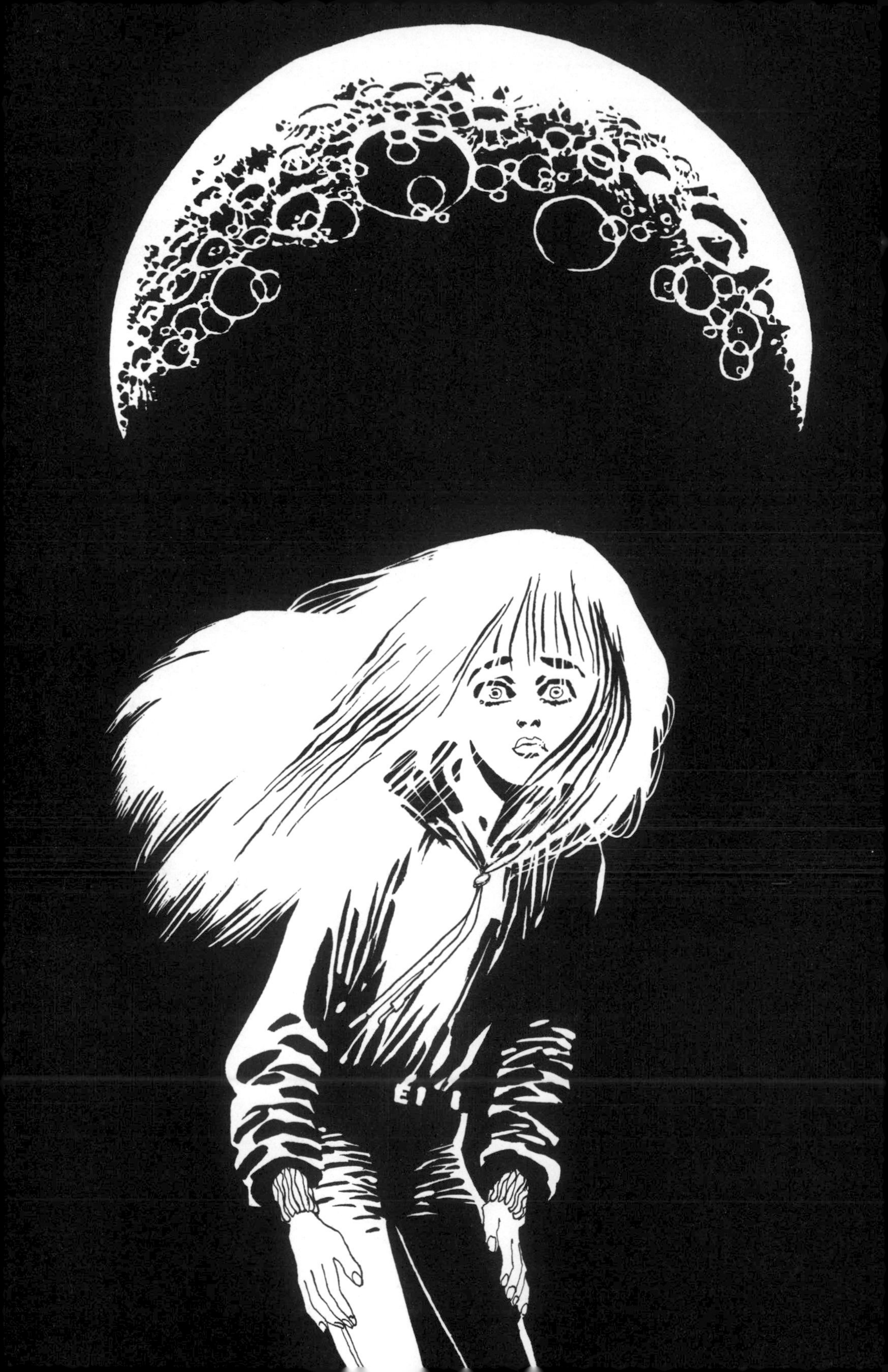

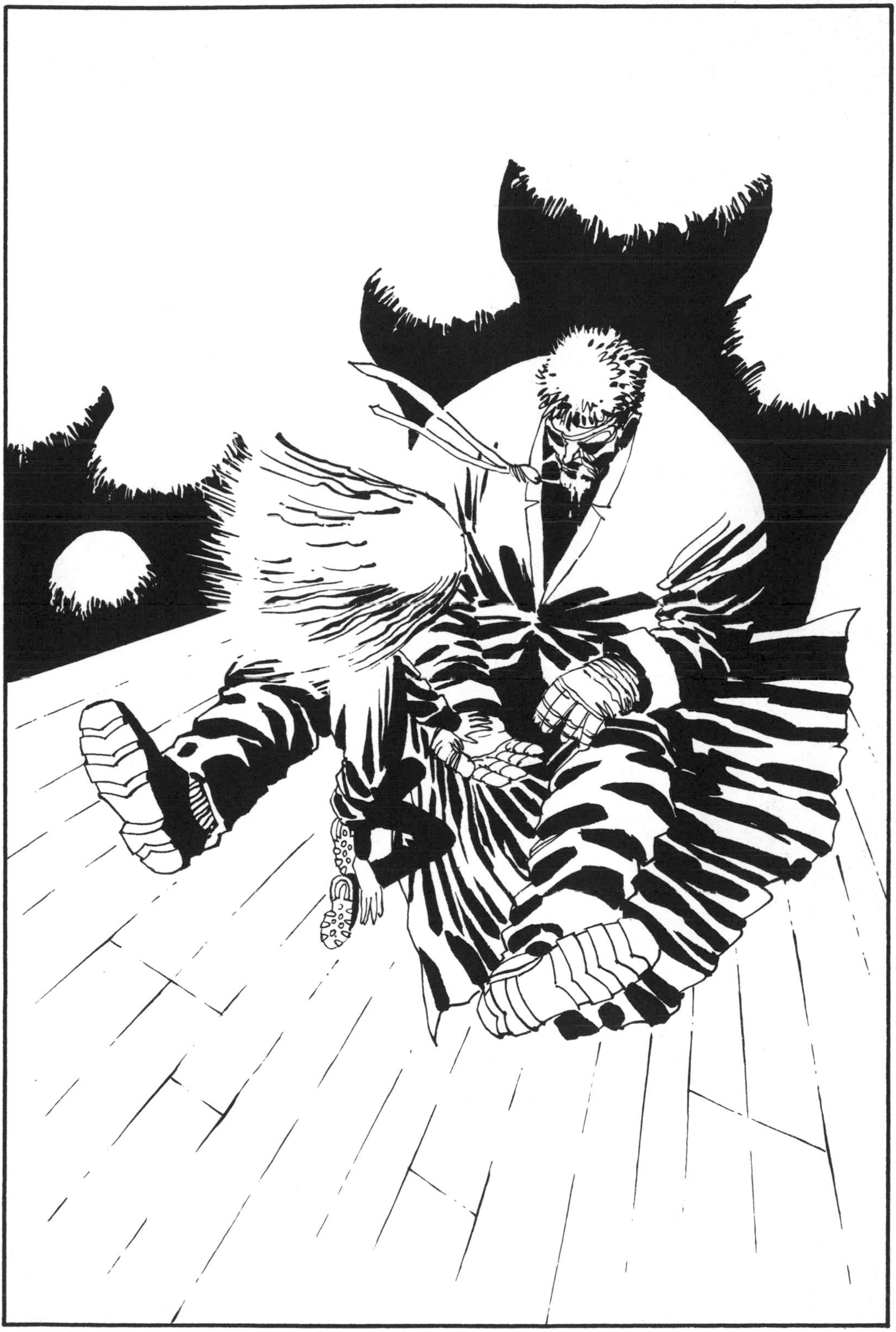

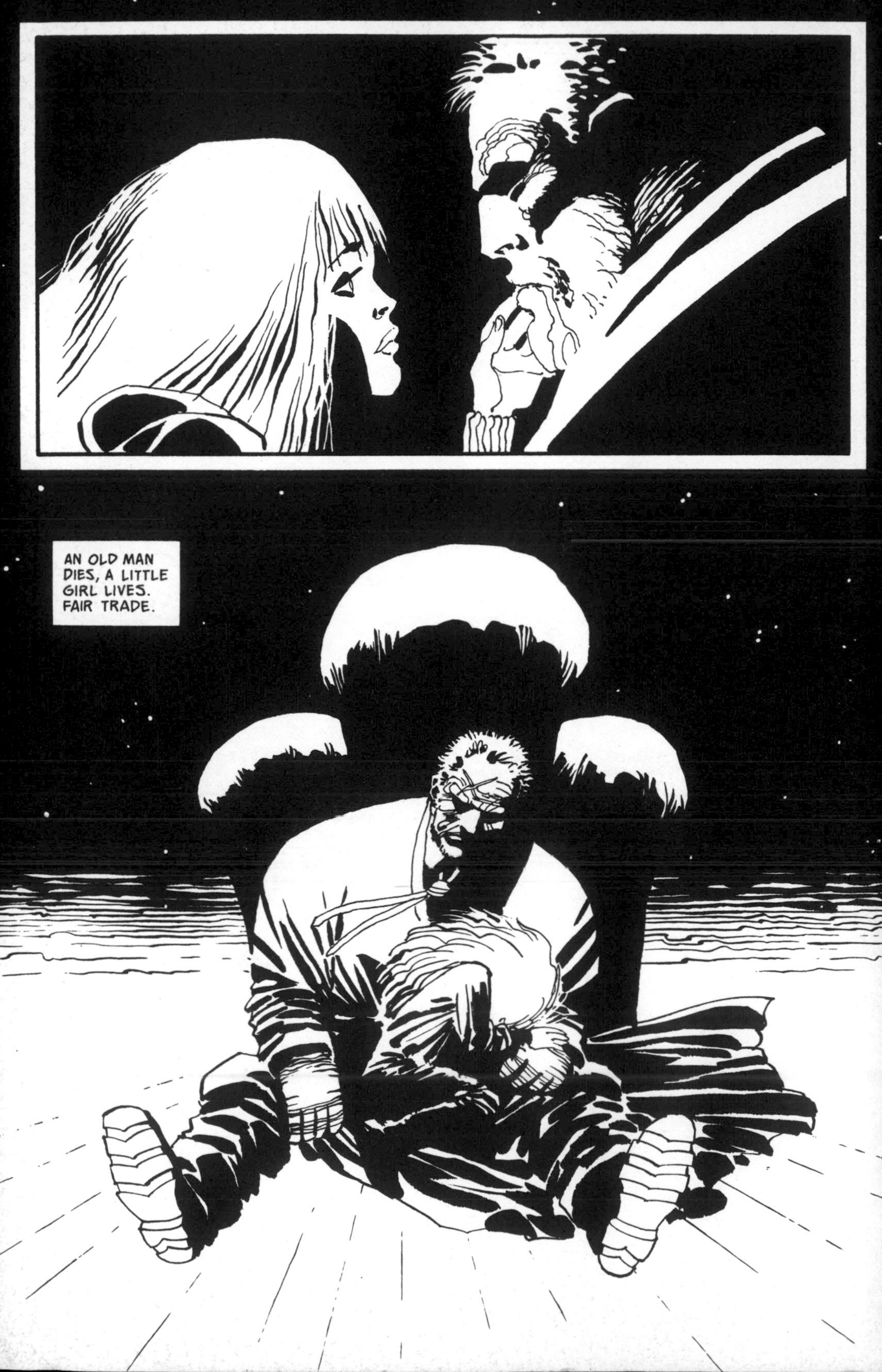
AN OLD MAN DIES, A LITTLE GIRL LIVES. FAIR TRADE.

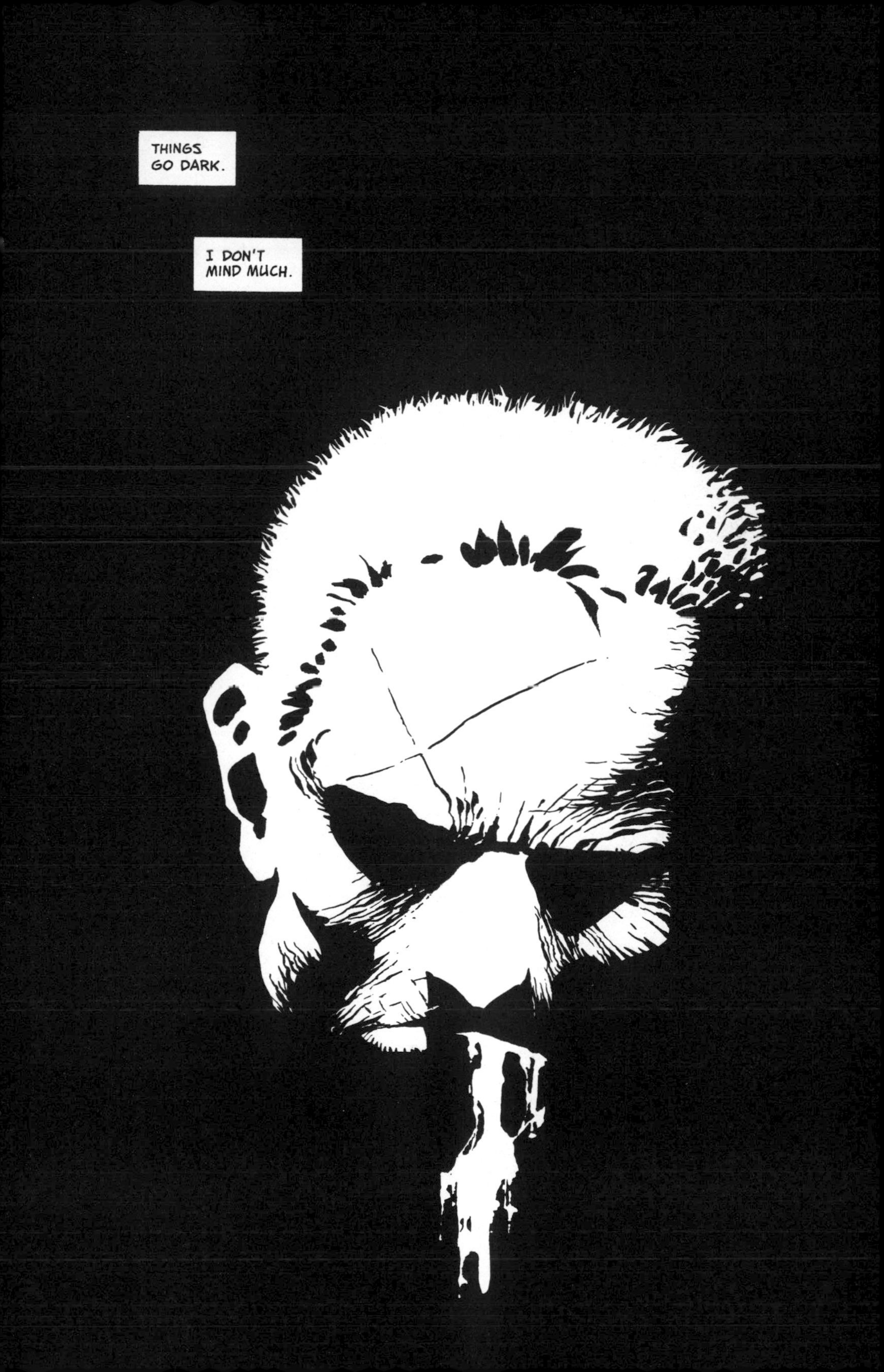
THINGS GO DARK.
I DON'T MIND MUCH.

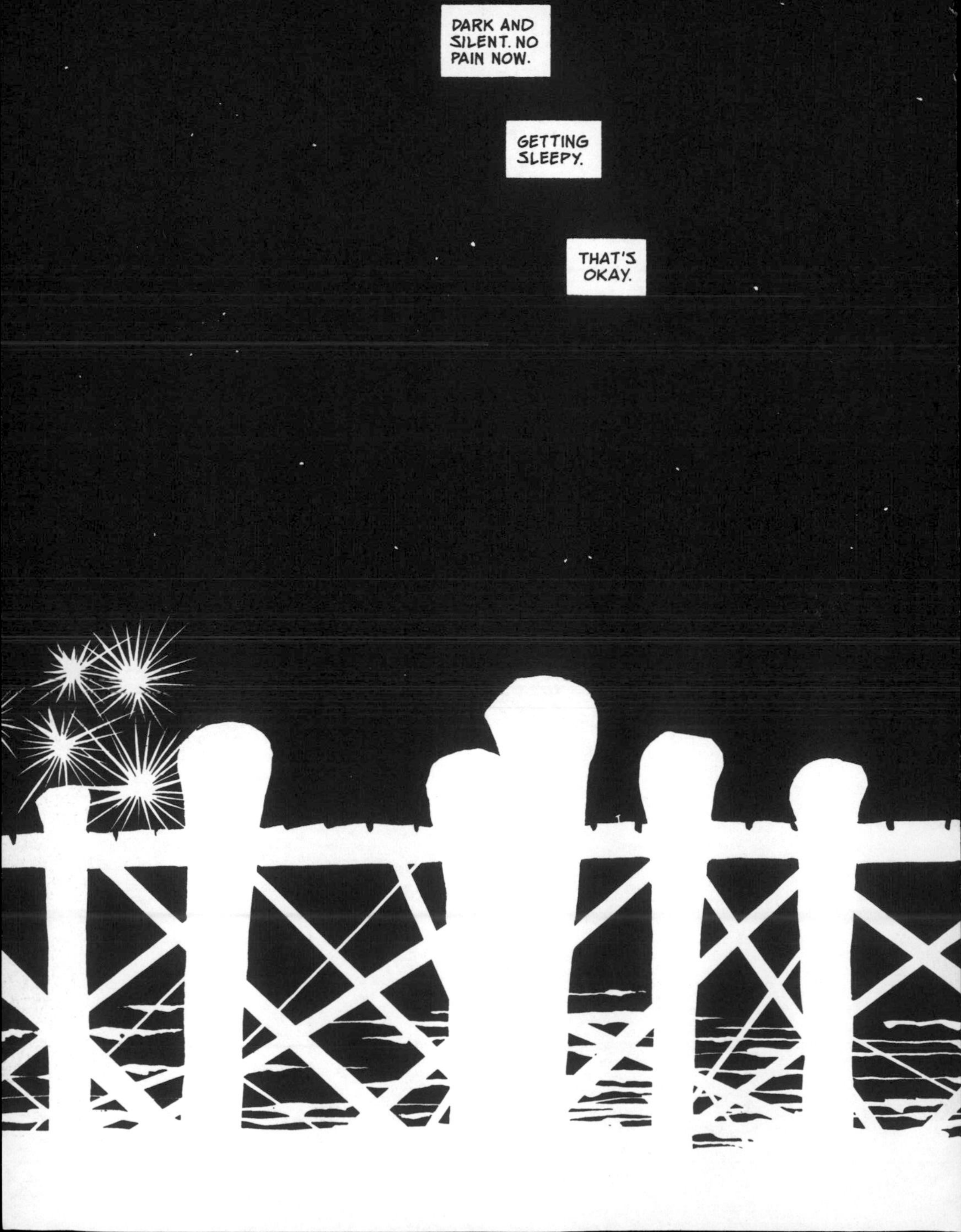
DARK AND SILENT. NO PAIN NOW.
GETTING SLEEPY.
THAT'S OKAY.

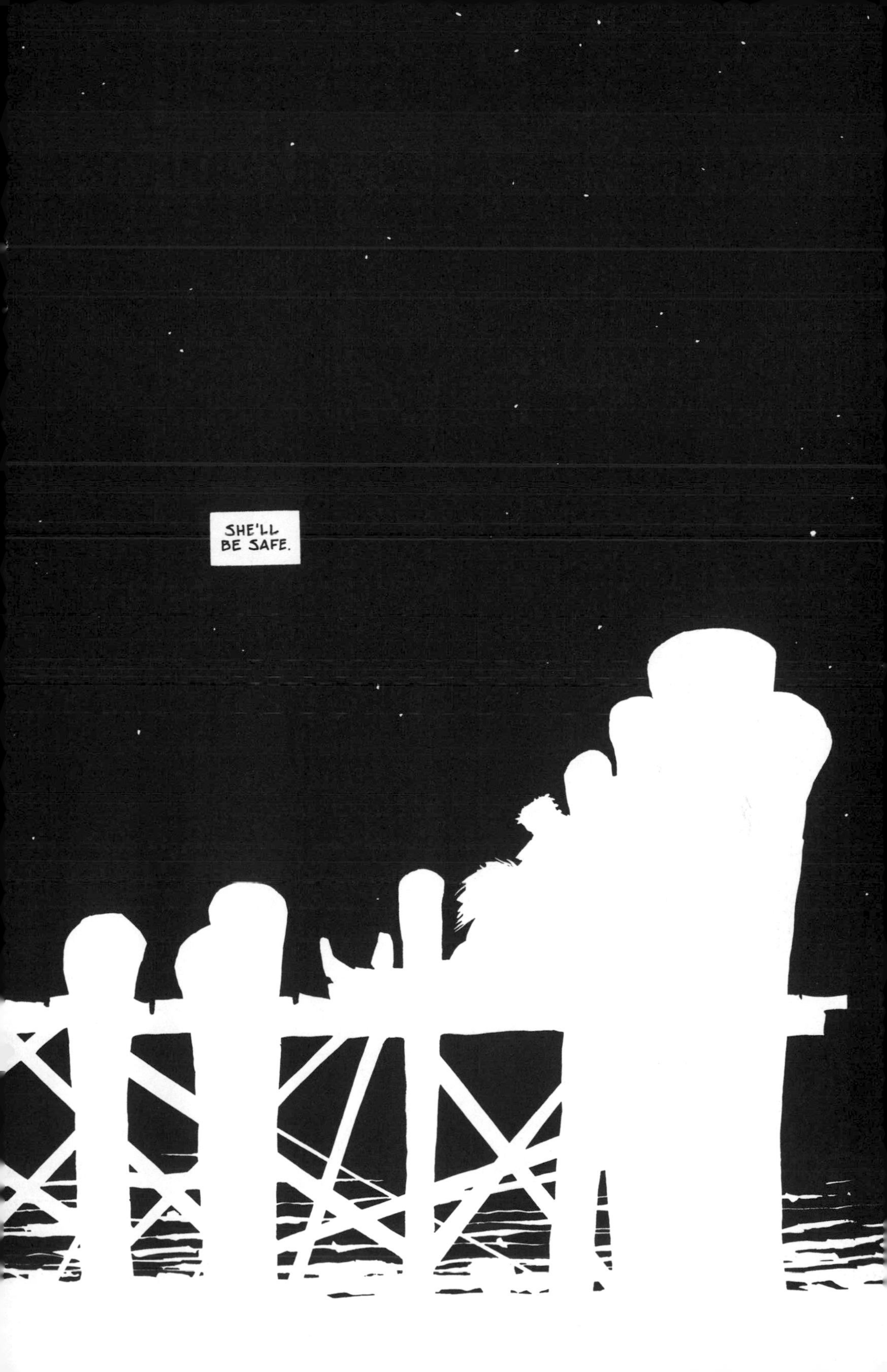
SHE'LL BE SAFE.

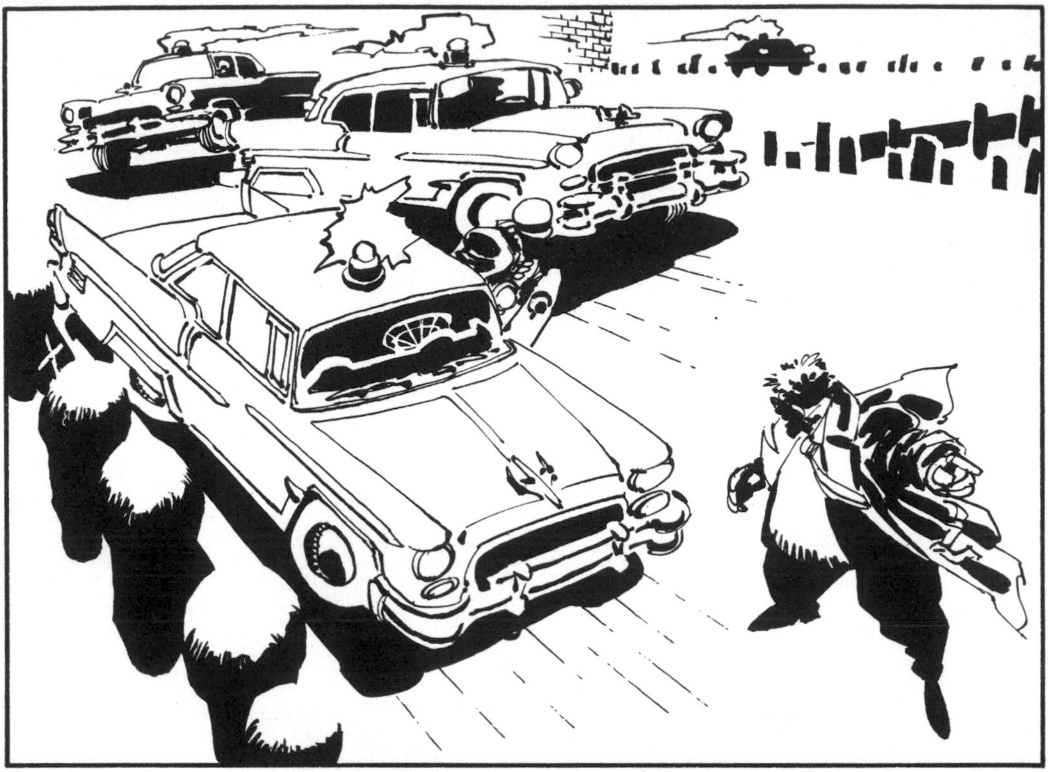

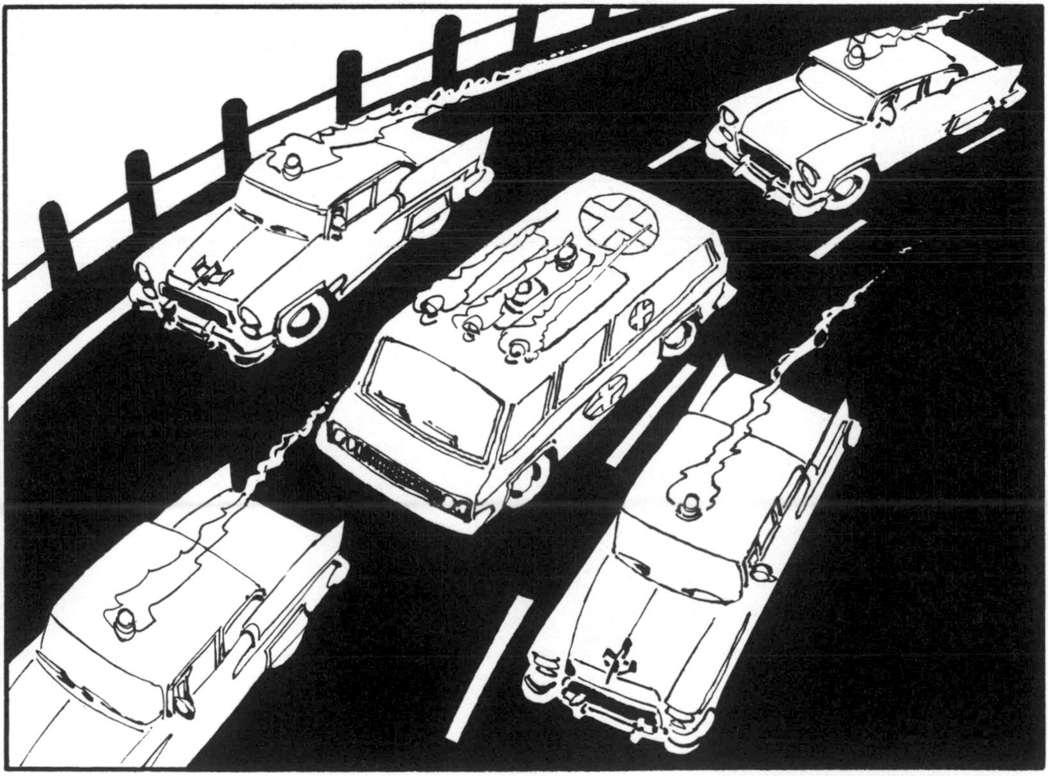

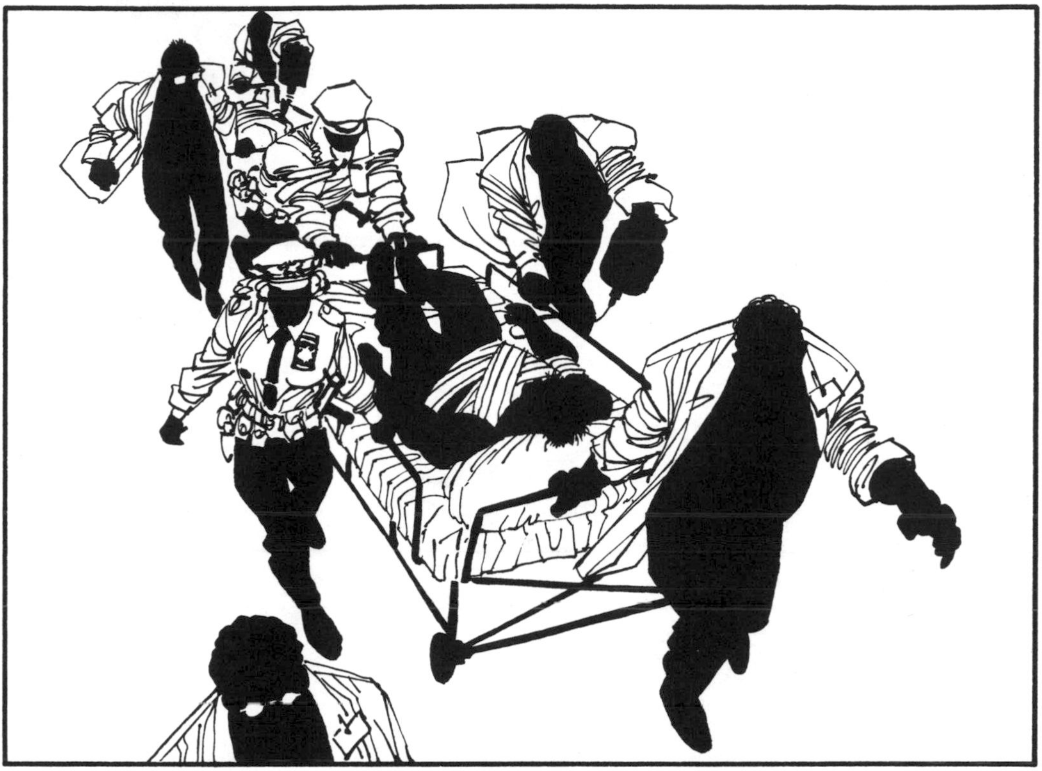

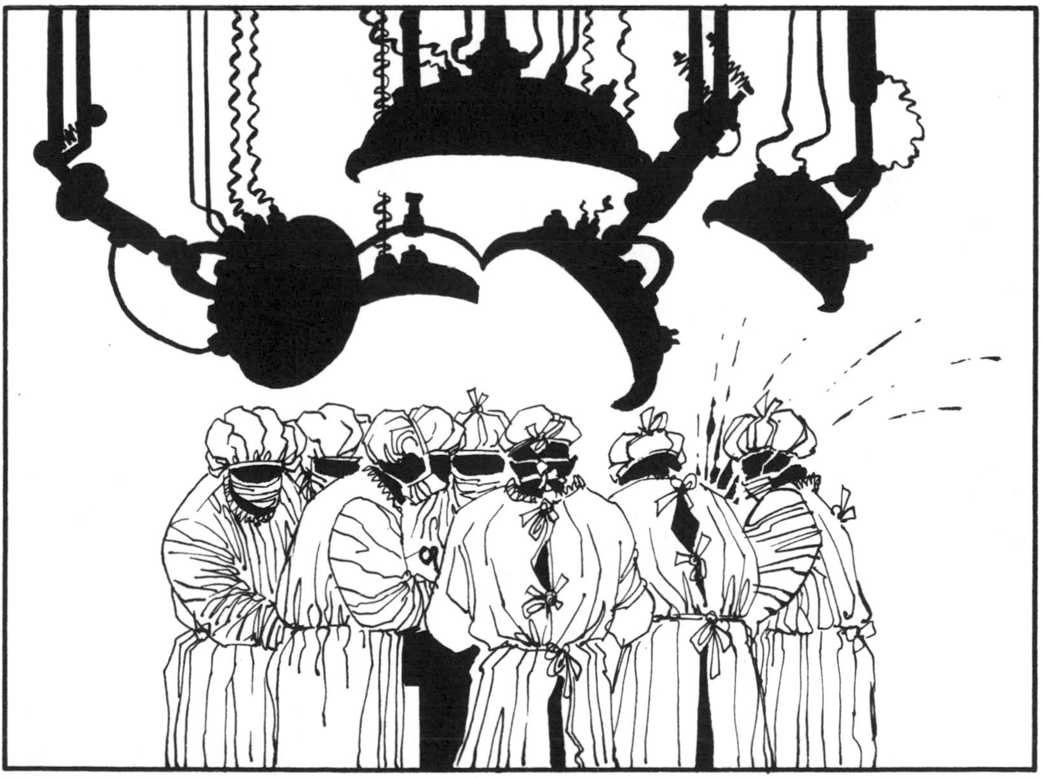

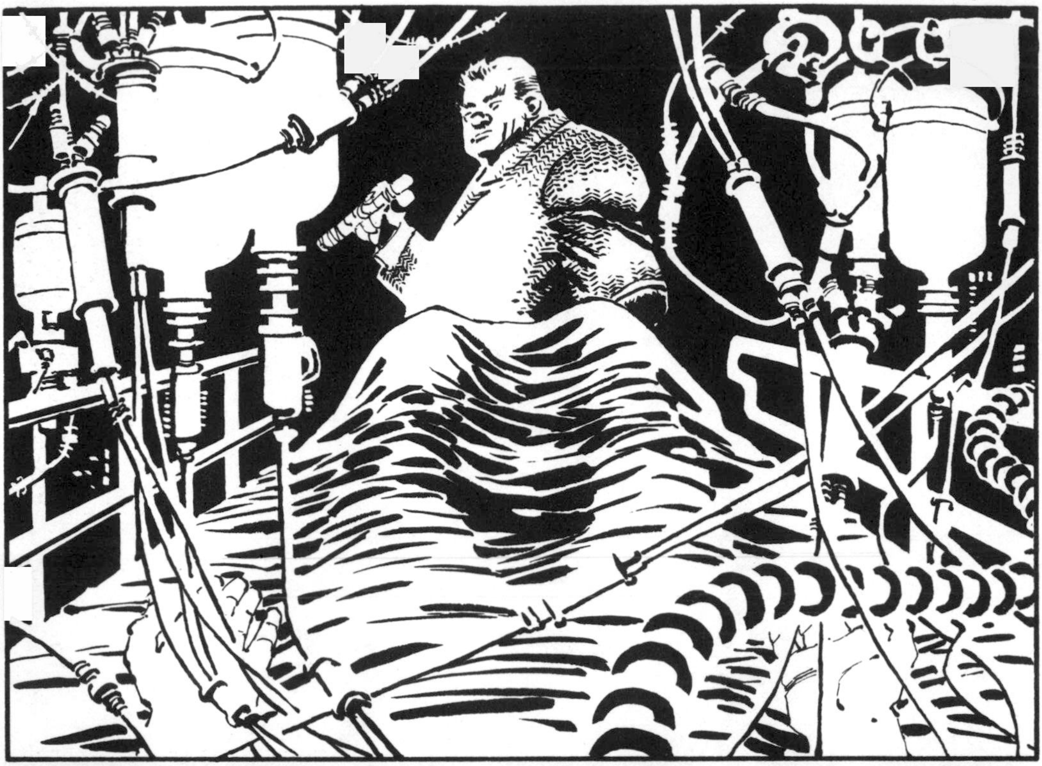

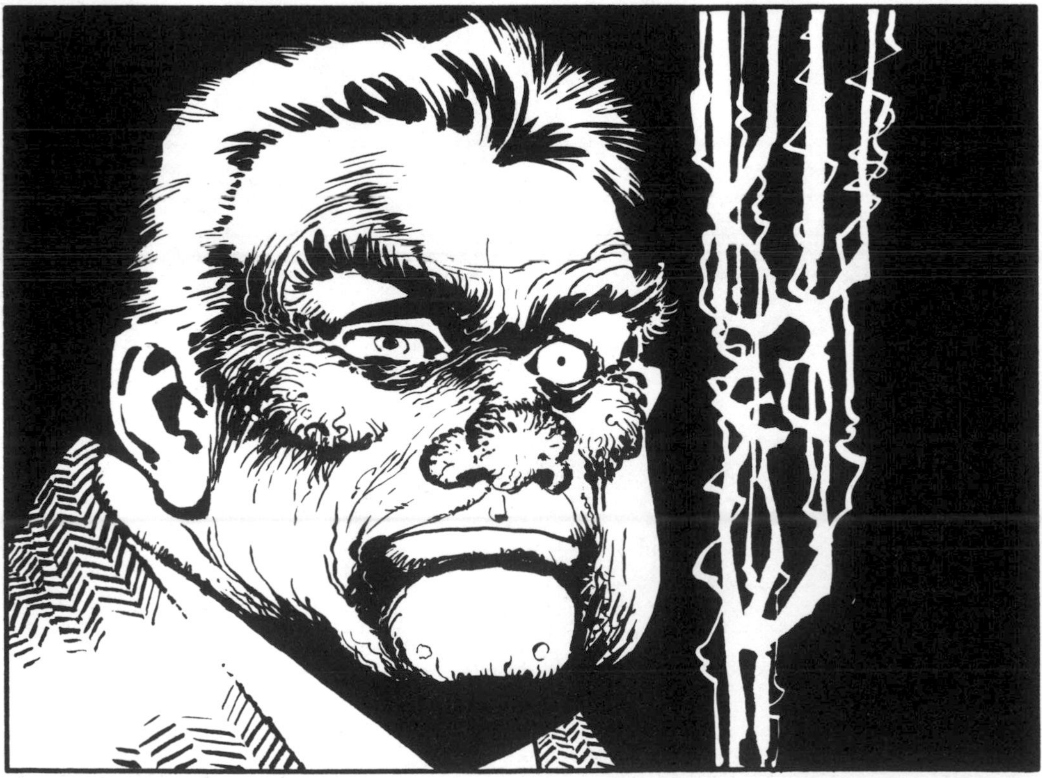

EVENING, OFFICER. I DON'T HAVE TO *INTRODUCE* MYSELF, DO I?...NAH. I DIDN'T THINK SO. YOU'RE A *GOOD CITIZEN*. A *RESPONSIBLE* CITIZEN. YOU KEEP YOURSELF *INFORMED*. YOU READ THE *PAPERS*. YOU'VE SEEN MY *PICTURE*.

THIS BEING AN *ELECTION* YEAR, YOU'VE SEEN *PLENTY* OF MY *PICTURE*.

YOU KNOW WHO I *AM*. YOU KNOW WHAT I CAN *DO*. AND I'M *DOING* YOU, HARTIGAN. *COLD* AND *HARD*, I'M *DOING* YOU.

oooh...I *KNOW* THAT *LOOK* IN YOUR *EYES*. LIKE A *CAT* NAILED TO A *TREE*. LIKE SOME PISSANT ROOKIE *LEGISLATOR* OUT TO SAVE THE *WORLD* WHO'S JUST GOTTEN HIS FIRST *LESSON* IN HOW THINGS ACTUALLY *WORK*.

YEAH, I KNOW THAT LOOK. I *LIKE* THAT LOOK. HELL, I *LIVE* FOR THAT LOOK. I SEEN IT A *THOUSAND* TIMES AND I *NEVER* GET ENOUGH OF IT. YOU *KNOW* YOU'RE GOOD AND *SCREWED*, RIGHT? COME *ON*. ADMIT IT. RIGHT NOW YOU'RE LYING THERE WISHING YOU'D *DIED* BACK ON THAT *DOCK*, AREN'T *YOU*, YOU GOD DAMN *COP*.?

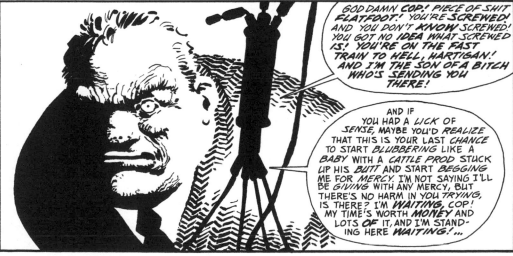

GOD DAMN *COP*.! PIECE OF SHIT *FLATFOOT*.! YOU'RE *SCREWED*.! AND *YOU* DON'T *KNOW* SCREWED! YOU GOT NO IDEA WHAT SCREWED *IS*.! YOU'RE ON THE *FAST TRAIN* TO HELL, HARTIGAN! AND *I'M* THE SON OF A BITCH WHO'S SENDING YOU *THERE*.!

AND IF YOU HAD A *LICK* OF *SENSE*, MAYBE YOU'D *REALIZE* THAT THIS IS YOUR LAST *CHANCE* TO START *BLUBBERING* LIKE A *BABY* WITH A *CATTLE PROD* STUCK UP HIS *BUTT* AND START *BEGGING* ME FOR *MERCY*. I'M NOT SAYING I'LL BE *GIVING* WITH ANY MERCY, BUT THERE'S NO HARM IN YOU *TRYING*, IS THERE? I'M *WAITING*, COP! MY TIME'S WORTH *MONEY* AND LOTS *OF* IT, AND I'M STANDING HERE *WAITING*! ...

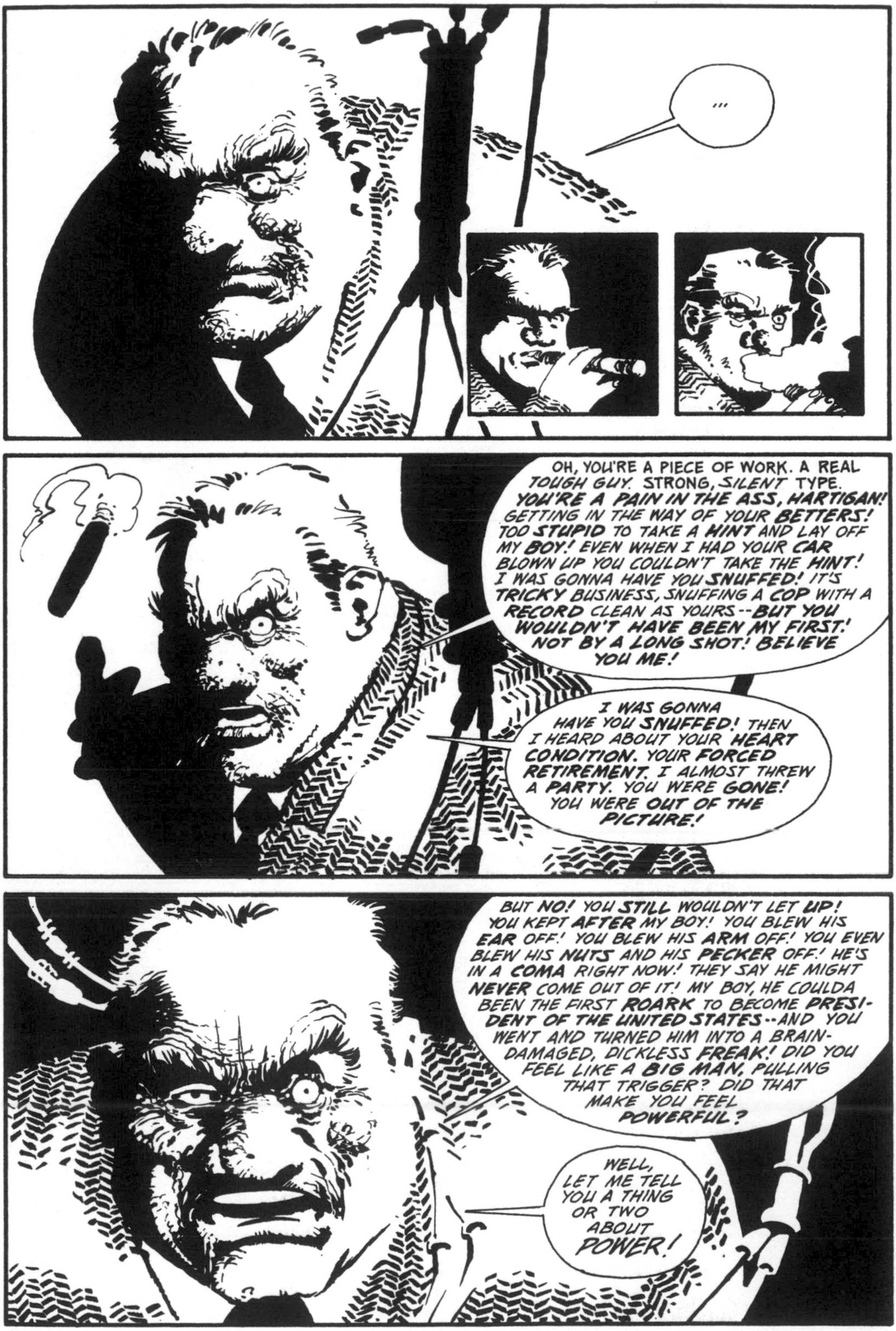
...
OH, YOU'RE A PIECE OF WORK. A REAL TOUGH GUY. STRONG, SILENT TYPE. YOU'RE A PAIN IN THE ASS, HARTIGAN! GETTING IN THE WAY OF YOUR BETTERS! TOO STUPID TO TAKE A HINT AND LAY OFF MY BOY! EVEN WHEN I HAD YOUR CAR BLOWN UP YOU COULDN'T TAKE THE HINT! I WAS GONNA HAVE YOU SNUFFED! IT'S TRICKY BUSINESS, SNUFFING A COP WITH A RECORD CLEAN AS YOURS--BUT YOU WOULDN'T HAVE BEEN MY FIRST! NOT BY A LONG SHOT! BELIEVE YOU ME!
I WAS GONNA HAVE YOU SNUFFED! THEN I HEARD ABOUT YOUR HEART CONDITION. YOUR FORCED RETIREMENT. I ALMOST THREW A PARTY. YOU WERE GONE! YOU WERE OUT OF THE PICTURE!
BUT NO! YOU STILL WOULDN'T LET UP! YOU KEPT AFTER MY BOY! YOU BLEW HIS EAR OFF! YOU BLEW HIS ARM OFF! YOU EVEN BLEW HIS NUTS AND HIS PECKER OFF! HE'S IN A COMA RIGHT NOW! THEY SAY HE MIGHT NEVER COME OUT OF IT! MY BOY, HE COULDA BEEN THE FIRST ROARK TO BECOME PRESI-DENT OF THE UNITED STATES--AND YOU WENT AND TURNED HIM INTO A BRAIN-DAMAGED, DICKLESS FREAK! DID YOU FEEL LIKE A BIG MAN, PULLING THAT TRIGGER? DID THAT MAKE YOU FEEL POWERFUL?
WELL, LET ME TELL YOU A THING OR TWO ABOUT POWER!

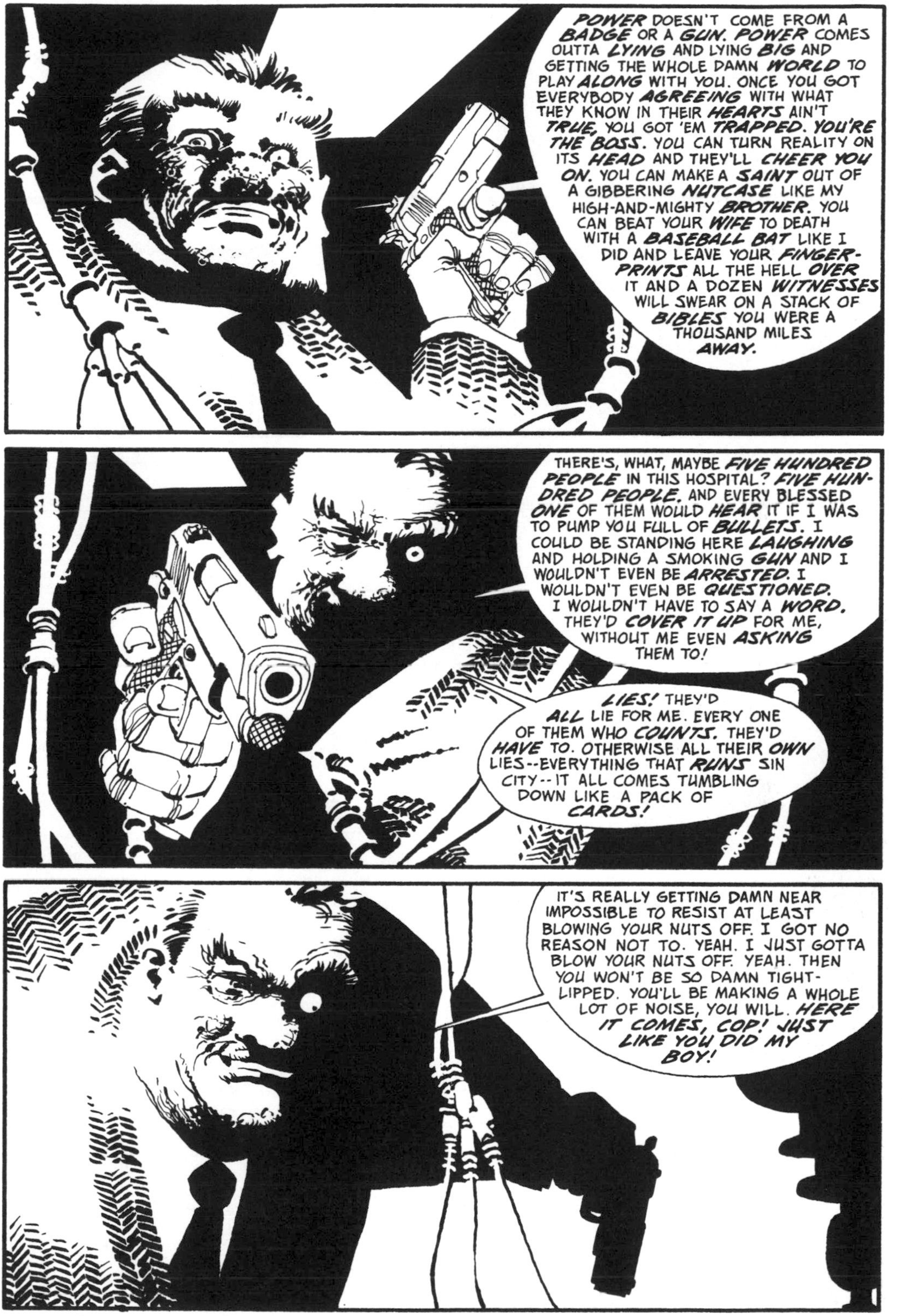
POWER DOESN'T COME FROM A BADGE OR A GUN. POWER COMES OUTTA LYING AND LYING BIG AND GETTING THE WHOLE DAMN WORLD TO PLAY ALONG WITH YOU. ONCE YOU GOT EVERYBODY AGREEING WITH WHAT THEY KNOW IN THEIR HEARTS AIN'T TRUE, YOU GOT 'EM TRAPPED. YOU'RE THE BOSS. YOU CAN TURN REALITY ON ITS HEAD AND THEY'LL CHEER YOU ON. YOU CAN MAKE A SAINT OUT OF A GIBBERING NUTCASE LIKE MY HIGH-AND-MIGHTY BROTHER. YOU CAN BEAT YOUR WIFE TO DEATH WITH A BASEBALL BAT LIKE I DID AND LEAVE YOUR FINGER-PRINTS ALL THE HELL OVER IT AND A DOZEN WITNESSES WILL SWEAR ON A STACK OF BIBLES YOU WERE A THOUSAND MILES AWAY.
THERE'S, WHAT, MAYBE FIVE HUNDRED PEOPLE IN THIS HOSPITAL? FIVE HUN-DRED PEOPLE. AND EVERY BLESSED ONE OF THEM WOULD HEAR IT IF I WAS TO PUMP YOU FULL OF BULLETS. I COULD BE STANDING HERE LAUGHING AND HOLDING A SMOKING GUN AND I WOULDN'T EVEN BE ARRESTED. I WOULDN'T EVEN BE QUESTIONED. I WOULDN'T HAVE TO SAY A WORD. THEY'D COVER IT UP FOR ME, WITHOUT ME EVEN ASKING THEM TO!
LIES! THEY'D ALL LIE FOR ME. EVERY ONE OF THEM WHO COUNTS. THEY'D HAVE TO. OTHERWISE ALL THEIR OWN LIES--EVERYTHING THAT RUNS SIN CITY--IT ALL COMES TUMBLING DOWN LIKE A PACK OF CARDS!
IT'S REALLY GETTING DAMN NEAR IMPOSSIBLE TO RESIST AT LEAST BLOWING YOUR NUTS OFF. I GOT NO REASON NOT TO. YEAH. I JUST GOTTA BLOW YOUR NUTS OFF. YEAH. THEN YOU WON'T BE SO DAMN TIGHT-LIPPED. YOU'LL BE MAKING A WHOLE LOT OF NOISE, YOU WILL. HERE IT COMES, COP! JUST LIKE YOU DID MY BOY!

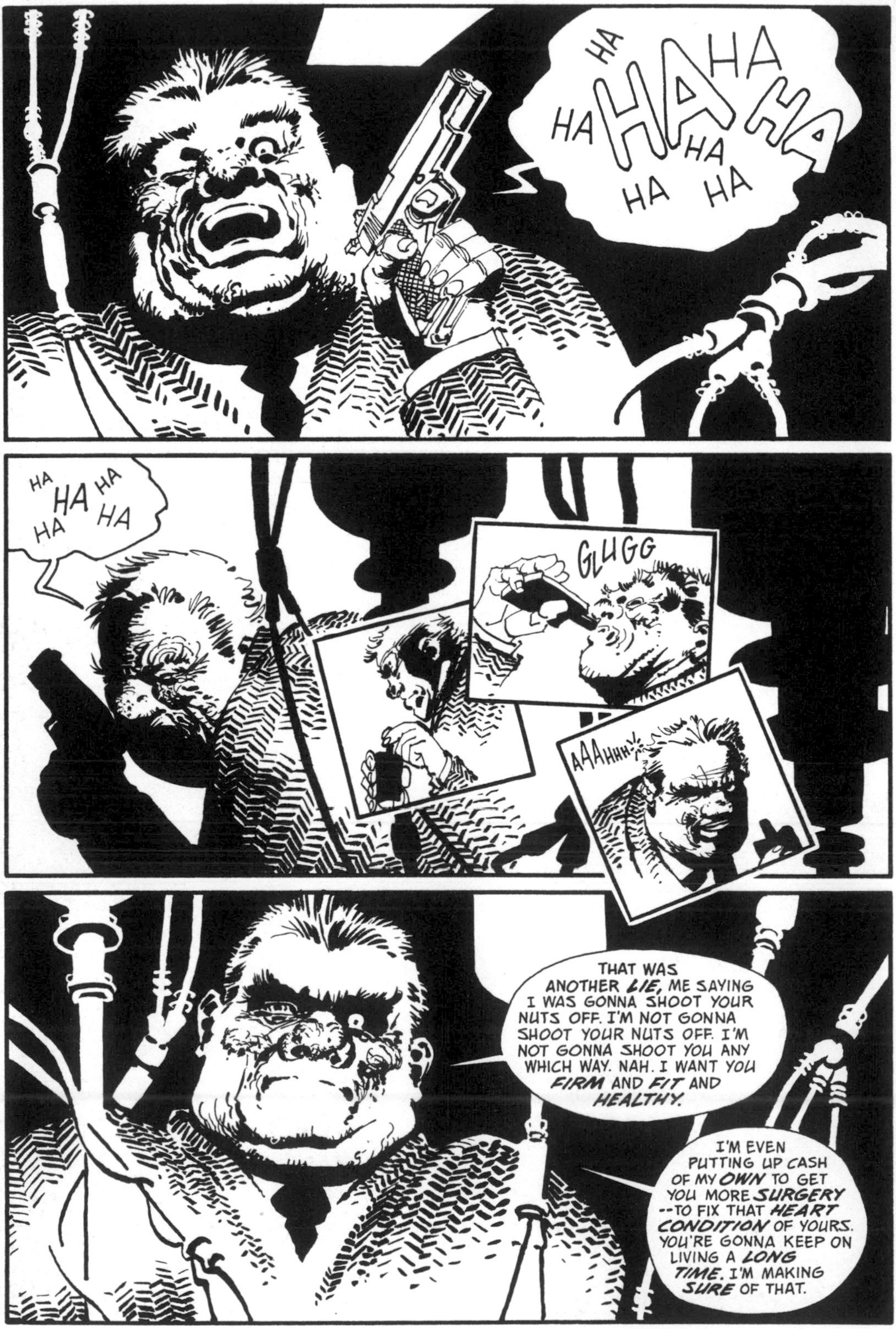
HA HA HA HA HA HA HA HA HA
HA HA HA HA HA
GLUGG
AAAHHH
THAT WAS ANOTHER LIE, ME SAYING I WAS GONNA SHOOT YOUR NUTS OFF. I'M NOT GONNA SHOOT YOUR NUTS OFF. I'M NOT GONNA SHOOT YOU ANY WHICH WAY. NAH. I WANT YOU FIRM AND FIT AND HEALTHY.
I'M EVEN PUTTING UP CASH OF MY OWN TO GET YOU MORE SURGERY --TO FIX THAT HEART CONDITION OF YOURS. YOU'RE GONNA KEEP ON LIVING A LONG TIME. I'M MAKING SURE OF THAT.

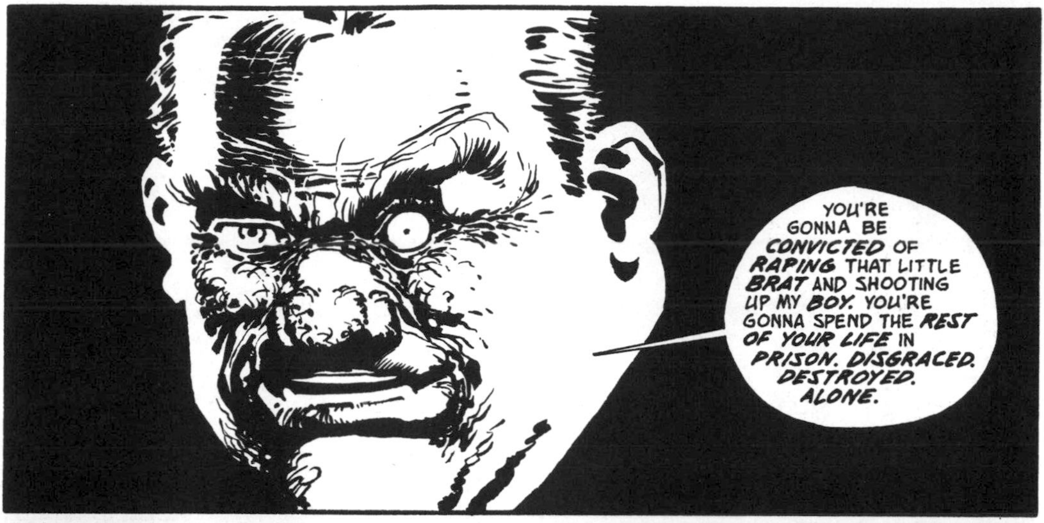
YOU'RE GONNA BE CONVICTED OF RAPING THAT LITTLE BRAT AND SHOOTING UP MY BOY. YOU'RE GONNA SPEND THE REST OF YOUR LIFE IN PRISON. DISGRACED. DESTROYED. ALONE.

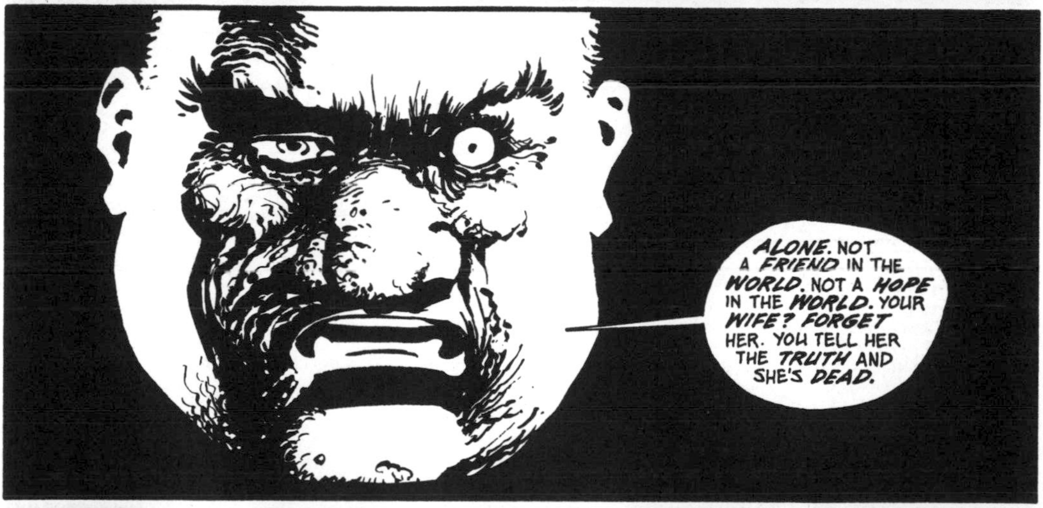
ALONE. NOT A FRIEND IN THE WORLD. NOT A HOPE IN THE WORLD. YOUR WIFE? FORGET HER. YOU TELL HER THE TRUTH AND SHE'S DEAD.

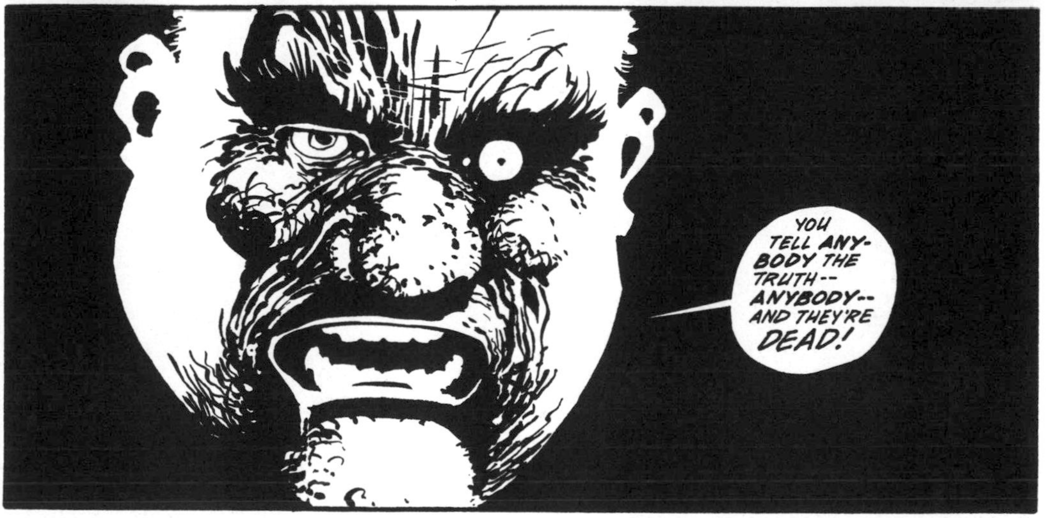
YOU TELL ANYBODY THE TRUTH-- ANYBODY-- AND THEY'RE DEAD!

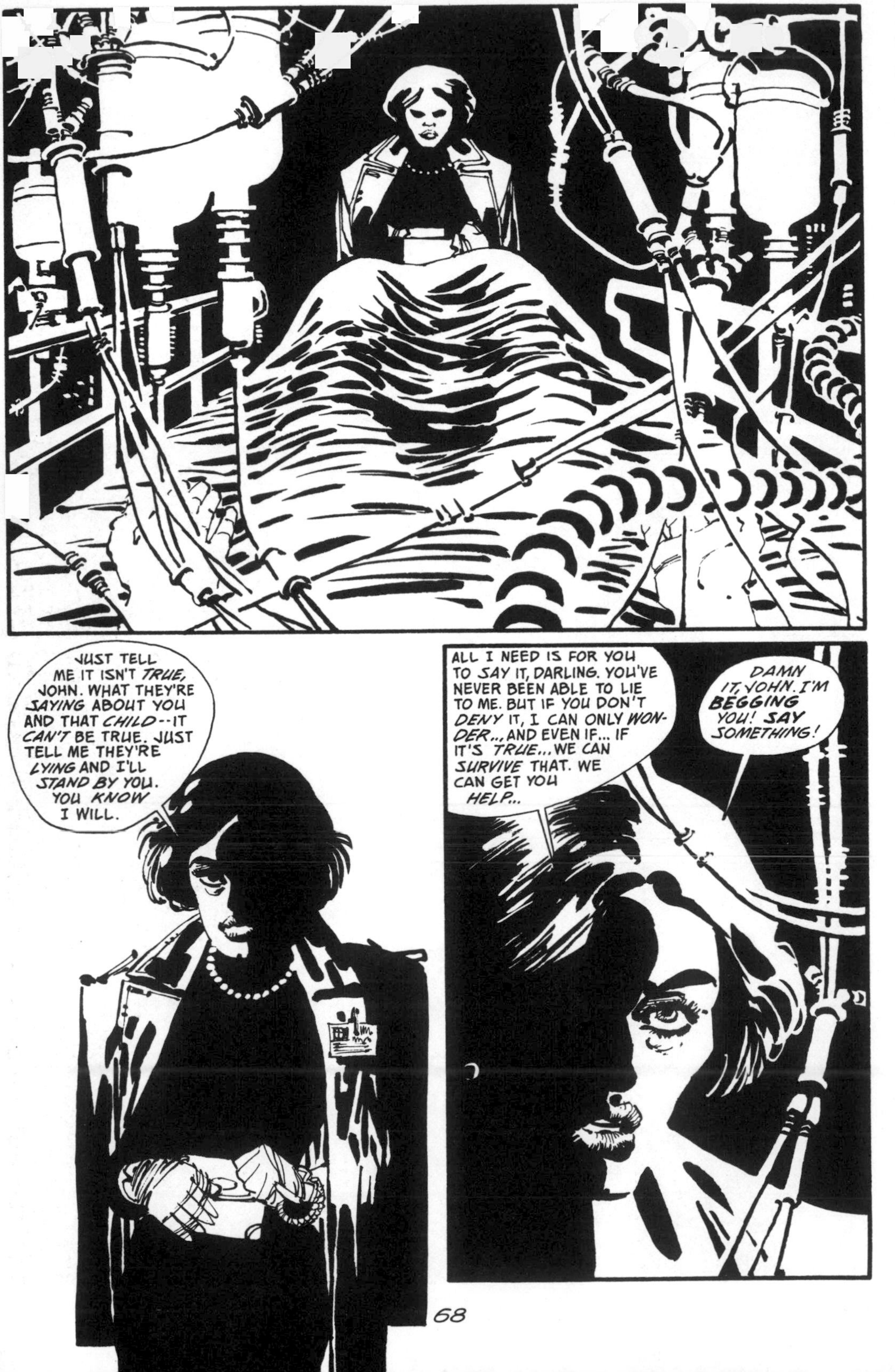
JUST TELL ME IT ISN'T TRUE, JOHN. WHAT THEY'RE SAYING ABOUT YOU AND THAT CHILD--IT CAN'T BE TRUE. JUST TELL ME THEY'RE LYING AND I'LL STAND BY YOU. YOU KNOW I WILL.
ALL I NEED IS FOR YOU TO SAY IT, DARLING. YOU'VE NEVER BEEN ABLE TO LIE TO ME. BUT IF YOU DON'T DENY IT, I CAN ONLY WONDER..., AND EVEN IF... IF IT'S TRUE... WE CAN SURVIVE THAT. WE CAN GET YOU HELP...
DAMN IT, JOHN. I'M BEGGING YOU! SAY SOMETHING!

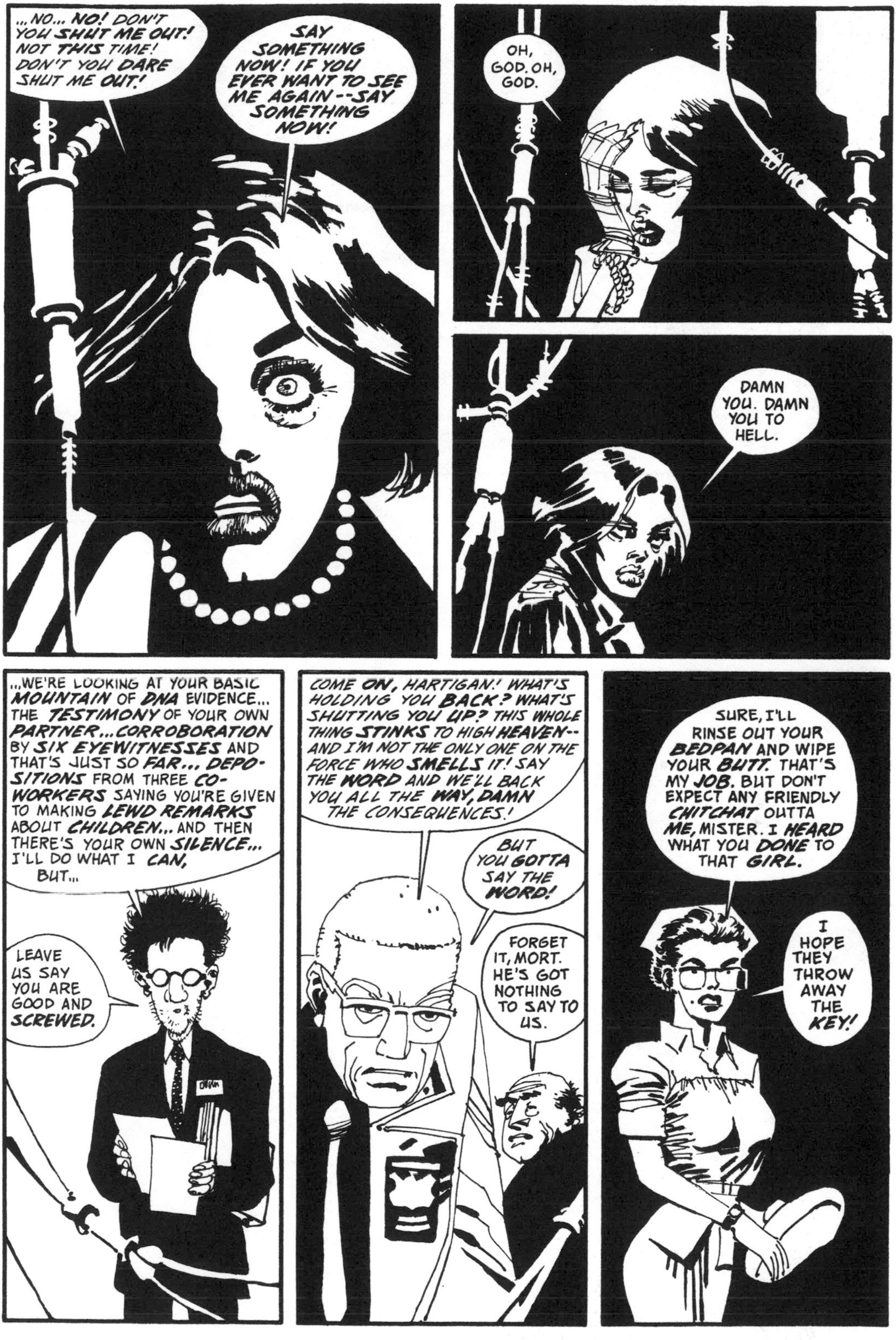
...NO... NO! DON'T YOU SHUT ME OUT! NOT THIS TIME! DON'T YOU DARE SHUT ME OUT!
SAY SOMETHING NOW! IF YOU EVER WANT TO SEE ME AGAIN--SAY SOMETHING NOW!
OH, GOD. OH, GOD.
DAMN YOU. DAMN YOU TO HELL.
...WE'RE LOOKING AT YOUR BASIC MOUNTAIN OF DNA EVIDENCE... THE TESTIMONY OF YOUR OWN PARTNER... CORROBORATION BY SIX EYEWITNESSES AND THAT'S JUST SO FAR... DEPOSITIONS FROM THREE CO-WORKERS SAYING YOU'RE GIVEN TO MAKING LEWD REMARKS ABOUT CHILDREN... AND THEN THERE'S YOUR OWN SILENCE... I'LL DO WHAT I CAN, BUT...
LEAVE US SAY YOU ARE GOOD AND SCREWED.
COME ON, HARTIGAN! WHAT'S HOLDING YOU BACK? WHAT'S SHUTTING YOU UP? THIS WHOLE THING STINKS TO HIGH HEAVEN--AND I'M NOT THE ONLY ONE ON THE FORCE WHO SMELLS IT! SAY THE WORD AND WE'LL BACK YOU ALL THE WAY, DAMN THE CONSEQUENCES!
BUT YOU GOTTA SAY THE WORD!
FORGET IT, MORT. HE'S GOT NOTHING TO SAY TO US.
SURE, I'LL RINSE OUT YOUR BEDPAN AND WIPE YOUR BUTT. THAT'S MY JOB. BUT DON'T EXPECT ANY FRIENDLY CHITCHAT OUTTA ME, MISTER. I HEARD WHAT YOU DONE TO THAT GIRL.
I HOPE THEY THROW AWAY THE KEY!

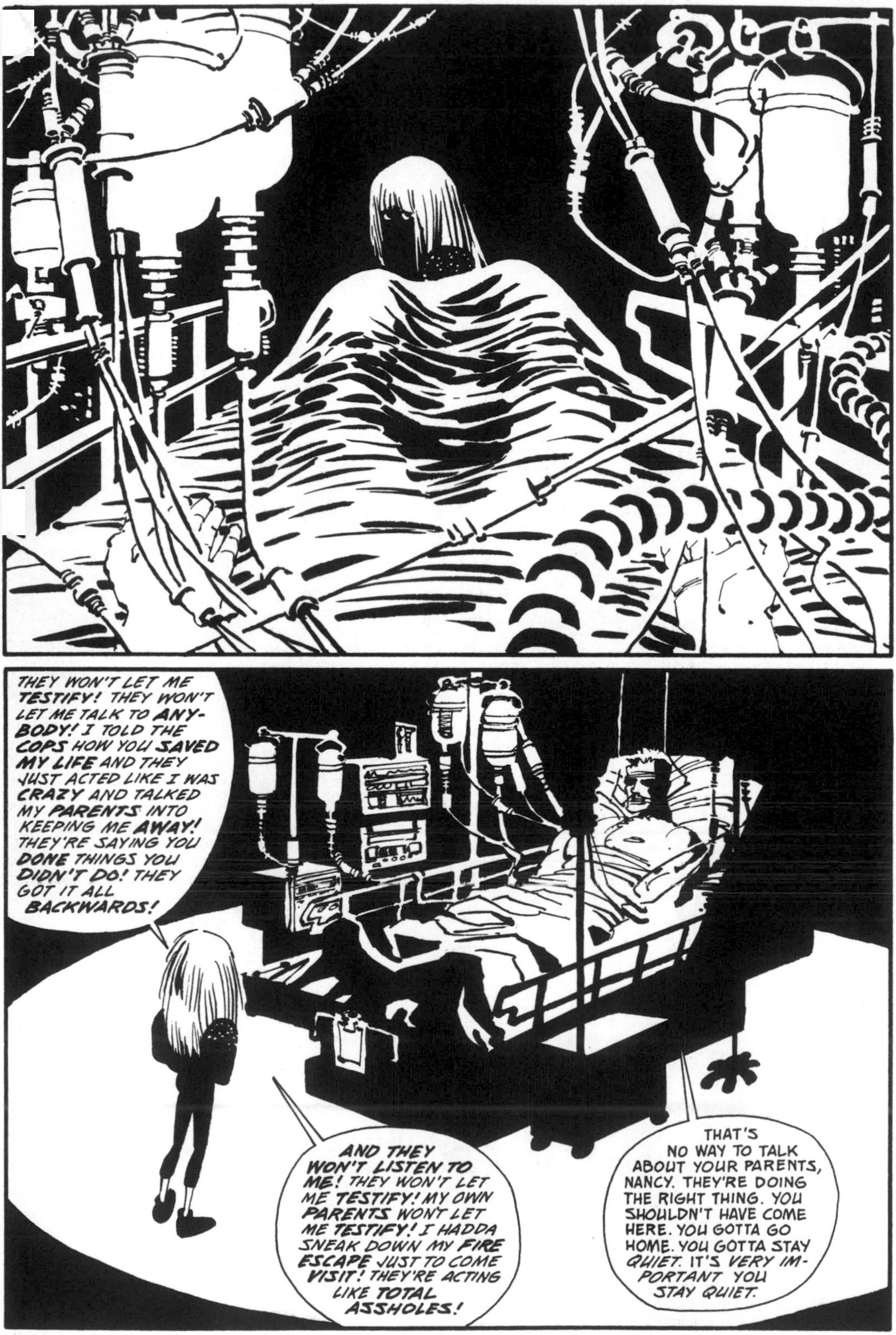
THEY WON'T LET ME TESTIFY! THEY WON'T LET ME TALK TO ANY-BODY! I TOLD THE COPS HOW YOU SAVED MY LIFE AND THEY JUST ACTED LIKE I WAS CRAZY AND TALKED MY PARENTS INTO KEEPING ME AWAY! THEY'RE SAYING YOU DONE THINGS YOU DIDN'T DO! THEY GOT IT ALL BACKWARDS!
AND THEY WON'T LISTEN TO ME! THEY WON'T LET ME TESTIFY! MY OWN PARENTS WON'T LET ME TESTIFY! I HADDA SNEAK DOWN MY FIRE ESCAPE JUST TO COME VISIT! THEY'RE ACTING LIKE TOTAL ASSHOLES!
THAT'S NO WAY TO TALK ABOUT YOUR PARENTS, NANCY. THEY'RE DOING THE RIGHT THING. YOU SHOULDN'T HAVE COME HERE. YOU GOTTA GO HOME. YOU GOTTA STAY QUIET. IT'S VERY IM-PORTANT YOU STAY QUIET.

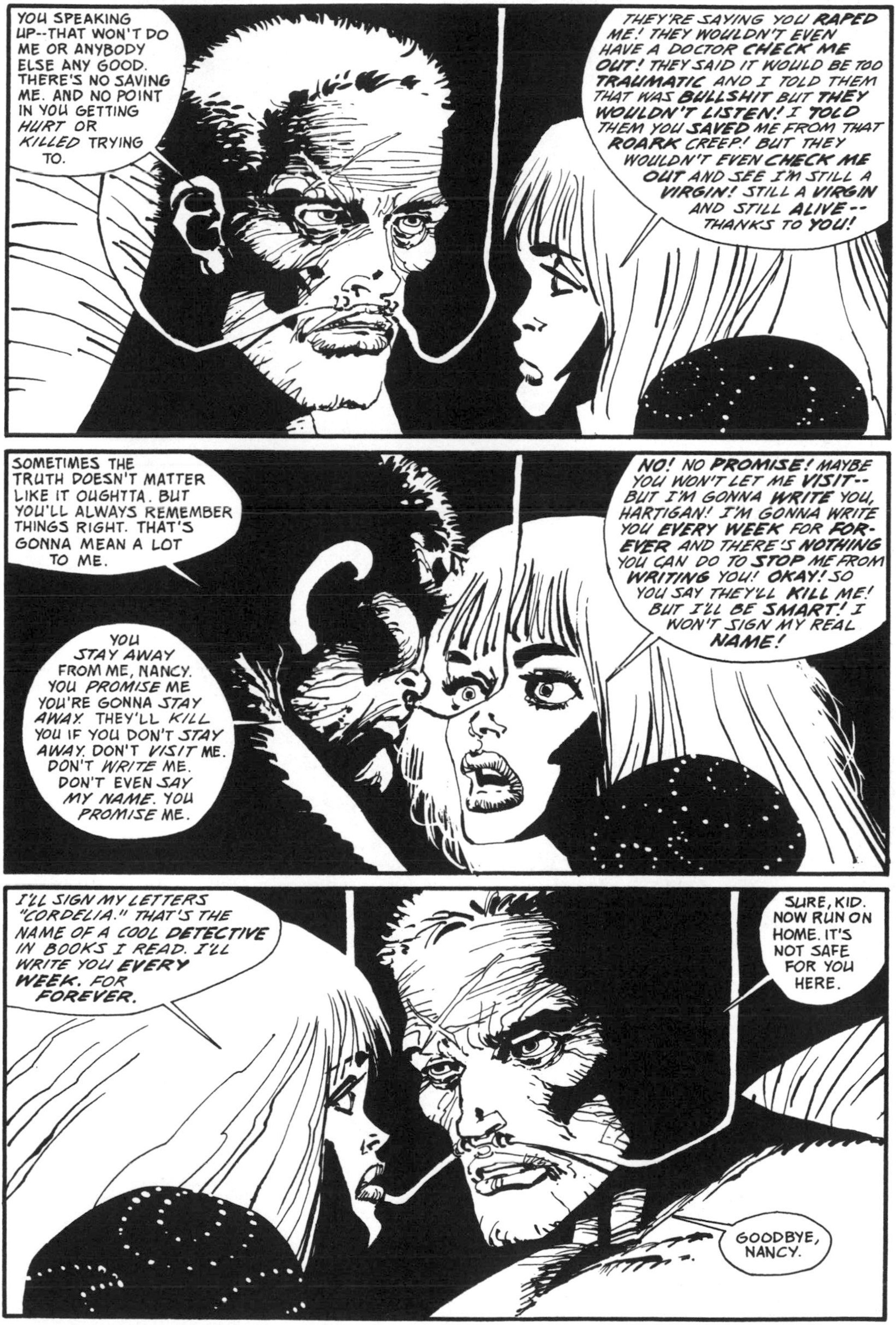
YOU SPEAKING UP--THAT WON'T DO ME OR ANYBODY ELSE ANY GOOD. THERE'S NO SAVING ME. AND NO POINT IN YOU GETTING HURT OR KILLED TRYING TO.
THEY'RE SAYING YOU RAPED ME! THEY WOULDN'T EVEN HAVE A DOCTOR CHECK ME OUT! THEY SAID IT WOULD BE TOO TRAUMATIC AND I TOLD THEM THAT WAS BULLSHIT BUT THEY WOULDN'T LISTEN! I TOLD THEM YOU SAVED ME FROM THAT ROARK CREEP! BUT THEY WOULDN'T EVEN CHECK ME OUT AND SEE I'M STILL A VIRGIN! STILL A VIRGIN AND STILL ALIVE-- THANKS TO YOU!
SOMETIMES THE TRUTH DOESN'T MATTER LIKE IT OUGHTTA. BUT YOU'LL ALWAYS REMEMBER THINGS RIGHT. THAT'S GONNA MEAN A LOT TO ME.
YOU STAY AWAY FROM ME, NANCY. YOU PROMISE ME YOU'RE GONNA STAY AWAY. THEY'LL KILL YOU IF YOU DON'T STAY AWAY. DON'T VISIT ME. DON'T WRITE ME. DON'T EVEN SAY MY NAME. YOU PROMISE ME.
NO! NO PROMISE! MAYBE YOU WON'T LET ME VISIT-- BUT I'M GONNA WRITE YOU, HARTIGAN! I'M GONNA WRITE YOU EVERY WEEK FOR FOREVER AND THERE'S NOTHING YOU CAN DO TO STOP ME FROM WRITING YOU! OKAY! SO YOU SAY THEY'LL KILL ME! BUT I'LL BE SMART! I WON'T SIGN MY REAL NAME!
I'LL SIGN MY LETTERS "CORDELIA." THAT'S THE NAME OF A COOL DETECTIVE IN BOOKS I READ. I'LL WRITE YOU EVERY WEEK. FOR FOREVER.
SURE, KID. NOW RUN ON HOME. IT'S NOT SAFE FOR YOU HERE.
GOODBYE, NANCY.

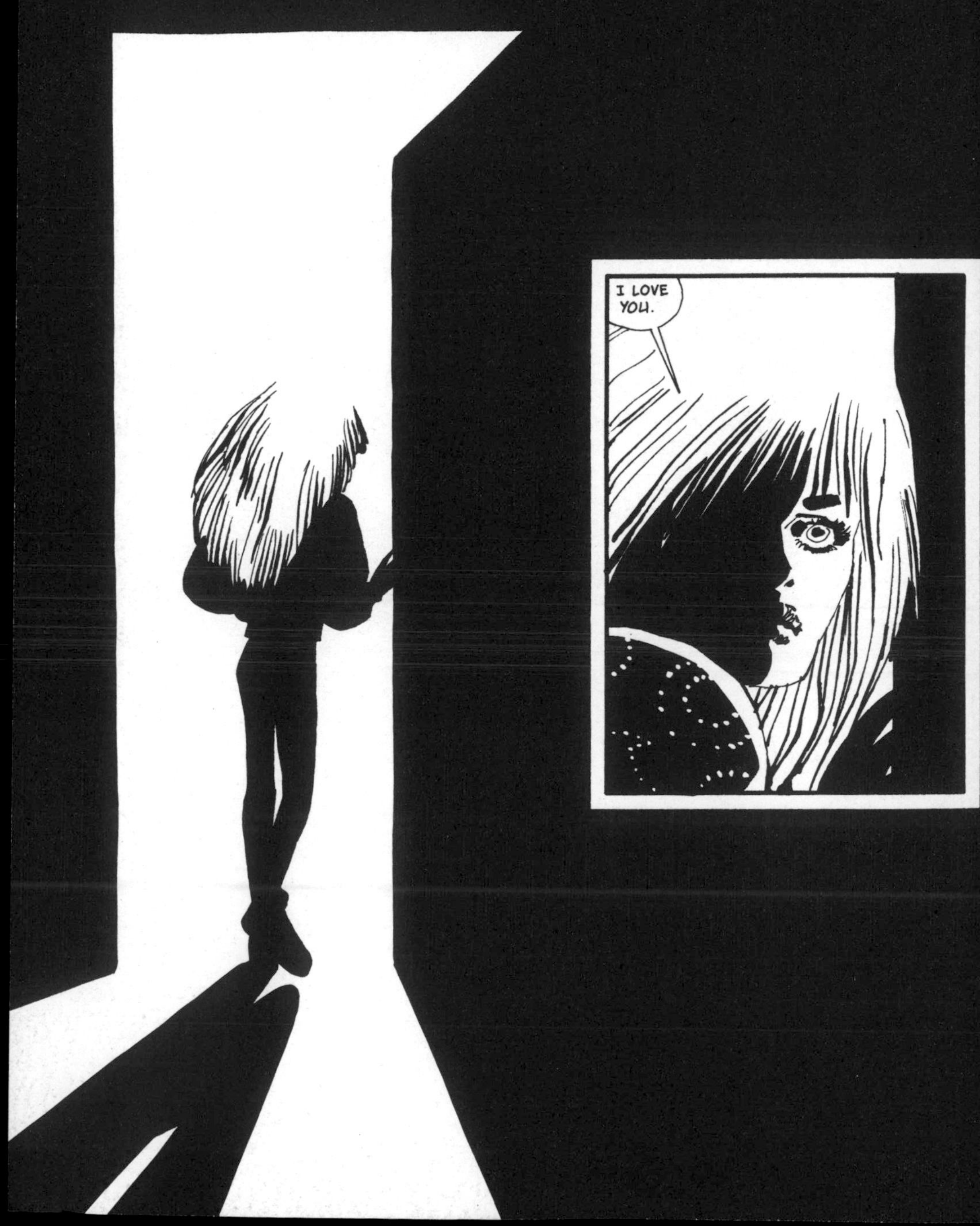
I LOVE YOU.

CHAPTER

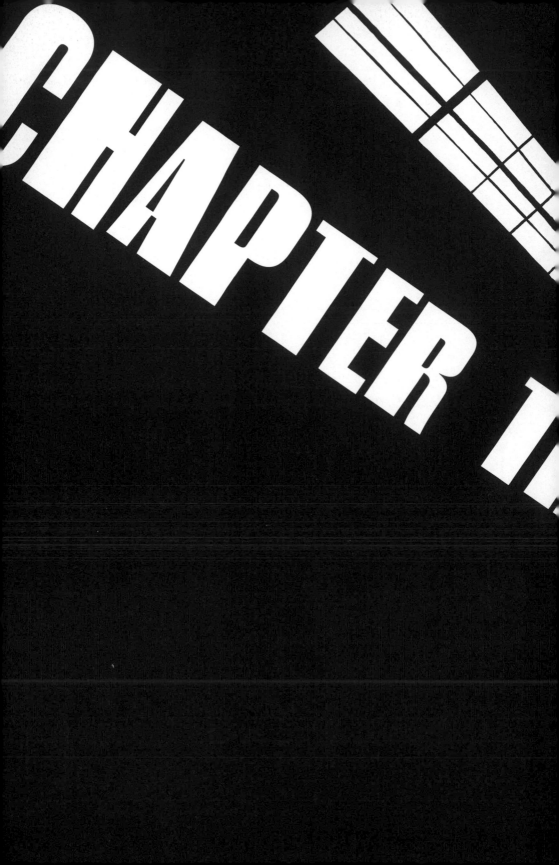

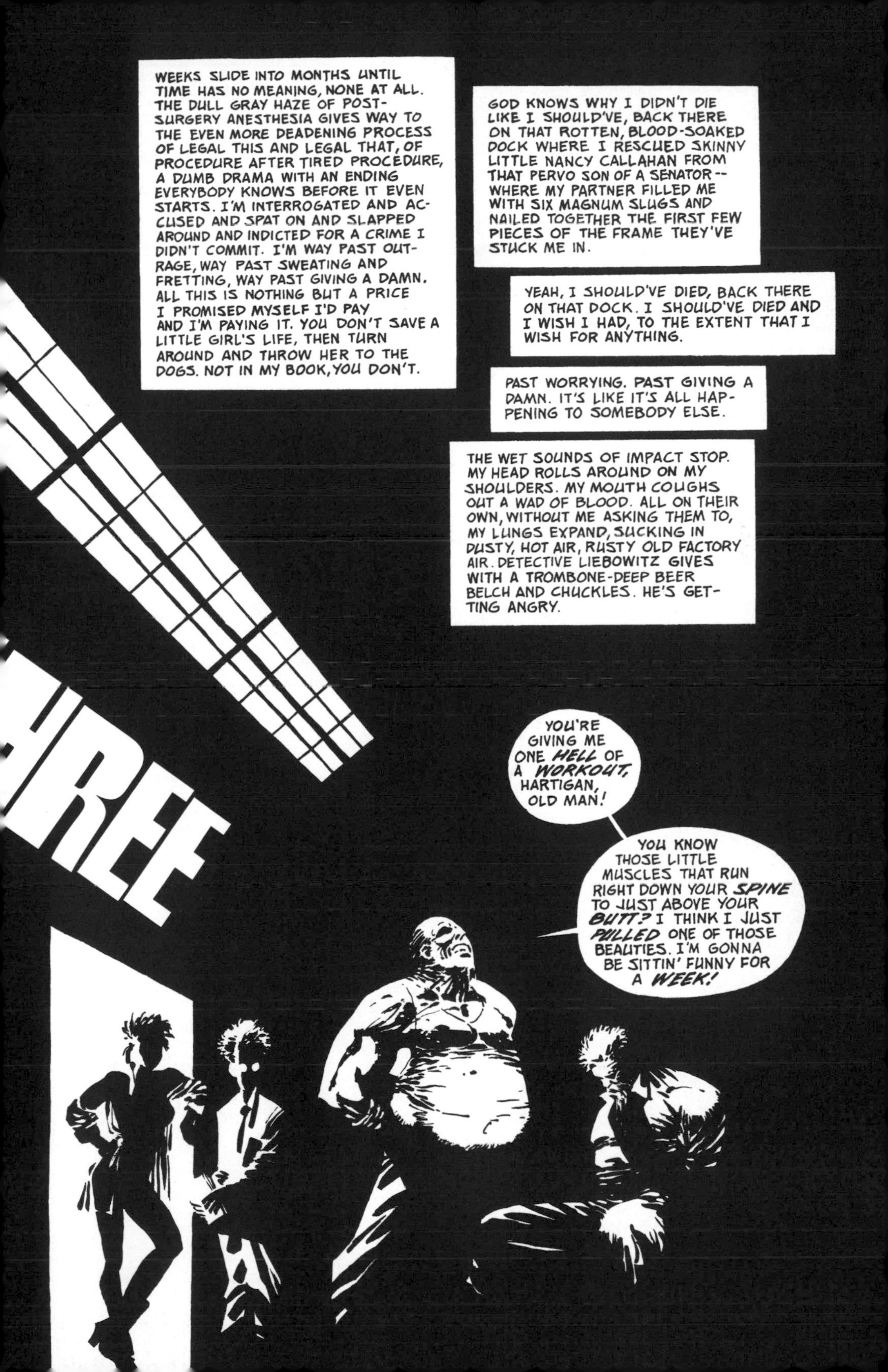

HREE
WEEKS SLIDE INTO MONTHS UNTIL TIME HAS NO MEANING, NONE AT ALL. THE DULL GRAY HAZE OF POST-SURGERY ANESTHESIA GIVES WAY TO THE EVEN MORE DEADENING PROCESS OF LEGAL THIS AND LEGAL THAT, OF PROCEDURE AFTER TIRED PROCEDURE, A DUMB DRAMA WITH AN ENDING EVERYBODY KNOWS BEFORE IT EVEN STARTS. I'M INTERROGATED AND ACCUSED AND SPAT ON AND SLAPPED AROUND AND INDICTED FOR A CRIME I DIDN'T COMMIT. I'M WAY PAST OUTRAGE, WAY PAST SWEATING AND FRETTING, WAY PAST GIVING A DAMN. ALL THIS IS NOTHING BUT A PRICE I PROMISED MYSELF I'D PAY AND I'M PAYING IT. YOU DON'T SAVE A LITTLE GIRL'S LIFE, THEN TURN AROUND AND THROW HER TO THE DOGS. NOT IN MY BOOK, YOU DON'T.
GOD KNOWS WHY I DIDN'T DIE LIKE I SHOULD'VE, BACK THERE ON THAT ROTTEN, BLOOD-SOAKED DOCK WHERE I RESCUED SKINNY LITTLE NANCY CALLAHAN FROM THAT PERVO SON OF A SENATOR -- WHERE MY PARTNER FILLED ME WITH SIX MAGNUM SLUGS AND NAILED TOGETHER THE FIRST FEW PIECES OF THE FRAME THEY'VE STUCK ME IN.
YEAH, I SHOULD'VE DIED, BACK THERE ON THAT DOCK. I SHOULD'VE DIED AND I WISH I HAD, TO THE EXTENT THAT I WISH FOR ANYTHING.
PAST WORRYING. PAST GIVING A DAMN. IT'S LIKE IT'S ALL HAPPENING TO SOMEBODY ELSE.
THE WET SOUNDS OF IMPACT STOP. MY HEAD ROLLS AROUND ON MY SHOULDERS. MY MOUTH COUGHS OUT A WAD OF BLOOD. ALL ON THEIR OWN, WITHOUT ME ASKING THEM TO, MY LUNGS EXPAND, SUCKING IN DUSTY, HOT AIR, RUSTY OLD FACTORY AIR. DETECTIVE LIEBOWITZ GIVES WITH A TROMBONE-DEEP BEER BELCH AND CHUCKLES. HE'S GETTING ANGRY.
YOU'RE GIVING ME ONE *HELL* OF A *WORKOUT,* HARTIGAN, OLD MAN!
YOU KNOW THOSE LITTLE MUSCLES THAT RUN RIGHT DOWN YOUR *SPINE* TO JUST ABOVE YOUR *BUTT?* I THINK I JUST *PULLED* ONE OF THOSE BEAUTIES. I'M GONNA BE SITTIN' FUNNY FOR A *WEEK!*

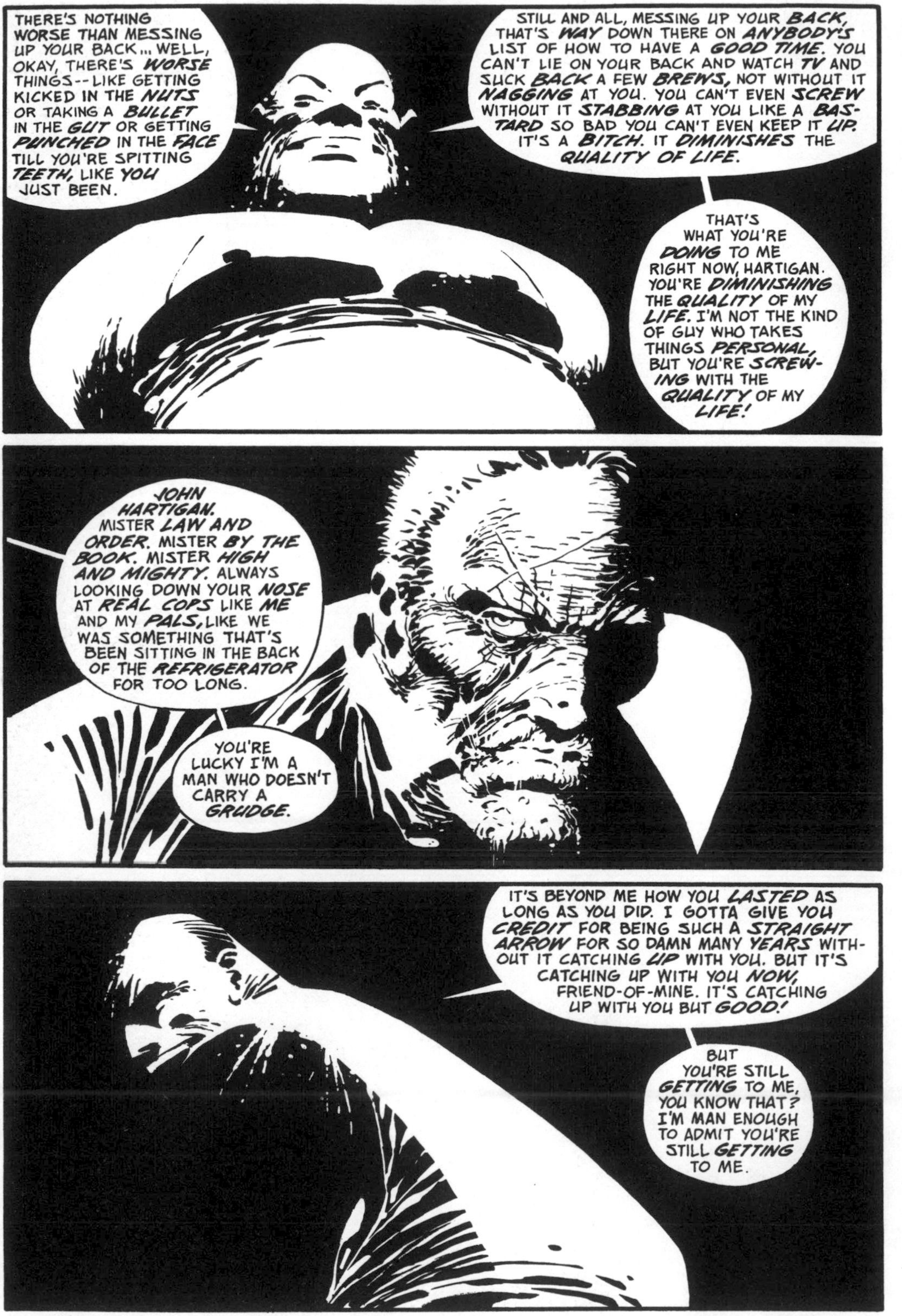
THERE'S NOTHING WORSE THAN MESSING UP YOUR BACK... WELL, OKAY, THERE'S WORSE THINGS--LIKE GETTING KICKED IN THE NUTS OR TAKING A BULLET IN THE GUT OR GETTING PUNCHED IN THE FACE TILL YOU'RE SPITTING TEETH, LIKE YOU JUST BEEN.
STILL AND ALL, MESSING UP YOUR BACK, THAT'S WAY DOWN THERE ON ANYBODY'S LIST OF HOW TO HAVE A GOOD TIME. YOU CAN'T LIE ON YOUR BACK AND WATCH TV AND SUCK BACK A FEW BREWS, NOT WITHOUT IT NAGGING AT YOU. YOU CAN'T EVEN SCREW WITHOUT IT STABBING AT YOU LIKE A BASTARD SO BAD YOU CAN'T EVEN KEEP IT UP. IT'S A BITCH. IT DIMINISHES THE QUALITY OF LIFE.
THAT'S WHAT YOU'RE DOING TO ME RIGHT NOW, HARTIGAN. YOU'RE DIMINISHING THE QUALITY OF MY LIFE. I'M NOT THE KIND OF GUY WHO TAKES THINGS PERSONAL, BUT YOU'RE SCREWING WITH THE QUALITY OF MY LIFE!
JOHN HARTIGAN. MISTER LAW AND ORDER. MISTER BY THE BOOK. MISTER HIGH AND MIGHTY. ALWAYS LOOKING DOWN YOUR NOSE AT REAL COPS LIKE ME AND MY PALS, LIKE WE WAS SOMETHING THAT'S BEEN SITTING IN THE BACK OF THE REFRIGERATOR FOR TOO LONG.
YOU'RE LUCKY I'M A MAN WHO DOESN'T CARRY A GRUDGE.
IT'S BEYOND ME HOW YOU LASTED AS LONG AS YOU DID. I GOTTA GIVE YOU CREDIT FOR BEING SUCH A STRAIGHT ARROW FOR SO DAMN MANY YEARS WITHOUT IT CATCHING UP WITH YOU. BUT IT'S CATCHING UP WITH YOU NOW, FRIEND-OF-MINE. IT'S CATCHING UP WITH YOU BUT GOOD!
BUT YOU'RE STILL GETTING TO ME, YOU KNOW THAT? I'M MAN ENOUGH TO ADMIT YOU'RE STILL GETTING TO ME.

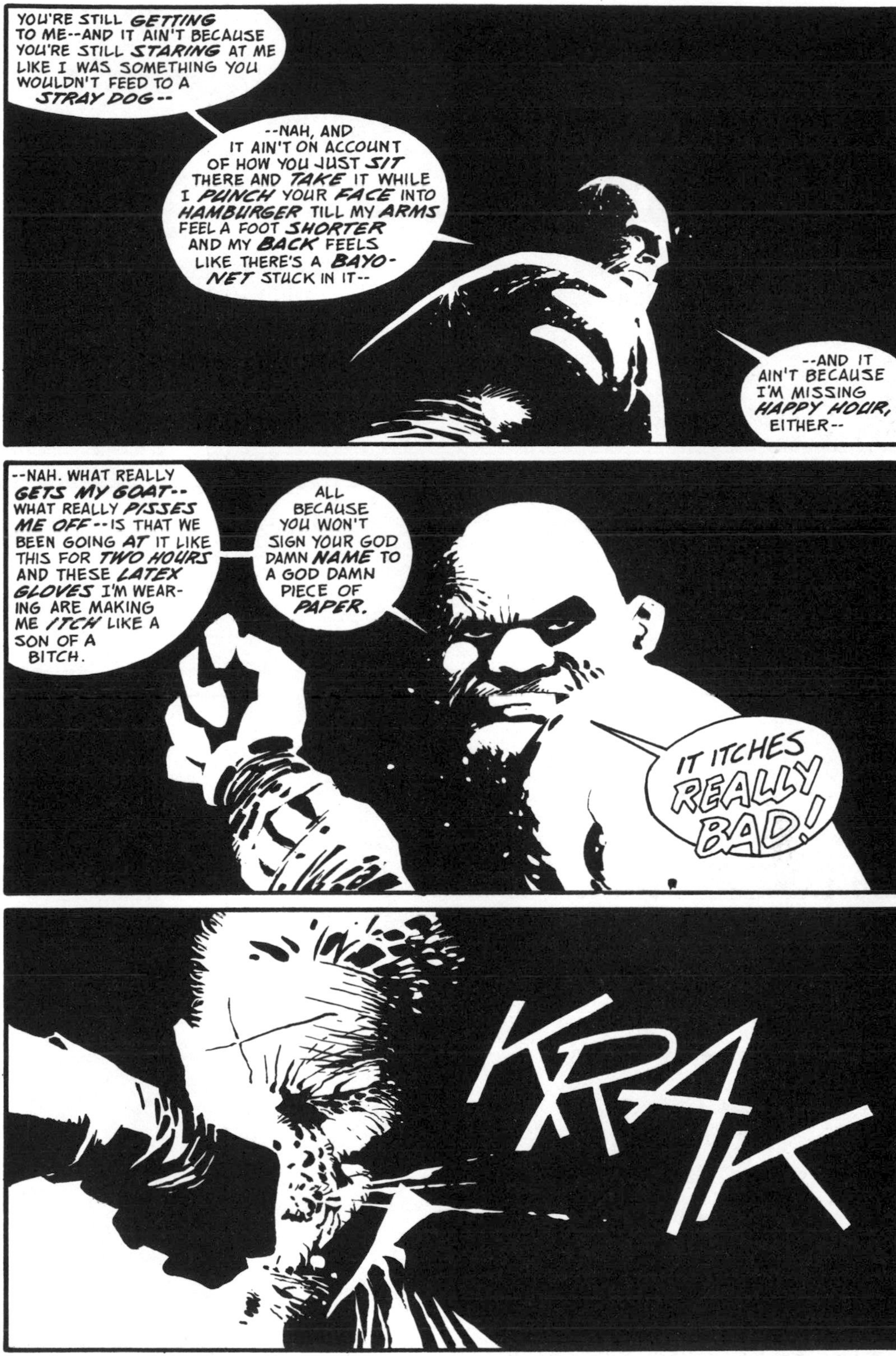
YOU'RE STILL GETTING TO ME--AND IT AIN'T BECAUSE YOU'RE STILL STARING AT ME LIKE I WAS SOMETHING YOU WOULDN'T FEED TO A STRAY DOG--
--NAH, AND IT AIN'T ON ACCOUNT OF HOW YOU JUST SIT THERE AND TAKE IT WHILE I PUNCH YOUR FACE INTO HAMBURGER TILL MY ARMS FEEL A FOOT SHORTER AND MY BACK FEELS LIKE THERE'S A BAYO-NET STUCK IN IT--
--AND IT AIN'T BECAUSE I'M MISSING HAPPY HOUR, EITHER--
--NAH. WHAT REALLY GETS MY GOAT--WHAT REALLY PISSES ME OFF--IS THAT WE BEEN GOING AT IT LIKE THIS FOR TWO HOURS AND THESE LATEX GLOVES I'M WEAR-ING ARE MAKING ME ITCH LIKE A SON OF A BITCH.
ALL BECAUSE YOU WON'T SIGN YOUR GOD DAMN NAME TO A GOD DAMN PIECE OF PAPER.
IT ITCHES REALLY BAD!
KRAK

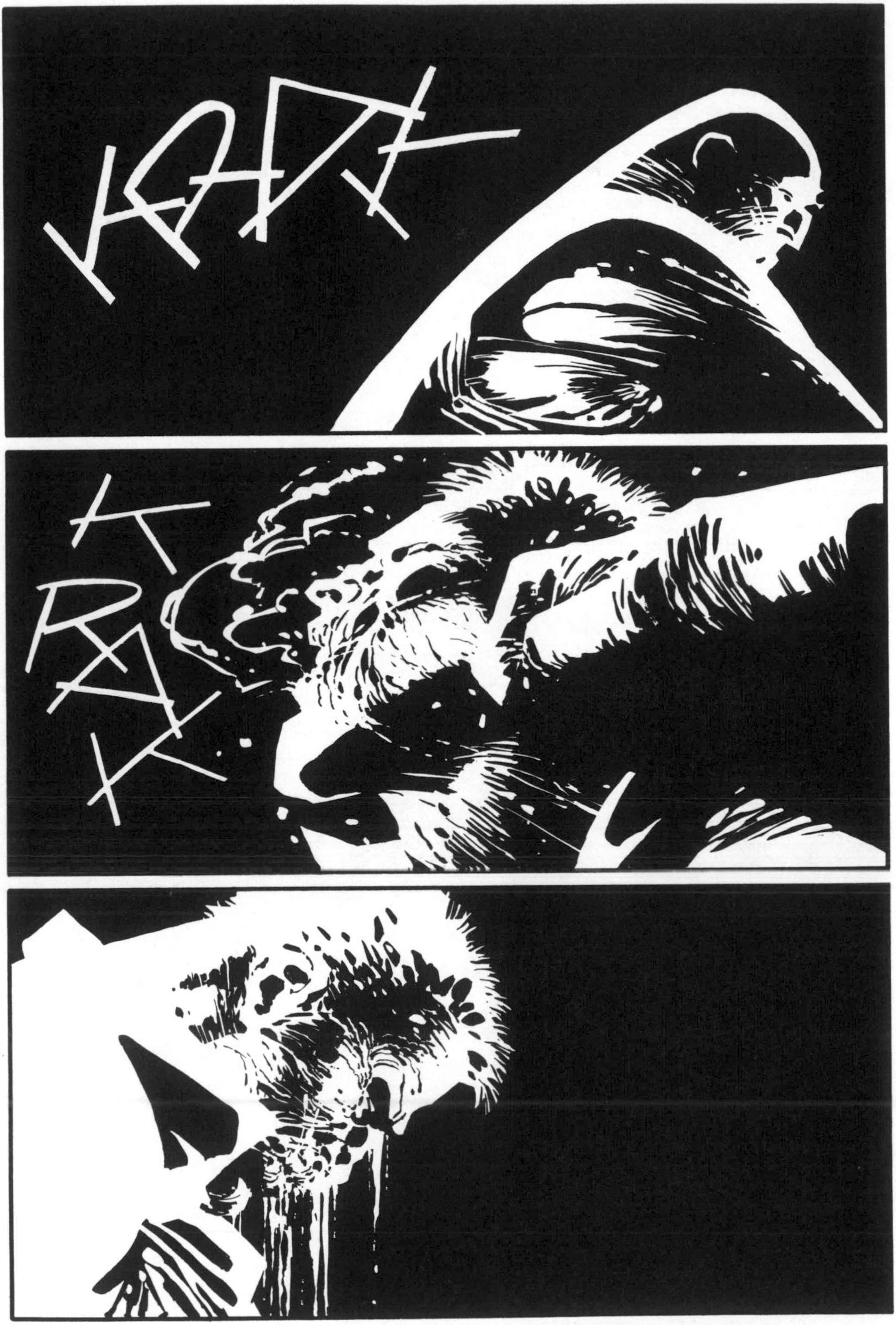
KRAK
KRAK

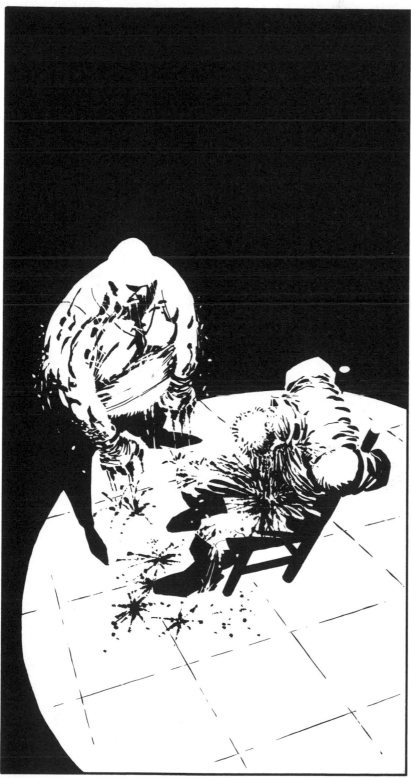

"I LOVE YOU"--
THAT WAS THE LAST
THING SKINNY LITTLE
NANCY CALLAHAN SAID
TO ME, WHEN SHE LEFT
MY HOSPITAL ROOM
ALL THOSE MONTHS
AGO.

SHE'S JUST A KID,
NANCY IS. JUST A
SCRAWNY ELEVEN-YEAR-
OLD WITH HER WHOLE
LIFE AHEAD OF HER.
HER WHOLE LIFE. I
SAVED IT BACK THEN
AND I'M STILL SAVING
IT, I'M STILL KEEPING
NANCY FROM GETTING
MURDERED, JUST BY
KEEPING MY MOUTH
SHUT AND NOT GIVING
THEM EVEN A WHISPER
OF A REASON TO DRAG
HER INTO THIS MESS.
THAT'S ABOUT ALL
THERE IS LEFT OF ME,
PROTECTING SKINNY
LITTLE NANCY
CALLAHAN.

PAST WORRYING. PAST
GIVING A DAMN. I'M A
HUSK, A SCARECROW,
A BEAT-UP, USED-UP
OLD MAN. THERE'S
NOTHING INSIDE OF
ME. NOTHING.
EXCEPT...

*...EXCEPT ONE TINY,
BURNING CHUNK OF
ME THAT WON'T LET
ME CAVE IN AND SIGN
A FALSE CONFESSION.*

*WHY DO THEY EVEN
WANT ME TO? THEY'VE
GOT ALL THE EVIDENCE
THEY NEED TO SEND
ME UP THE RIVER FOR
THE REST OF MY LIFE.
WHAT THEY DIDN'T
PLANT THEY MANU-
FACTURED, TONS OF
IT, ENOUGH TO CON-
VICT A HUNDRED
MEN. WHY THE HELL
DO THEY NEED ME TO
PUT MY SIGNATURE
ON THEIR PACK OF
LIES? I DON'T KNOW
WHY IT MATTERS TO ME
AND I DON'T KNOW
WHY IT MATTERS
TO THEM.*

THEY WANT A
CONFESSION.

THEY WON'T GET IT.

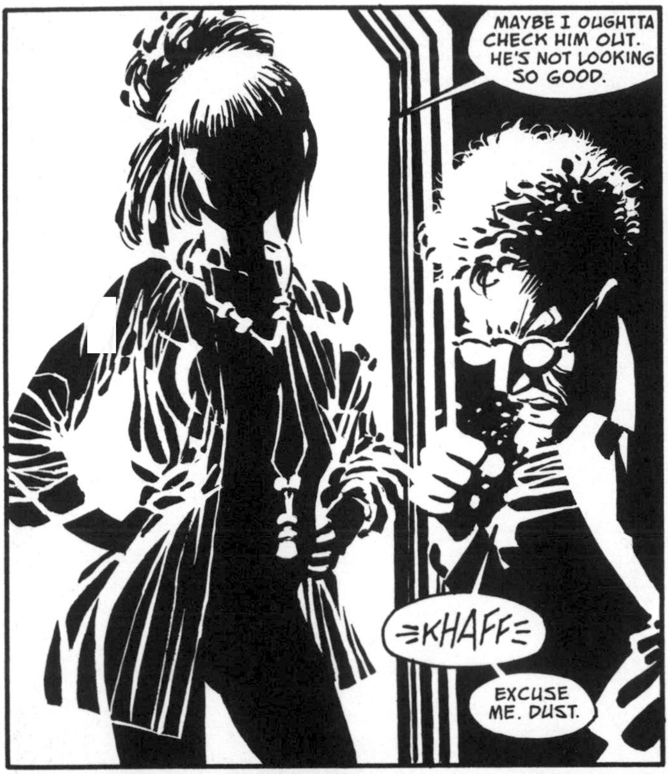
MAYBE I OUGHTTA CHECK HIM OUT. HE'S NOT LOOKING SO GOOD.
KHAFF
EXCUSE ME. DUST.

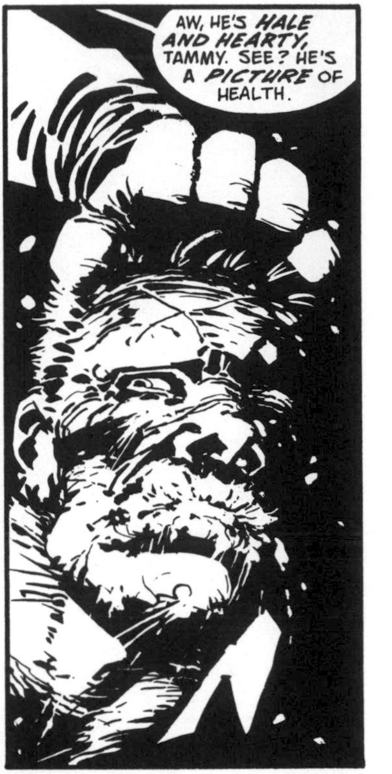
AW, HE'S HALE AND HEARTY, TAMMY. SEE? HE'S A PICTURE OF HEALTH.

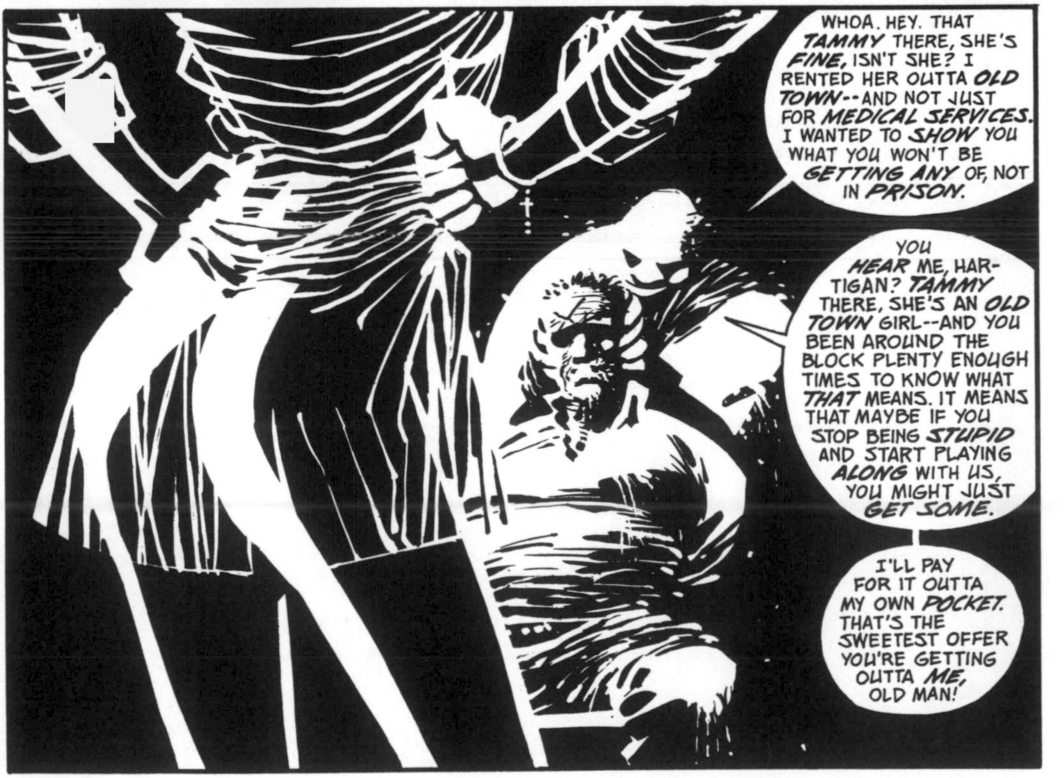
WHOA. HEY. THAT TAMMY THERE, SHE'S FINE, ISN'T SHE? I RENTED HER OUTTA OLD TOWN--AND NOT JUST FOR MEDICAL SERVICES. I WANTED TO SHOW YOU WHAT YOU WON'T BE GETTING ANY OF, NOT IN PRISON.
YOU HEAR ME, HARTIGAN? TAMMY THERE, SHE'S AN OLD TOWN GIRL--AND YOU BEEN AROUND THE BLOCK PLENTY ENOUGH TIMES TO KNOW WHAT THAT MEANS. IT MEANS THAT MAYBE IF YOU STOP BEING STUPID AND START PLAYING ALONG WITH US, YOU MIGHT JUST GET SOME.
I'LL PAY FOR IT OUTTA MY OWN POCKET. THAT'S THE SWEETEST OFFER YOU'RE GETTING OUTTA ME, OLD MAN!

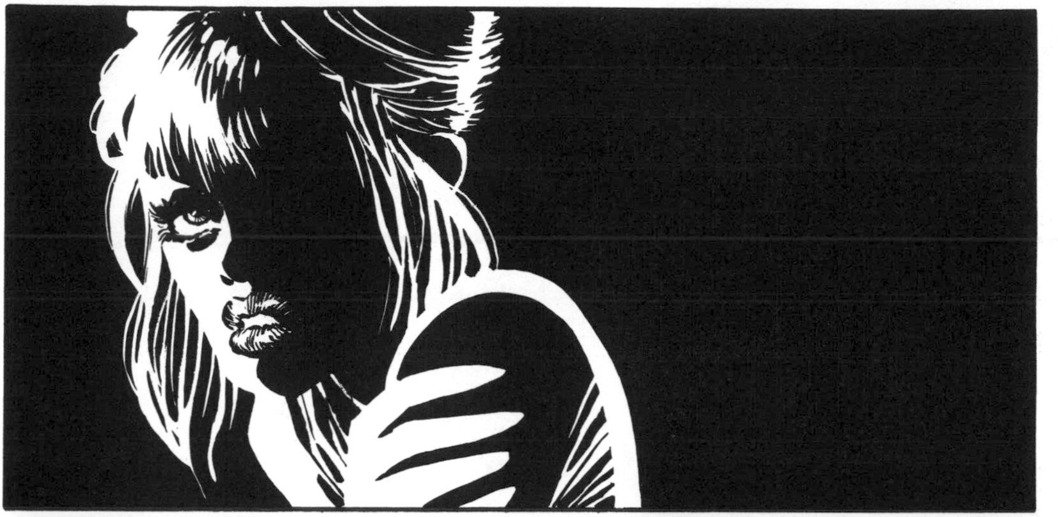

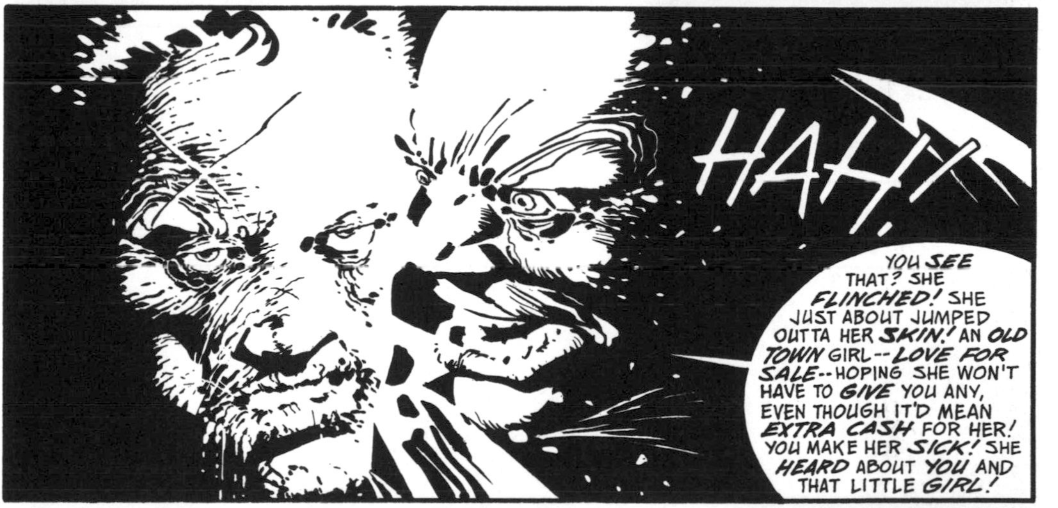
HAH!
YOU SEE THAT? SHE FLINCHED! SHE JUST ABOUT JUMPED OUTTA HER SKIN! AN OLD TOWN GIRL--LOVE FOR SALE--HOPING SHE WON'T HAVE TO GIVE YOU ANY, EVEN THOUGH IT'D MEAN EXTRA CASH FOR HER! YOU MAKE HER SICK! SHE HEARD ABOUT YOU AND THAT LITTLE GIRL!

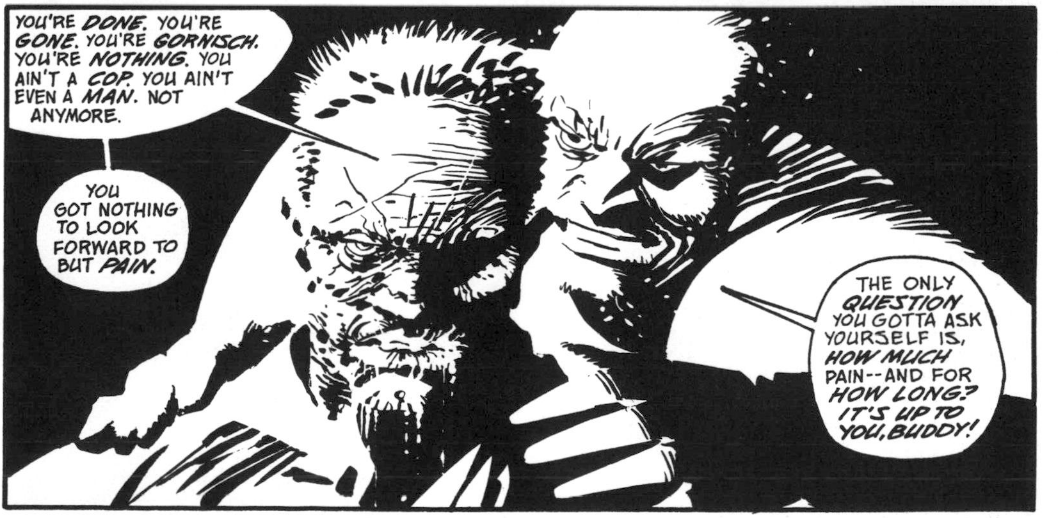
YOU'RE DONE. YOU'RE GONE. YOU'RE GORNISCH. YOU'RE NOTHING. YOU AIN'T A COP. YOU AIN'T EVEN A MAN. NOT ANYMORE.
YOU GOT NOTHING TO LOOK FORWARD TO BUT PAIN.
THE ONLY QUESTION YOU GOTTA ASK YOURSELF IS, HOW MUCH PAIN--AND FOR HOW LONG? IT'S UP TO YOU, BUDDY!

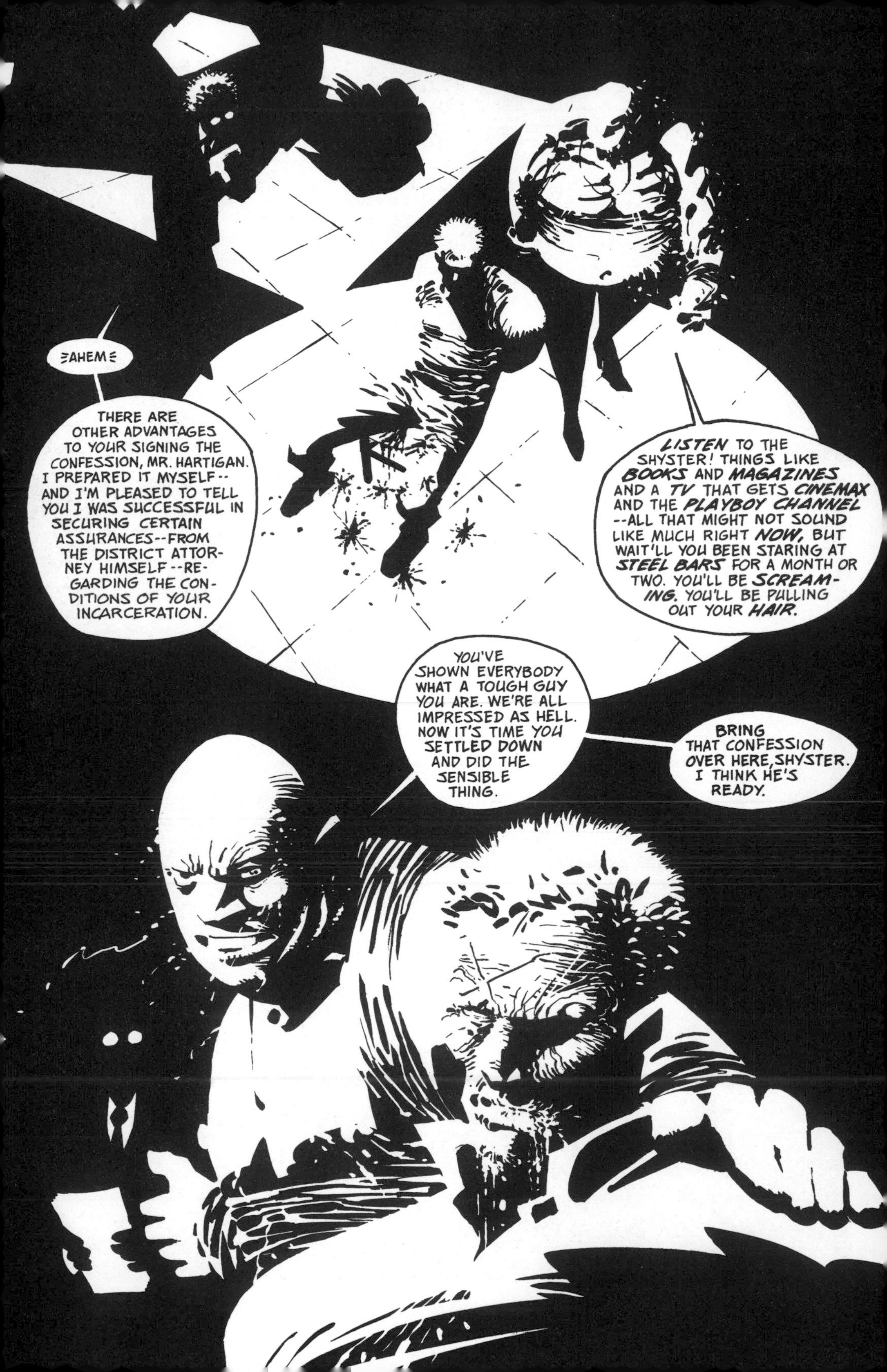

≡AHEM≡
THERE ARE OTHER ADVANTAGES TO YOUR SIGNING THE CONFESSION, MR. HARTIGAN. I PREPARED IT MYSELF-- AND I'M PLEASED TO TELL YOU I WAS SUCCESSFUL IN SECURING CERTAIN ASSURANCES--FROM THE DISTRICT ATTORNEY HIMSELF--REGARDING THE CONDITIONS OF YOUR INCARCERATION.
LISTEN TO THE SHYSTER! THINGS LIKE BOOKS AND MAGAZINES AND A TV THAT GETS CINEMAX AND THE PLAYBOY CHANNEL --ALL THAT MIGHT NOT SOUND LIKE MUCH RIGHT NOW, BUT WAIT'LL YOU BEEN STARING AT STEEL BARS FOR A MONTH OR TWO. YOU'LL BE SCREAMING. YOU'LL BE PULLING OUT YOUR HAIR.
YOU'VE SHOWN EVERYBODY WHAT A TOUGH GUY YOU ARE. WE'RE ALL IMPRESSED AS HELL. NOW IT'S TIME YOU SETTLED DOWN AND DID THE SENSIBLE THING.
BRING THAT CONFESSION OVER HERE, SHYSTER. I THINK HE'S READY.

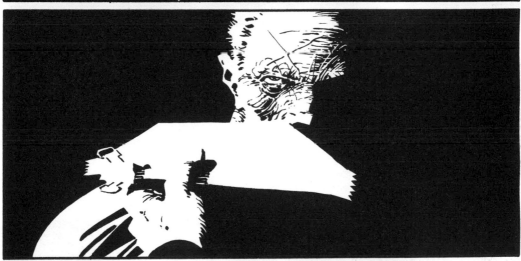

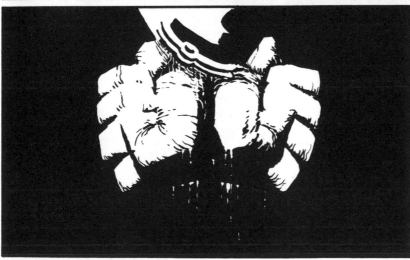

ALL I'VE GOTTA DO
IS NOD MY HEAD AND
LIEBOWITZ WILL STOP
PUNCHING ME AND
THE CUFFS WILL
COME OFF.

THEY'RE GONNA
CONVICT ME ANYWAY.
THERE'S NOTHING I
CAN DO TO CHANGE
THAT.

THERE'S NO REASON
ON EARTH TO KEEP
STANDING MY
GROUND.

THERE'S NOTHING TO
GAIN. NOTHING.

NOTHING BUT MORE
PAIN, JUST LIKE
LIEBOWITZ SAID.

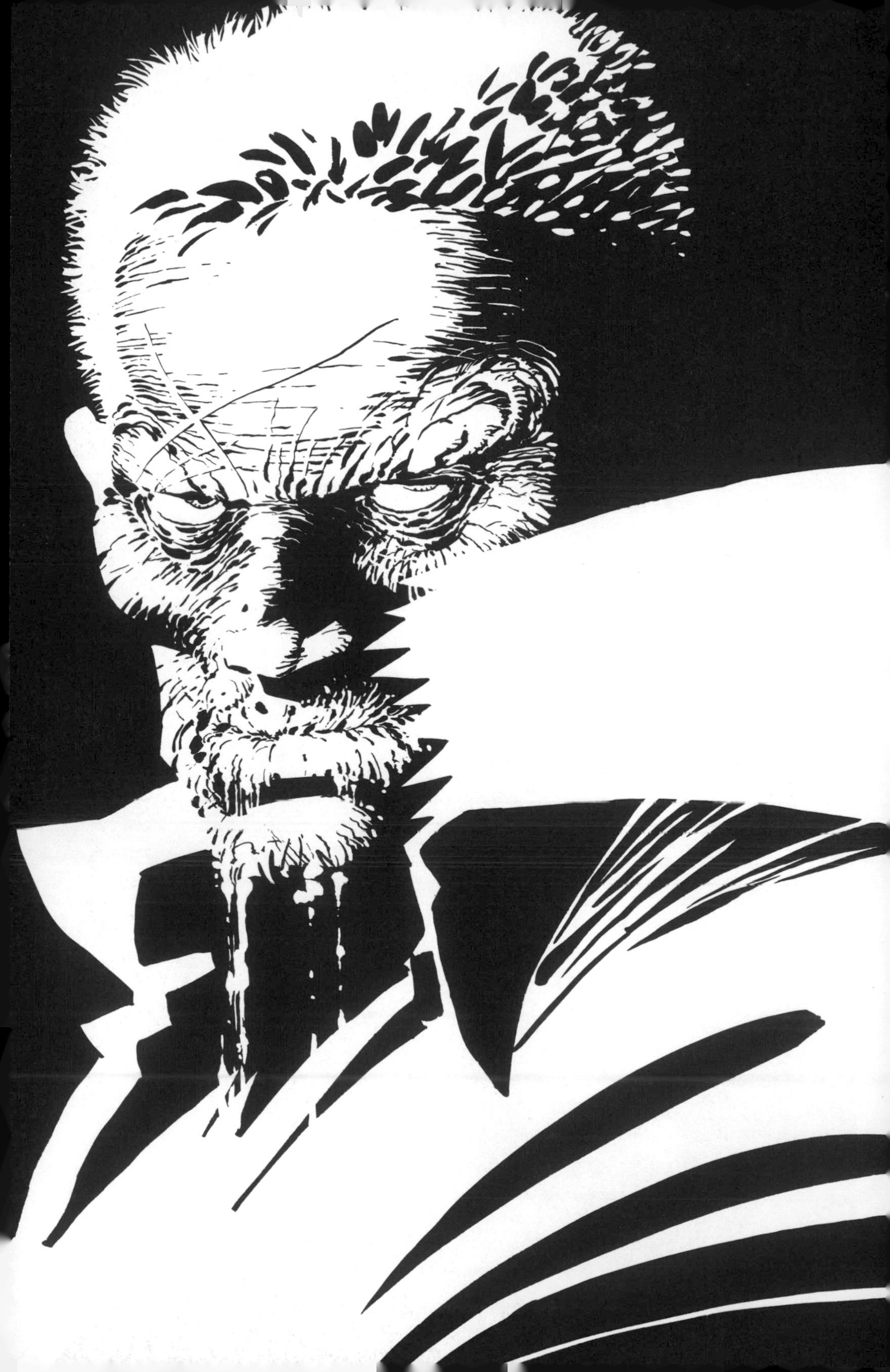

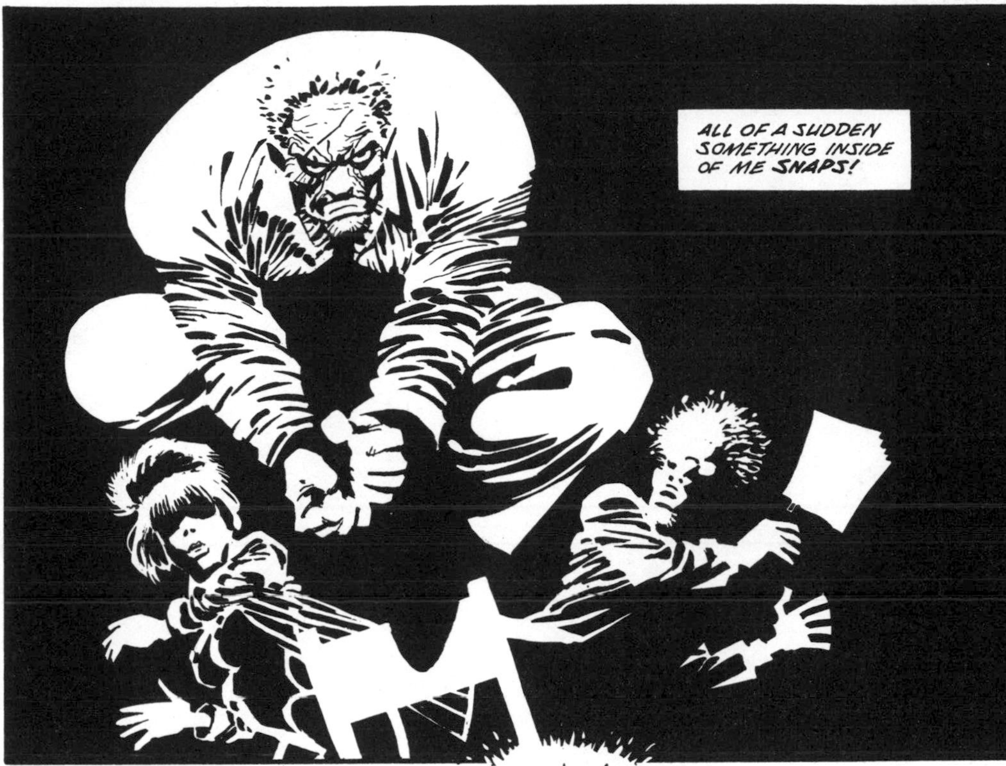
ALL OF A SUDDEN SOMETHING INSIDE OF ME SNAPS!

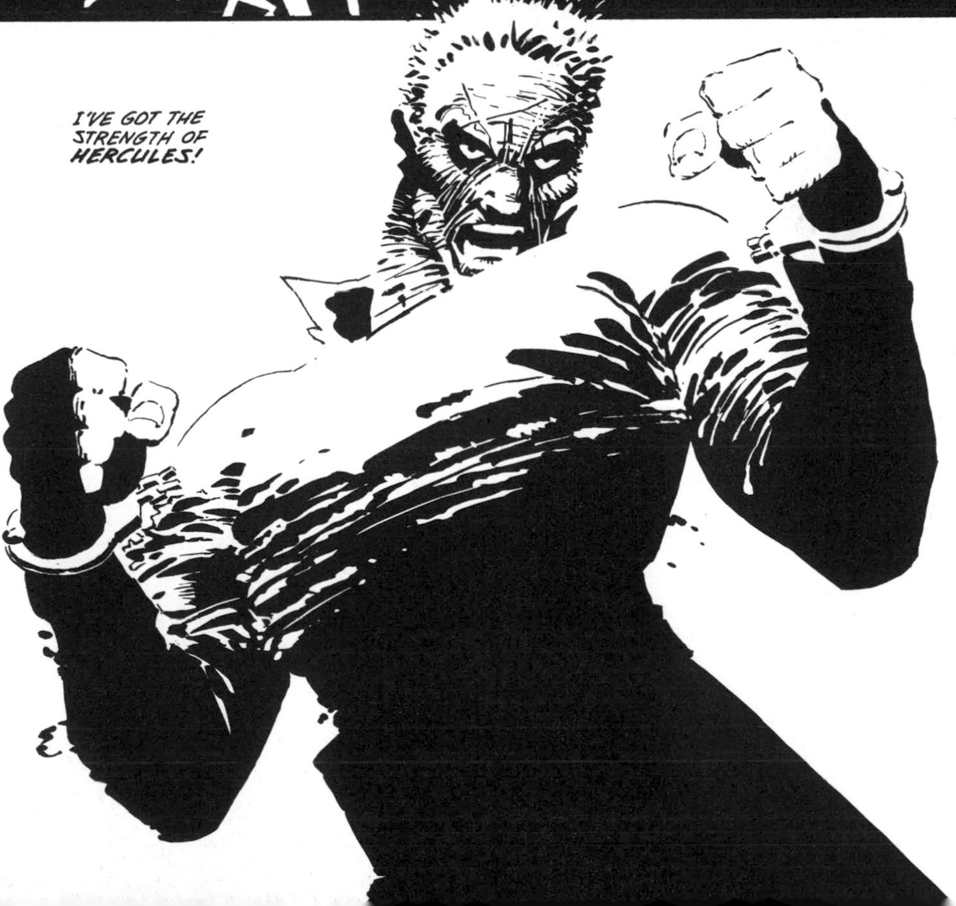
I'VE GOT THE STRENGTH OF HERCULES!

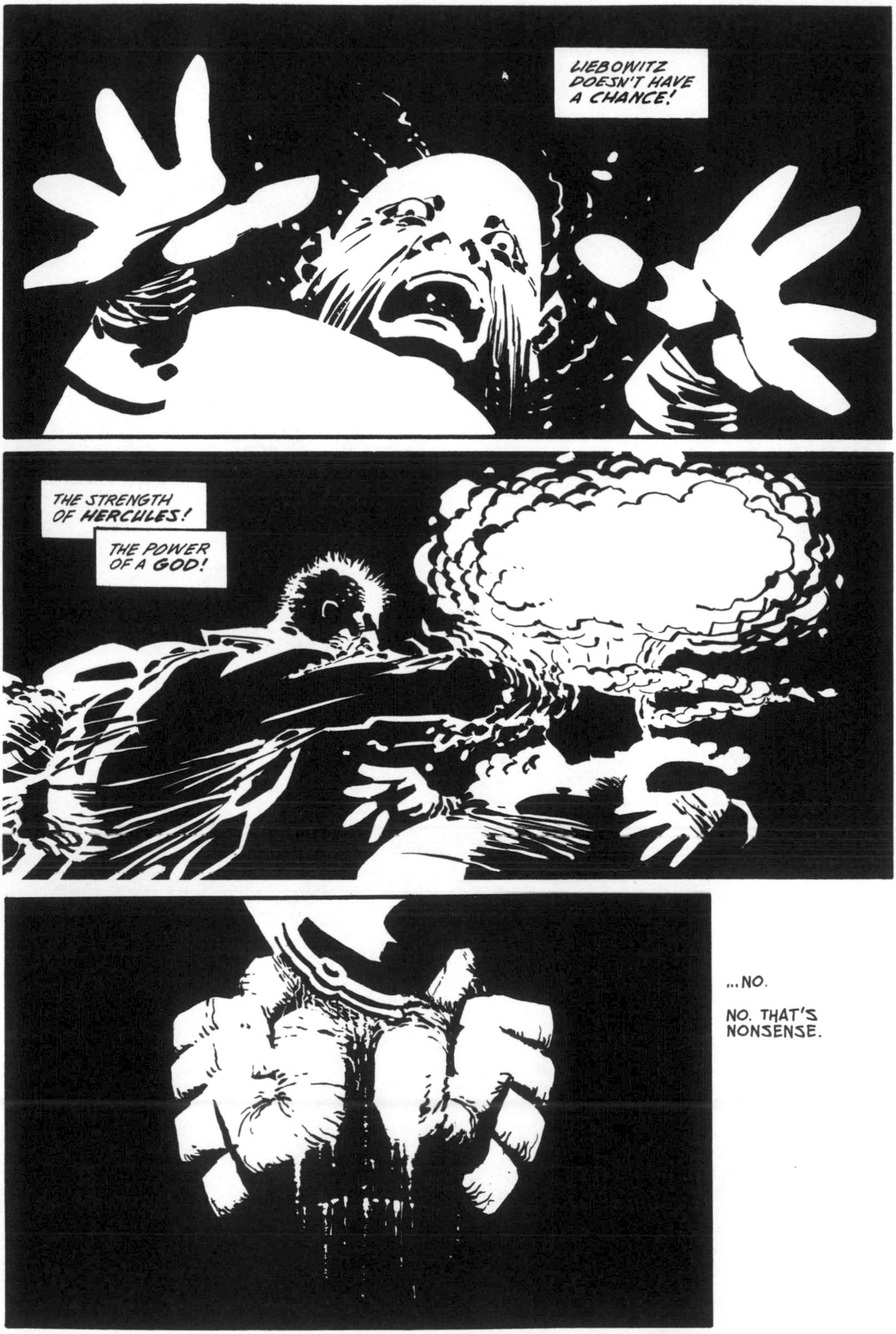
LIEBOWITZ DOESN'T HAVE A CHANCE!
THE STRENGTH OF HERCULES!
THE POWER OF A GOD!
...NO.
NO. THAT'S NONSENSE.

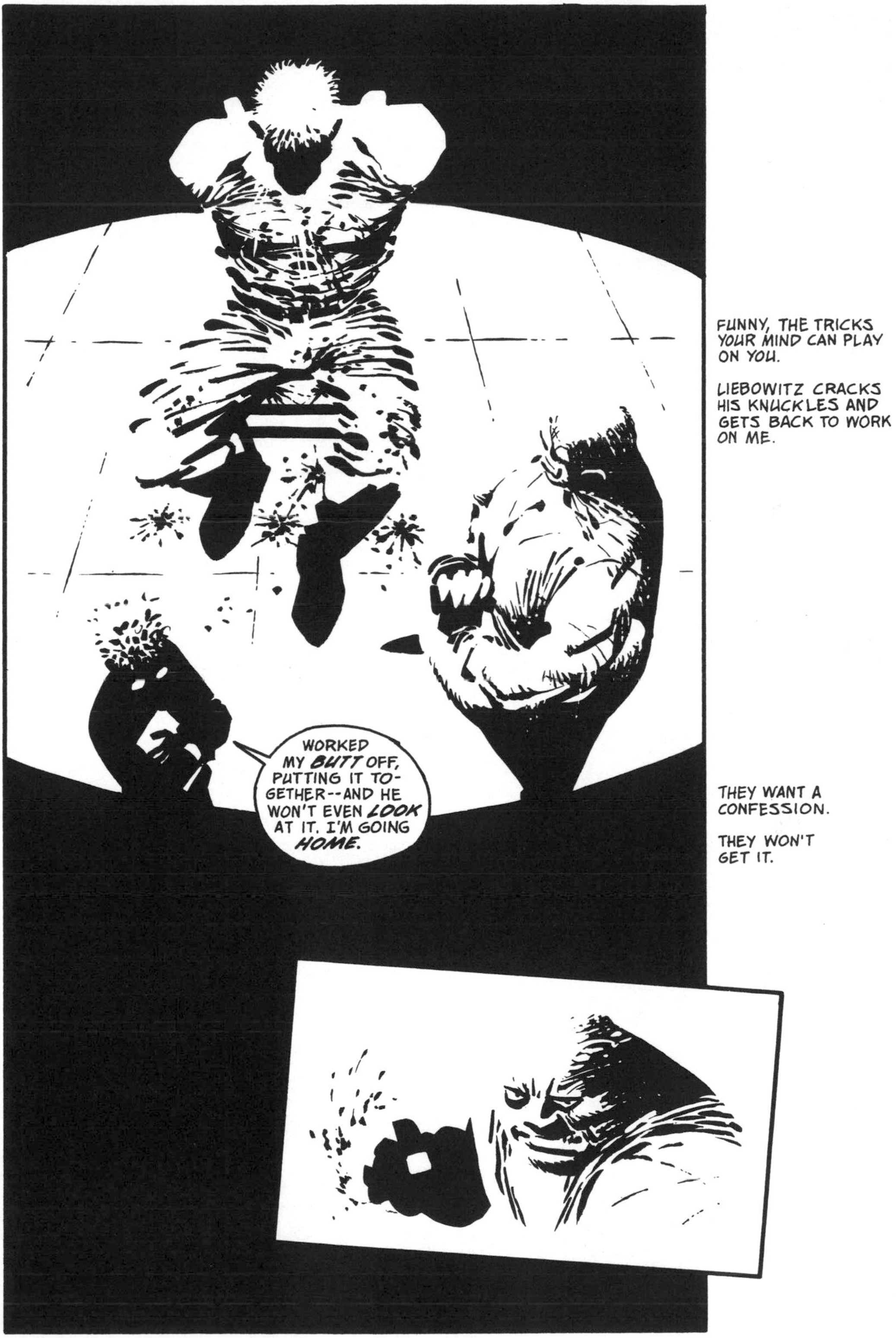
FUNNY, THE TRICKS YOUR MIND CAN PLAY ON YOU.
LIEBOWITZ CRACKS HIS KNUCKLES AND GETS BACK TO WORK ON ME.
WORKED MY BUTT OFF, PUTTING IT TO-GETHER--AND HE WON'T EVEN LOOK AT IT. I'M GOING HOME.
THEY WANT A CONFESSION.
THEY WON'T GET IT.

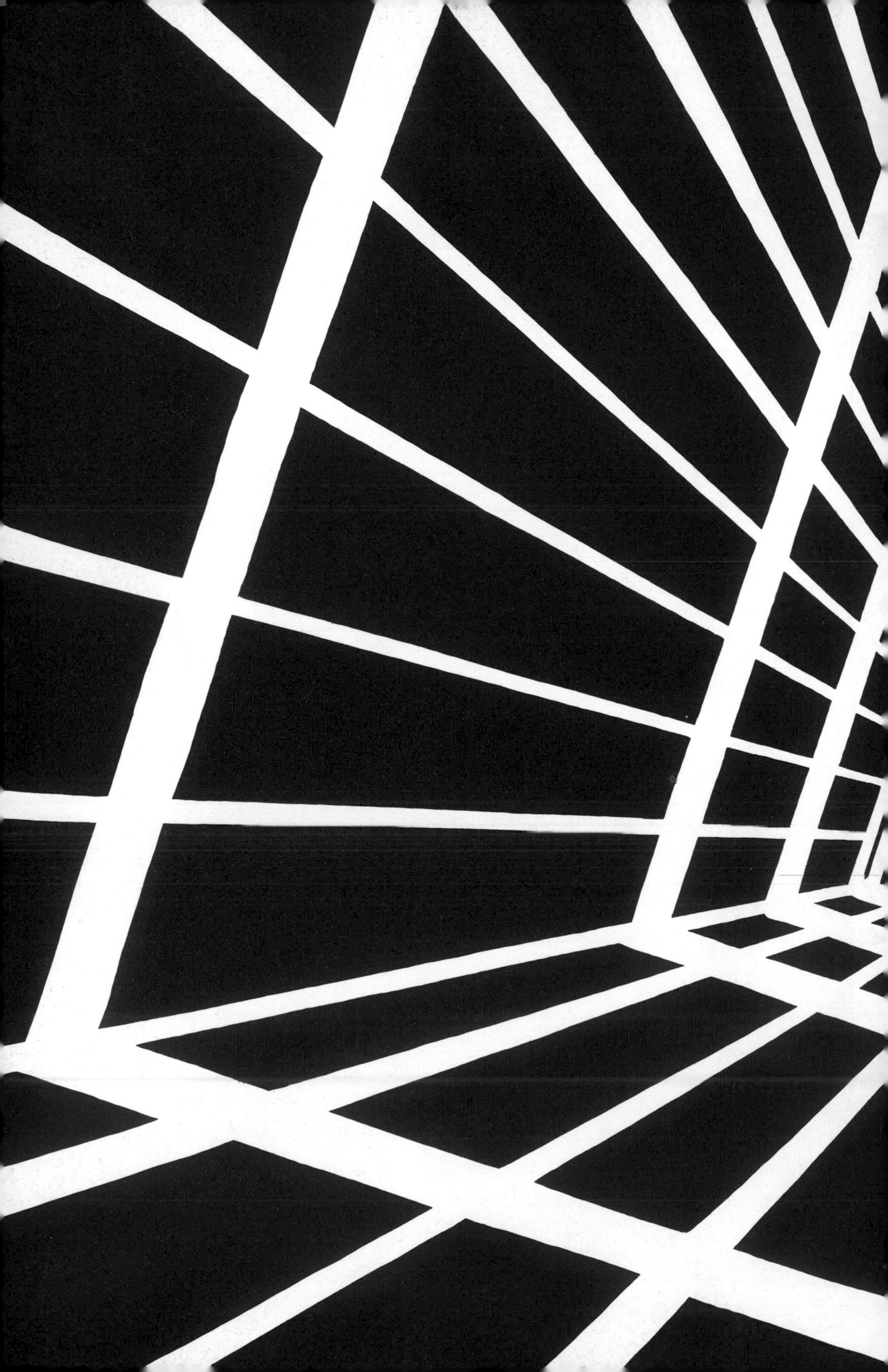

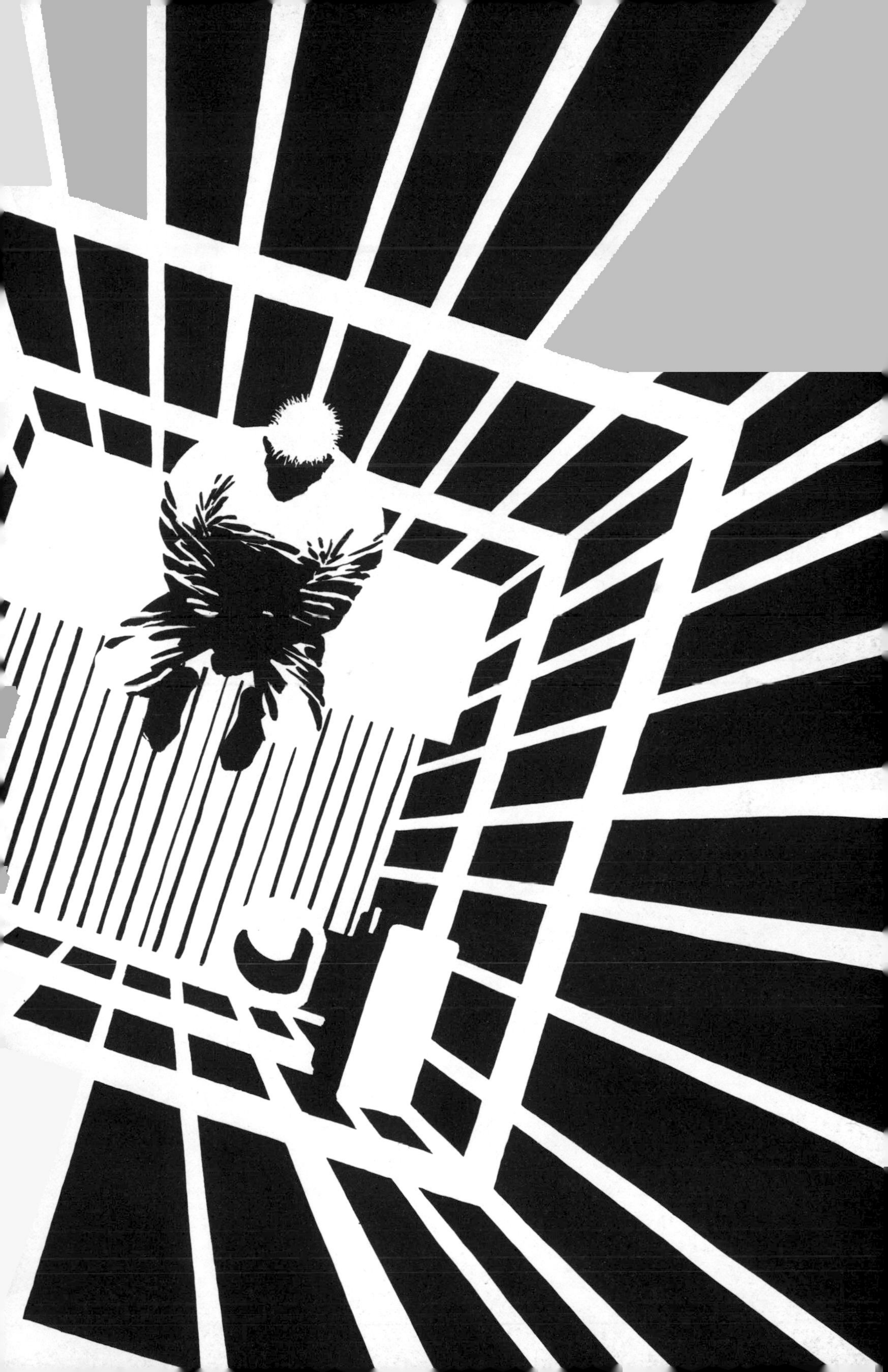

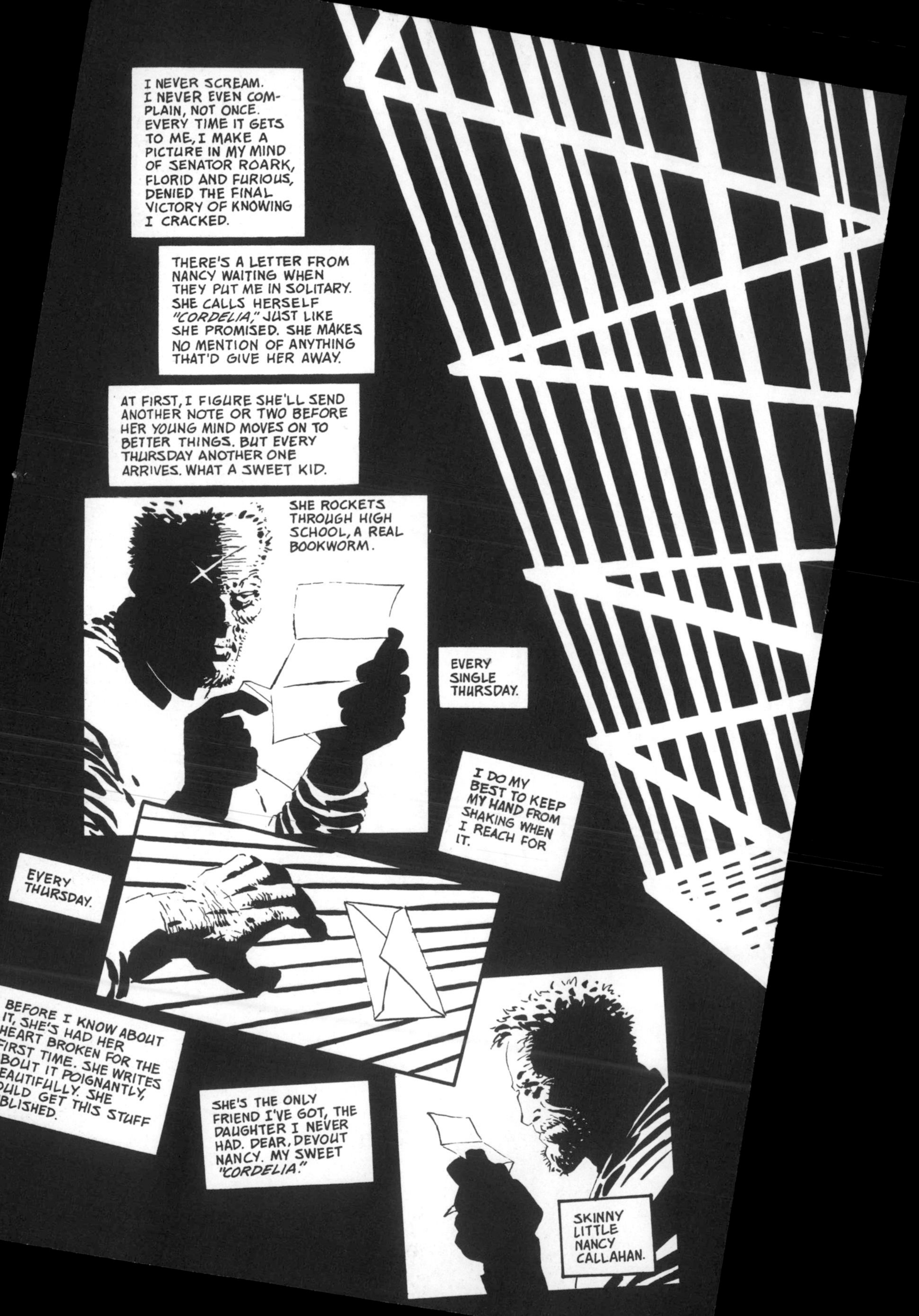
I NEVER SCREAM. I NEVER EVEN COMPLAIN, NOT ONCE. EVERY TIME IT GETS TO ME, I MAKE A PICTURE IN MY MIND OF SENATOR ROARK, FLORID AND FURIOUS, DENIED THE FINAL VICTORY OF KNOWING I CRACKED.
THERE'S A LETTER FROM NANCY WAITING WHEN THEY PUT ME IN SOLITARY. SHE CALLS HERSELF *"CORDELIA,"* JUST LIKE SHE PROMISED. SHE MAKES NO MENTION OF ANYTHING THAT'D GIVE HER AWAY.
AT FIRST, I FIGURE SHE'LL SEND ANOTHER NOTE OR TWO BEFORE HER *YOUNG* MIND MOVES ON TO BETTER THINGS. BUT EVERY THURSDAY ANOTHER ONE ARRIVES. WHAT A SWEET KID.
SHE ROCKETS THROUGH HIGH SCHOOL, A REAL BOOKWORM.
EVERY SINGLE THURSDAY.
I DO MY BEST TO KEEP MY HAND FROM SHAKING WHEN I REACH FOR IT.
EVERY THURSDAY.
BEFORE I KNOW ABOUT IT, SHE'S HAD HER HEART BROKEN FOR THE FIRST TIME. SHE WRITES ABOUT IT POIGNANTLY, BEAUTIFULLY. SHE COULD GET THIS STUFF PUBLISHED.
SHE'S THE ONLY FRIEND I'VE GOT, THE DAUGHTER I NEVER HAD. DEAR, DEVOUT NANCY. MY SWEET *"CORDELIA."*
SKINNY LITTLE NANCY CALLAHAN.

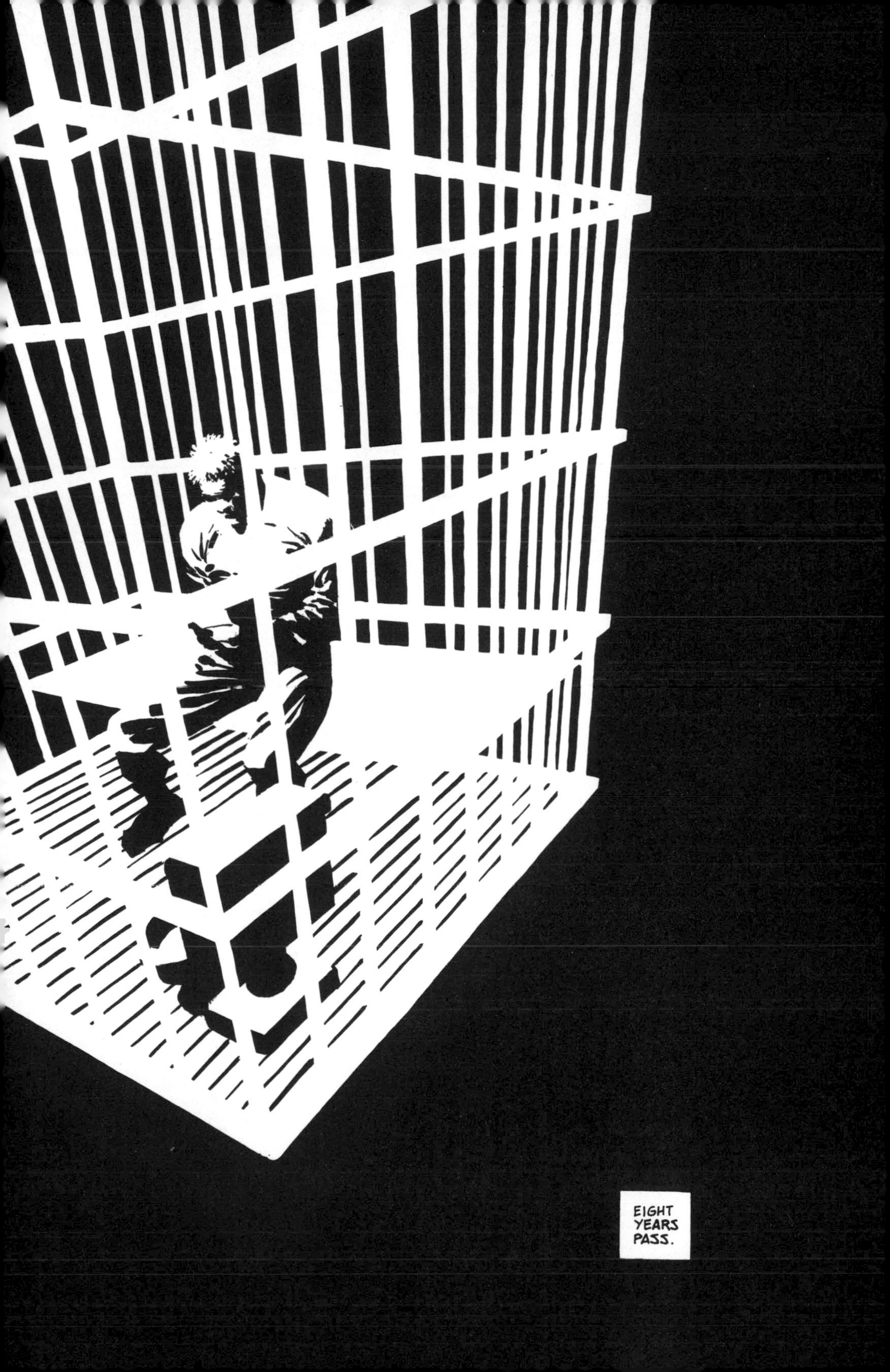
EIGHT YEARS PASS.

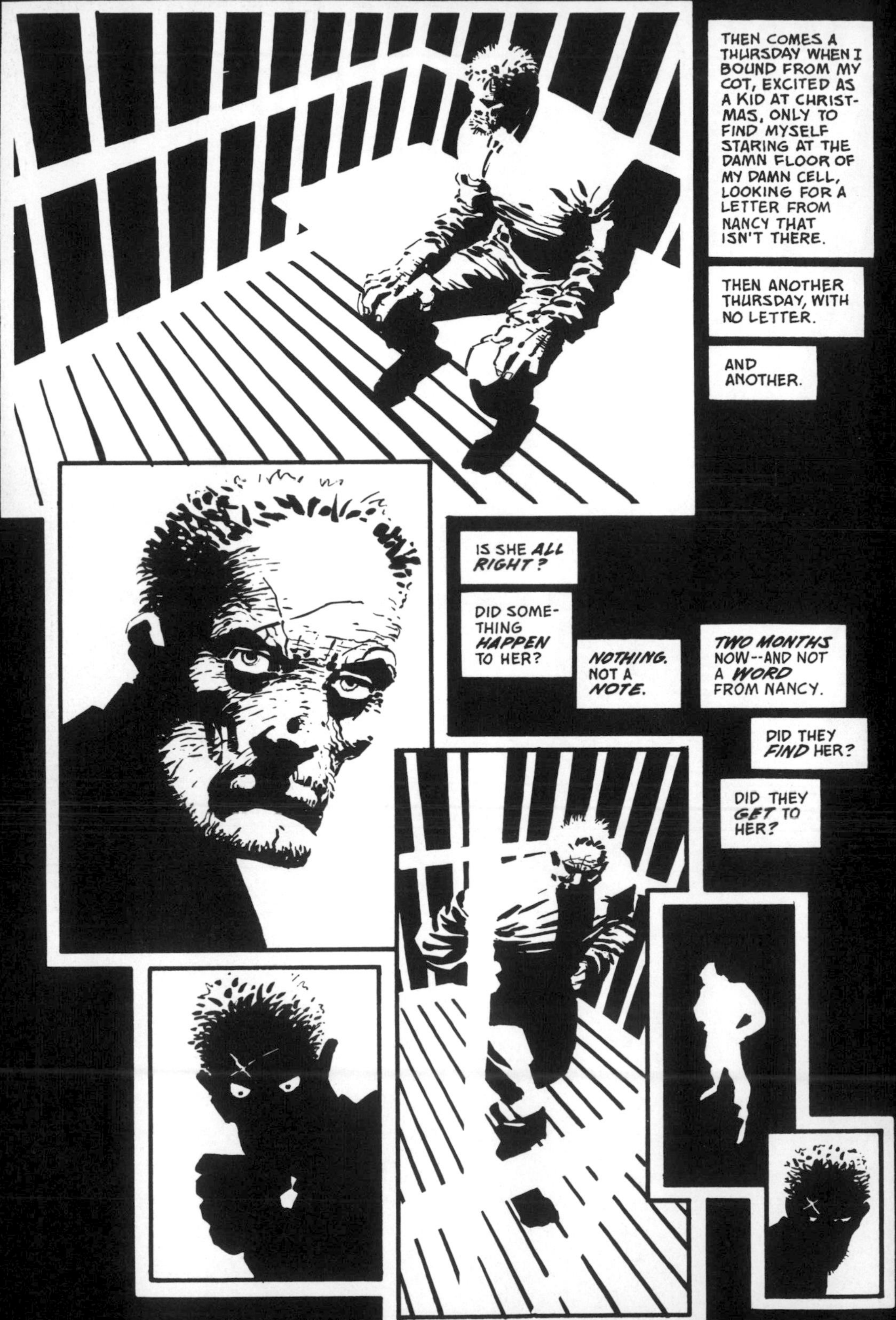
THEN COMES A THURSDAY WHEN I BOUND FROM MY COT, EXCITED AS A KID AT CHRISTMAS, ONLY TO FIND MYSELF STARING AT THE DAMN FLOOR OF MY DAMN CELL, LOOKING FOR A LETTER FROM NANCY THAT ISN'T THERE.
THEN ANOTHER THURSDAY, WITH NO LETTER.
AND ANOTHER.
IS SHE ALL RIGHT?
DID SOMETHING HAPPEN TO HER?
NOTHING. NOT A NOTE.
TWO MONTHS NOW--AND NOT A WORD FROM NANCY.
DID THEY FIND HER?
DID THEY GET TO HER?

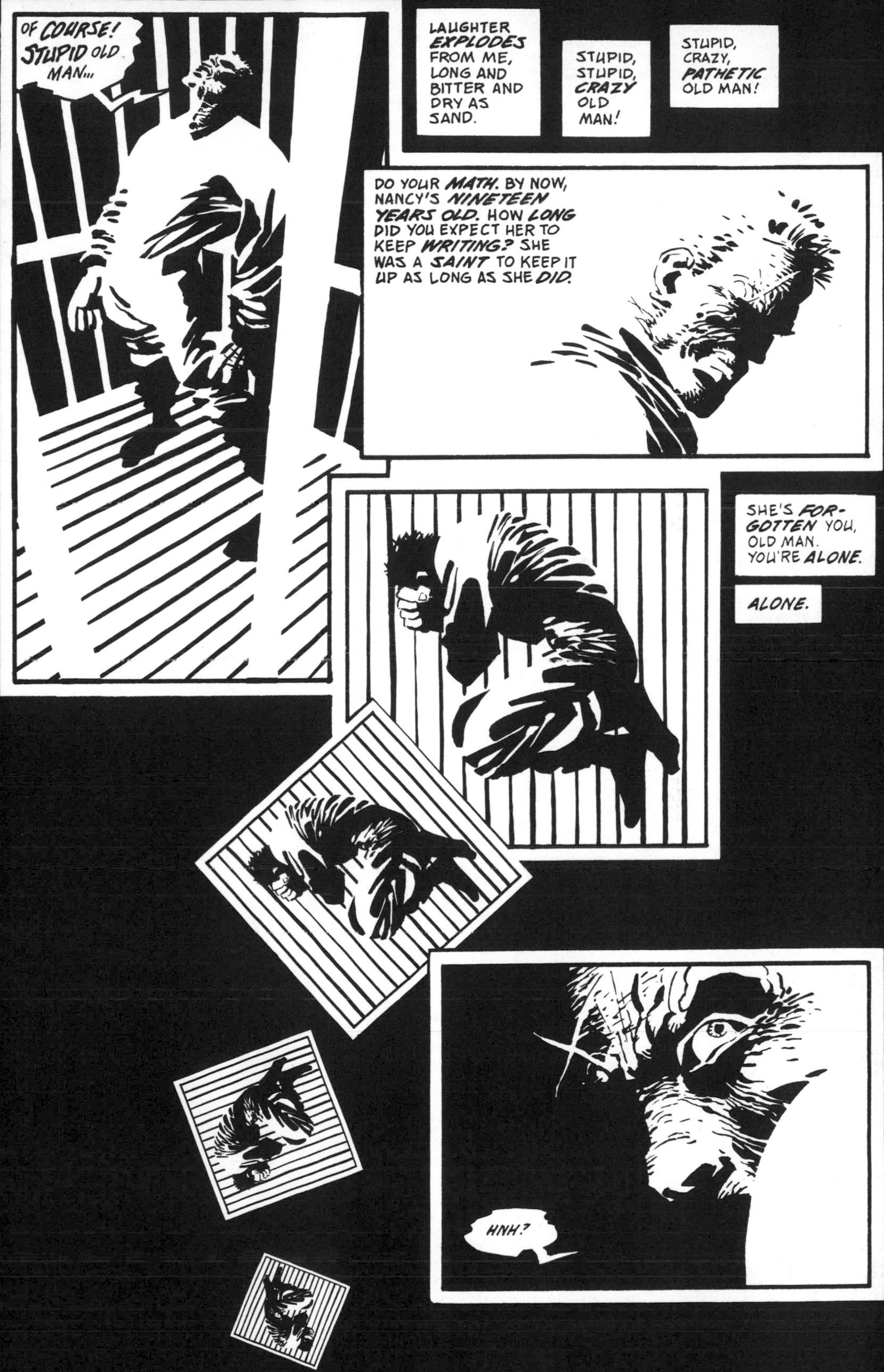
OF COURSE! STUPID OLD MAN...
LAUGHTER EXPLODES FROM ME, LONG AND BITTER AND DRY AS SAND.
STUPID, STUPID, CRAZY OLD MAN!
STUPID, CRAZY, PATHETIC OLD MAN!
DO YOUR MATH. BY NOW, NANCY'S NINETEEN YEARS OLD. HOW LONG DID YOU EXPECT HER TO KEEP WRITING? SHE WAS A SAINT TO KEEP IT UP AS LONG AS SHE DID.
SHE'S FOR-GOTTEN YOU, OLD MAN. YOU'RE ALONE.
ALONE.
HNH?

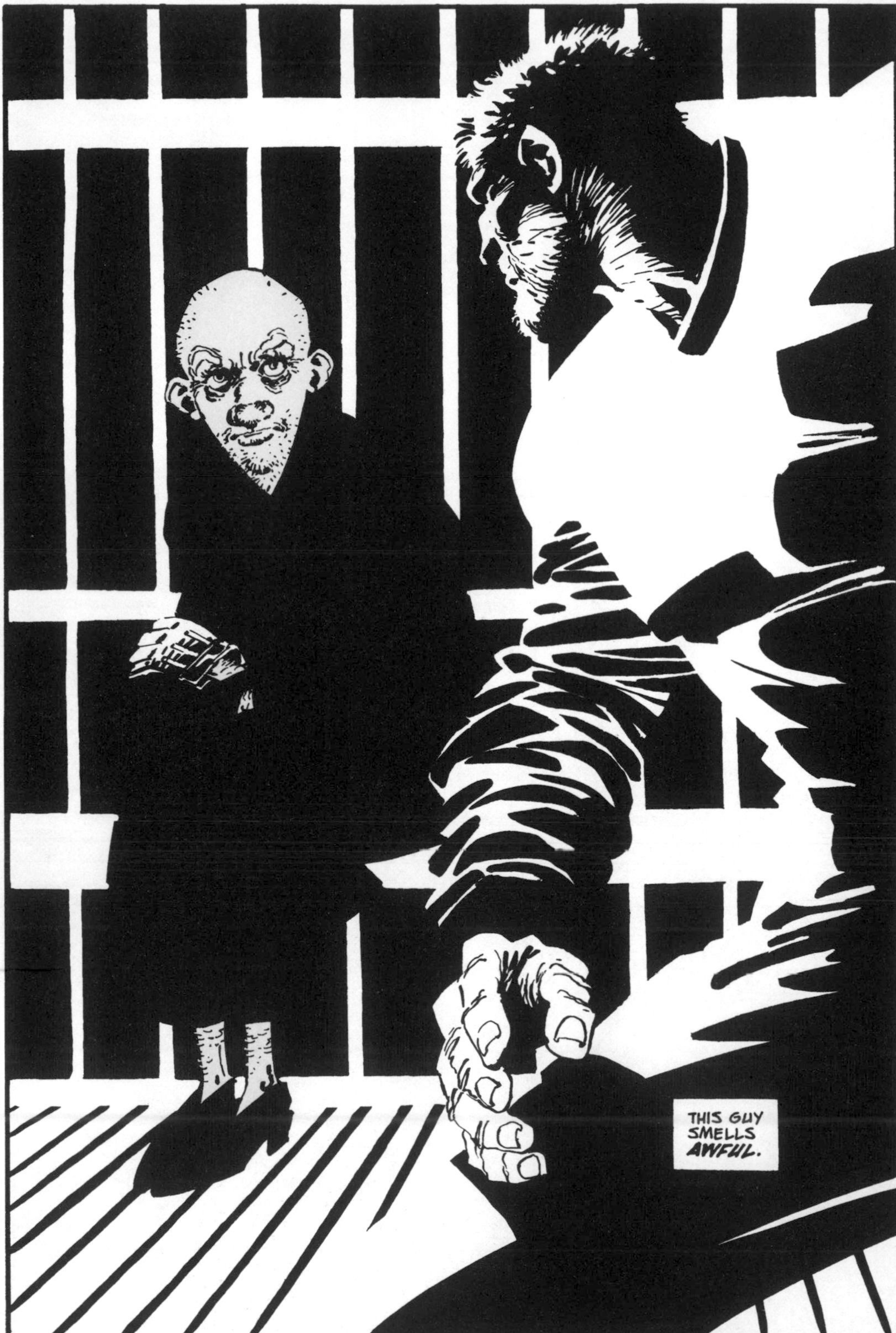
THIS GUY SMELLS AWFUL.

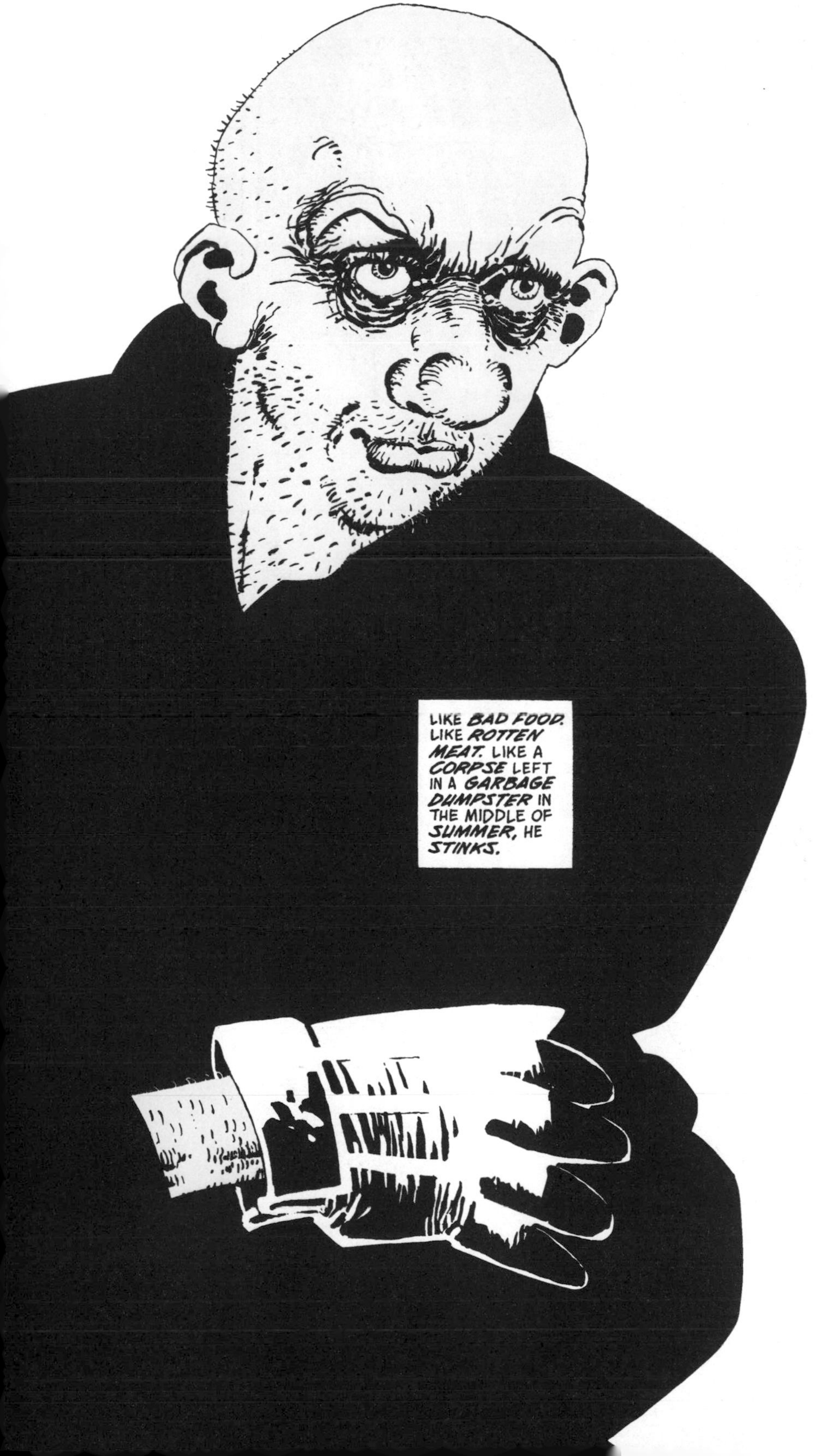
LIKE BAD FOOD. LIKE ROTTEN MEAT. LIKE A CORPSE LEFT IN A GARBAGE DUMPSTER IN THE MIDDLE OF SUMMER, HE STINKS.

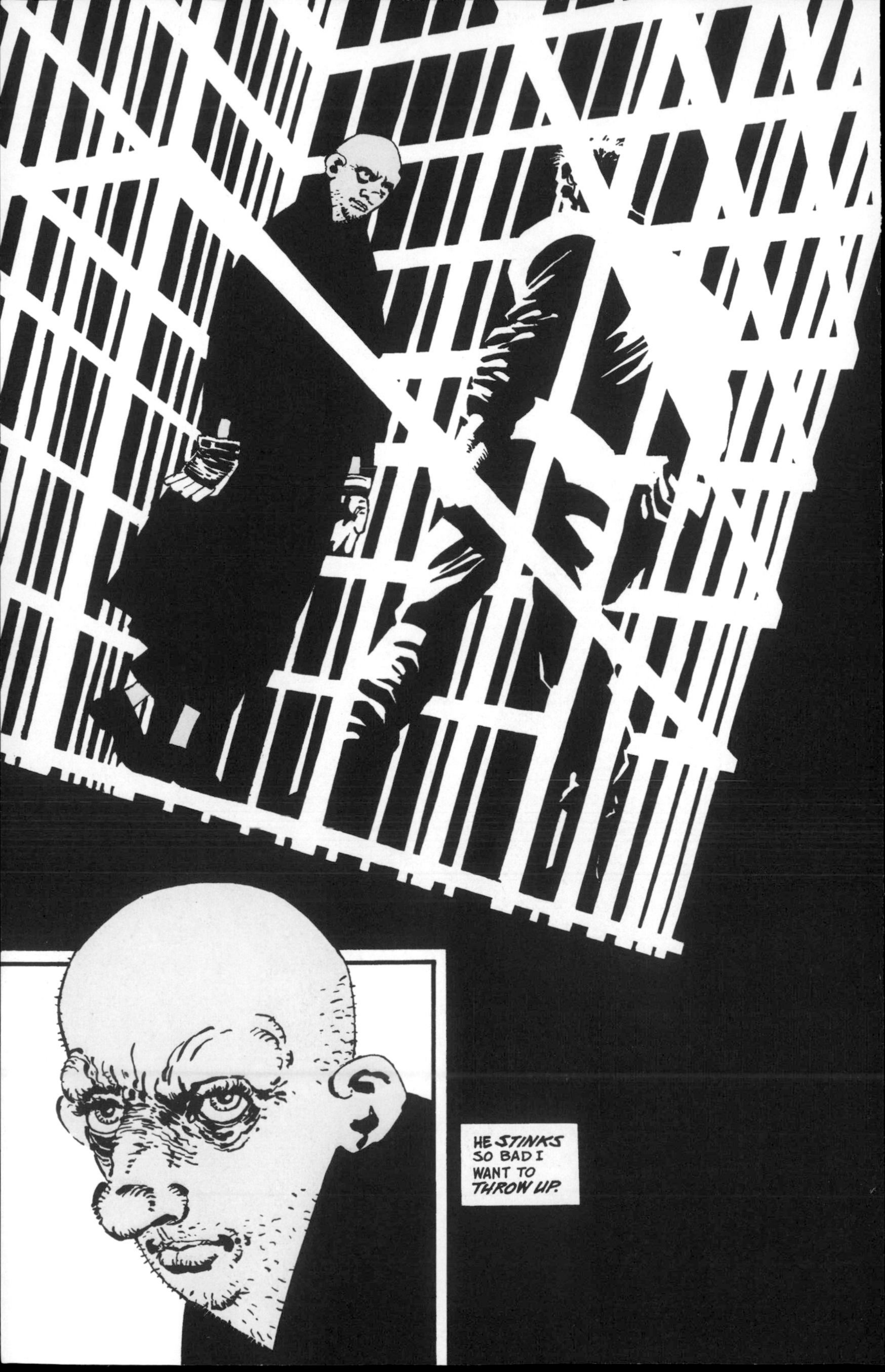
HE STINKS SO BAD I WANT TO THROW UP.

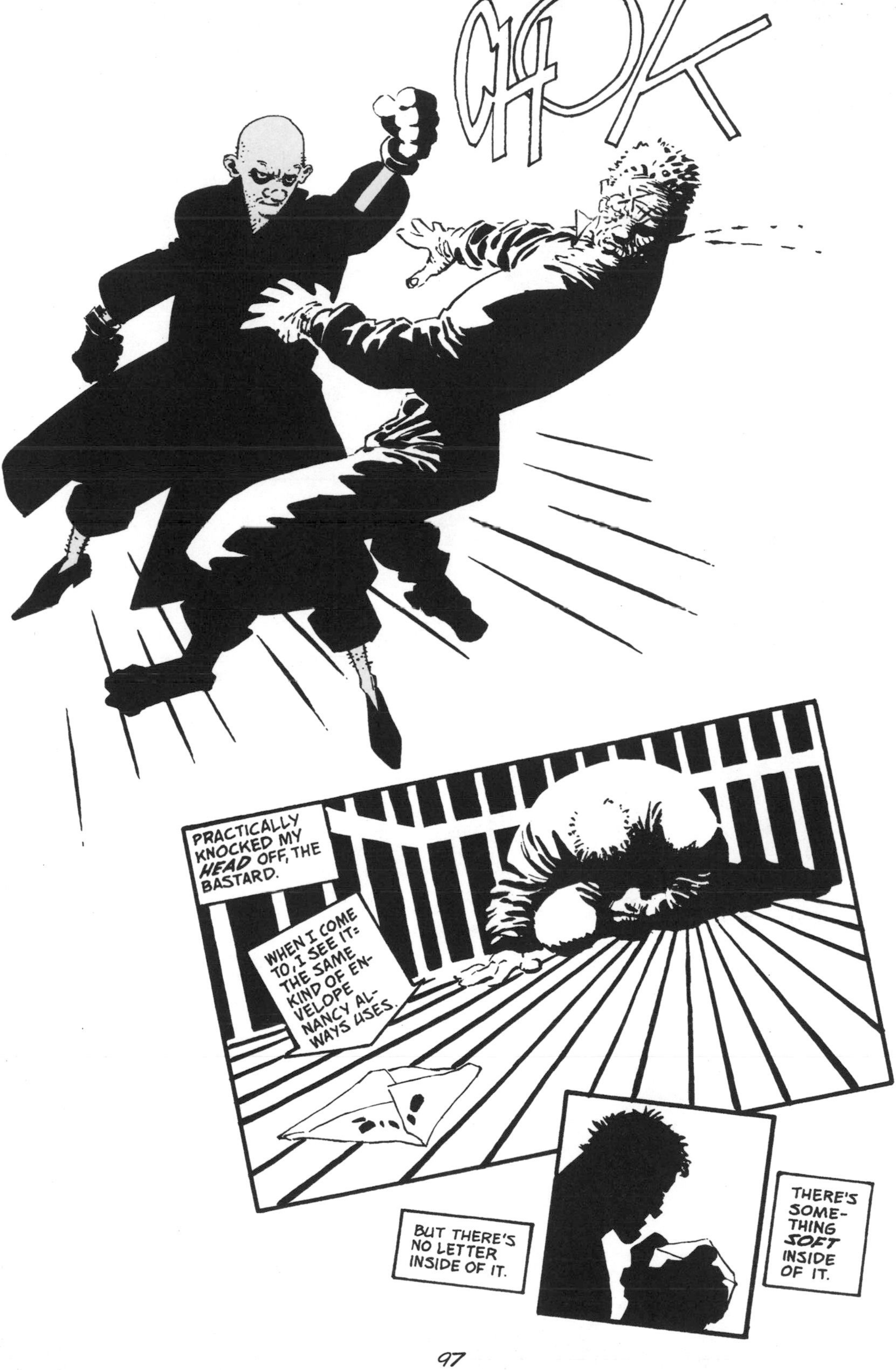
CHOK
PRACTICALLY KNOCKED MY HEAD OFF, THE BASTARD.
WHEN I COME TO, I SEE IT: THE SAME KIND OF ENVELOPE NANCY ALWAYS USES.
BUT THERE'S NO LETTER INSIDE OF IT.
THERE'S SOMETHING SOFT INSIDE OF IT.

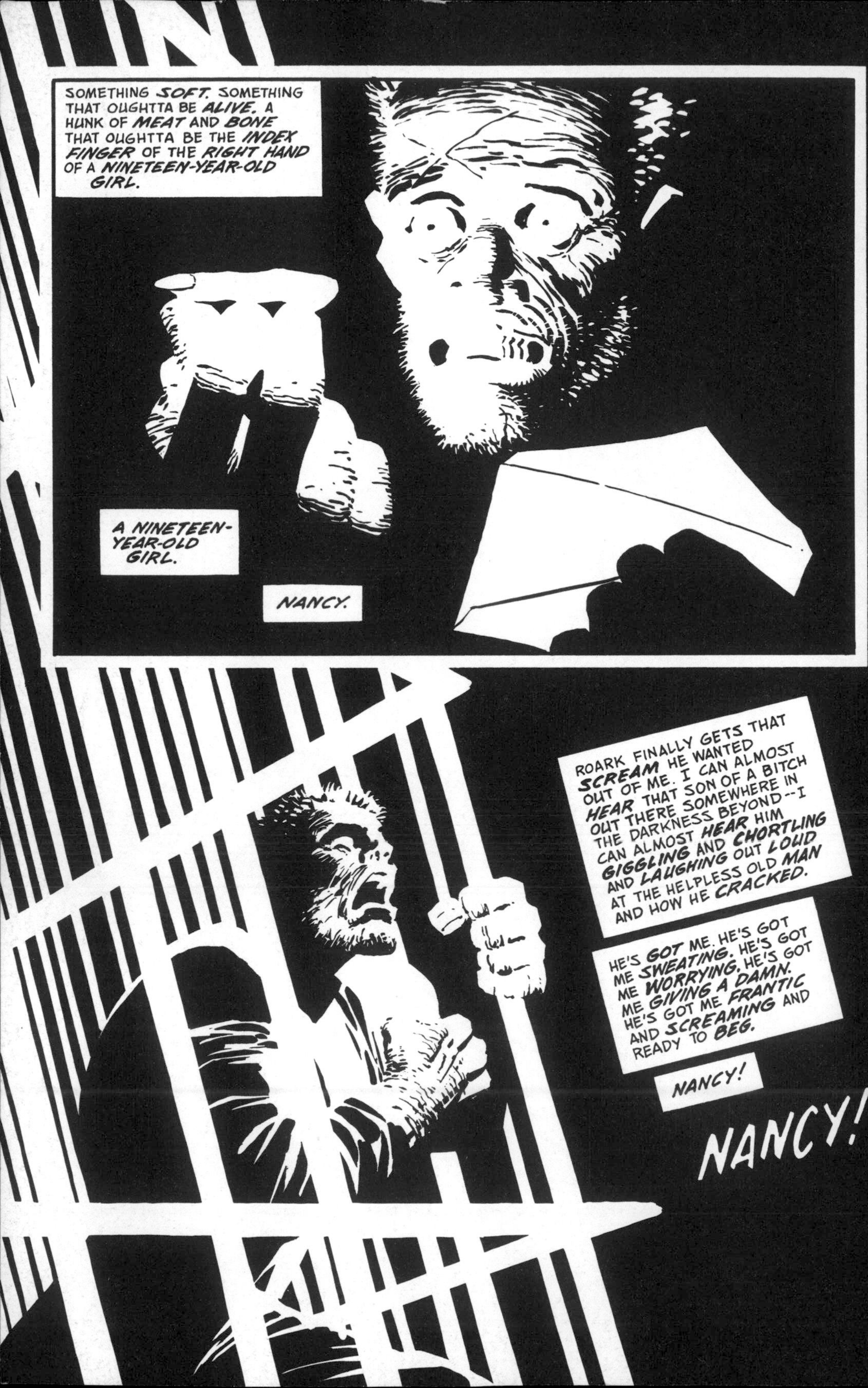
SOMETHING SOFT. SOMETHING THAT OUGHTTA BE ALIVE. A HUNK OF MEAT AND BONE THAT OUGHTTA BE THE INDEX FINGER OF THE RIGHT HAND OF A NINETEEN-YEAR-OLD GIRL.
A NINETEEN-YEAR-OLD GIRL.
NANCY.
ROARK FINALLY GETS THAT SCREAM HE WANTED OUT OF ME. I CAN ALMOST HEAR THAT SON OF A BITCH OUT THERE SOMEWHERE IN THE DARKNESS BEYOND--I CAN ALMOST HEAR HIM GIGGLING AND CHORTLING AND LAUGHING OUT LOUD AT THE HELPLESS OLD MAN AND HOW HE CRACKED.
HE'S GOT ME. HE'S GOT ME SWEATING. HE'S GOT ME WORRYING. HE'S GOT ME GIVING A DAMN. HE'S GOT ME FRANTIC AND SCREAMING AND READY TO BEG.
NANCY!
NANCY!

CHAPTER FOUR

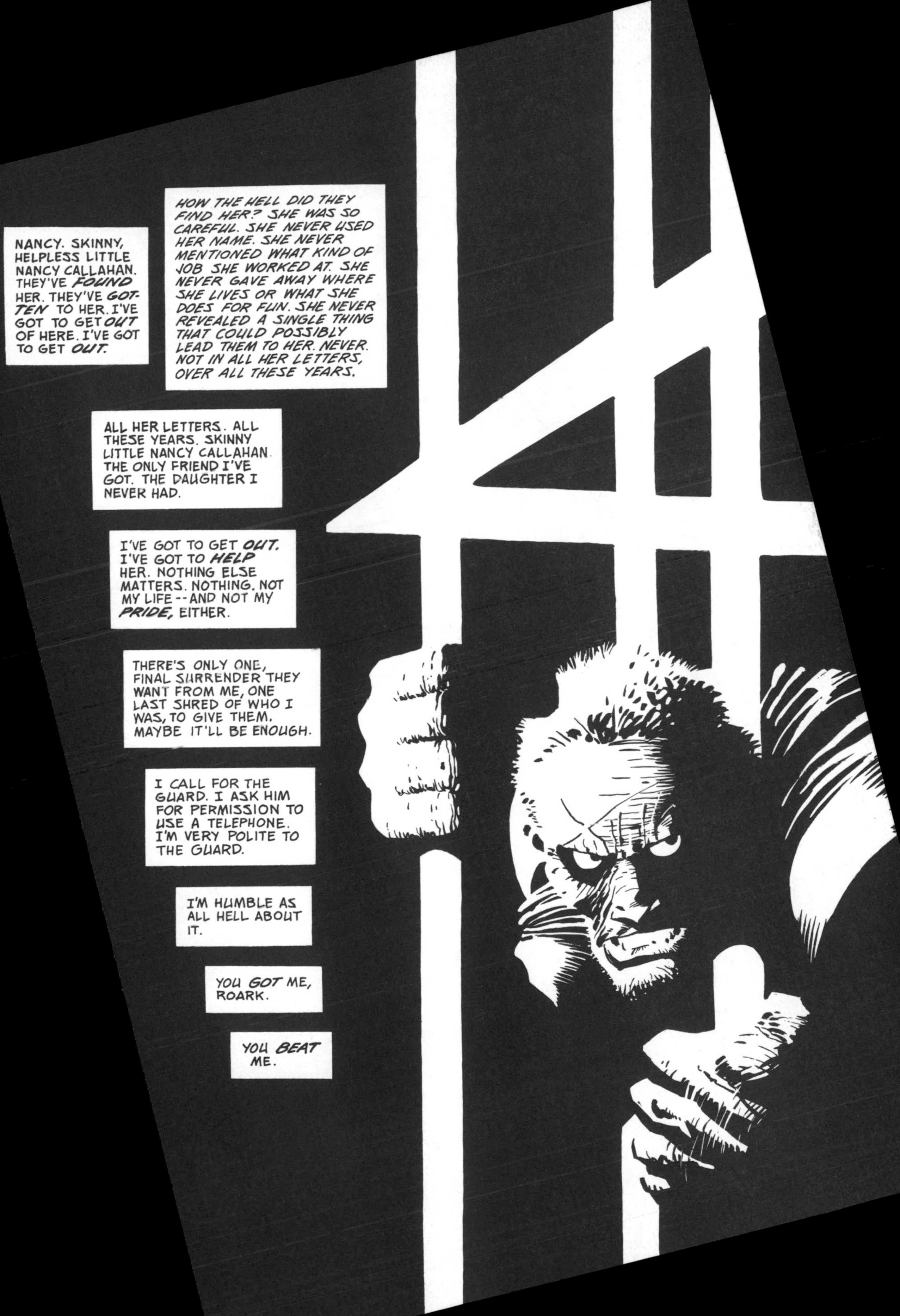
NANCY. SKINNY, HELPLESS LITTLE NANCY CALLAHAN. THEY'VE FOUND HER. THEY'VE GOT-TEN TO HER. I'VE GOT TO GET OUT OF HERE. I'VE GOT TO GET OUT.
HOW THE HELL DID THEY FIND HER? SHE WAS SO CAREFUL. SHE NEVER USED HER NAME. SHE NEVER MENTIONED WHAT KIND OF JOB SHE WORKED AT. SHE NEVER GAVE AWAY WHERE SHE LIVES OR WHAT SHE DOES FOR FUN. SHE NEVER REVEALED A SINGLE THING THAT COULD POSSIBLY LEAD THEM TO HER. NEVER. NOT IN ALL HER LETTERS, OVER ALL THESE YEARS.
ALL HER LETTERS. ALL THESE YEARS. SKINNY LITTLE NANCY CALLAHAN. THE ONLY FRIEND I'VE GOT. THE DAUGHTER I NEVER HAD.
I'VE GOT TO GET OUT. I'VE GOT TO HELP HER. NOTHING ELSE MATTERS. NOTHING. NOT MY LIFE -- AND NOT MY PRIDE, EITHER.
THERE'S ONLY ONE, FINAL SURRENDER THEY WANT FROM ME, ONE LAST SHRED OF WHO I WAS, TO GIVE THEM. MAYBE IT'LL BE ENOUGH.
I CALL FOR THE GUARD. I ASK HIM FOR PERMISSION TO USE A TELEPHONE. I'M VERY POLITE TO THE GUARD.
I'M HUMBLE AS ALL HELL ABOUT IT.
YOU GOT ME, ROARK.
YOU BEAT ME.

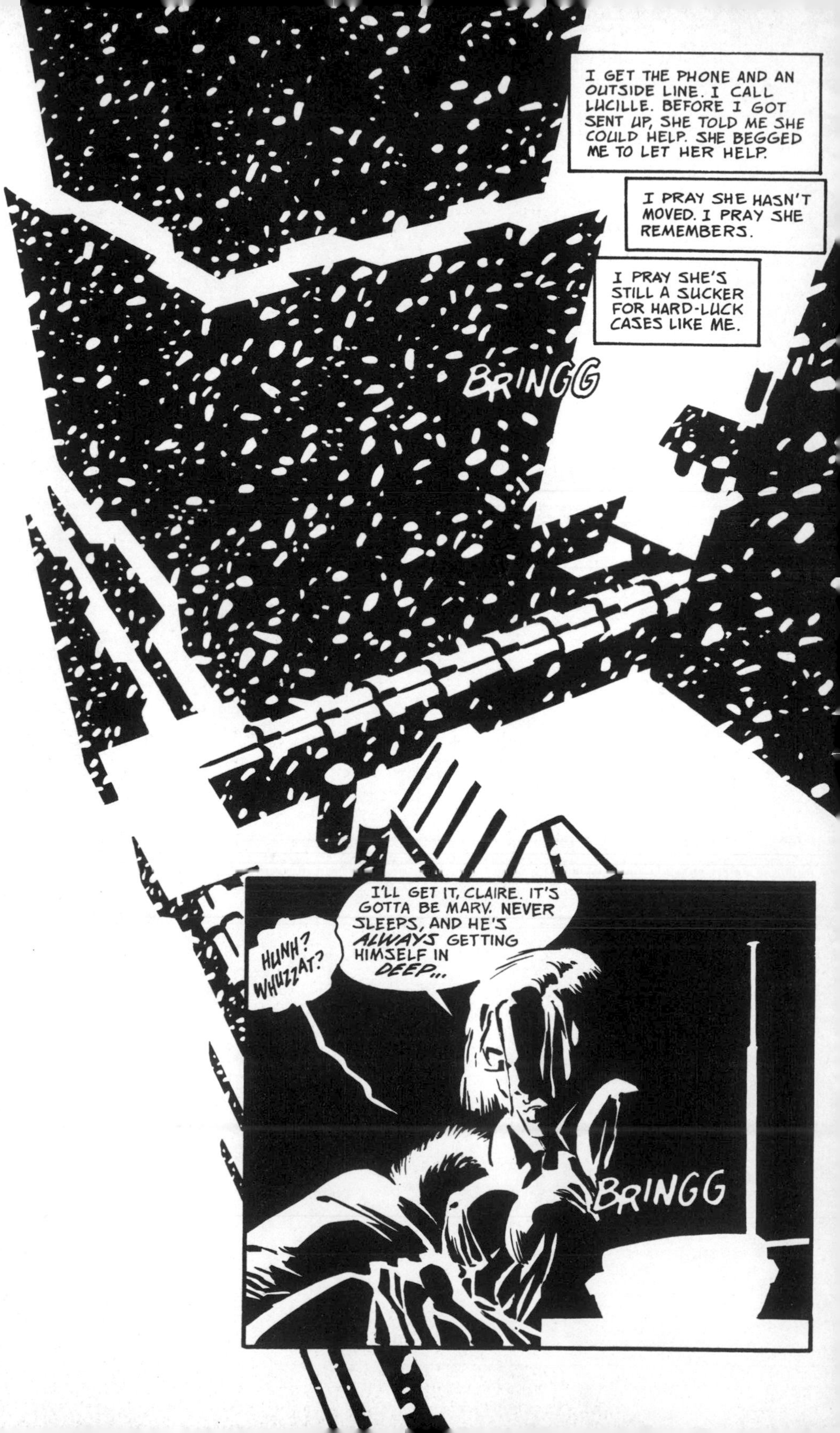
I GET THE PHONE AND AN OUTSIDE LINE. I CALL LUCILLE. BEFORE I GOT SENT UP, SHE TOLD ME SHE COULD HELP. SHE BEGGED ME TO LET HER HELP.
I PRAY SHE HASN'T MOVED. I PRAY SHE REMEMBERS.
I PRAY SHE'S STILL A SUCKER FOR HARD-LUCK CASES LIKE ME.
BRINGG
HUNH? WHUZZAT?
I'LL GET IT, CLAIRE. IT'S GOTTA BE MARV. NEVER SLEEPS, AND HE'S ALWAYS GETTING HIMSELF IN DEEP...
BRINGG

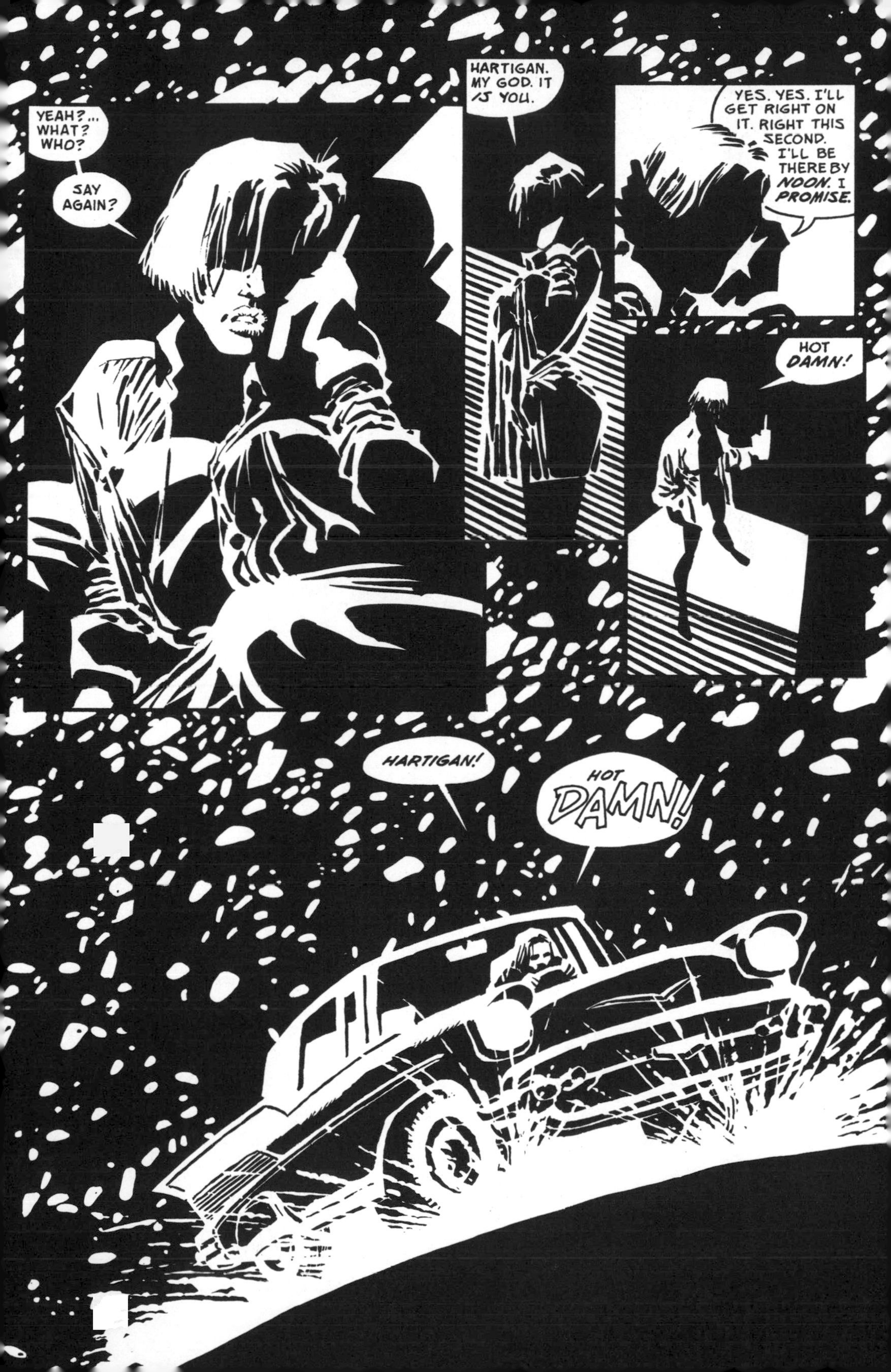
YEAH?... WHAT? WHO?
SAY AGAIN?
HARTIGAN. MY GOD. IT IS YOU.
YES. YES. I'LL GET RIGHT ON IT. RIGHT THIS SECOND. I'LL BE THERE BY NOON. I PROMISE.
HOT DAMN!
HARTIGAN!
HOT DAMN!

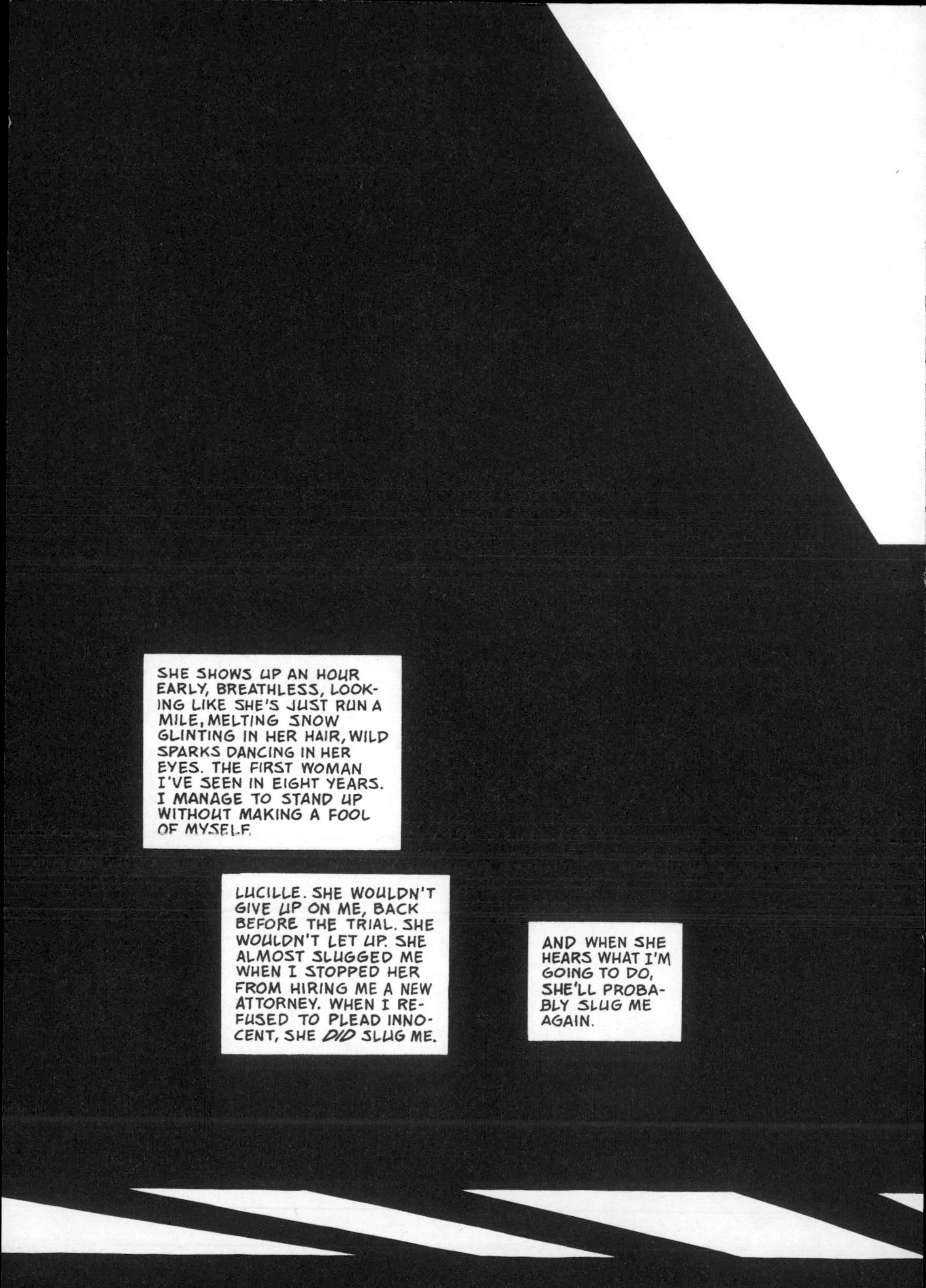
SHE SHOWS UP AN HOUR EARLY, BREATHLESS, LOOKING LIKE SHE'S JUST RUN A MILE, MELTING SNOW GLINTING IN HER HAIR, WILD SPARKS DANCING IN HER EYES. THE FIRST WOMAN I'VE SEEN IN EIGHT YEARS. I MANAGE TO STAND UP WITHOUT MAKING A FOOL OF MYSELF.
LUCILLE. SHE WOULDN'T GIVE UP ON ME, BACK BEFORE THE TRIAL. SHE WOULDN'T LET UP. SHE ALMOST SLUGGED ME WHEN I STOPPED HER FROM HIRING ME A NEW ATTORNEY. WHEN I REFUSED TO PLEAD INNOCENT, SHE *DID* SLUG ME.
AND WHEN SHE HEARS WHAT I'M GOING TO DO, SHE'LL PROBABLY SLUG ME AGAIN.

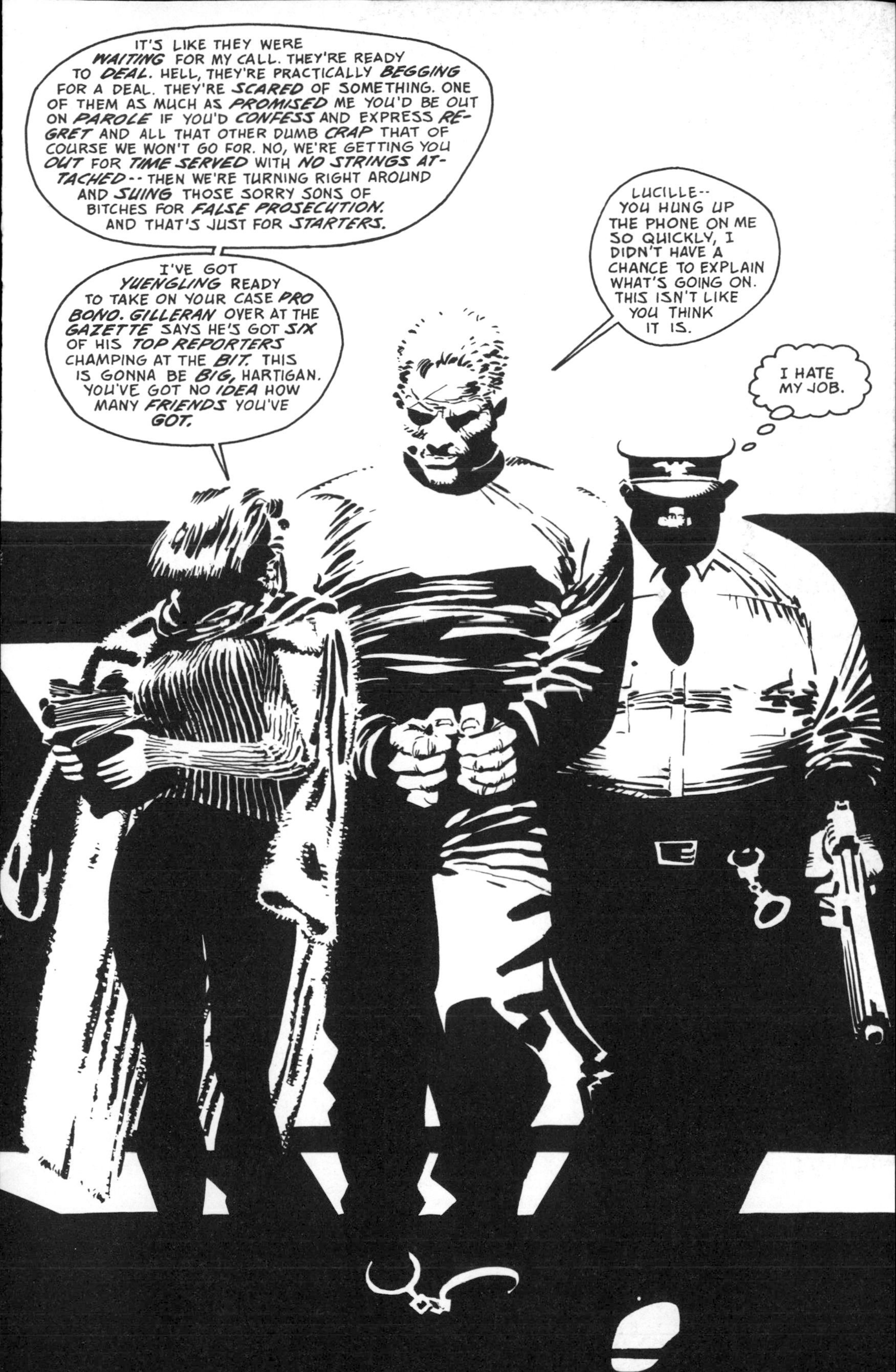
IT'S LIKE THEY WERE WAITING FOR MY CALL. THEY'RE READY TO DEAL. HELL, THEY'RE PRACTICALLY BEGGING FOR A DEAL. THEY'RE SCARED OF SOMETHING. ONE OF THEM AS MUCH AS PROMISED ME YOU'D BE OUT ON PAROLE IF YOU'D CONFESS AND EXPRESS REGRET AND ALL THAT OTHER DUMB CRAP THAT OF COURSE WE WON'T GO FOR. NO, WE'RE GETTING YOU OUT FOR TIME SERVED WITH NO STRINGS ATTACHED-- THEN WE'RE TURNING RIGHT AROUND AND SUING THOSE SORRY SONS OF BITCHES FOR FALSE PROSECUTION. AND THAT'S JUST FOR STARTERS.
I'VE GOT YUENGLING READY TO TAKE ON YOUR CASE PRO BONO. GILLERAN OVER AT THE GAZETTE SAYS HE'S GOT SIX OF HIS TOP REPORTERS CHAMPING AT THE BIT. THIS IS GONNA BE BIG, HARTIGAN. YOU'VE GOT NO IDEA HOW MANY FRIENDS YOU'VE GOT.
LUCILLE-- YOU HUNG UP THE PHONE ON ME SO QUICKLY, I DIDN'T HAVE A CHANCE TO EXPLAIN WHAT'S GOING ON. THIS ISN'T LIKE YOU THINK IT IS.
I HATE MY JOB.

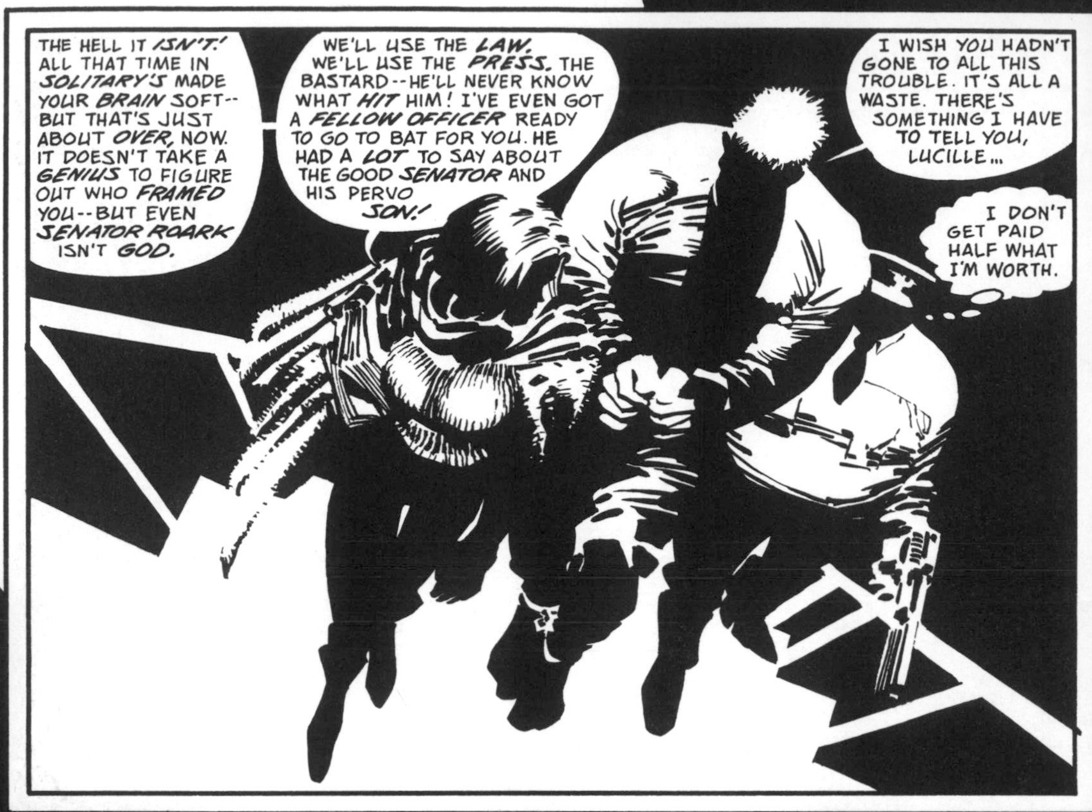
THE HELL IT ISN'T! ALL THAT TIME IN SOLITARY'S MADE YOUR BRAIN SOFT-- BUT THAT'S JUST ABOUT OVER, NOW. IT DOESN'T TAKE A GENIUS TO FIGURE OUT WHO FRAMED YOU--BUT EVEN SENATOR ROARK ISN'T GOD.
WE'LL USE THE LAW. WE'LL USE THE PRESS. THE BASTARD--HE'LL NEVER KNOW WHAT HIT HIM! I'VE EVEN GOT A FELLOW OFFICER READY TO GO TO BAT FOR YOU. HE HAD A LOT TO SAY ABOUT THE GOOD SENATOR AND HIS PERVO SON!
I WISH YOU HADN'T GONE TO ALL THIS TROUBLE. IT'S ALL A WASTE. THERE'S SOMETHING I HAVE TO TELL YOU, LUCILLE...
I DON'T GET PAID HALF WHAT I'M WORTH.
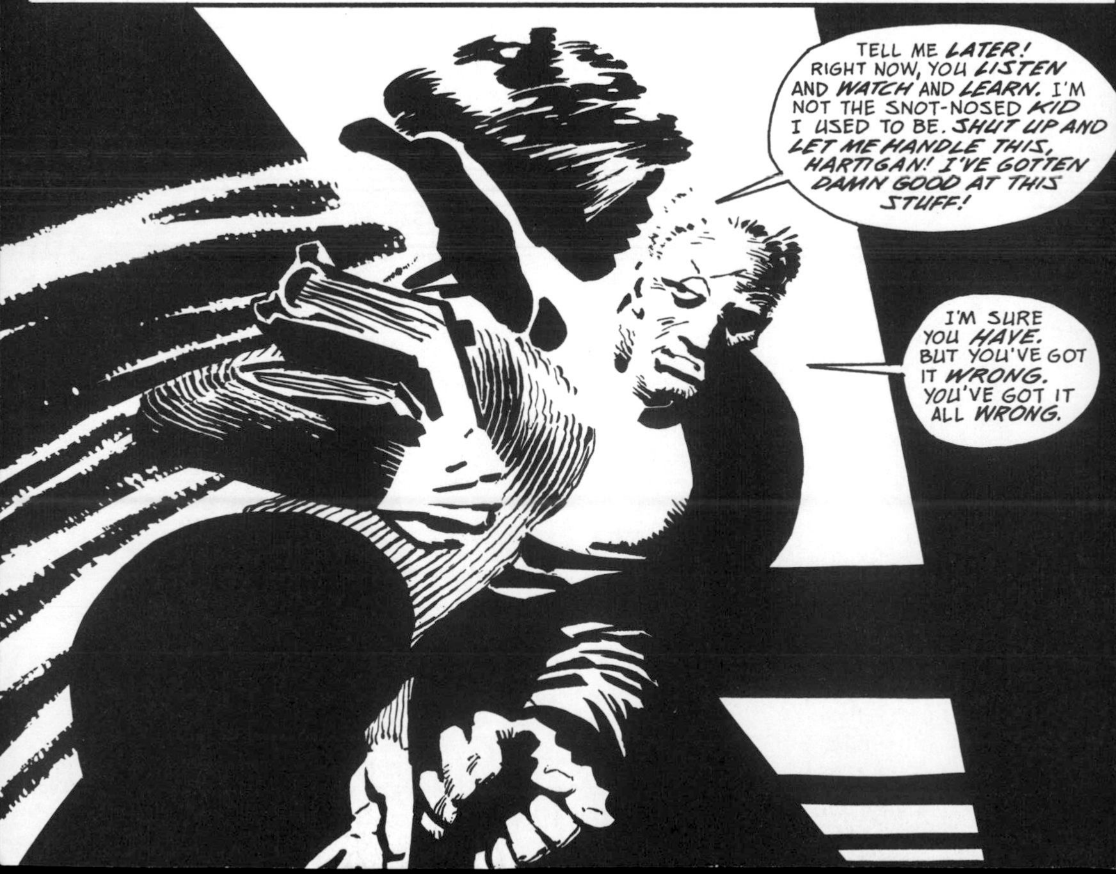
TELL ME LATER! RIGHT NOW, YOU LISTEN AND WATCH AND LEARN. I'M NOT THE SNOT-NOSED KID I USED TO BE. SHUT UP AND LET ME HANDLE THIS, HARTIGAN! I'VE GOTTEN DAMN GOOD AT THIS STUFF!
I'M SURE YOU HAVE. BUT YOU'VE GOT IT WRONG. YOU'VE GOT IT ALL WRONG.

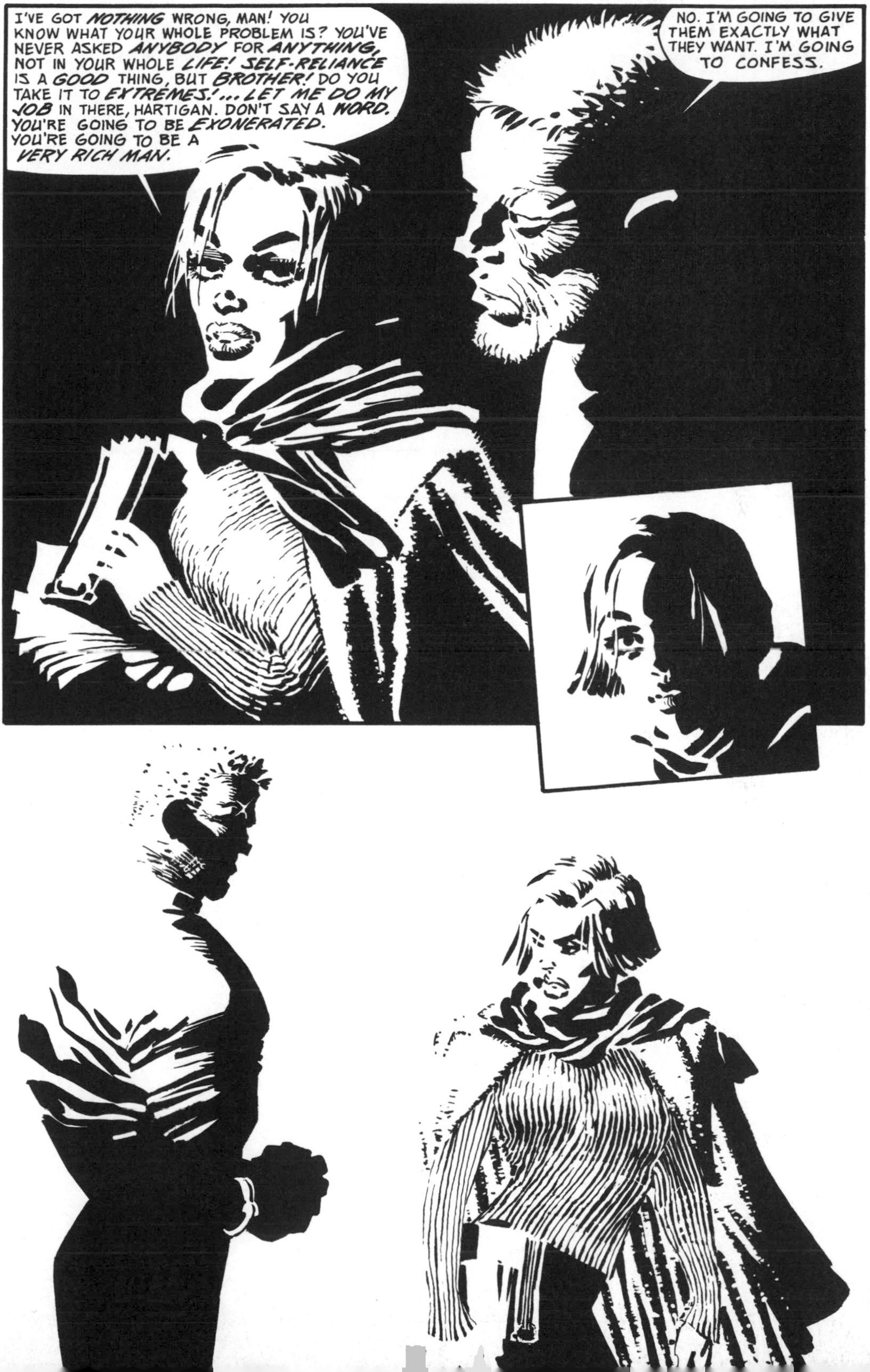
I'VE GOT NOTHING WRONG, MAN! YOU KNOW WHAT YOUR WHOLE PROBLEM IS? YOU'VE NEVER ASKED ANYBODY FOR ANYTHING, NOT IN YOUR WHOLE LIFE! SELF-RELIANCE IS A GOOD THING, BUT BROTHER! DO YOU TAKE IT TO EXTREMES! ...LET ME DO MY JOB IN THERE, HARTIGAN. DON'T SAY A WORD. YOU'RE GOING TO BE EXONERATED. YOU'RE GOING TO BE A VERY RICH MAN.
NO. I'M GOING TO GIVE THEM EXACTLY WHAT THEY WANT. I'M GOING TO CONFESS.

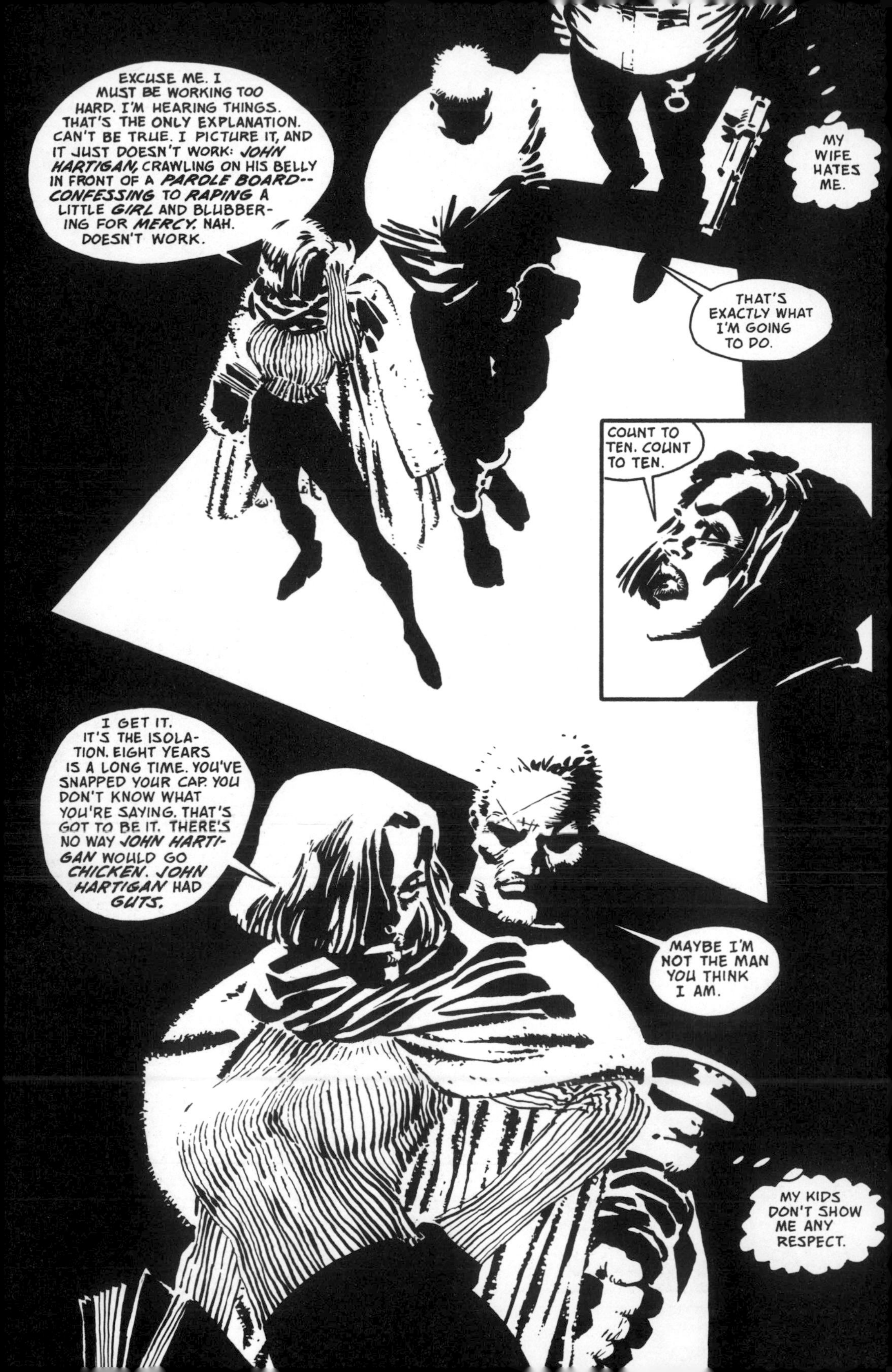
EXCUSE ME. I MUST BE WORKING TOO HARD. I'M HEARING THINGS. THAT'S THE ONLY EXPLANATION. CAN'T BE TRUE. I PICTURE IT, AND IT JUST DOESN'T WORK: JOHN HARTIGAN, CRAWLING ON HIS BELLY IN FRONT OF A PAROLE BOARD-- CONFESSING TO RAPING A LITTLE GIRL AND BLUBBERING FOR MERCY. NAH. DOESN'T WORK.
MY WIFE HATES ME.
THAT'S EXACTLY WHAT I'M GOING TO DO.
COUNT TO TEN. COUNT TO TEN.
I GET IT. IT'S THE ISOLATION. EIGHT YEARS IS A LONG TIME. YOU'VE SNAPPED YOUR CAP. YOU DON'T KNOW WHAT YOU'RE SAYING. THAT'S GOT TO BE IT. THERE'S NO WAY JOHN HARTIGAN WOULD GO CHICKEN. JOHN HARTIGAN HAD GUTS.
MAYBE I'M NOT THE MAN YOU THINK I AM.
MY KIDS DON'T SHOW ME ANY RESPECT.

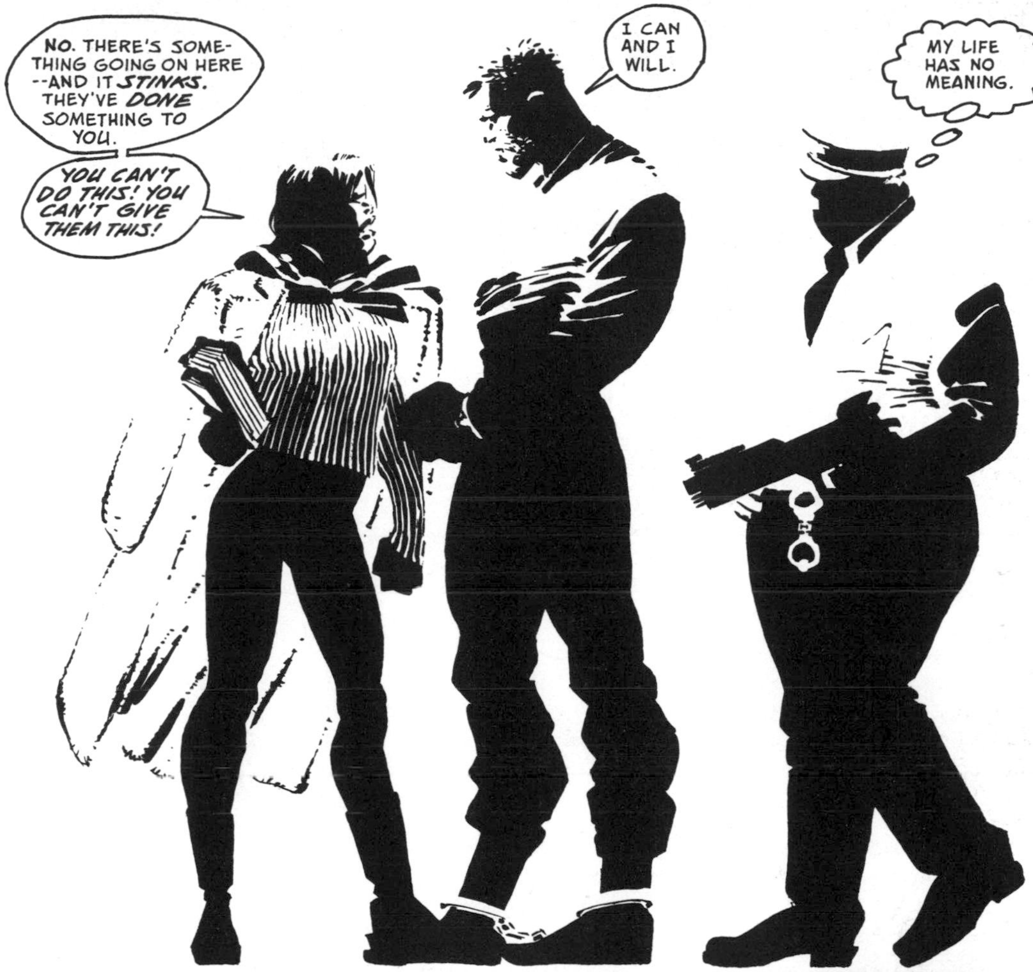
NO. THERE'S SOME-THING GOING ON HERE --AND IT STINKS. THEY'VE DONE SOMETHING TO YOU.
YOU CAN'T DO THIS! YOU CAN'T GIVE THEM THIS!
I CAN AND I WILL.
MY LIFE HAS NO MEANING.

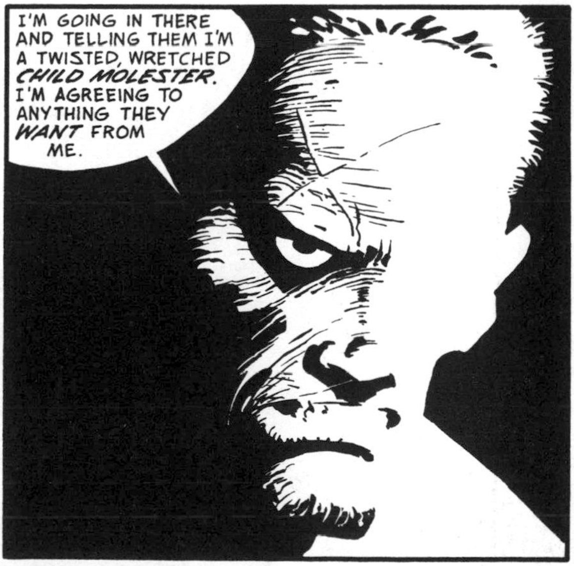
I'M GOING IN THERE AND TELLING THEM I'M A TWISTED, WRETCHED CHILD MOLESTER. I'M AGREEING TO ANYTHING THEY WANT FROM ME.

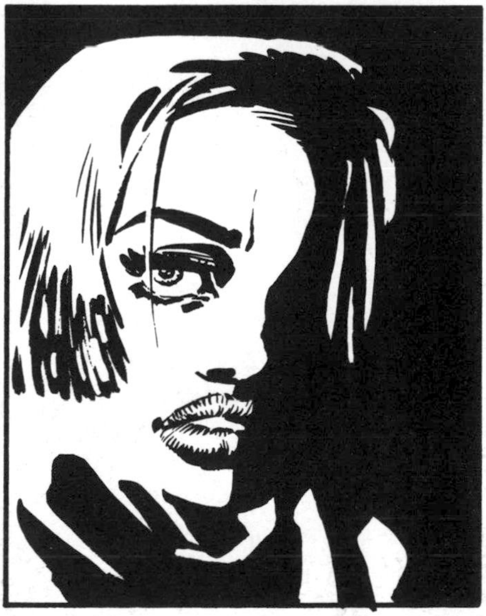

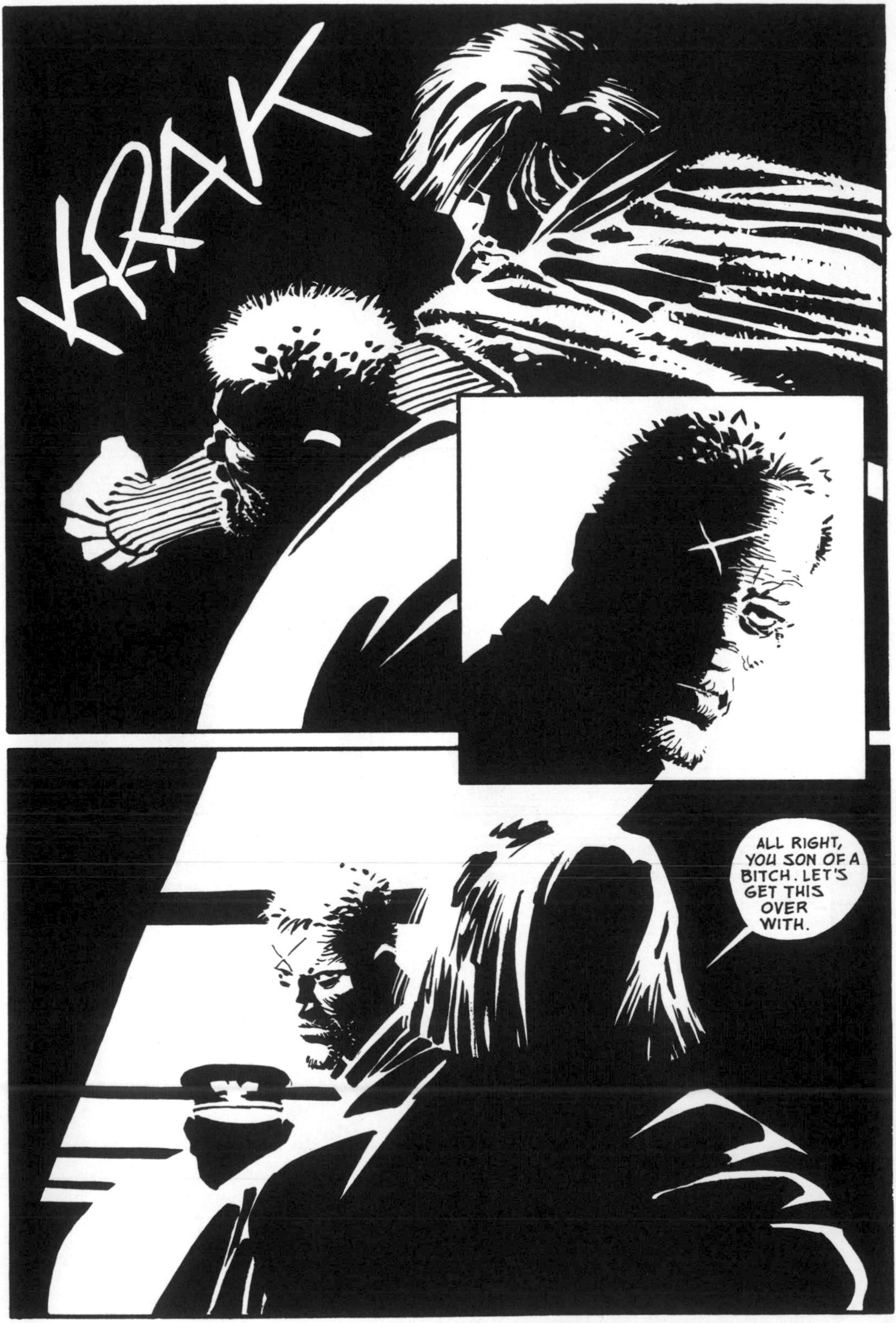
KRAK
ALL RIGHT, YOU SON OF A BITCH. LET'S GET THIS OVER WITH.

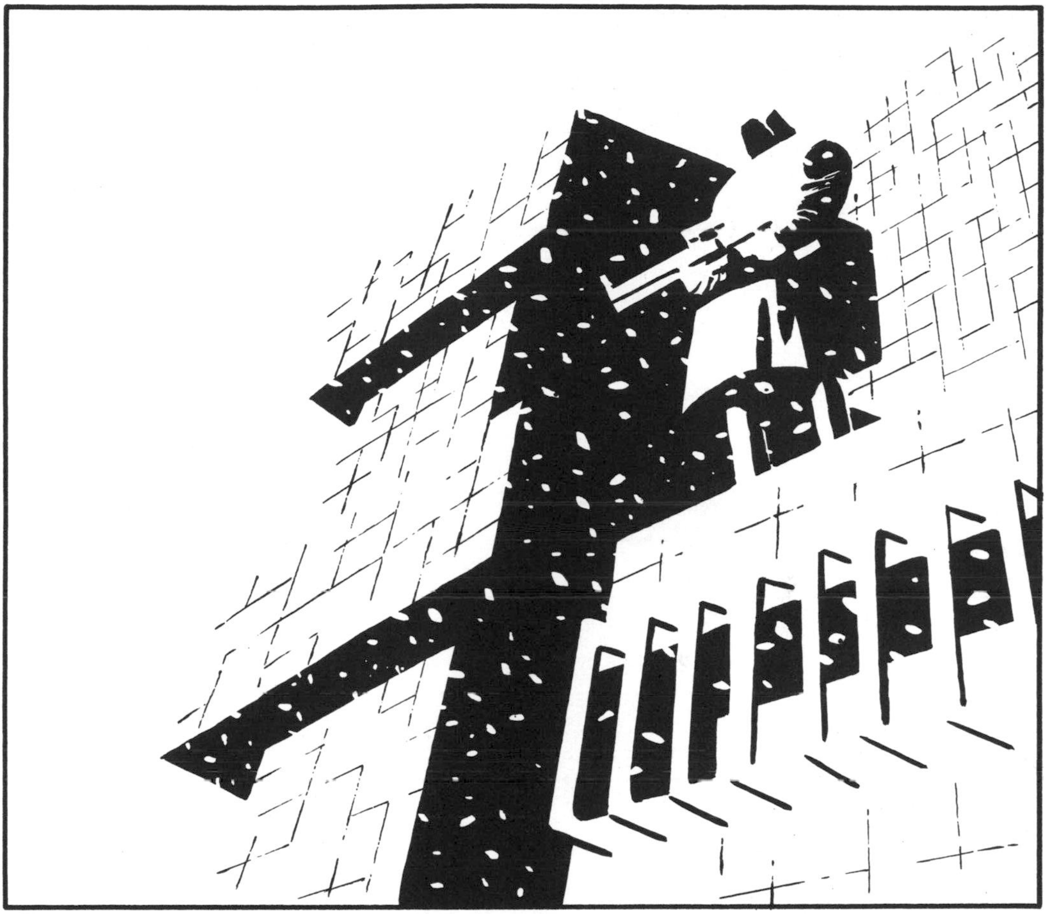

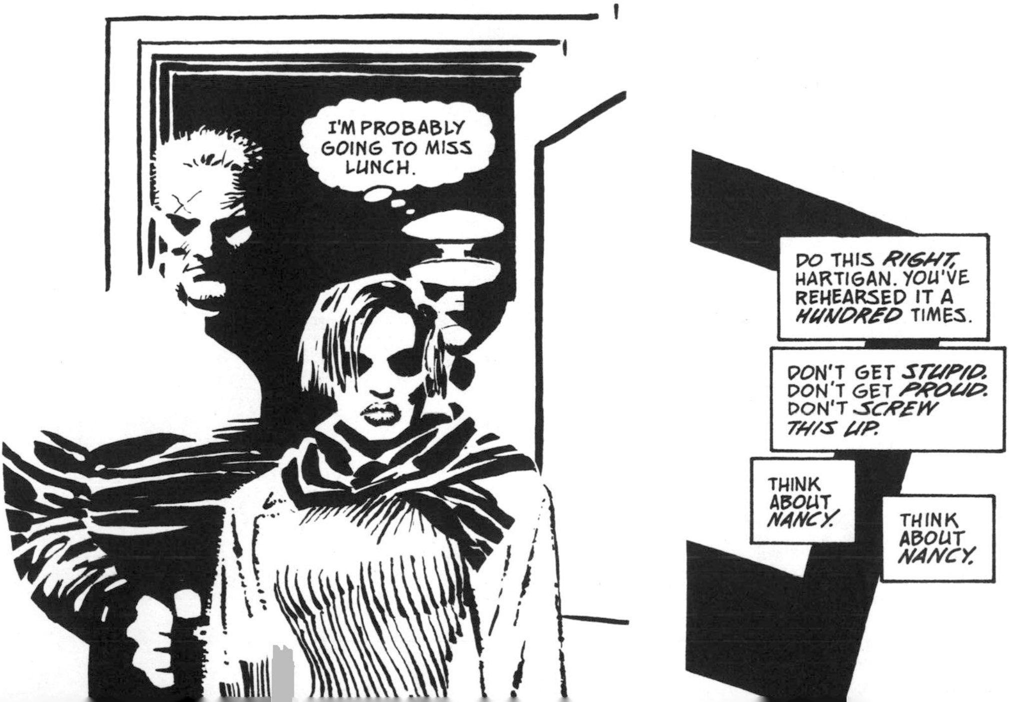
I'M PROBABLY GOING TO MISS LUNCH.
DO THIS RIGHT, HARTIGAN. YOU'VE REHEARSED IT A HUNDRED TIMES.
DON'T GET STUPID. DON'T GET PROUD. DON'T SCREW THIS UP.
THINK ABOUT NANCY.
THINK ABOUT NANCY.

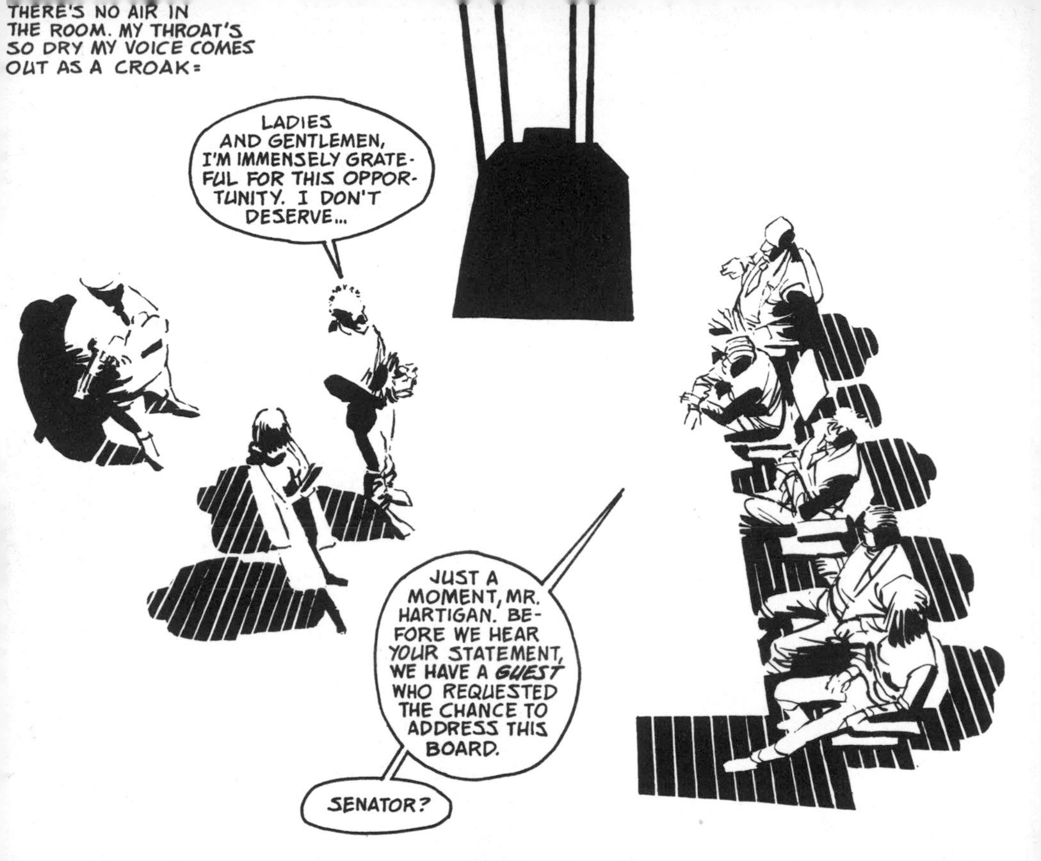
THERE'S NO AIR IN THE ROOM. MY THROAT'S SO DRY MY VOICE COMES OUT AS A CROAK=
LADIES AND GENTLEMEN, I'M IMMENSELY GRATE-FUL FOR THIS OPPOR-TUNITY. I DON'T DESERVE...
JUST A MOMENT, MR. HARTIGAN. BE-FORE WE HEAR YOUR STATEMENT, WE HAVE A GUEST WHO REQUESTED THE CHANCE TO ADDRESS THIS BOARD.
SENATOR?
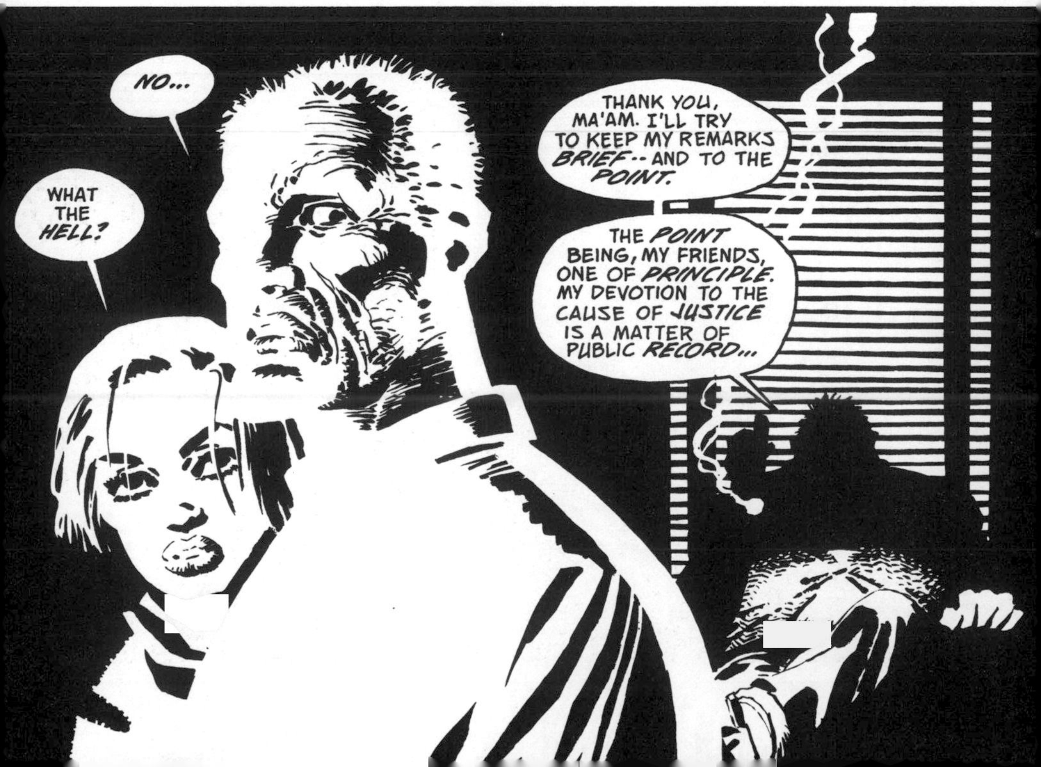
NO...
WHAT THE HELL?
THANK YOU, MA'AM. I'LL TRY TO KEEP MY REMARKS BRIEF-- AND TO THE POINT.
THE POINT BEING, MY FRIENDS, ONE OF PRINCIPLE. MY DEVOTION TO THE CAUSE OF JUSTICE IS A MATTER OF PUBLIC RECORD...

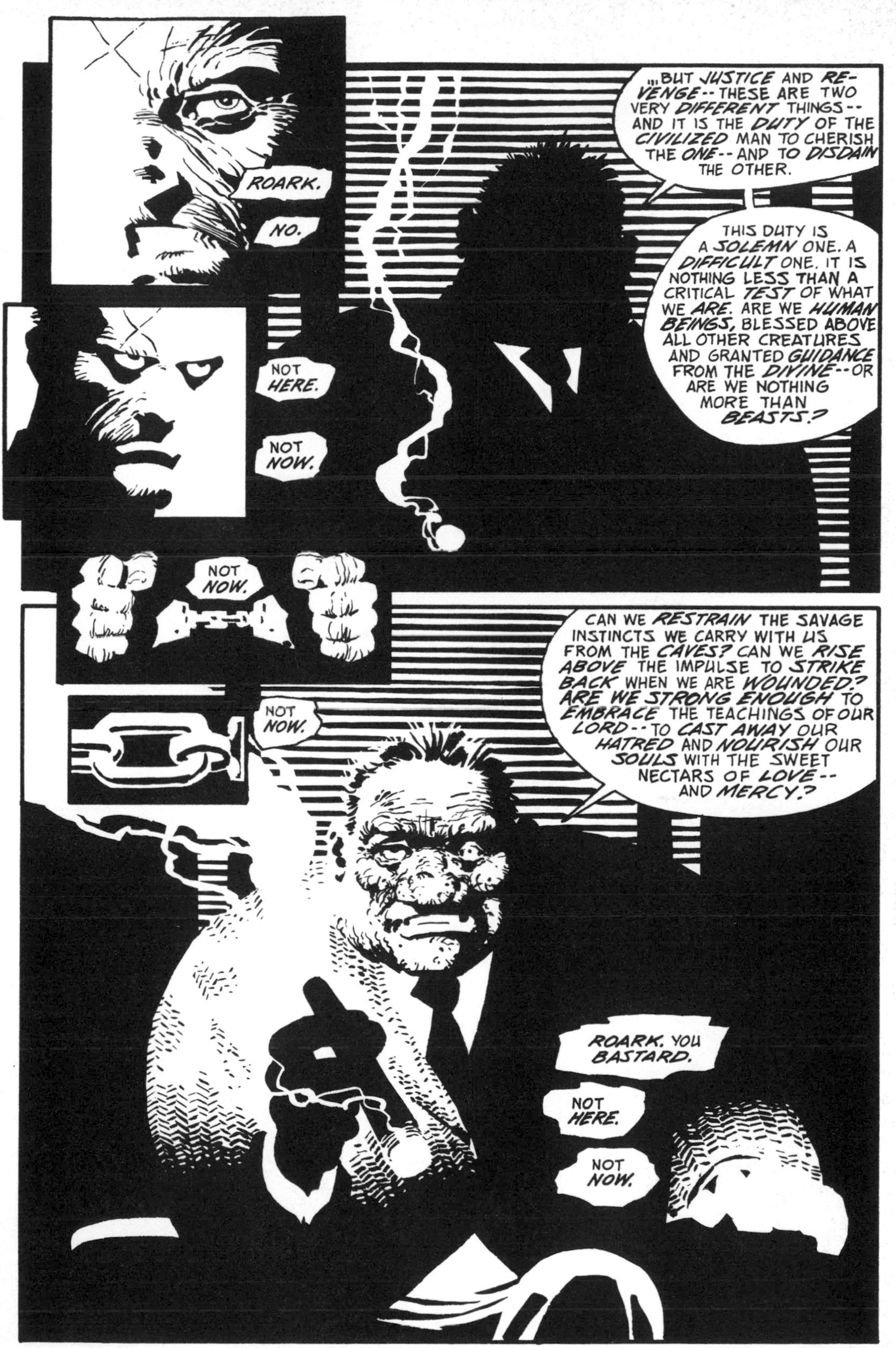
...BUT JUSTICE AND REVENGE--THESE ARE TWO VERY DIFFERENT THINGS--AND IT IS THE DUTY OF THE CIVILIZED MAN TO CHERISH THE ONE--AND TO DISDAIN THE OTHER.
ROARK.
NO.
THIS DUTY IS A SOLEMN ONE. A DIFFICULT ONE. IT IS NOTHING LESS THAN A CRITICAL TEST OF WHAT WE ARE. ARE WE HUMAN BEINGS, BLESSED ABOVE ALL OTHER CREATURES AND GRANTED GUIDANCE FROM THE DIVINE--OR ARE WE NOTHING MORE THAN BEASTS?
NOT HERE.
NOT NOW.
NOT NOW.
CAN WE RESTRAIN THE SAVAGE INSTINCTS WE CARRY WITH US FROM THE CAVES? CAN WE RISE ABOVE THE IMPULSE TO STRIKE BACK WHEN WE ARE WOUNDED? ARE WE STRONG ENOUGH TO EMBRACE THE TEACHINGS OF OUR LORD--TO CAST AWAY OUR HATRED AND NOURISH OUR SOULS WITH THE SWEET NECTARS OF LOVE--AND MERCY?
NOT NOW.
ROARK. YOU BASTARD.
NOT HERE.
NOT NOW.

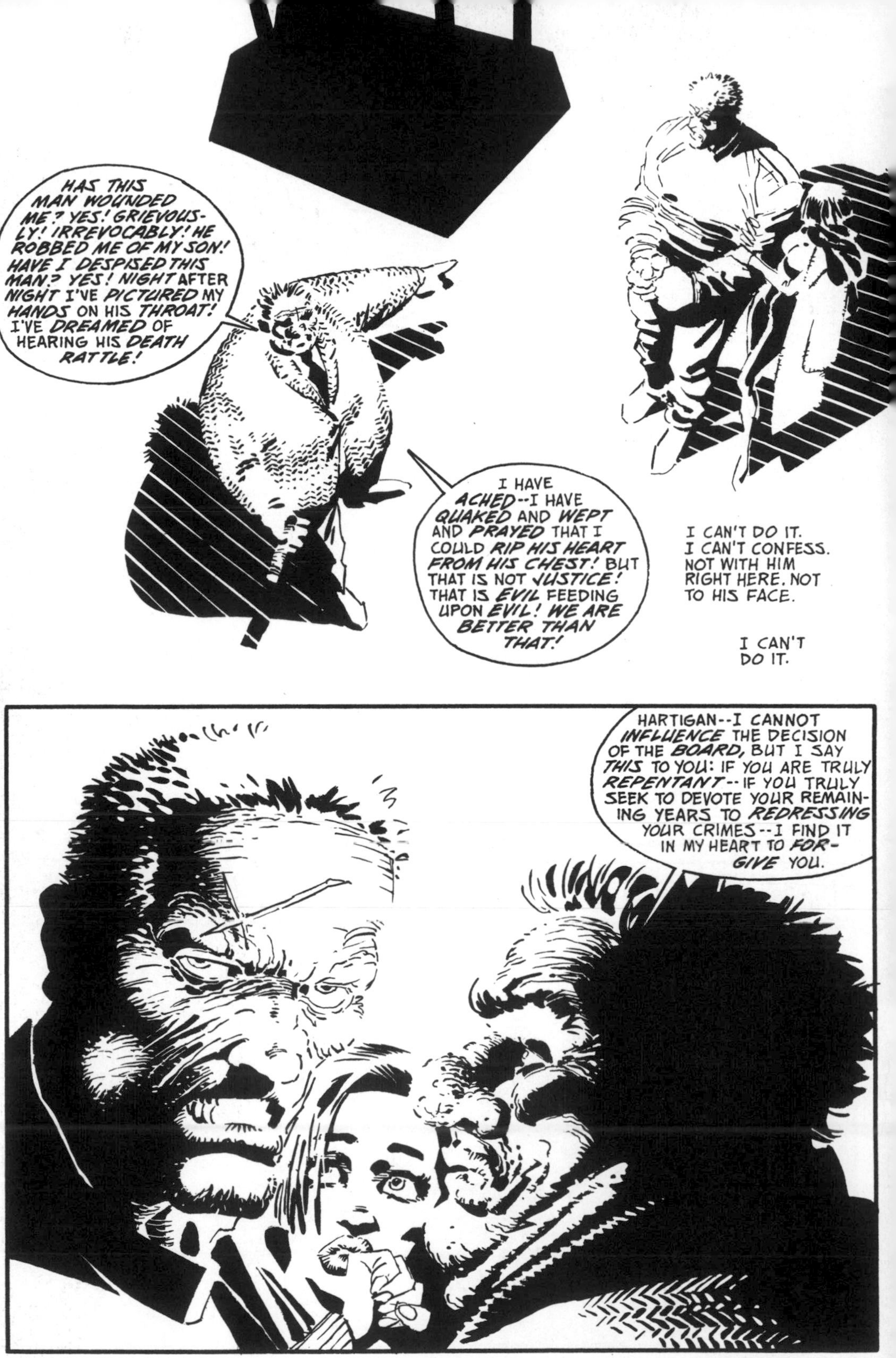
HAS THIS MAN WOUNDED ME? YES! GRIEVOUS-LY! IRREVOCABLY! HE ROBBED ME OF MY SON! HAVE I DESPISED THIS MAN? YES! NIGHT AFTER NIGHT I'VE PICTURED MY HANDS ON HIS THROAT! I'VE DREAMED OF HEARING HIS DEATH RATTLE!
I HAVE ACHED--I HAVE QUAKED AND WEPT AND PRAYED THAT I COULD RIP HIS HEART FROM HIS CHEST! BUT THAT IS NOT JUSTICE! THAT IS EVIL FEEDING UPON EVIL! WE ARE BETTER THAN THAT!
I CAN'T DO IT. I CAN'T CONFESS. NOT WITH HIM RIGHT HERE. NOT TO HIS FACE.
I CAN'T DO IT.
HARTIGAN--I CANNOT INFLUENCE THE DECISION OF THE BOARD, BUT I SAY THIS TO YOU: IF YOU ARE TRULY REPENTANT--IF YOU TRULY SEEK TO DEVOTE YOUR REMAIN-ING YEARS TO REDRESSING YOUR CRIMES--I FIND IT IN MY HEART TO FOR-GIVE YOU.

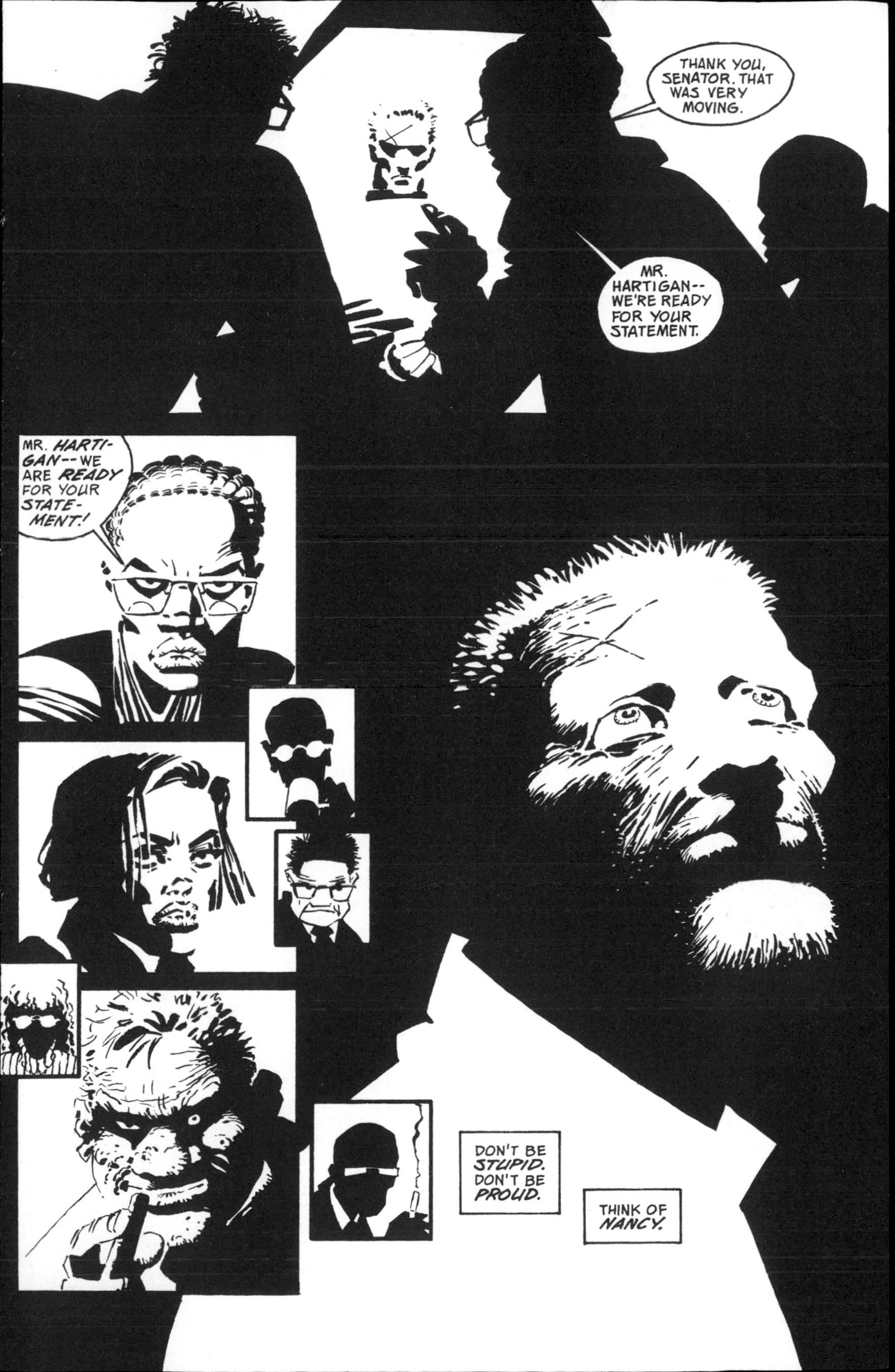
THANK YOU, SENATOR. THAT WAS VERY MOVING.
MR. HARTIGAN-- WE'RE READY FOR YOUR STATEMENT.
MR. HARTIGAN-- WE ARE READY FOR YOUR STATEMENT!
DON'T BE STUPID. DON'T BE PROUD.
THINK OF NANCY.

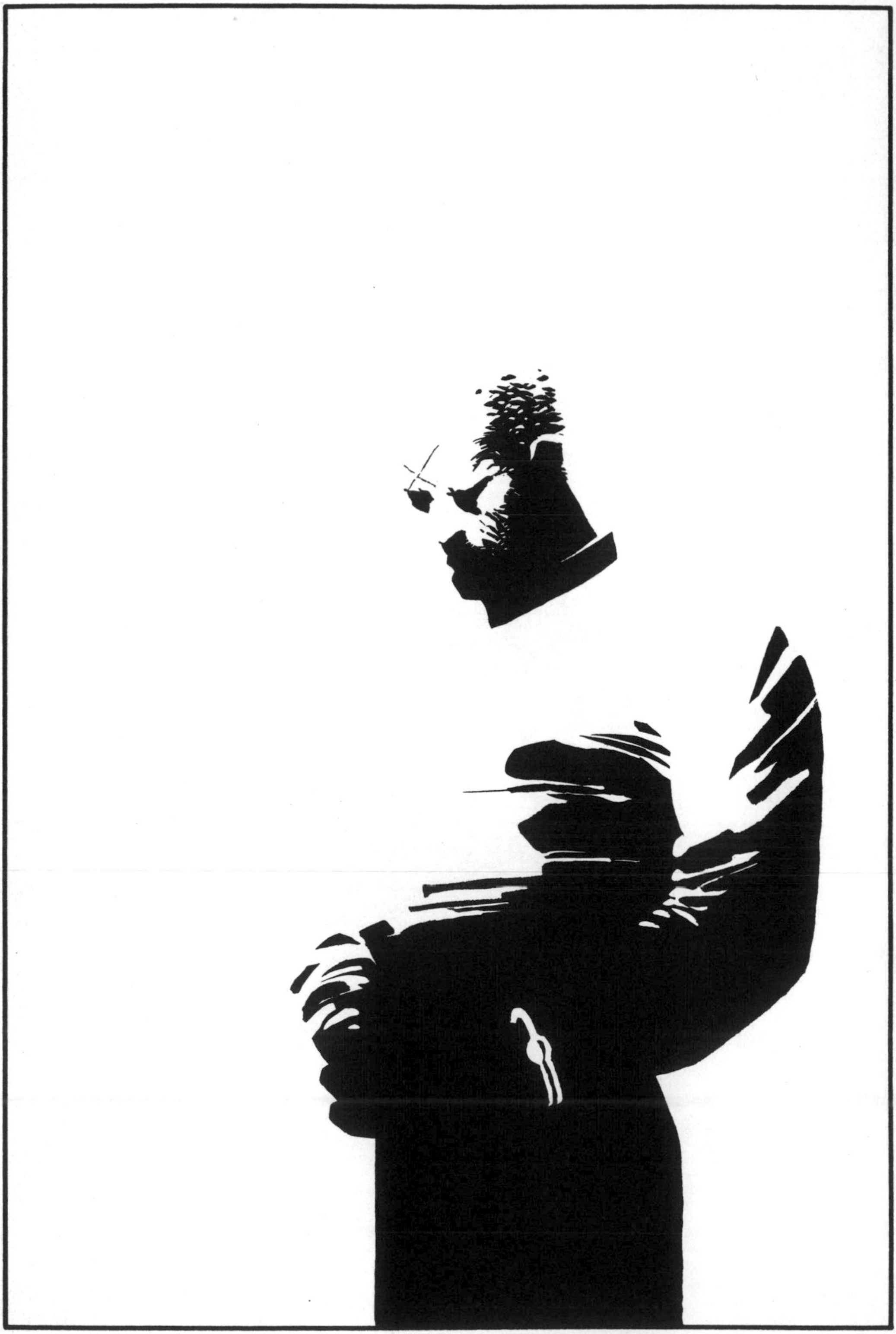

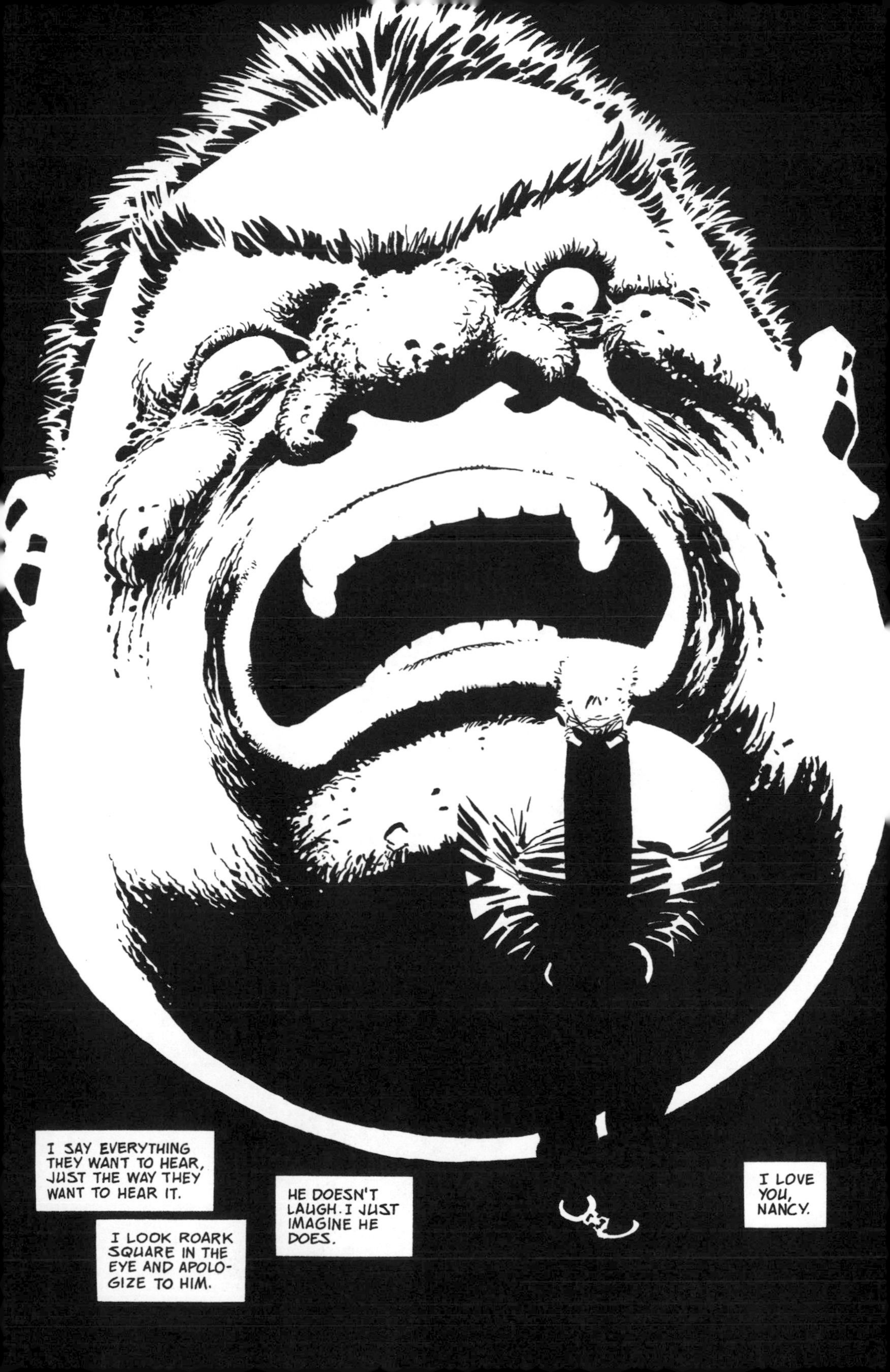
I SAY EVERYTHING THEY WANT TO HEAR, JUST THE WAY THEY WANT TO HEAR IT.
I LOOK ROARK SQUARE IN THE EYE AND APOLO-GIZE TO HIM.
HE DOESN'T LAUGH. I JUST IMAGINE HE DOES.
I LOVE YOU, NANCY.

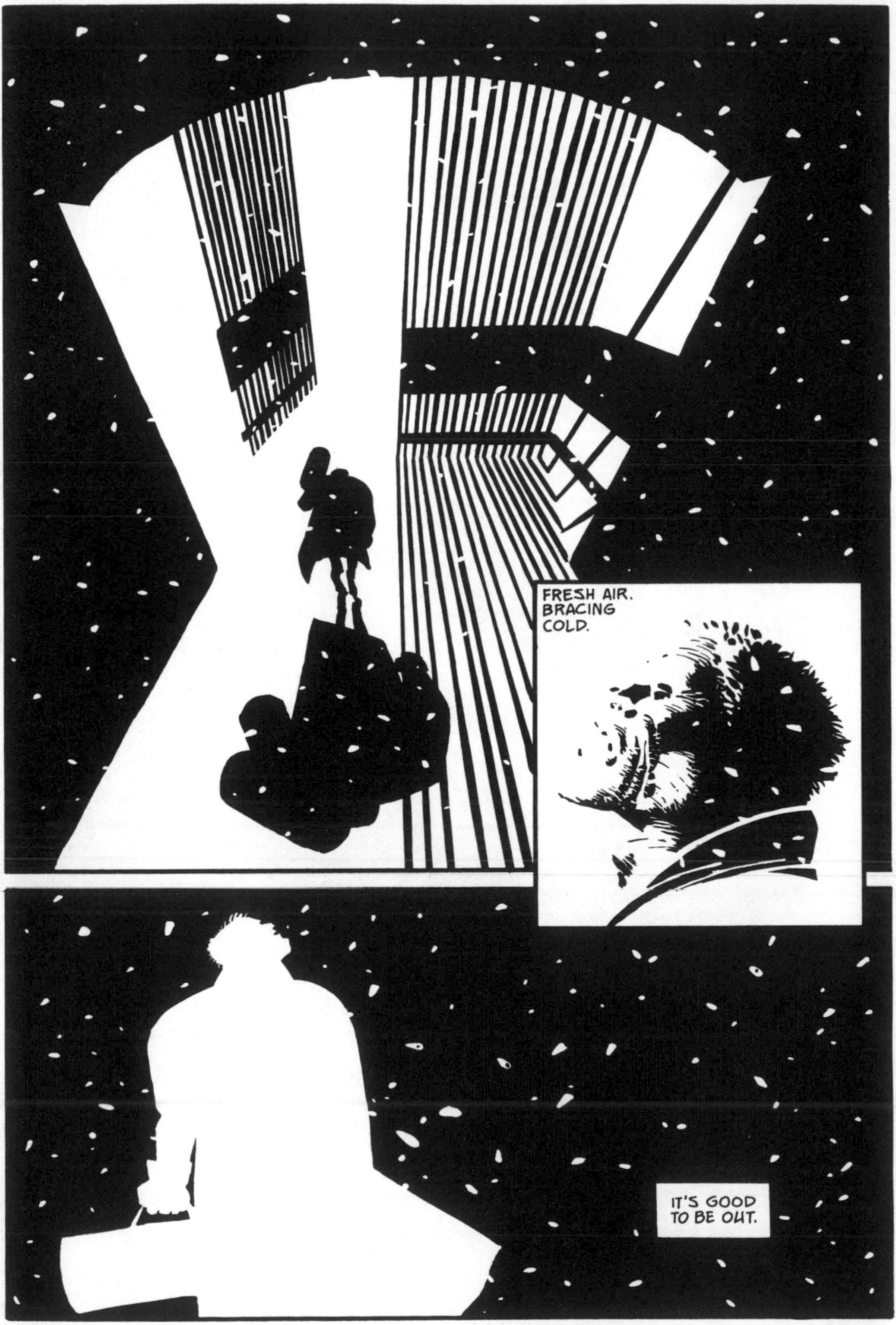
FRESH AIR. BRACING COLD.
IT'S GOOD TO BE OUT.

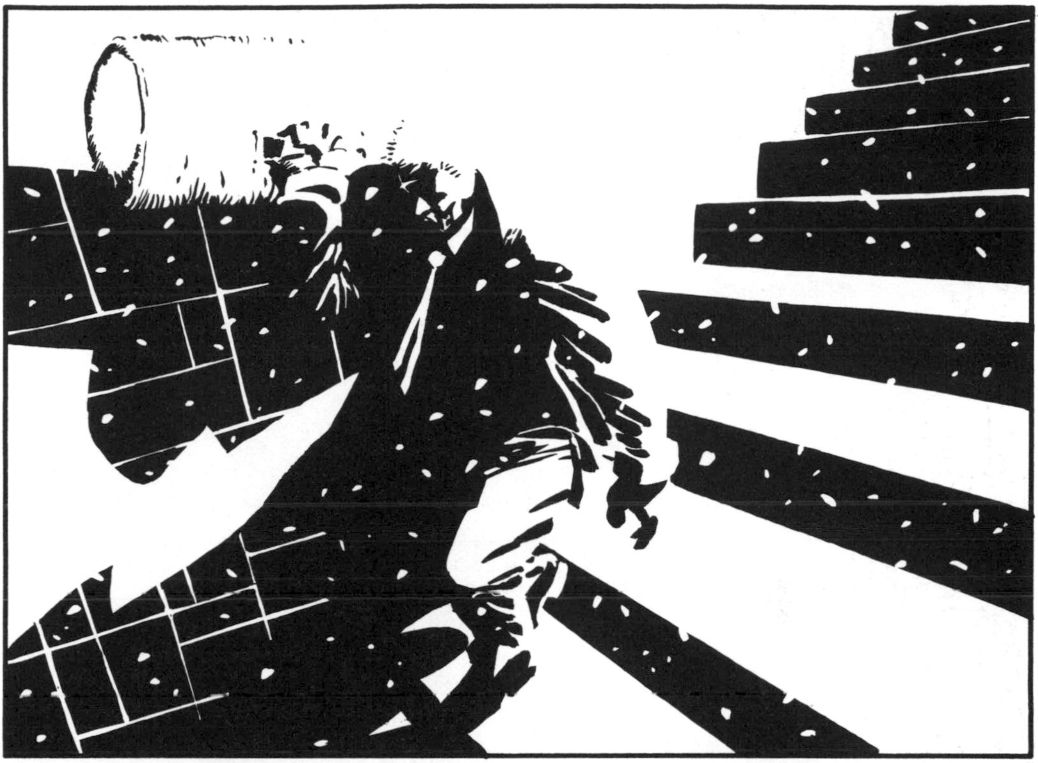

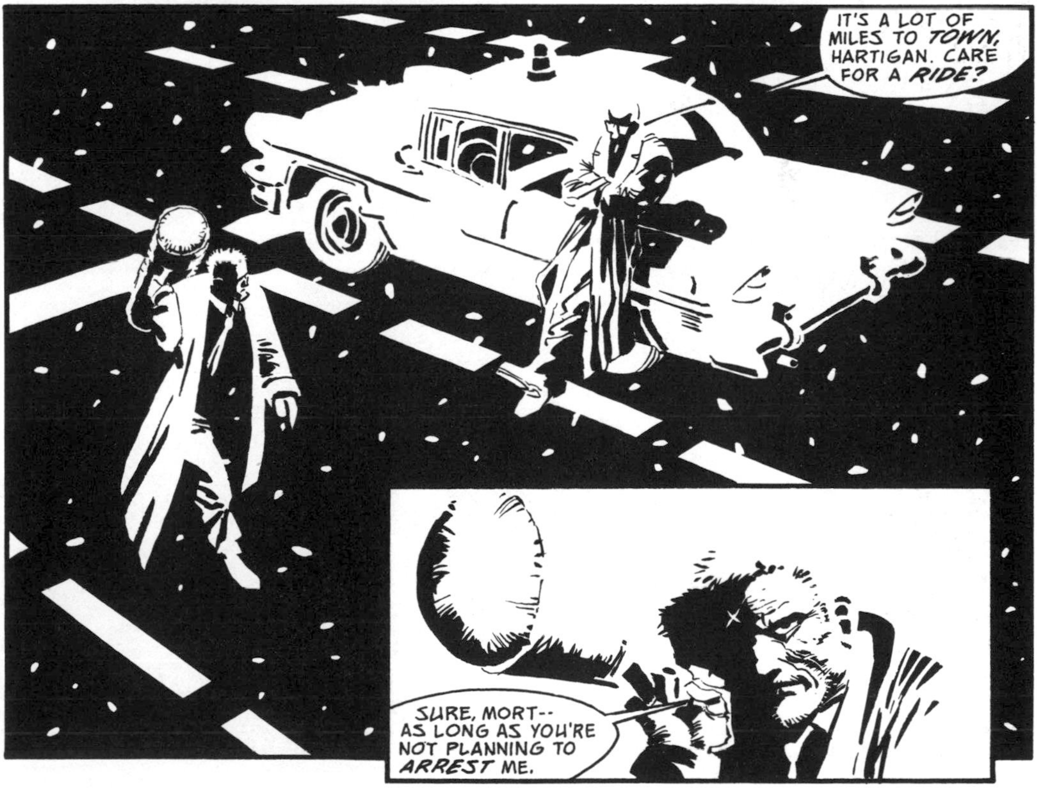
IT'S A LOT OF MILES TO TOWN, HARTIGAN. CARE FOR A RIDE?
SURE, MORT-- AS LONG AS YOU'RE NOT PLANNING TO ARREST ME.

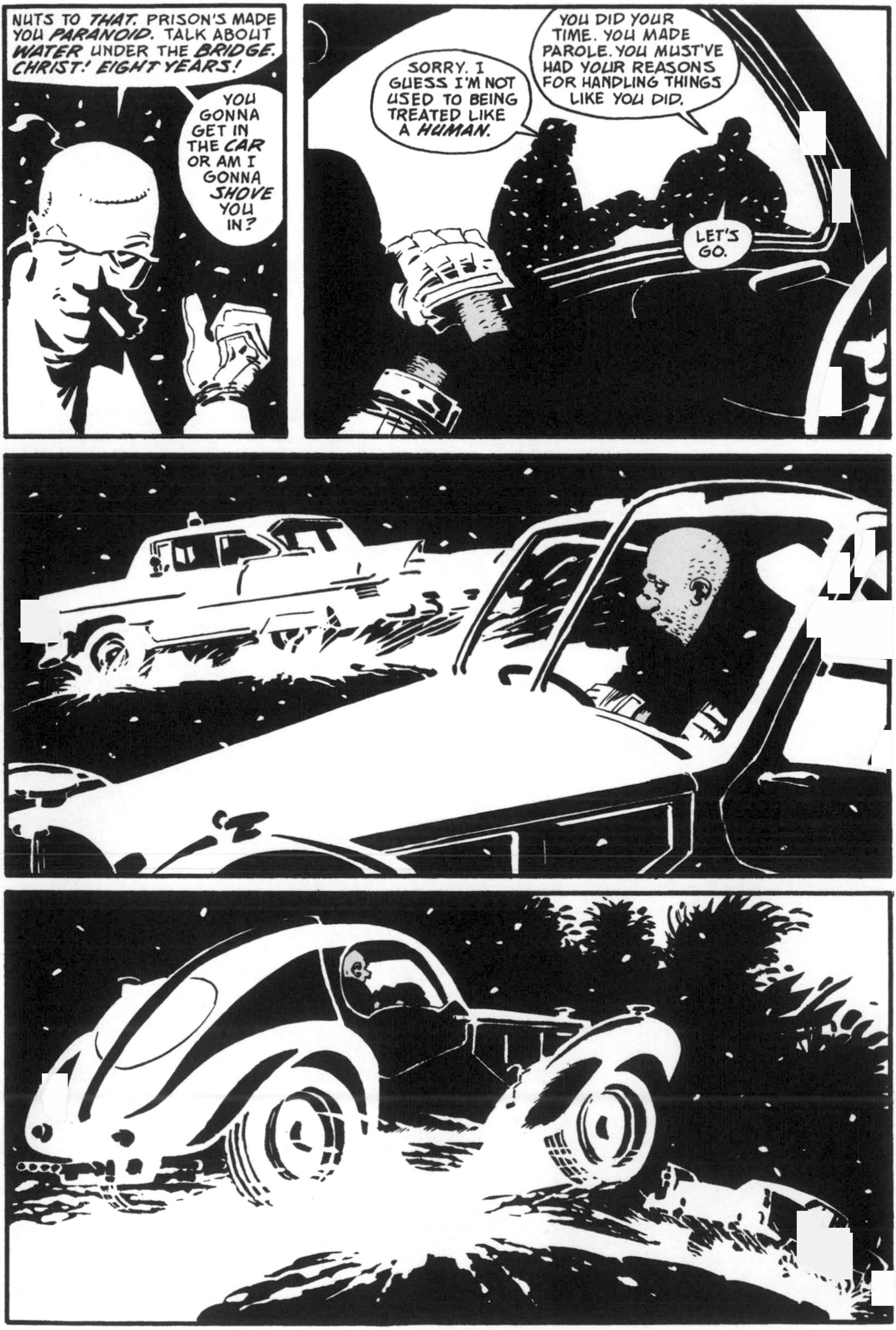
NUTS TO THAT. PRISON'S MADE YOU PARANOID. TALK ABOUT WATER UNDER THE BRIDGE. CHRIST! EIGHT YEARS!
YOU GONNA GET IN THE CAR OR AM I GONNA SHOVE YOU IN?
SORRY. I GUESS I'M NOT USED TO BEING TREATED LIKE A HUMAN.
YOU DID YOUR TIME. YOU MADE PAROLE. YOU MUST'VE HAD YOUR REASONS FOR HANDLING THINGS LIKE YOU DID.
LET'S GO.

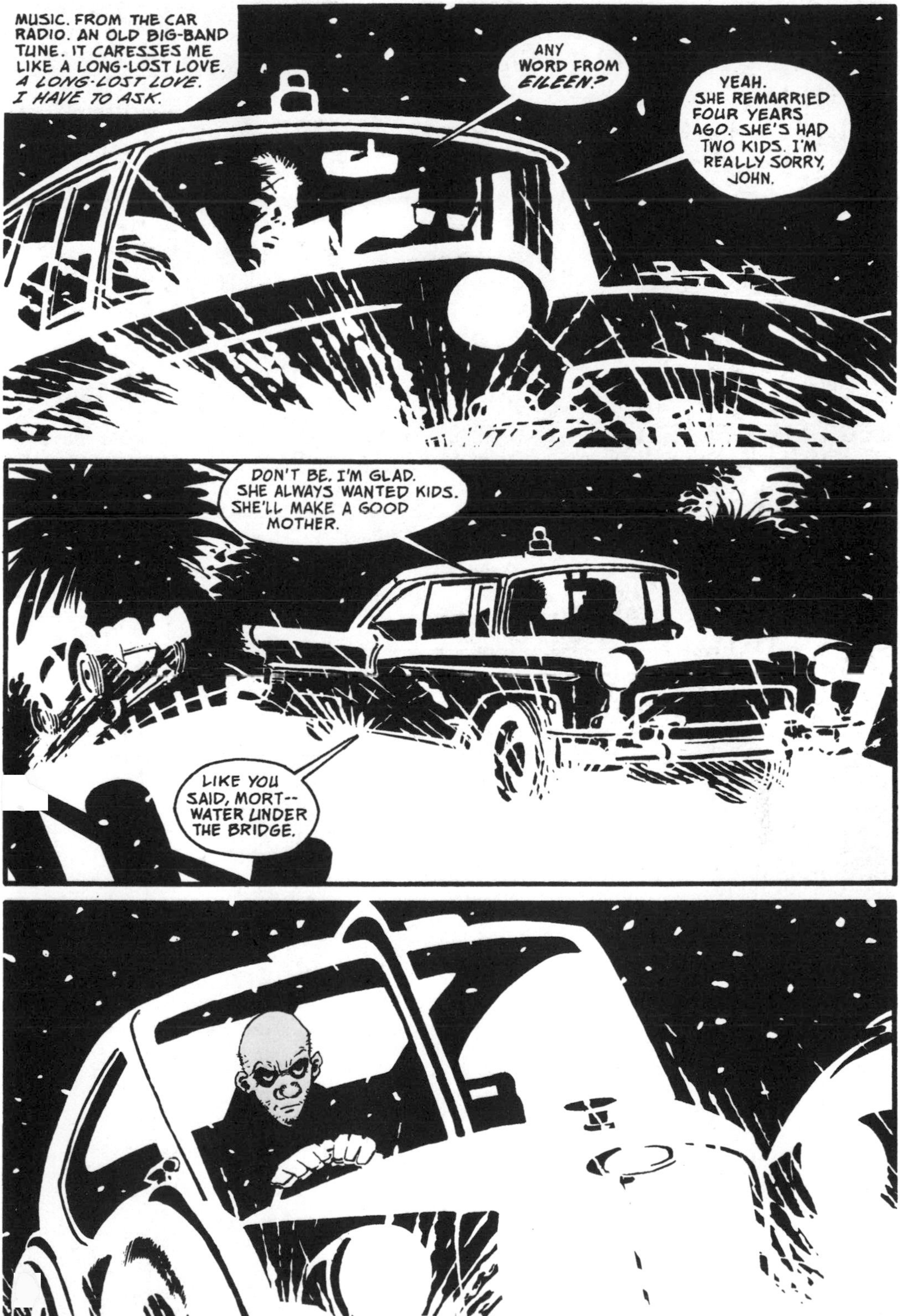
MUSIC. FROM THE CAR RADIO. AN OLD BIG-BAND TUNE. IT CARESSES ME LIKE A LONG-LOST LOVE. *A LONG-LOST LOVE. I HAVE TO ASK.*
ANY WORD FROM *EILEEN?*
YEAH. SHE REMARRIED FOUR YEARS AGO. SHE'S HAD TWO KIDS. I'M REALLY SORRY, JOHN.
DON'T BE. I'M GLAD. SHE ALWAYS WANTED KIDS. SHE'LL MAKE A GOOD MOTHER.
LIKE YOU SAID, MORT-- WATER UNDER THE BRIDGE.

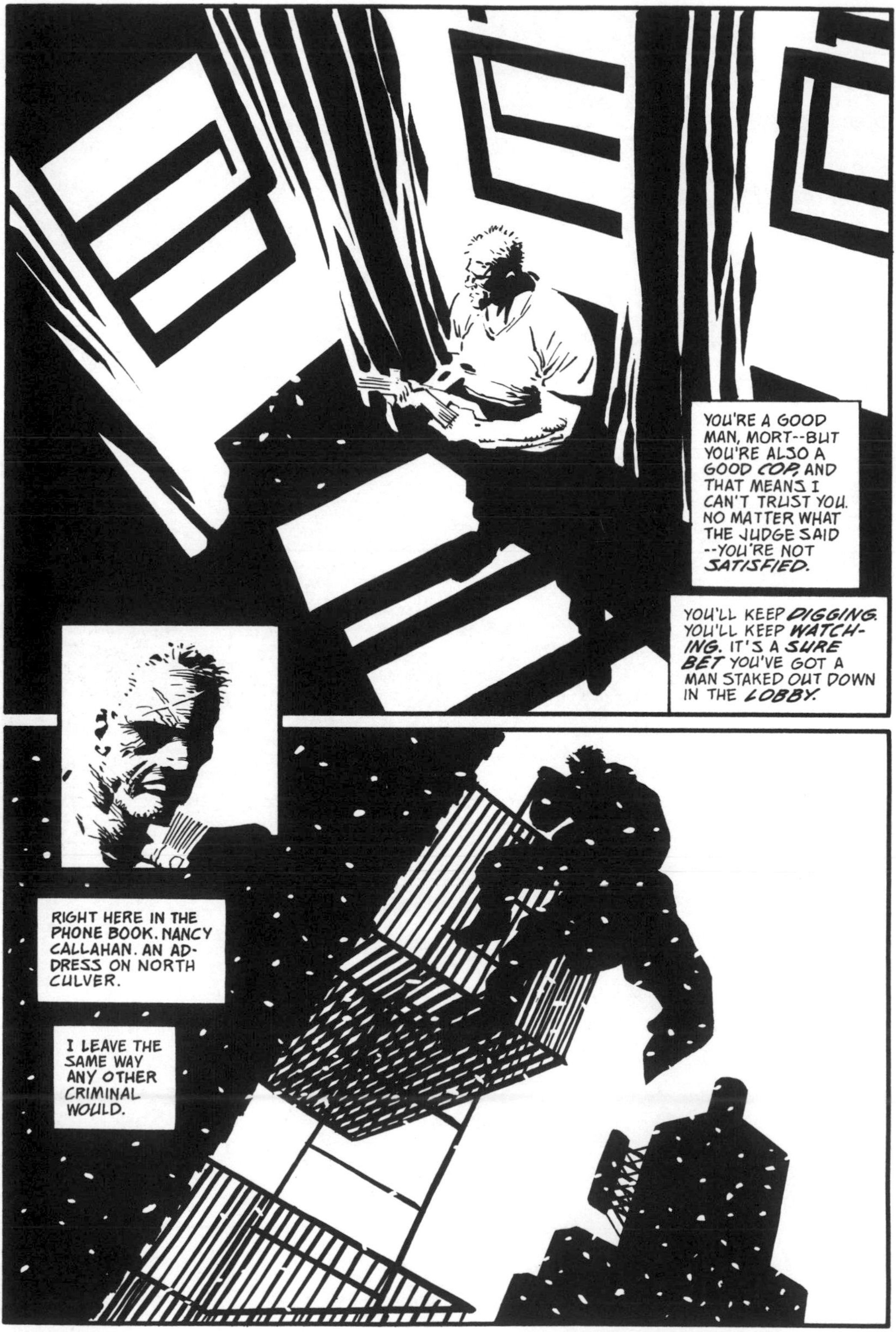
YOU'RE A GOOD MAN, MORT--BUT YOU'RE ALSO A GOOD COP, AND THAT MEANS I CAN'T TRUST YOU. NO MATTER WHAT THE JUDGE SAID --YOU'RE NOT SATISFIED.
YOU'LL KEEP DIGGING. YOU'LL KEEP WATCHING. IT'S A SURE BET YOU'VE GOT A MAN STAKED OUT DOWN IN THE LOBBY.
RIGHT HERE IN THE PHONE BOOK. NANCY CALLAHAN. AN ADDRESS ON NORTH CULVER.
I LEAVE THE SAME WAY ANY OTHER CRIMINAL WOULD.

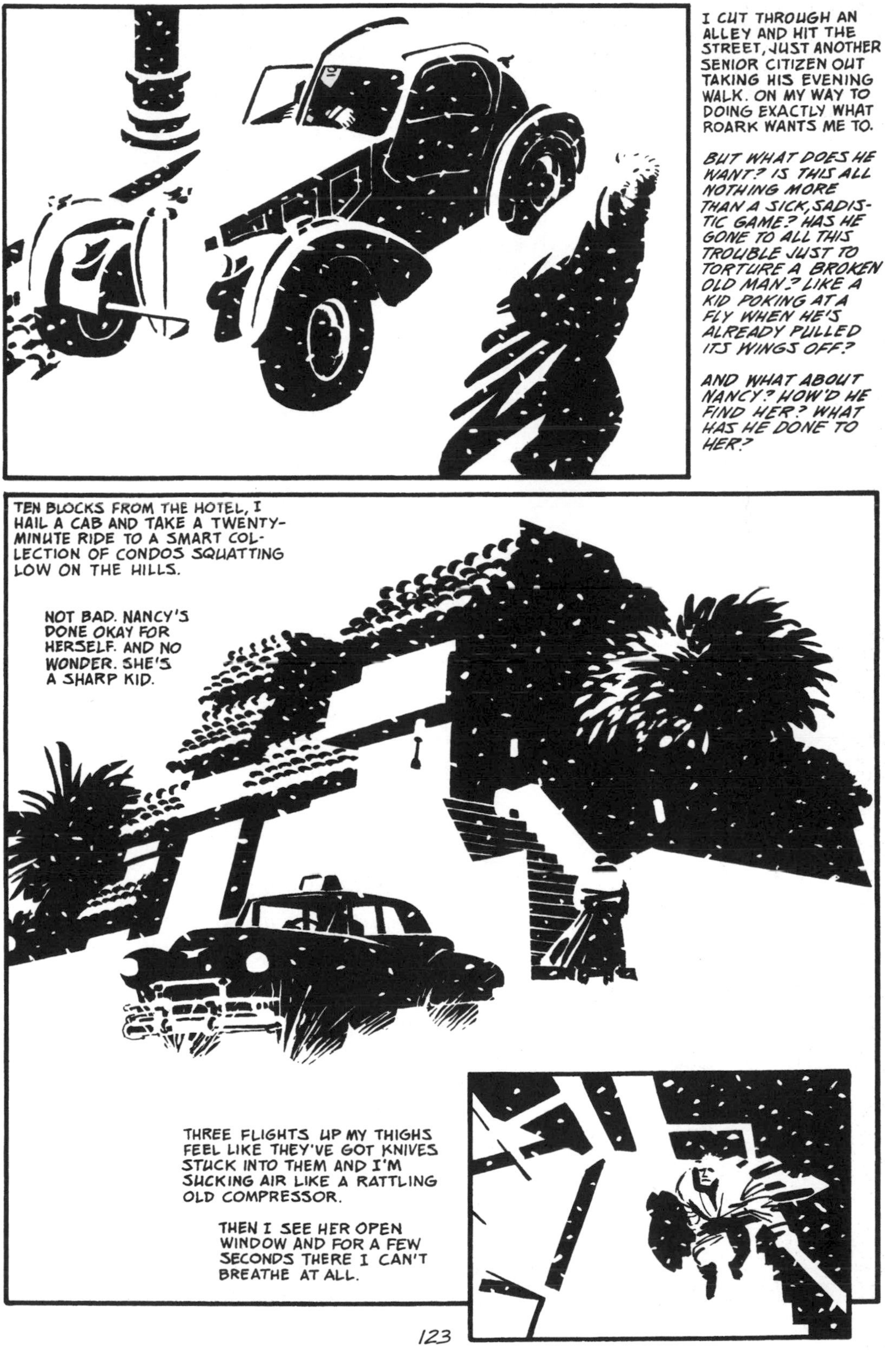
I CUT THROUGH AN ALLEY AND HIT THE STREET, JUST ANOTHER SENIOR CITIZEN OUT TAKING HIS EVENING WALK. ON MY WAY TO DOING EXACTLY WHAT ROARK WANTS ME TO.
BUT WHAT DOES HE WANT? IS THIS ALL NOTHING MORE THAN A SICK, SADISTIC GAME? HAS HE GONE TO ALL THIS TROUBLE JUST TO TORTURE A BROKEN OLD MAN? LIKE A KID POKING AT A FLY WHEN HE'S ALREADY PULLED ITS WINGS OFF?
AND WHAT ABOUT NANCY? HOW'D HE FIND HER? WHAT HAS HE DONE TO HER?
TEN BLOCKS FROM THE HOTEL, I HAIL A CAB AND TAKE A TWENTY-MINUTE RIDE TO A SMART COLLECTION OF CONDOS SQUATTING LOW ON THE HILLS.
NOT BAD. NANCY'S DONE OKAY FOR HERSELF. AND NO WONDER. SHE'S A SHARP KID.
THREE FLIGHTS UP MY THIGHS FEEL LIKE THEY'VE GOT KNIVES STUCK INTO THEM AND I'M SUCKING AIR LIKE A RATTLING OLD COMPRESSOR.
THEN I SEE HER OPEN WINDOW AND FOR A FEW SECONDS THERE I CAN'T BREATHE AT ALL.

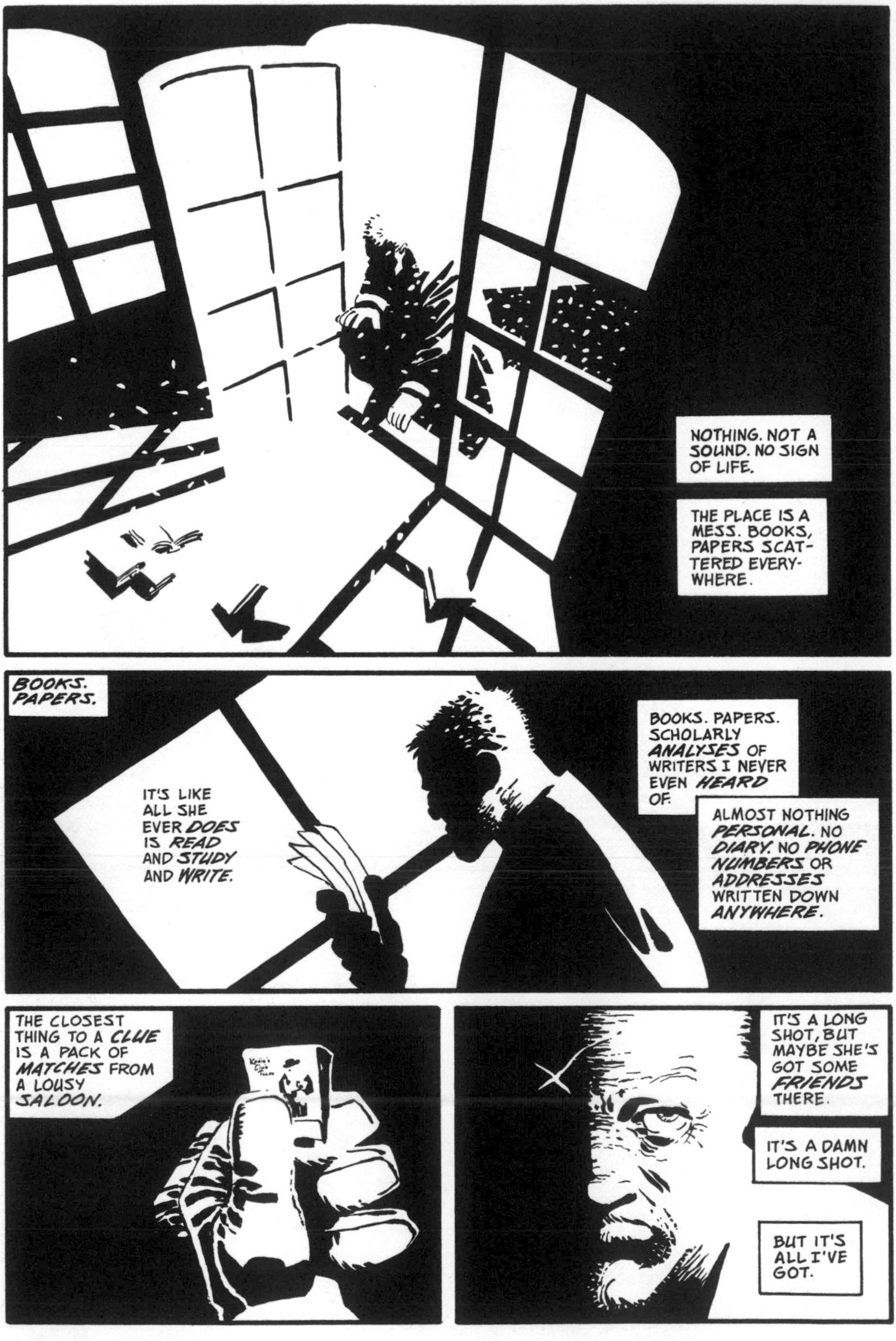
NOTHING. NOT A SOUND. NO SIGN OF LIFE.
THE PLACE IS A MESS. BOOKS, PAPERS SCATTERED EVERYWHERE.
BOOKS. PAPERS.
IT'S LIKE ALL SHE EVER DOES IS READ AND STUDY AND WRITE.
BOOKS. PAPERS. SCHOLARLY ANALYSES OF WRITERS I NEVER EVEN HEARD OF.
ALMOST NOTHING PERSONAL. NO DIARY. NO PHONE NUMBERS OR ADDRESSES WRITTEN DOWN ANYWHERE.
THE CLOSEST THING TO A CLUE IS A PACK OF MATCHES FROM A LOUSY SALOON.
IT'S A LONG SHOT, BUT MAYBE SHE'S GOT SOME FRIENDS THERE.
IT'S A DAMN LONG SHOT.
BUT IT'S ALL I'VE GOT.

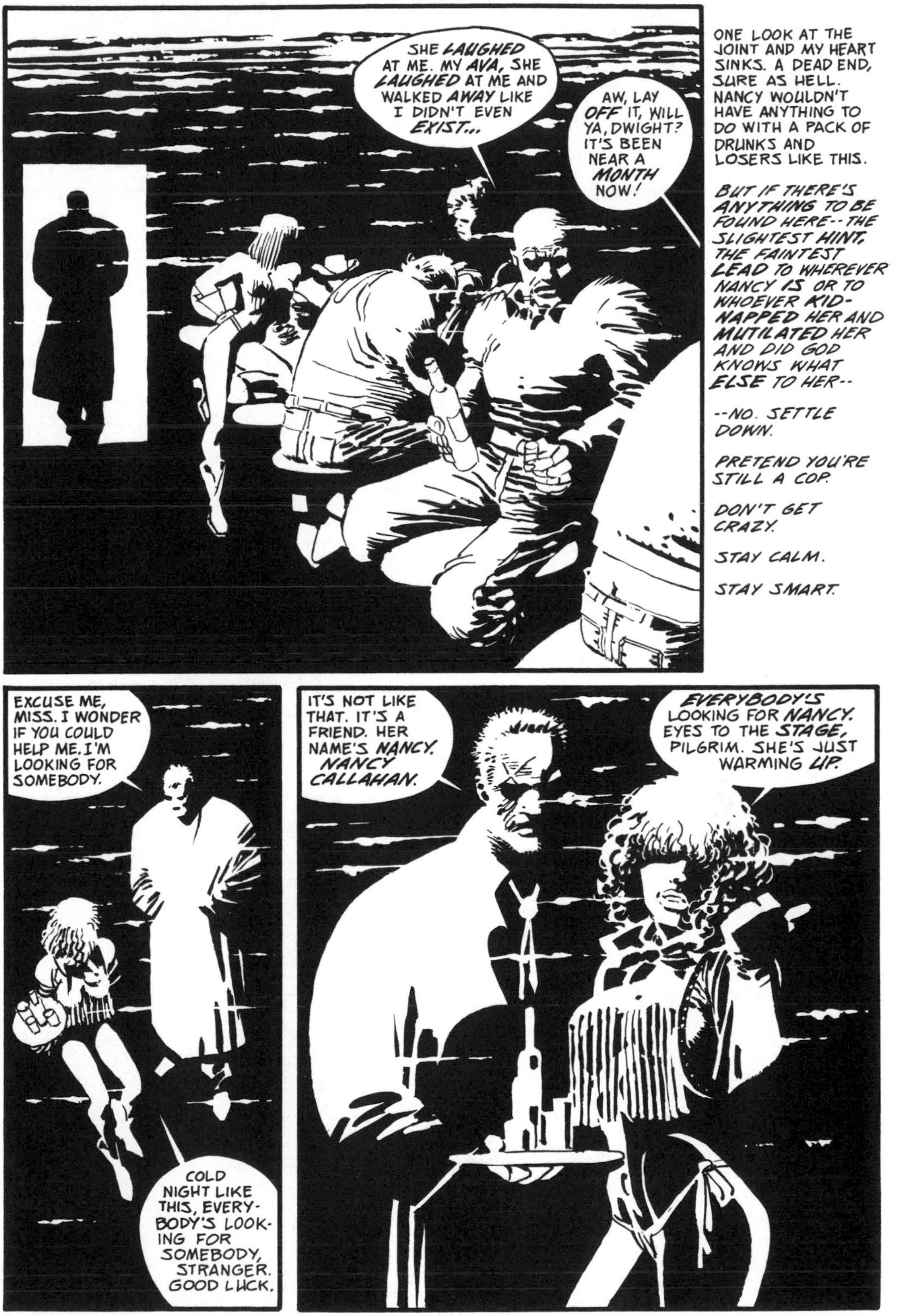
SHE LAUGHED AT ME. MY AVA, SHE LAUGHED AT ME AND WALKED AWAY LIKE I DIDN'T EVEN EXIST...
AW, LAY OFF IT, WILL YA, DWIGHT? IT'S BEEN NEAR A MONTH NOW!
ONE LOOK AT THE JOINT AND MY HEART SINKS. A DEAD END, SURE AS HELL. NANCY WOULDN'T HAVE ANYTHING TO DO WITH A PACK OF DRUNKS AND LOSERS LIKE THIS.
BUT IF THERE'S ANYTHING TO BE FOUND HERE--THE SLIGHTEST HINT, THE FAINTEST LEAD TO WHEREVER NANCY IS OR TO WHOEVER KID-NAPPED HER AND MUTILATED HER AND DID GOD KNOWS WHAT ELSE TO HER--
--NO. SETTLE DOWN.
PRETEND YOU'RE STILL A COP.
DON'T GET CRAZY.
STAY CALM.
STAY SMART.
EXCUSE ME, MISS. I WONDER IF YOU COULD HELP ME. I'M LOOKING FOR SOMEBODY.
COLD NIGHT LIKE THIS, EVERY-BODY'S LOOK-ING FOR SOMEBODY, STRANGER. GOOD LUCK.
IT'S NOT LIKE THAT. IT'S A FRIEND. HER NAME'S NANCY. NANCY CALLAHAN.
EVERYBODY'S LOOKING FOR NANCY. EYES TO THE STAGE, PILGRIM. SHE'S JUST WARMING UP.

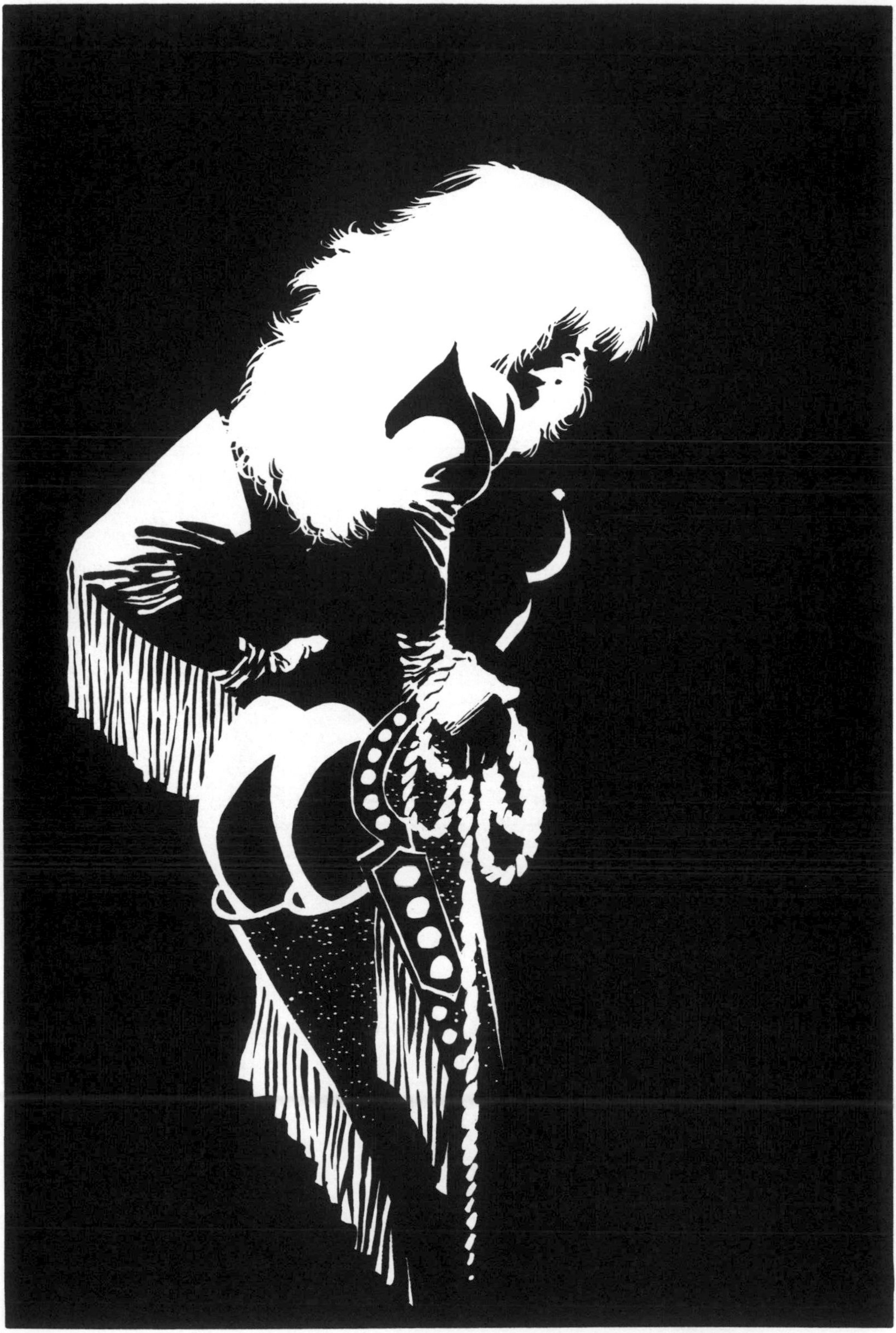

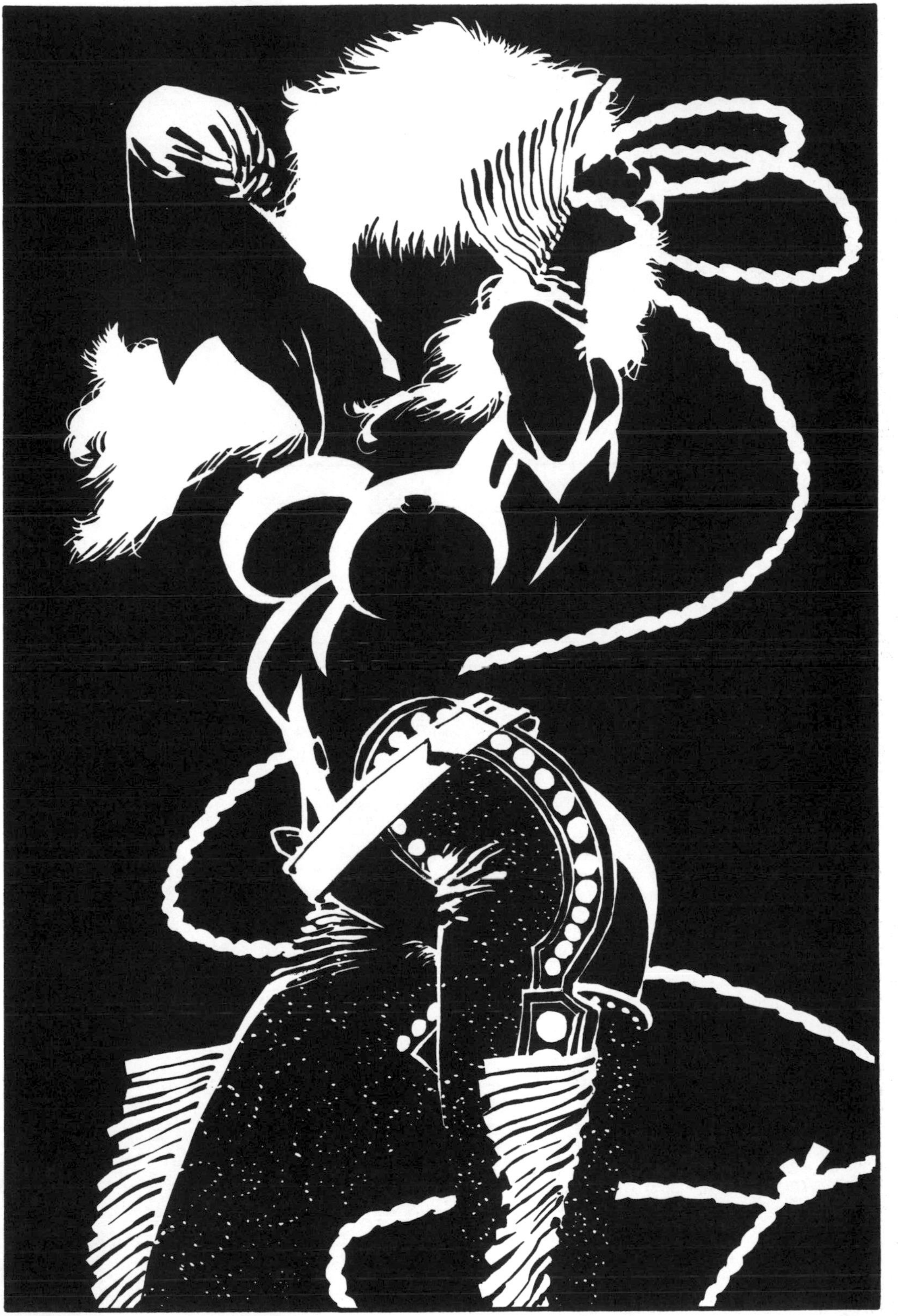

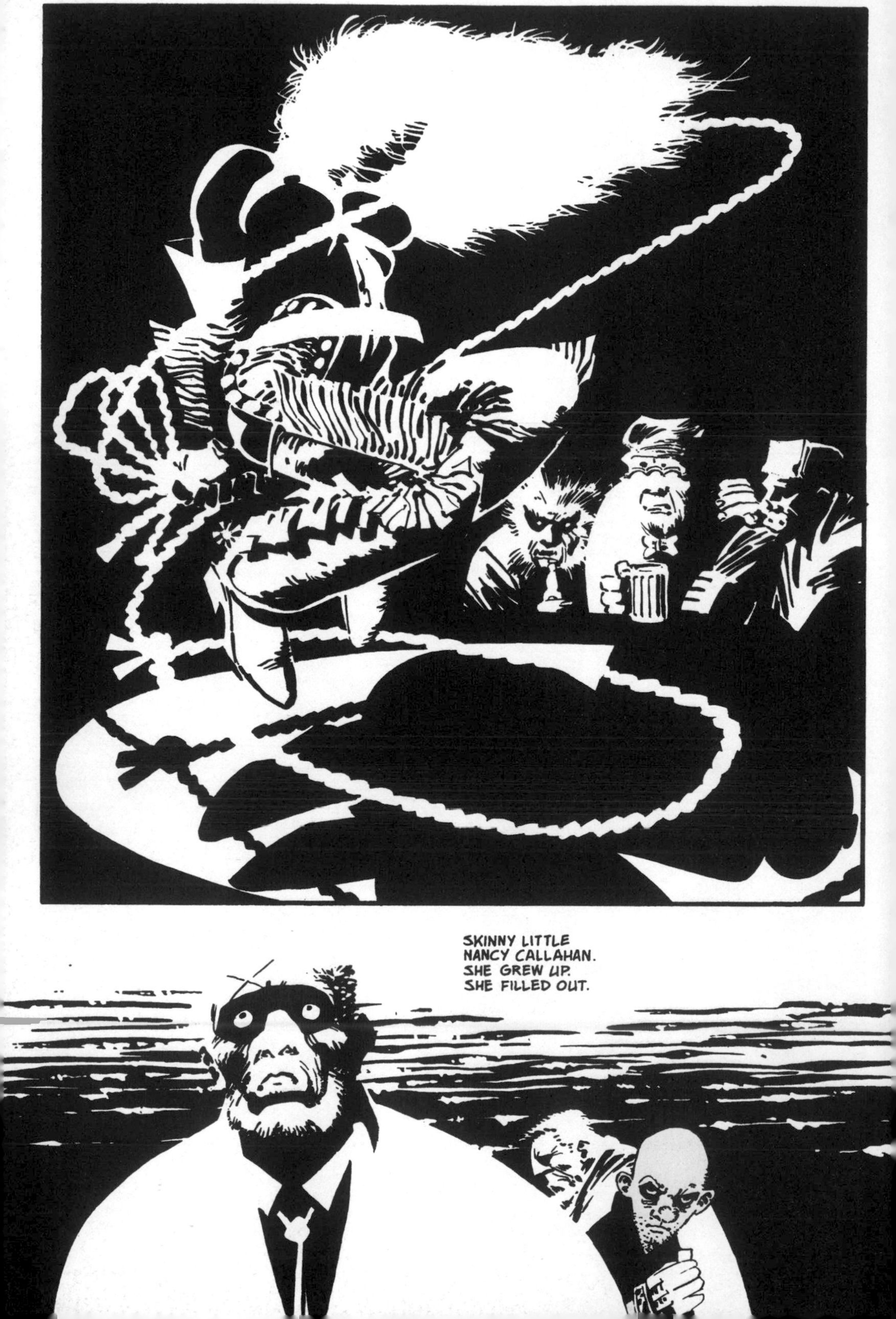
SKINNY LITTLE
NANCY CALLAHAN.
SHE GREW UP.
SHE FILLED OUT.

CHAPTER FI

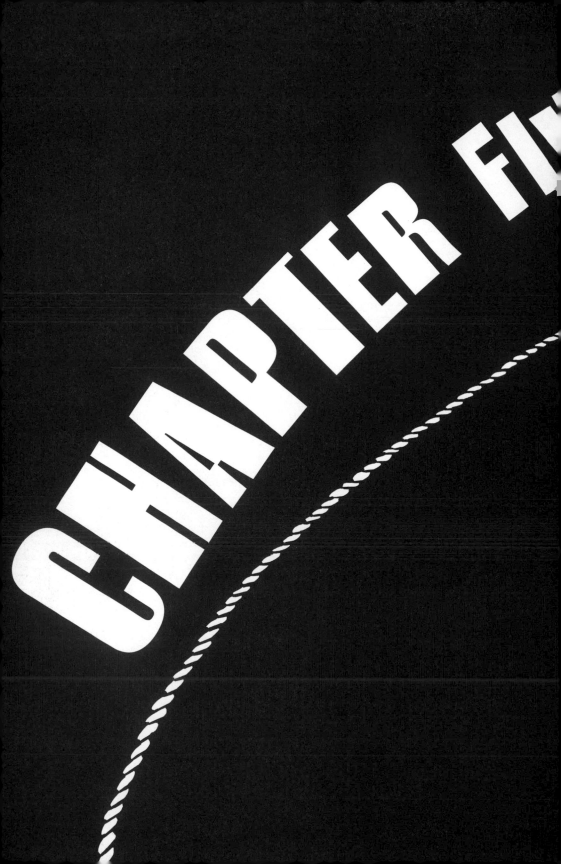

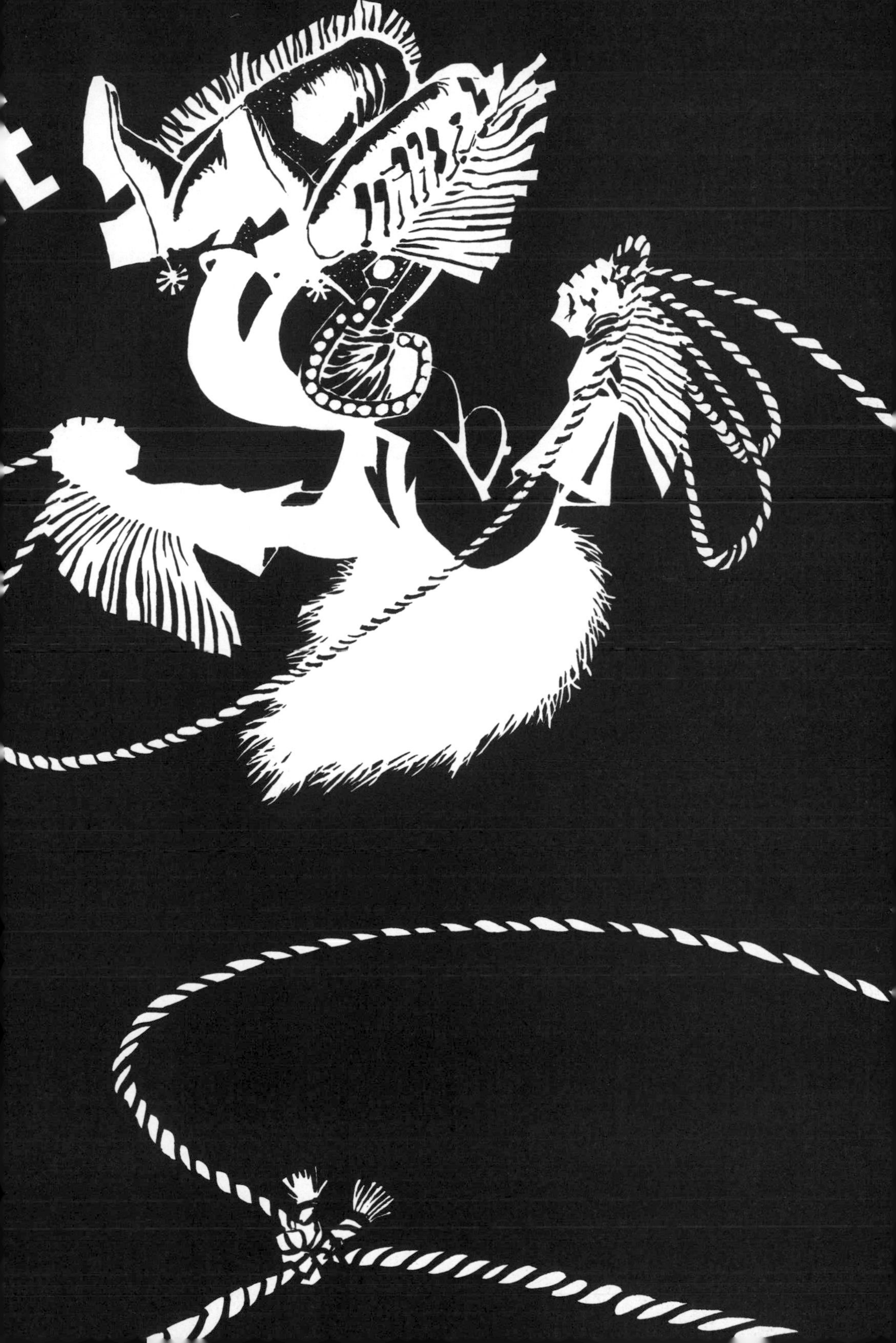

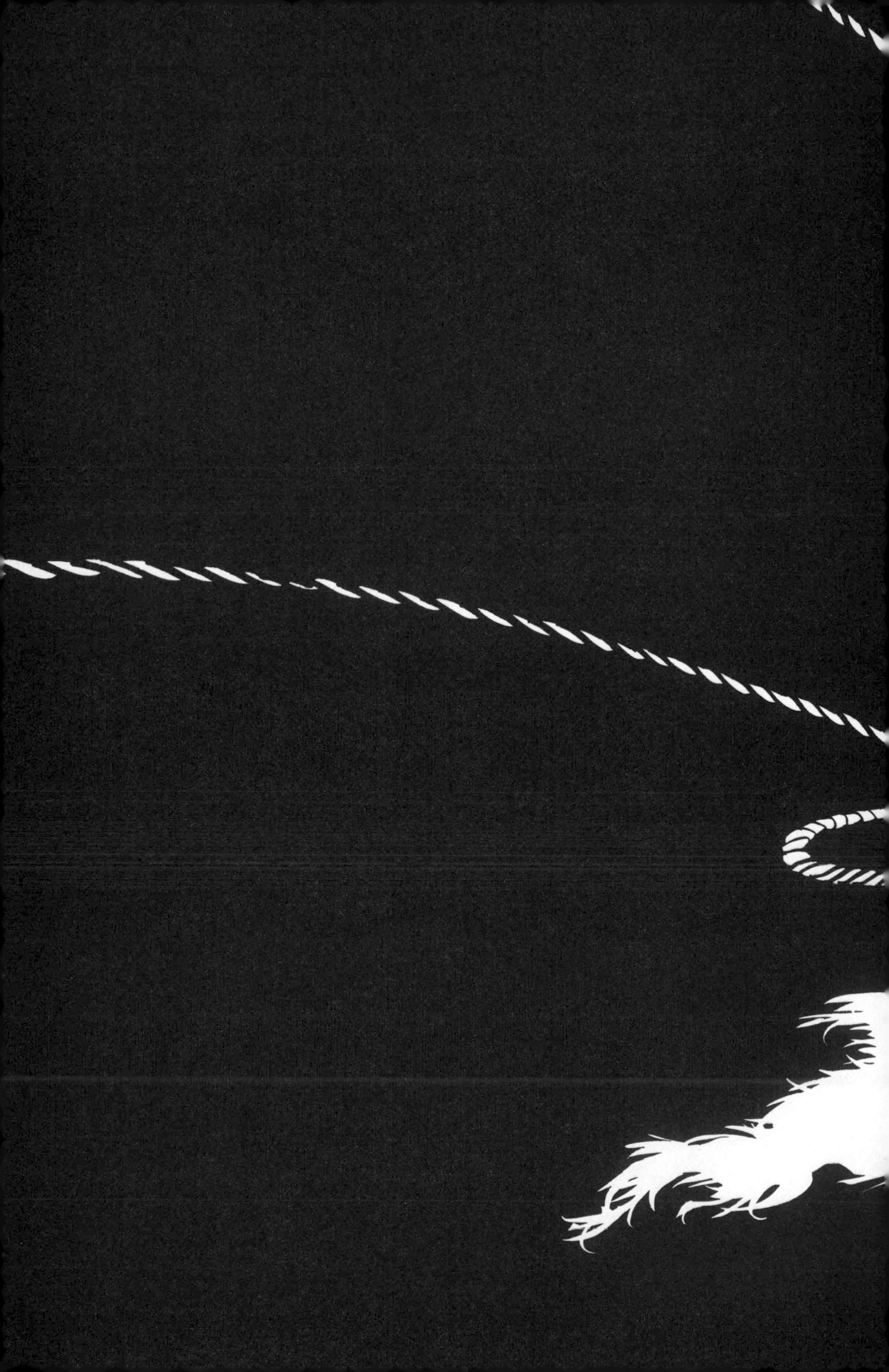

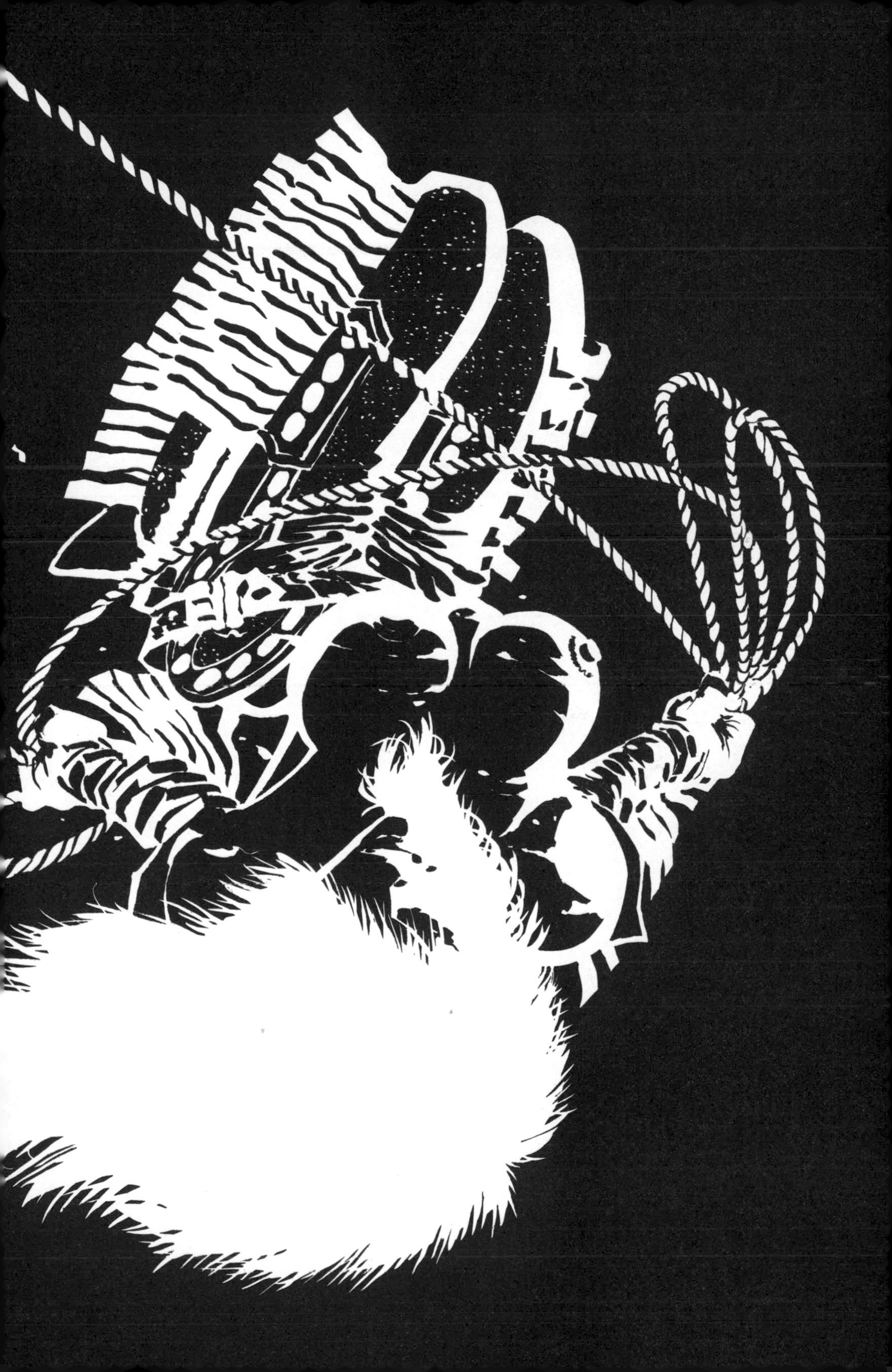

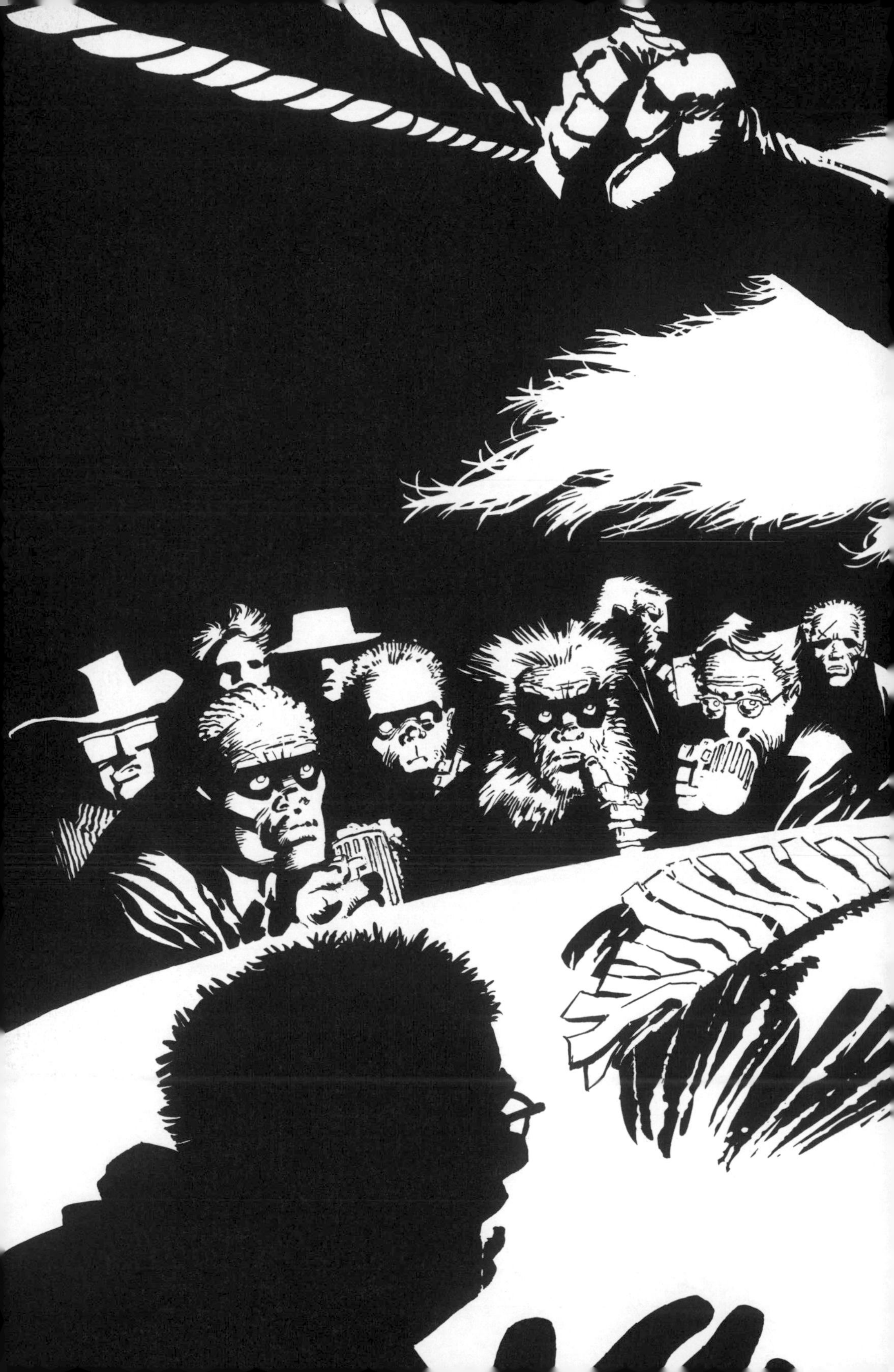

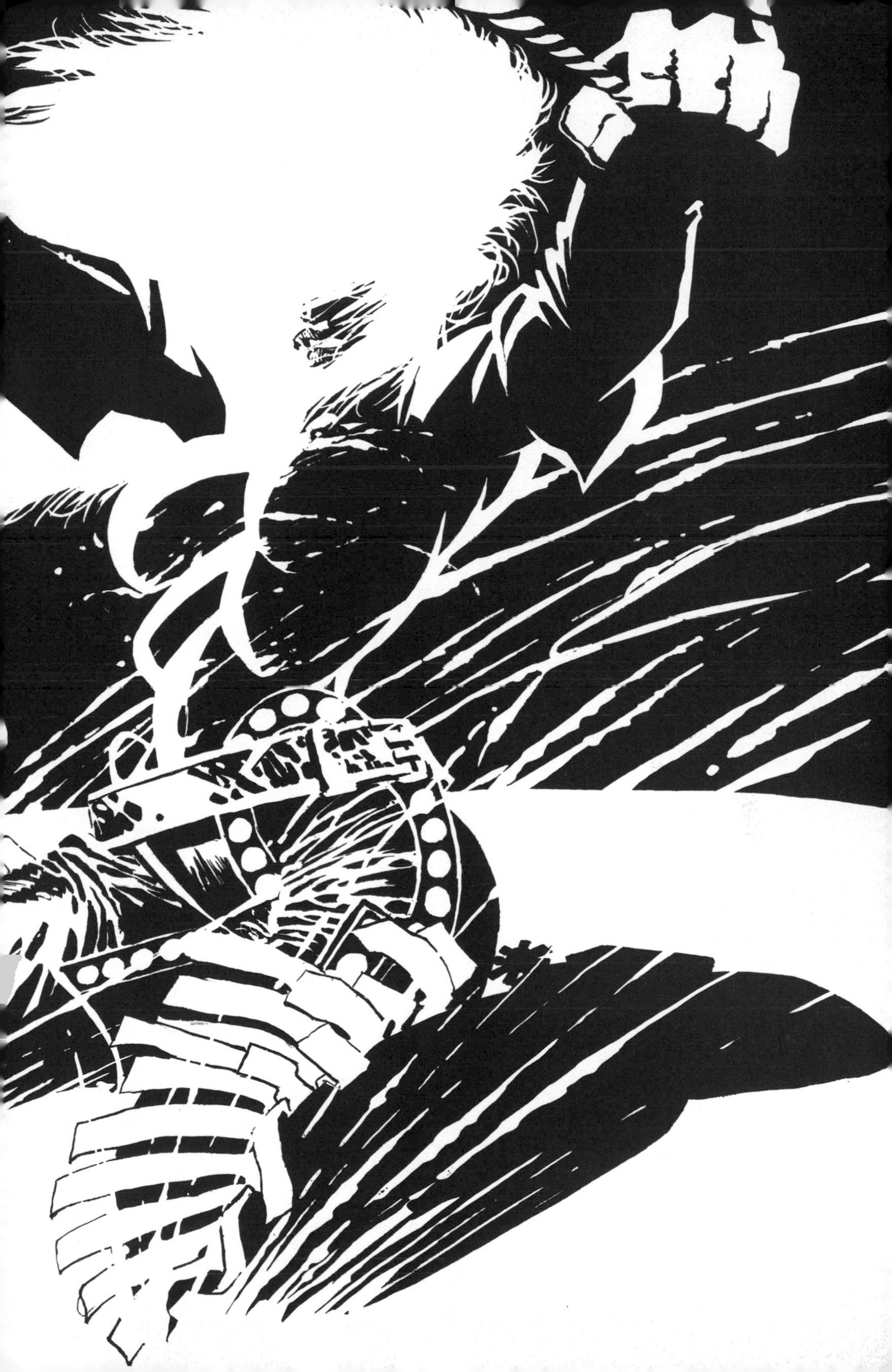

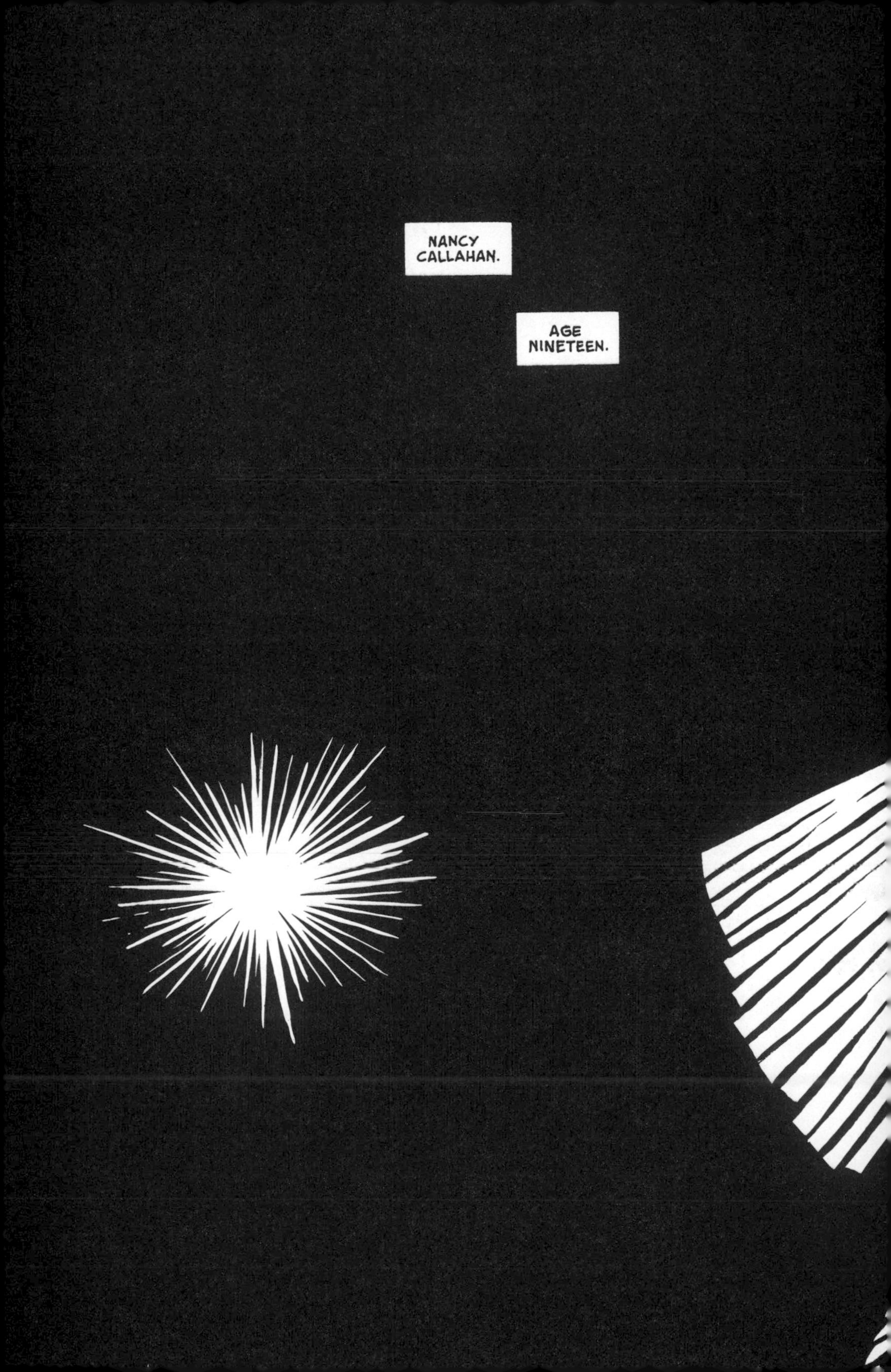
NANCY CALLAHAN.
AGE NINETEEN.

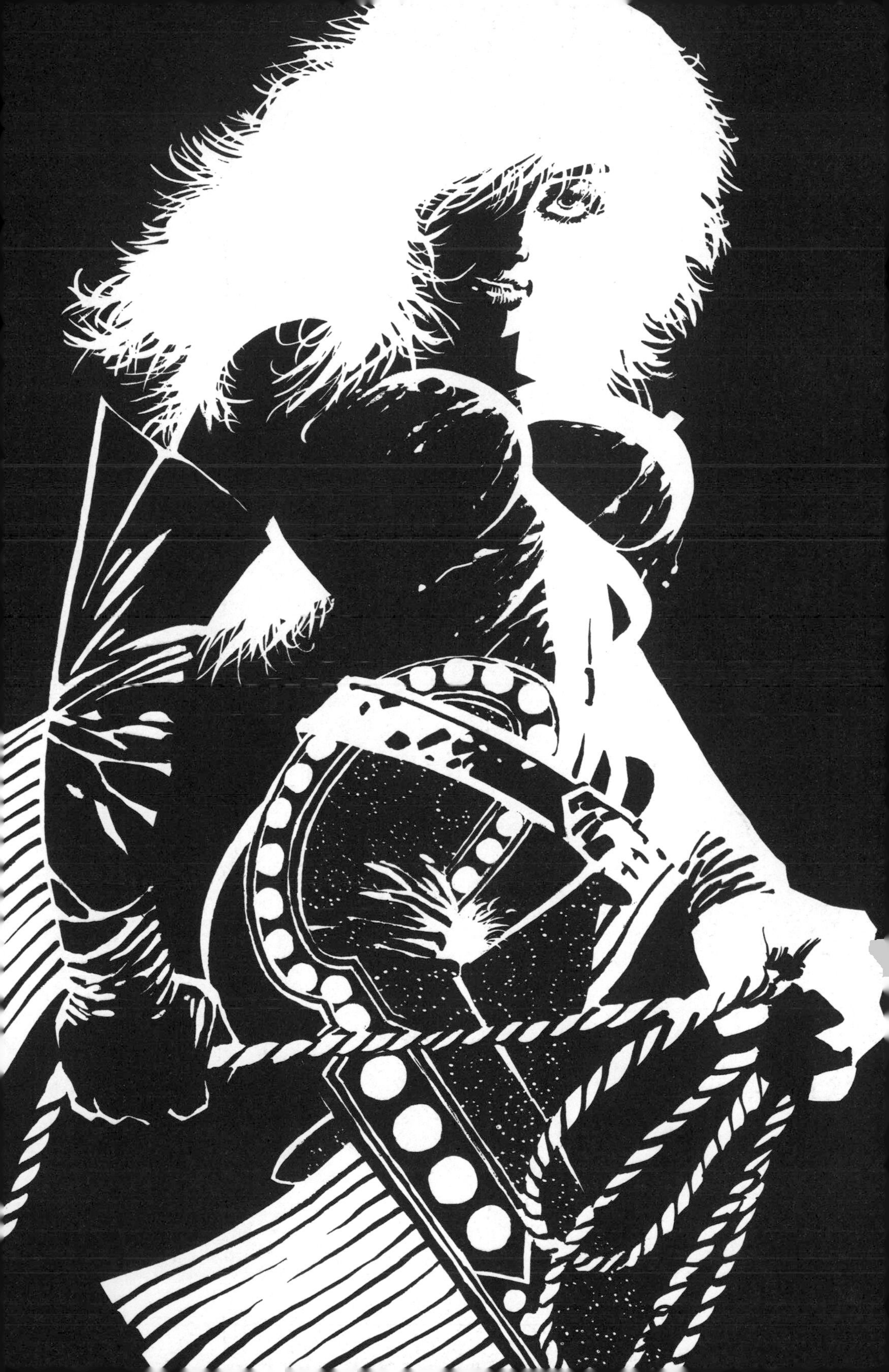

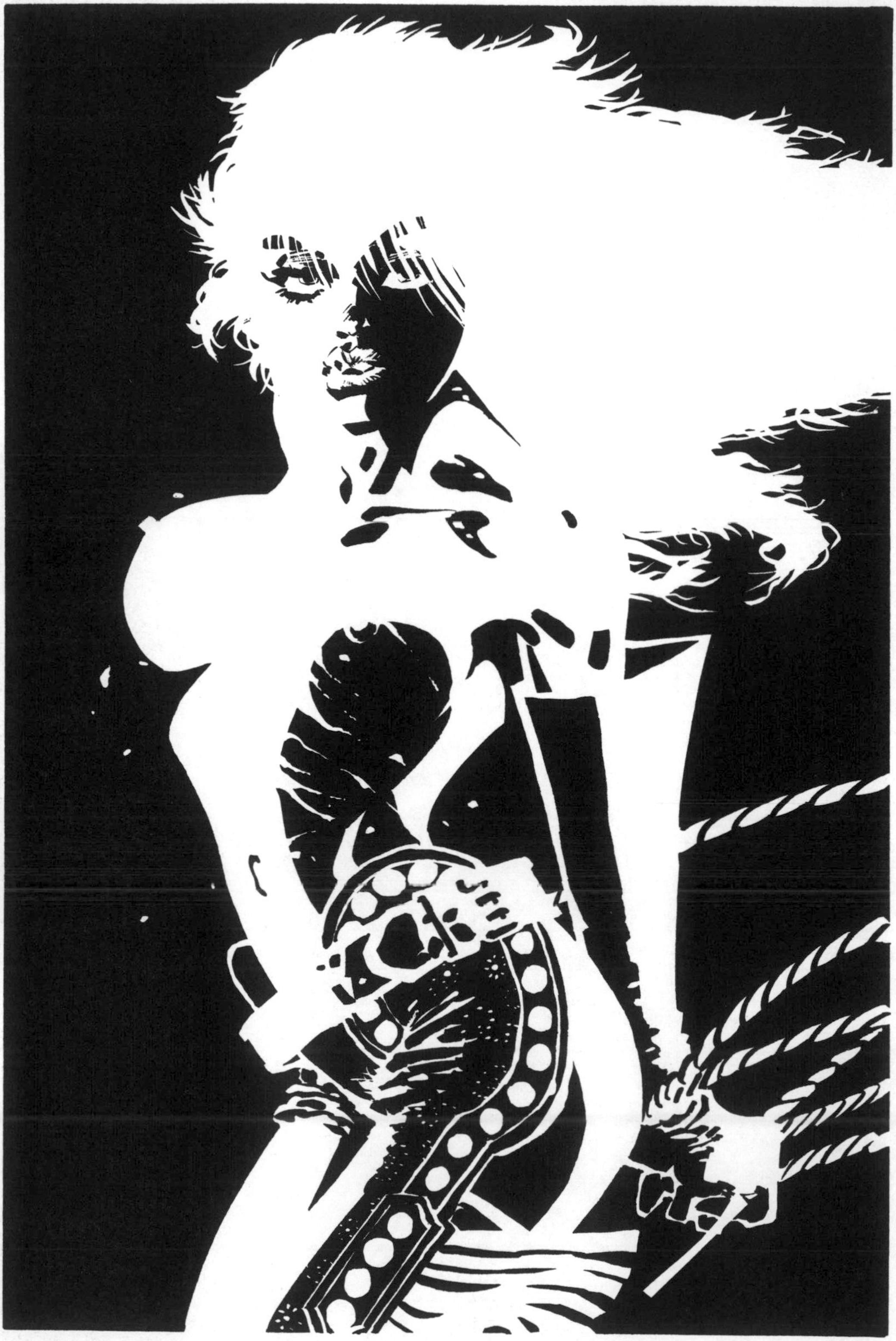

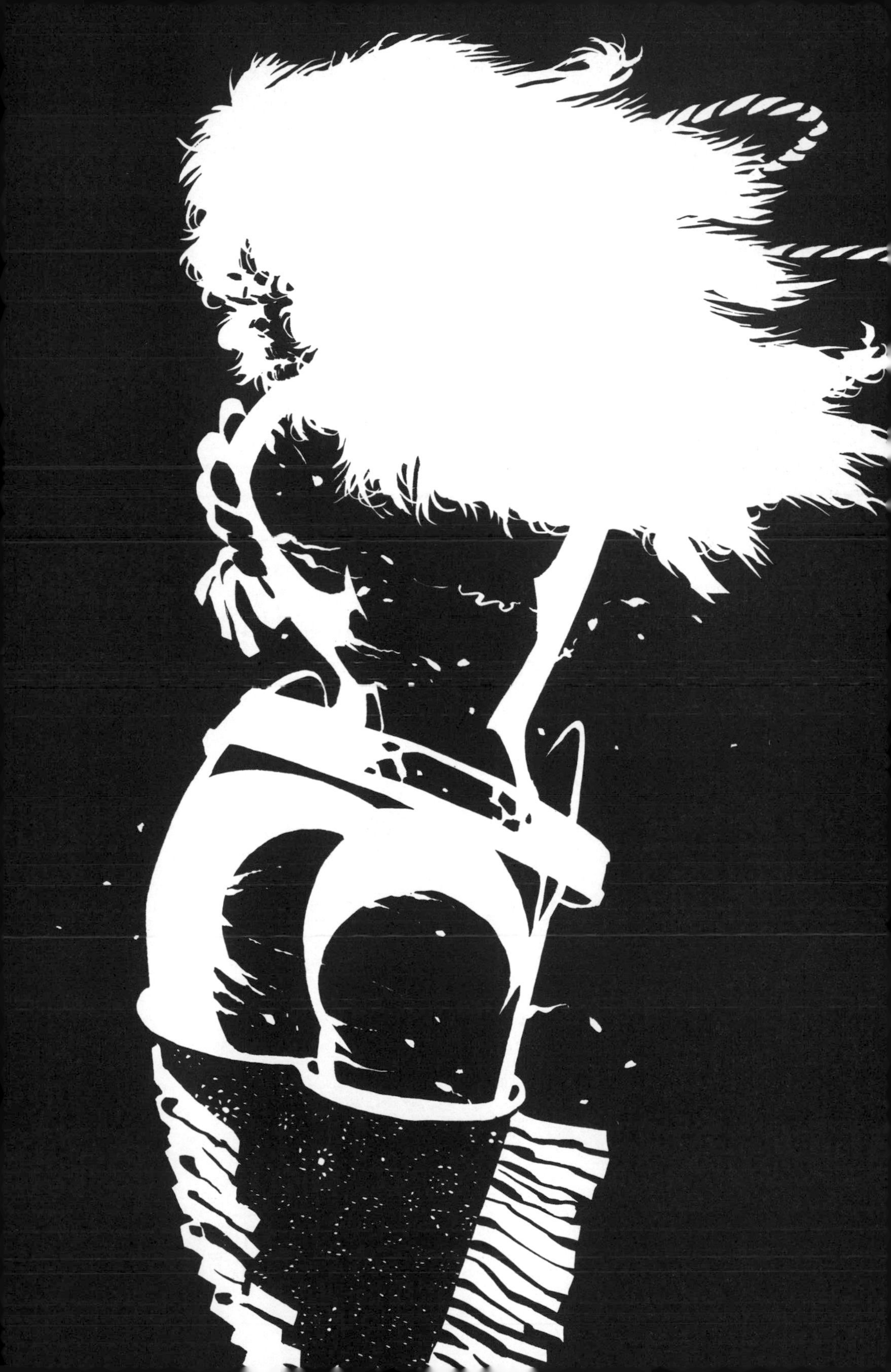

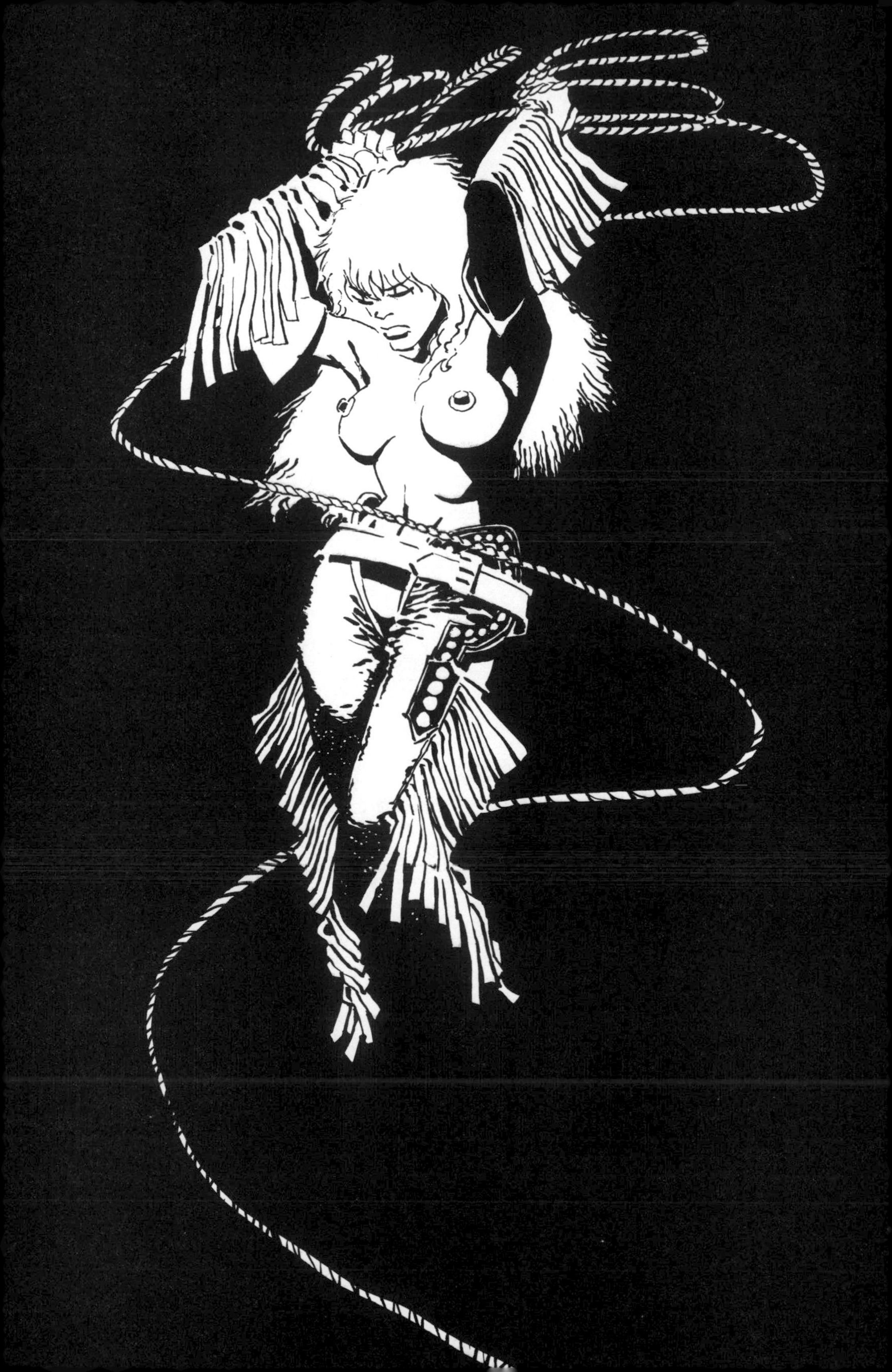

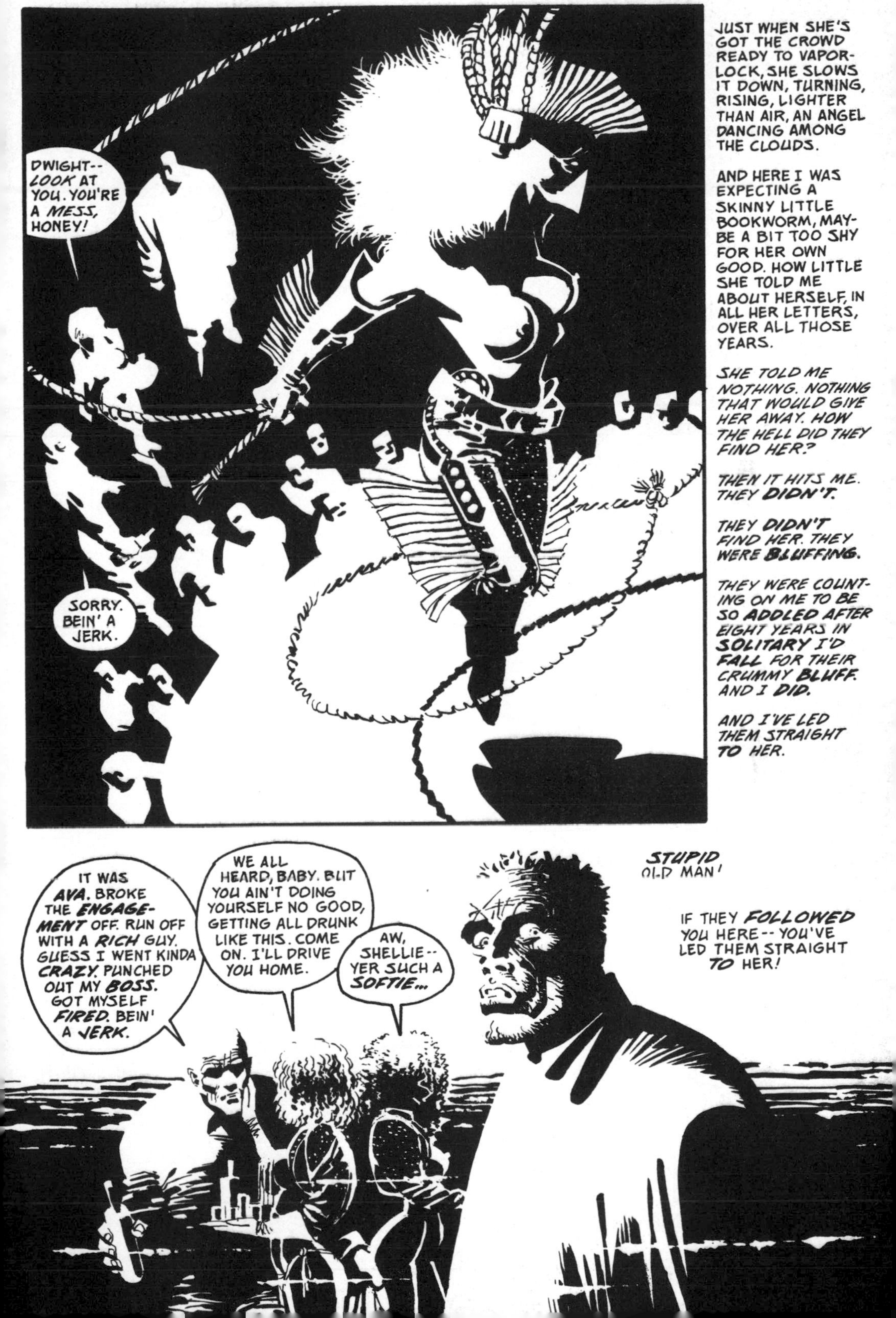
JUST WHEN SHE'S GOT THE CROWD READY TO VAPOR-LOCK, SHE SLOWS IT DOWN, TURNING, RISING, LIGHTER THAN AIR, AN ANGEL DANCING AMONG THE CLOUDS.
DWIGHT-- LOOK AT YOU. YOU'RE A MESS, HONEY!
AND HERE I WAS EXPECTING A SKINNY LITTLE BOOKWORM, MAY-BE A BIT TOO SHY FOR HER OWN GOOD. HOW LITTLE SHE TOLD ME ABOUT HERSELF, IN ALL HER LETTERS, OVER ALL THOSE YEARS.
SHE TOLD ME NOTHING. NOTHING THAT WOULD GIVE HER AWAY. HOW THE HELL DID THEY FIND HER?
SORRY. BEIN' A JERK.
THEN IT HITS ME. THEY DIDN'T.
THEY DIDN'T FIND HER. THEY WERE BLUFFING.
THEY WERE COUNT-ING ON ME TO BE SO ADDLED AFTER EIGHT YEARS IN SOLITARY I'D FALL FOR THEIR CRUMMY BLUFF. AND I DID.
AND I'VE LED THEM STRAIGHT TO HER.
IT WAS AVA. BROKE THE ENGAGE-MENT OFF. RUN OFF WITH A RICH GUY. GUESS I WENT KINDA CRAZY. PUNCHED OUT MY BOSS. GOT MYSELF FIRED. BEIN' A JERK.
WE ALL HEARD, BABY. BUT YOU AIN'T DOING YOURSELF NO GOOD, GETTING ALL DRUNK LIKE THIS. COME ON. I'LL DRIVE YOU HOME.
AW, SHELLIE-- YER SUCH A SOFTIE...
STUPID OLD MAN!
IF THEY FOLLOWED YOU HERE-- YOU'VE LED THEM STRAIGHT TO HER!

FROM RIGHT *BEHIND ME*--

--THAT *SMELL...*

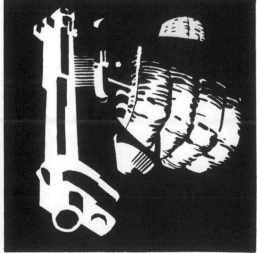

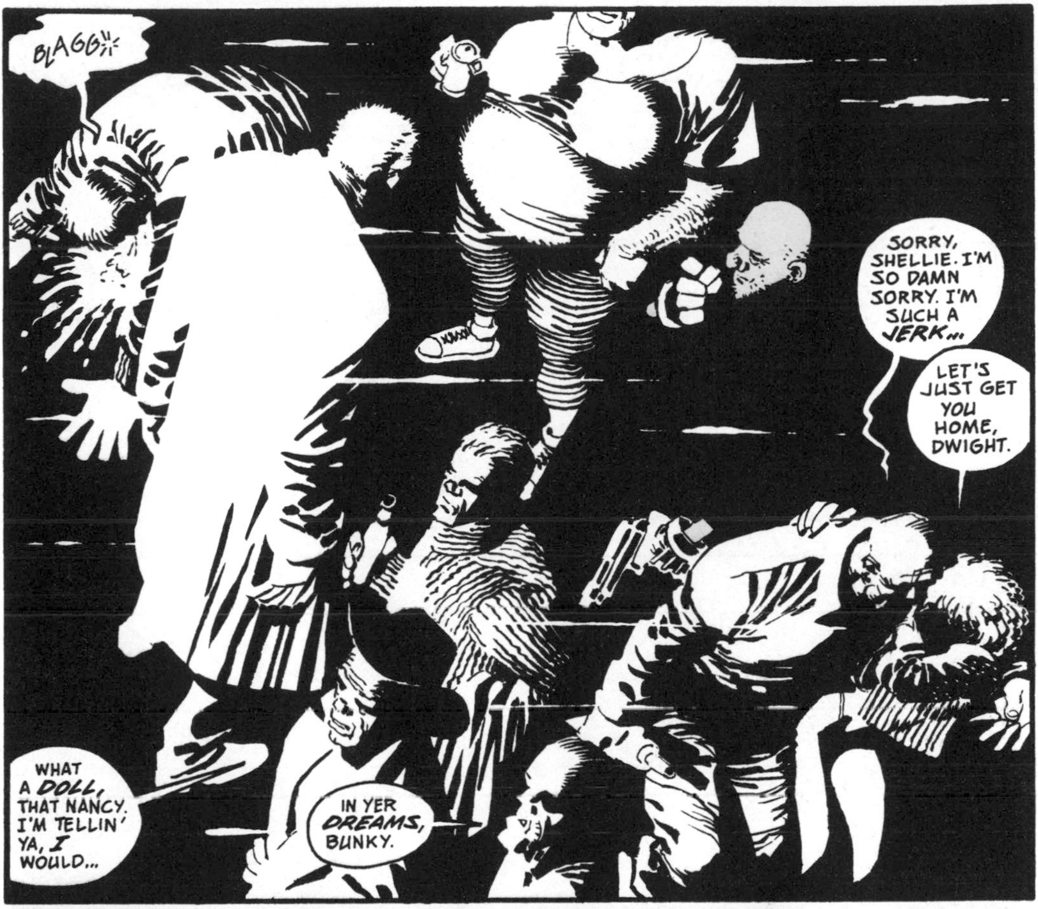
BLAGG!!
SORRY, SHELLIE. I'M SO DAMN SORRY. I'M SUCH A *JERK*...
LET'S JUST GET YOU HOME, DWIGHT.
WHAT A *DOLL*, THAT NANCY. I'M TELLIN' YA, *I* WOULD...
IN YER *DREAMS*, BUNKY.

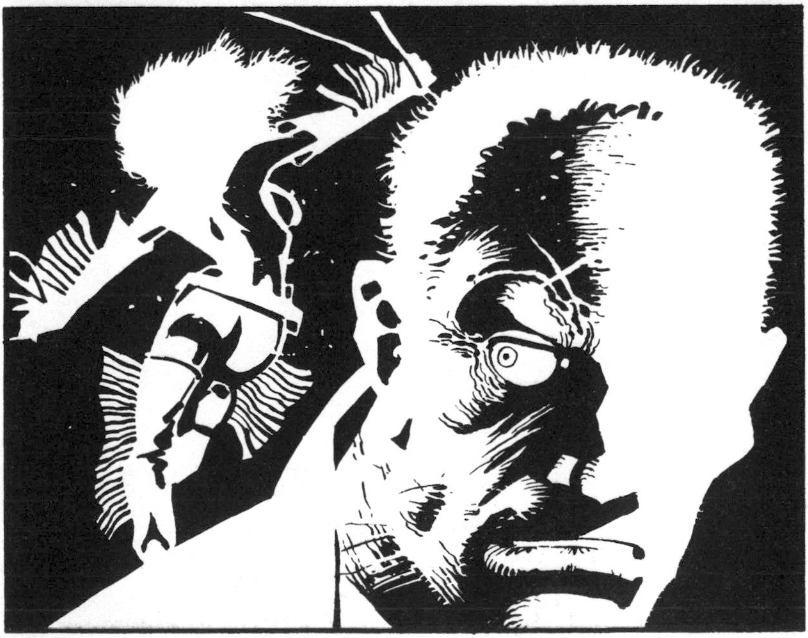

STAY STEADY, OLD MAN. STAY SHARP. YOU HAVEN'T QUITE MANAGED TO COM-PLETELY SCREW EVERYTHING UP. NOT QUITE. NOT YET.

SHE HASN'T SPOTTED YOU YET. YOU'RE JUST A HORNY EX-CON WATCHING AN EXOTIC DANCER.

STAY CALM. SHE HASN'T SPOTTED YOU YET.

STAY CALM. TURN AROUND AND WALK OUT THE DOOR--AND SHE'LL BE *SAFE*.

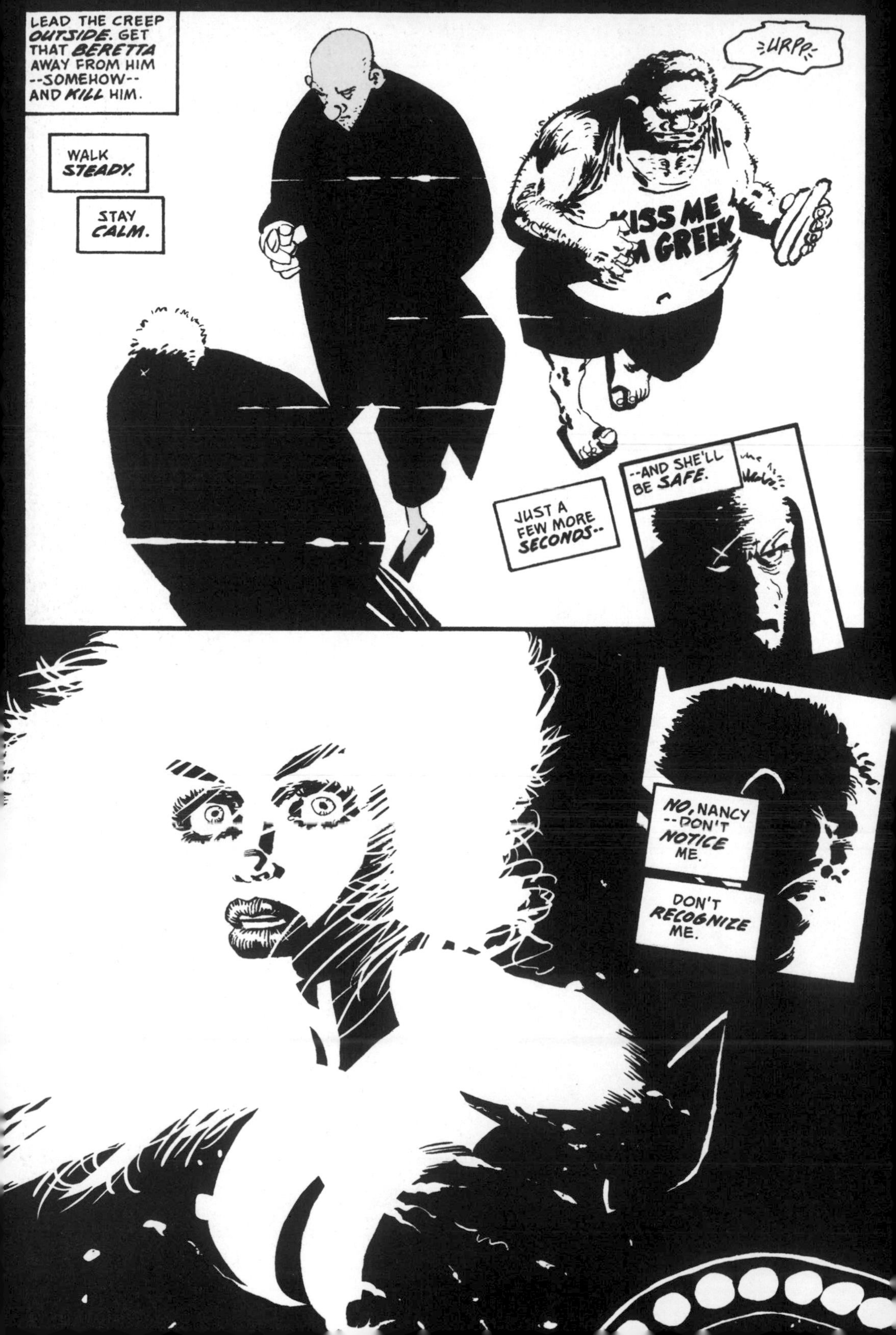
LEAD THE CREEP OUTSIDE. GET THAT BERETTA AWAY FROM HIM --SOMEHOW-- AND KILL HIM.
URPP
WALK STEADY.
STAY CALM.
KISS ME I'M GREEK
JUST A FEW MORE SECONDS--
--AND SHE'LL BE SAFE.
NO, NANCY --DON'T NOTICE ME.
DON'T RECOGNIZE ME.

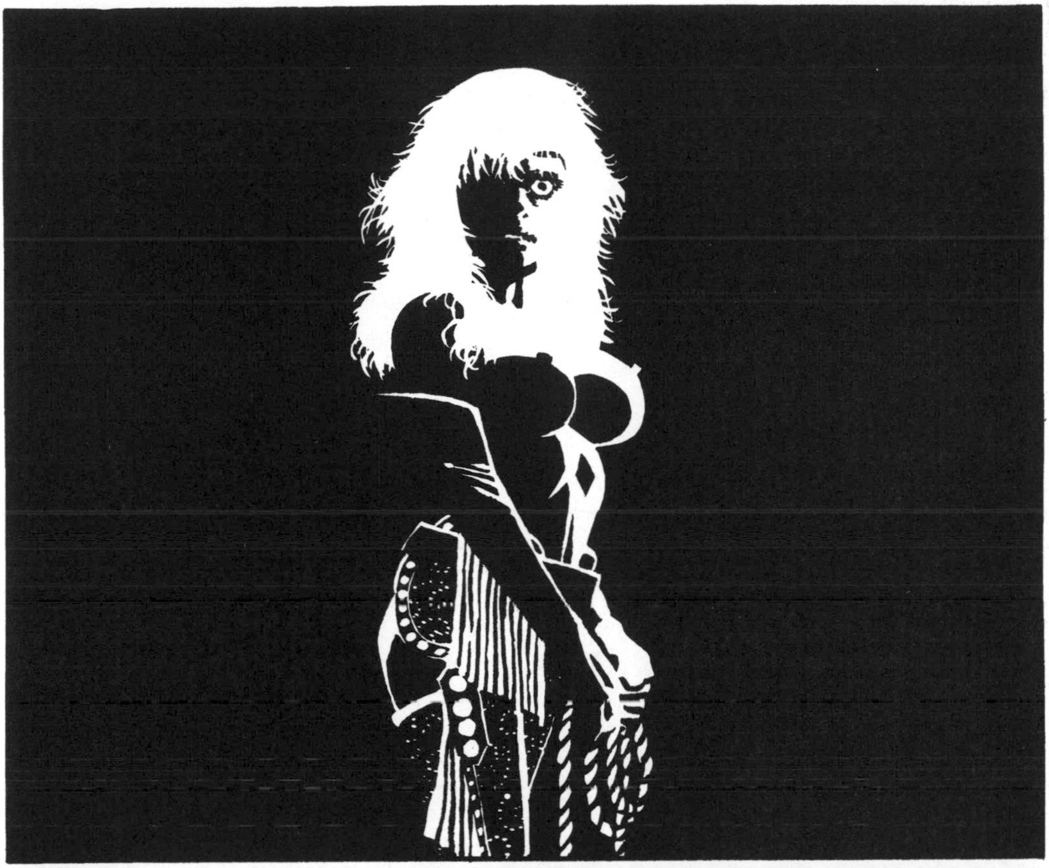

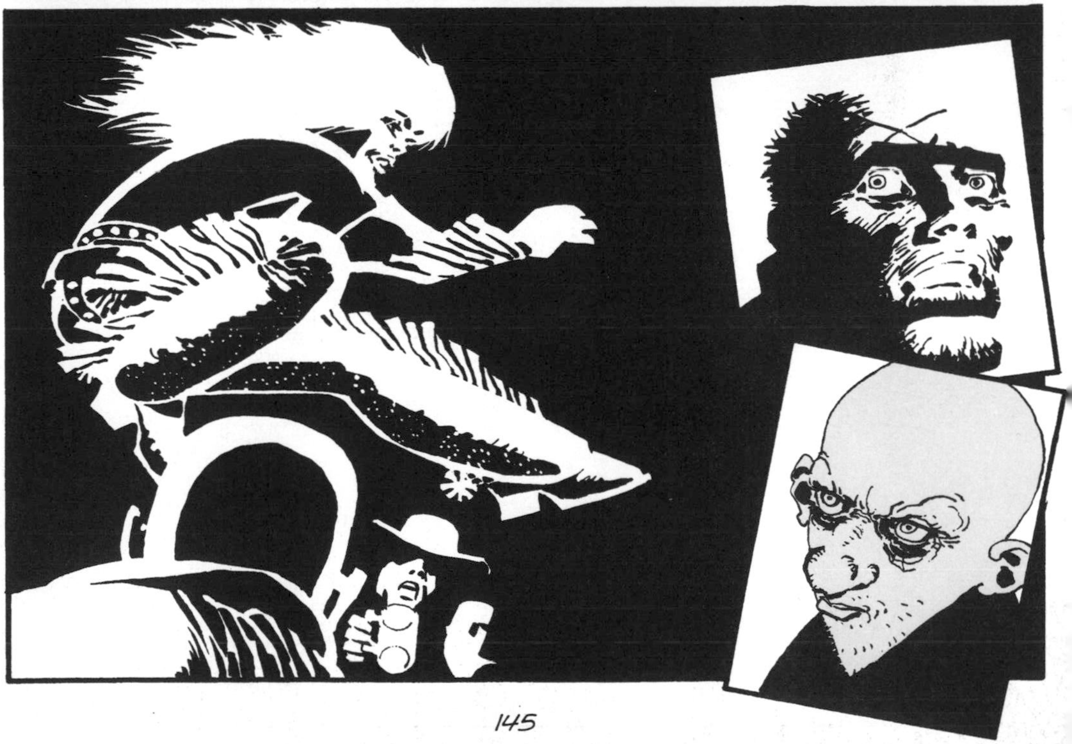

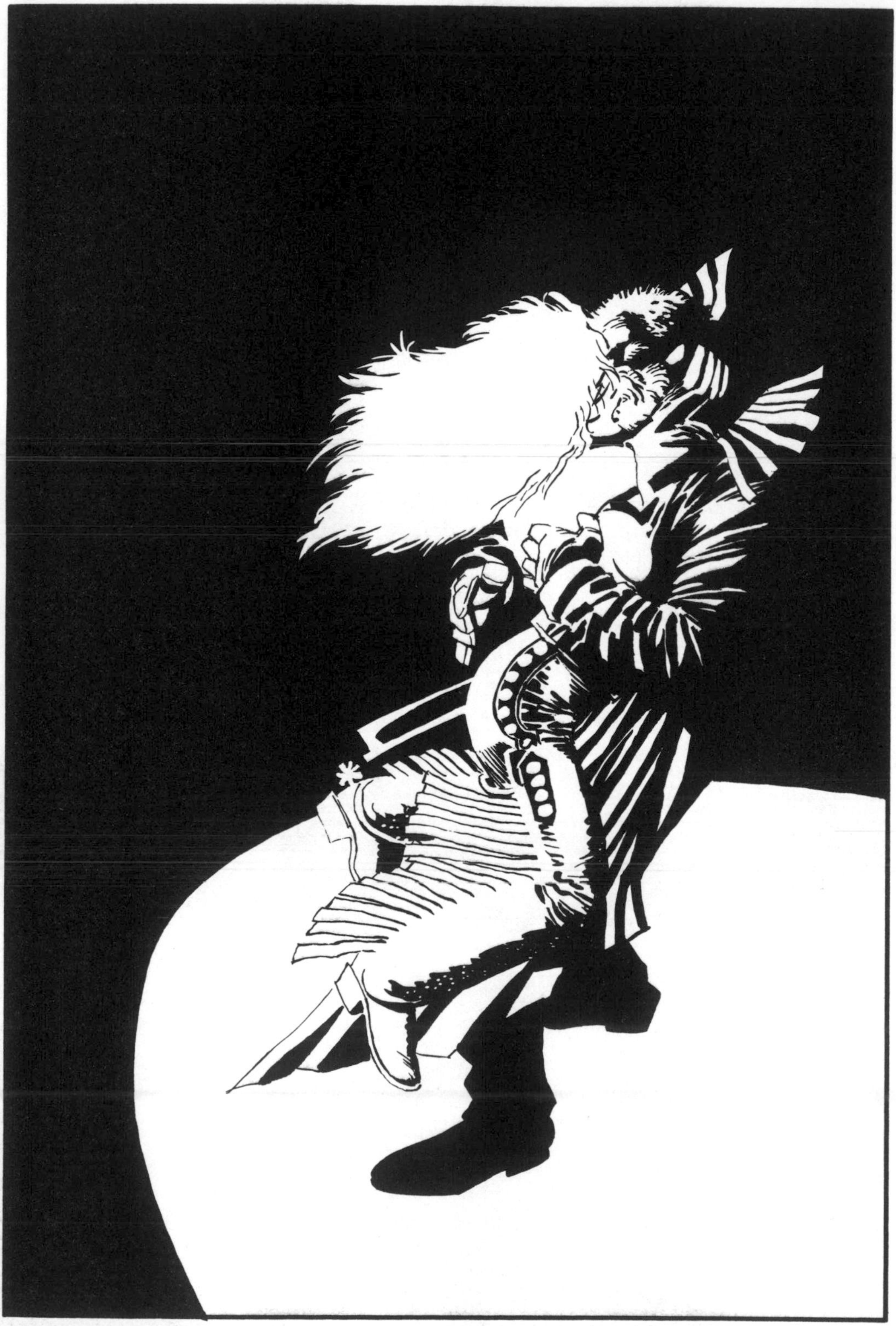

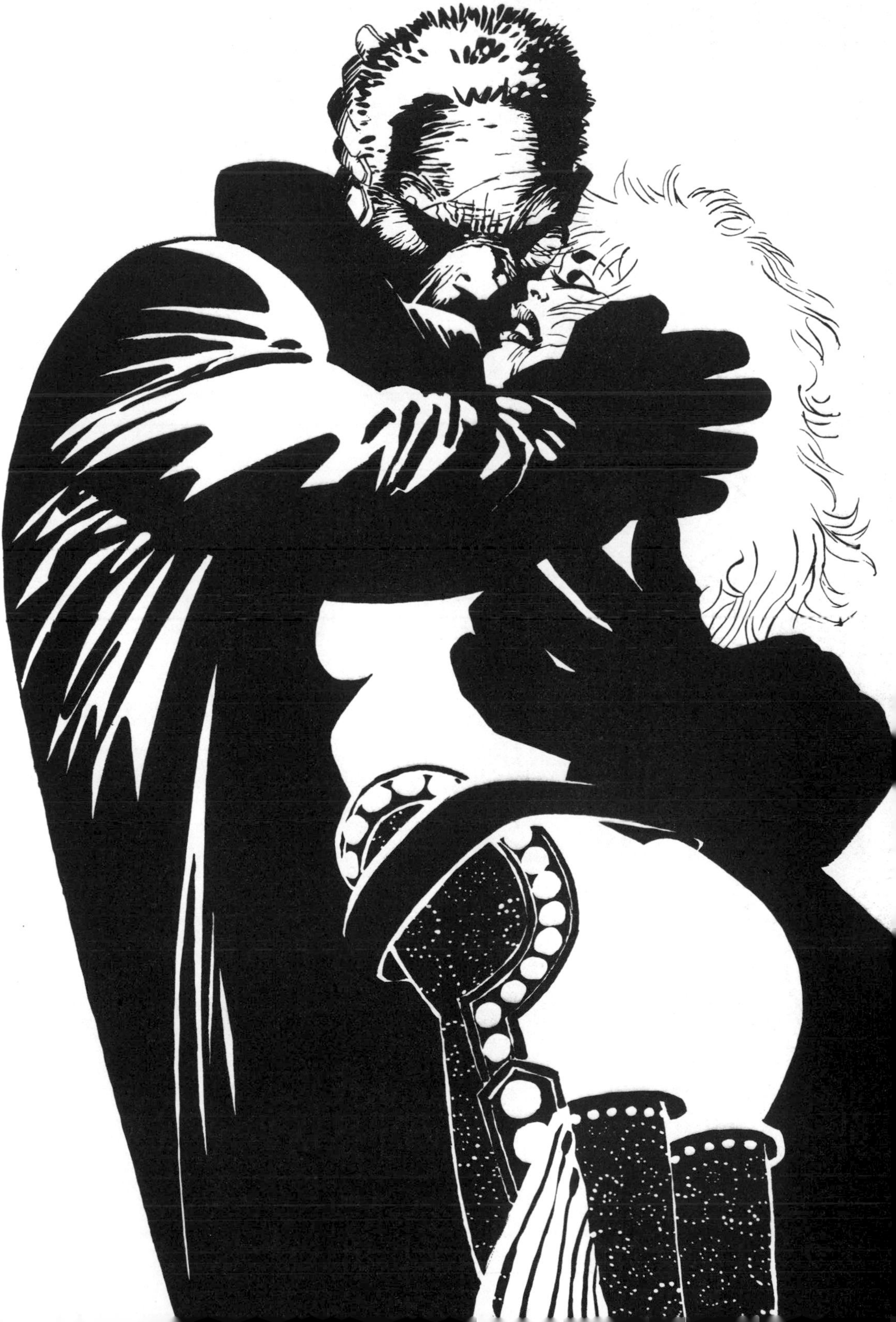

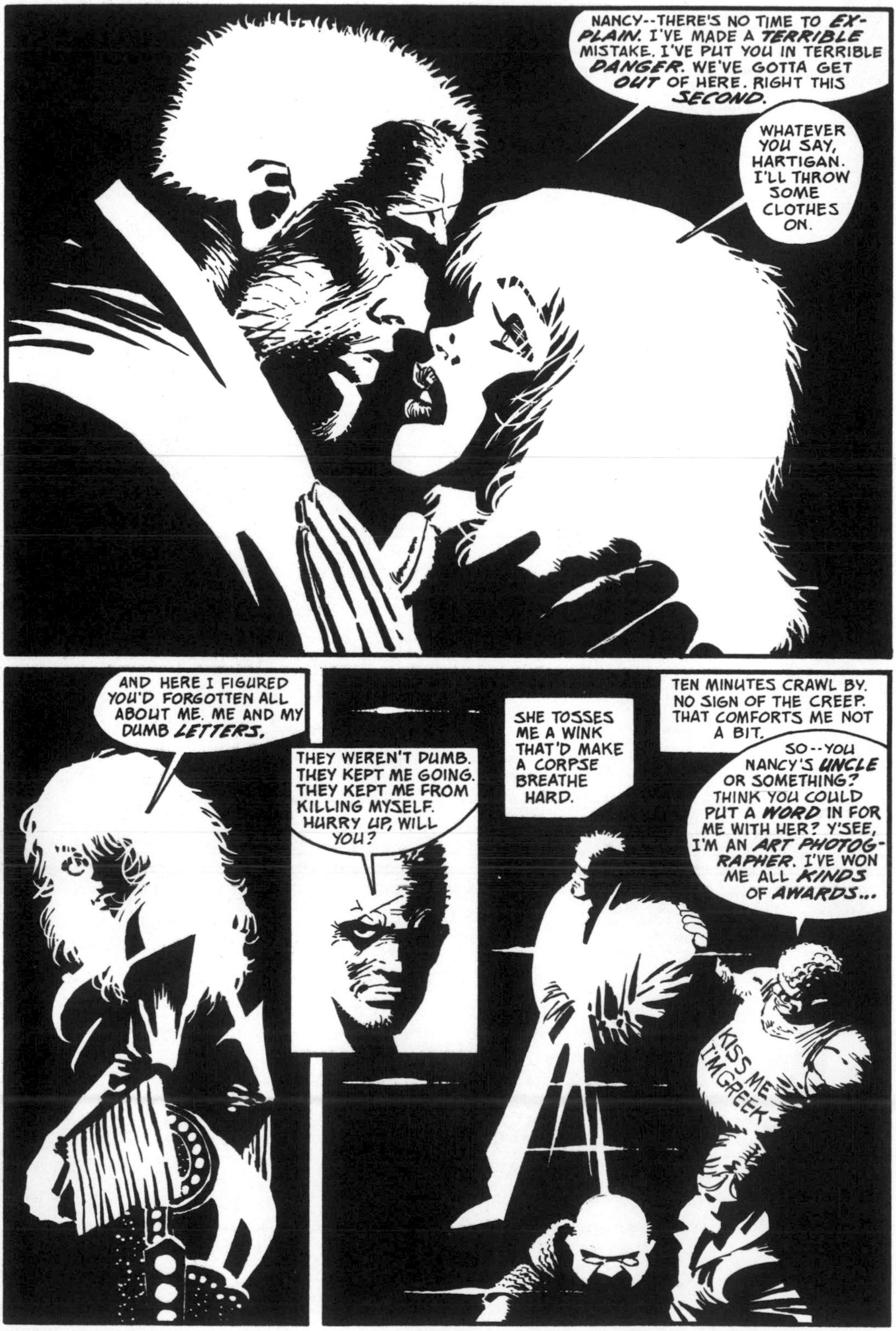
NANCY--THERE'S NO TIME TO EX-PLAIN. I'VE MADE A TERRIBLE MISTAKE. I'VE PUT YOU IN TERRIBLE DANGER. WE'VE GOTTA GET OUT OF HERE. RIGHT THIS SECOND.
WHATEVER YOU SAY, HARTIGAN. I'LL THROW SOME CLOTHES ON.
AND HERE I FIGURED YOU'D FORGOTTEN ALL ABOUT ME. ME AND MY DUMB LETTERS.
THEY WEREN'T DUMB. THEY KEPT ME GOING. THEY KEPT ME FROM KILLING MYSELF. HURRY UP, WILL YOU?
SHE TOSSES ME A WINK THAT'D MAKE A CORPSE BREATHE HARD.
TEN MINUTES CRAWL BY. NO SIGN OF THE CREEP. THAT COMFORTS ME NOT A BIT.
SO--YOU NANCY'S UNCLE OR SOMETHING? THINK YOU COULD PUT A WORD IN FOR ME WITH HER? Y'SEE, I'M AN ART PHOTOG-RAPHER. I'VE WON ME ALL KINDS OF AWARDS...
KISS ME I'M GREEK

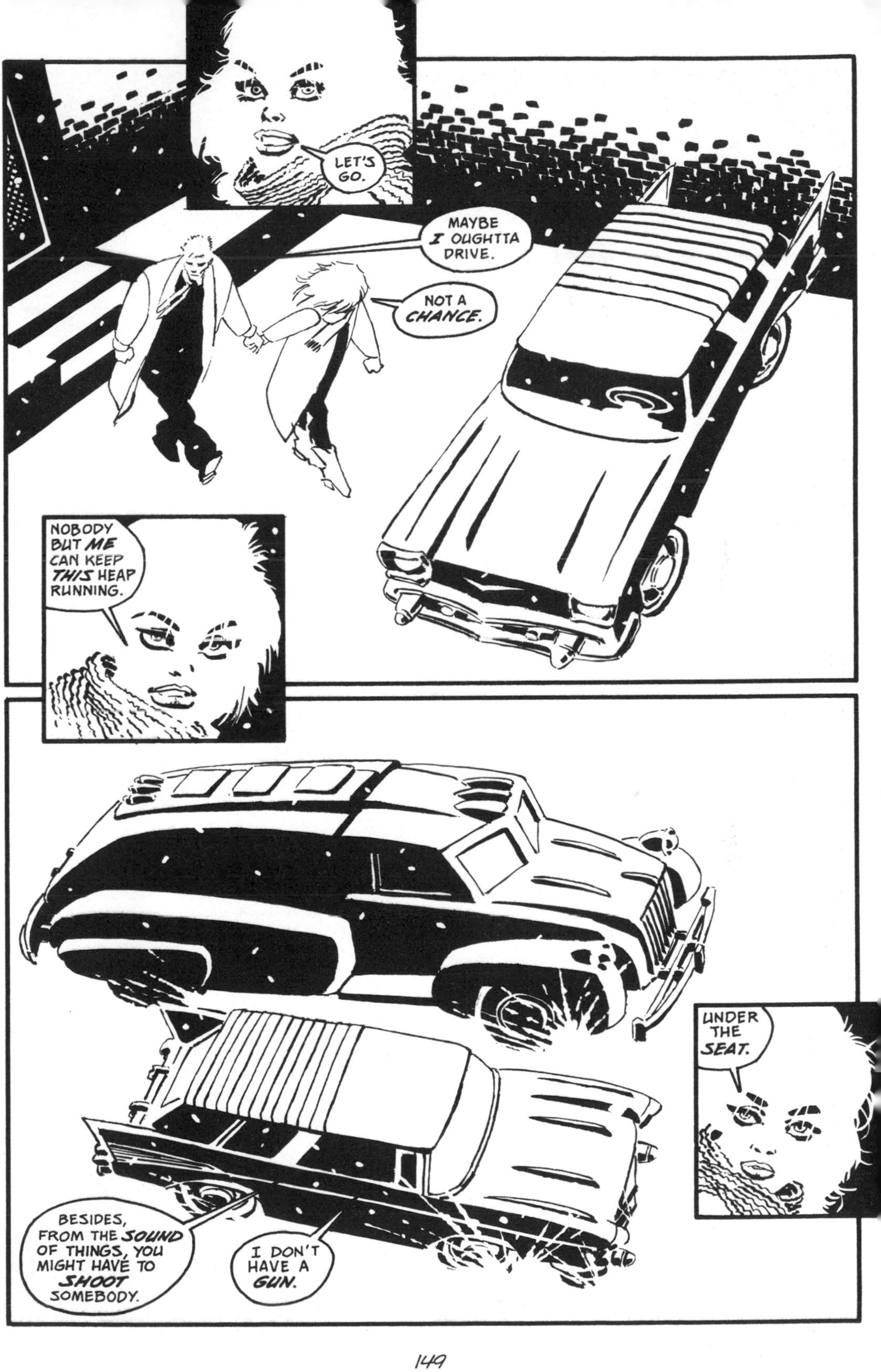
LET'S GO.
MAYBE I OUGHTTA DRIVE.
NOT A CHANCE.
NOBODY BUT ME CAN KEEP THIS HEAP RUNNING.
UNDER THE SEAT.
BESIDES, FROM THE SOUND OF THINGS, YOU MIGHT HAVE TO SHOOT SOMEBODY.
I DON'T HAVE A GUN.

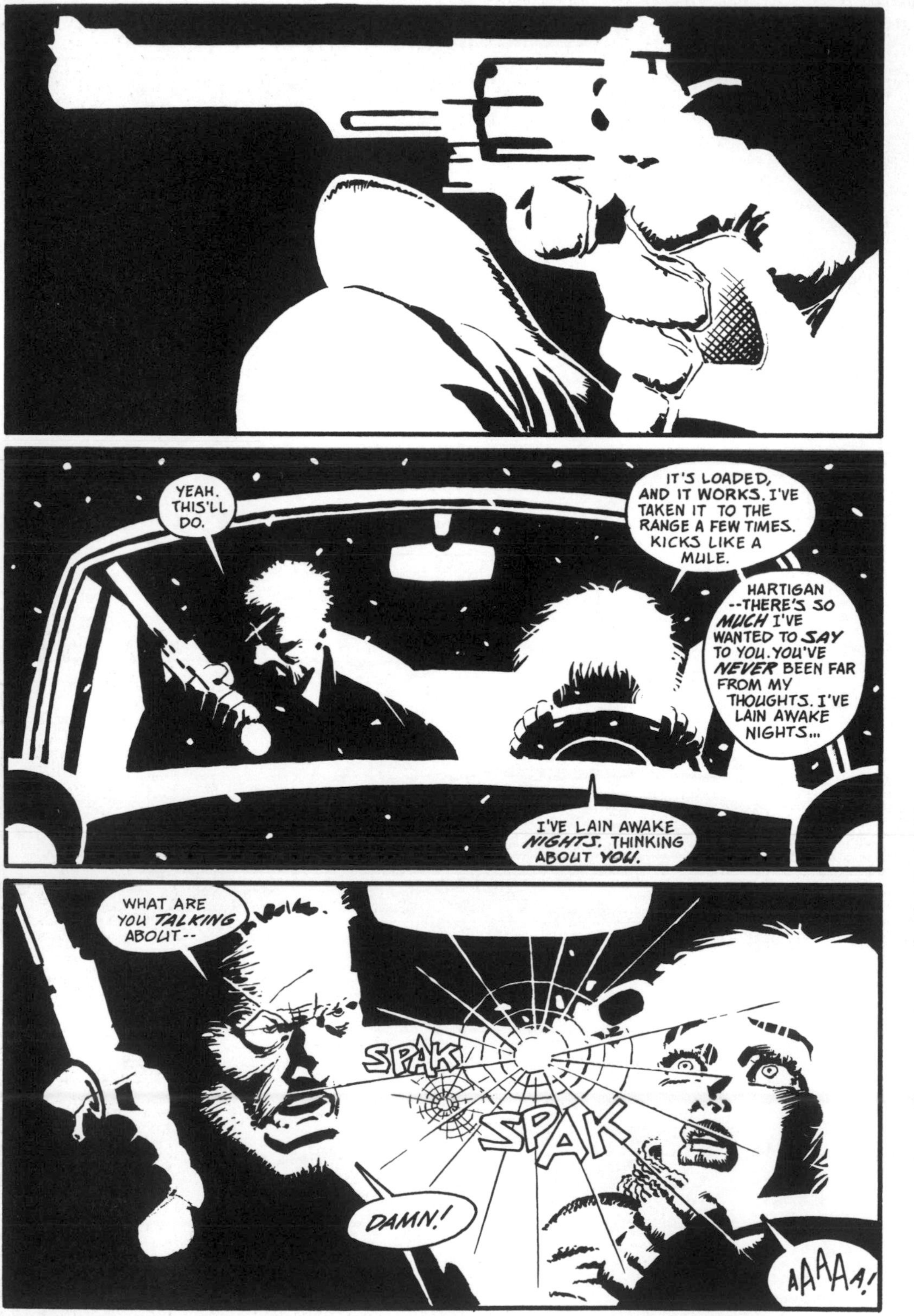
YEAH. THIS'LL DO.
IT'S LOADED, AND IT WORKS. I'VE TAKEN IT TO THE RANGE A FEW TIMES. KICKS LIKE A MULE.
HARTIGAN --THERE'S SO MUCH I'VE WANTED TO SAY TO YOU. YOU'VE NEVER BEEN FAR FROM MY THOUGHTS. I'VE LAIN AWAKE NIGHTS...
I'VE LAIN AWAKE NIGHTS. THINKING ABOUT YOU.
WHAT ARE YOU TALKING ABOUT--
SPAK
SPAK
DAMN!
AAAAA!

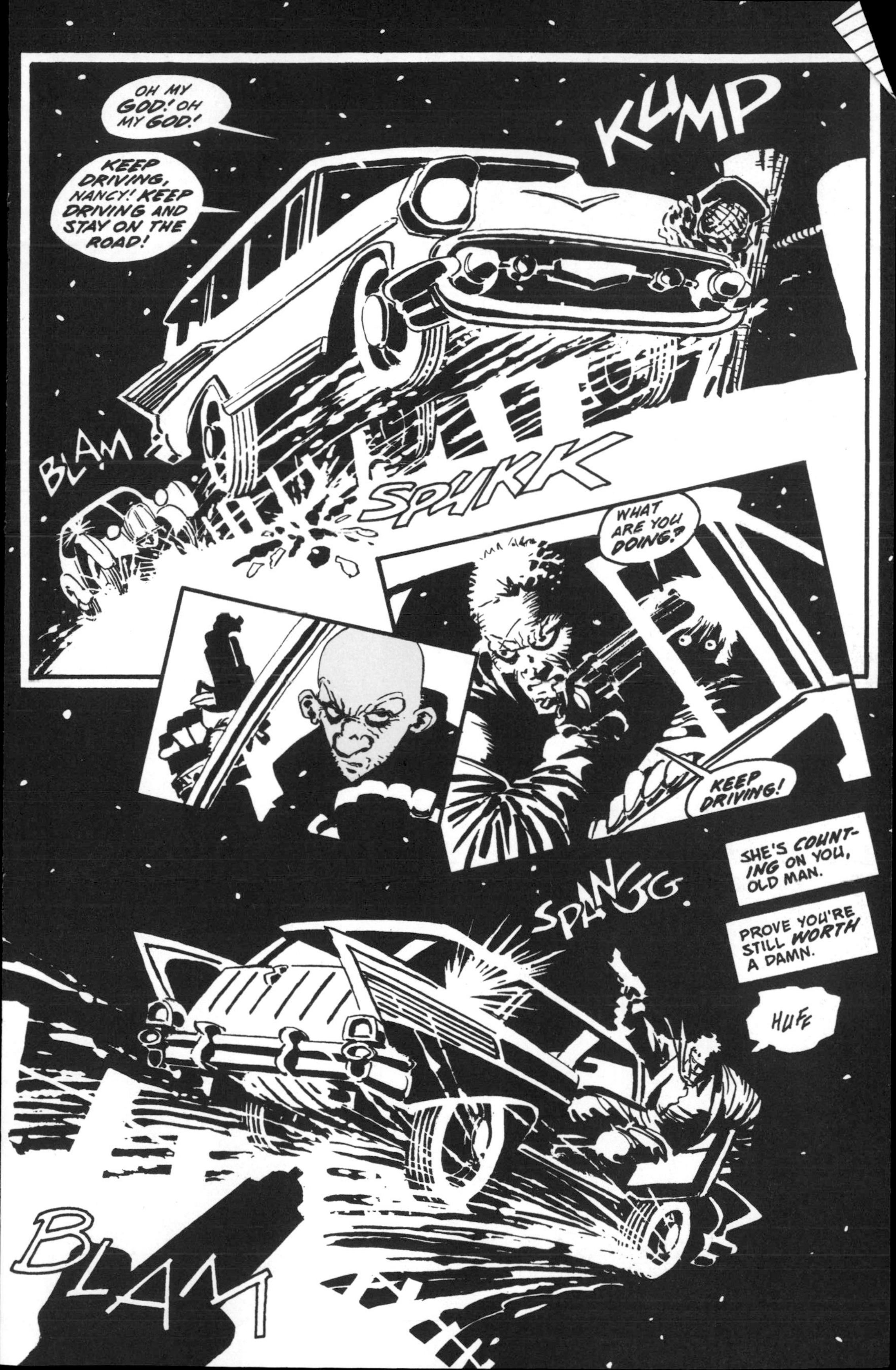
OH MY GOD! OH MY GOD!
KEEP DRIVING, NANCY! KEEP DRIVING AND STAY ON THE ROAD!
KUMP
BLAM
SPLIKK
WHAT ARE YOU DOING?
KEEP DRIVING!
SHE'S COUNTING ON YOU, OLD MAN.
PROVE YOU'RE STILL WORTH A DAMN.
SPANGG
HUFF
BLAM

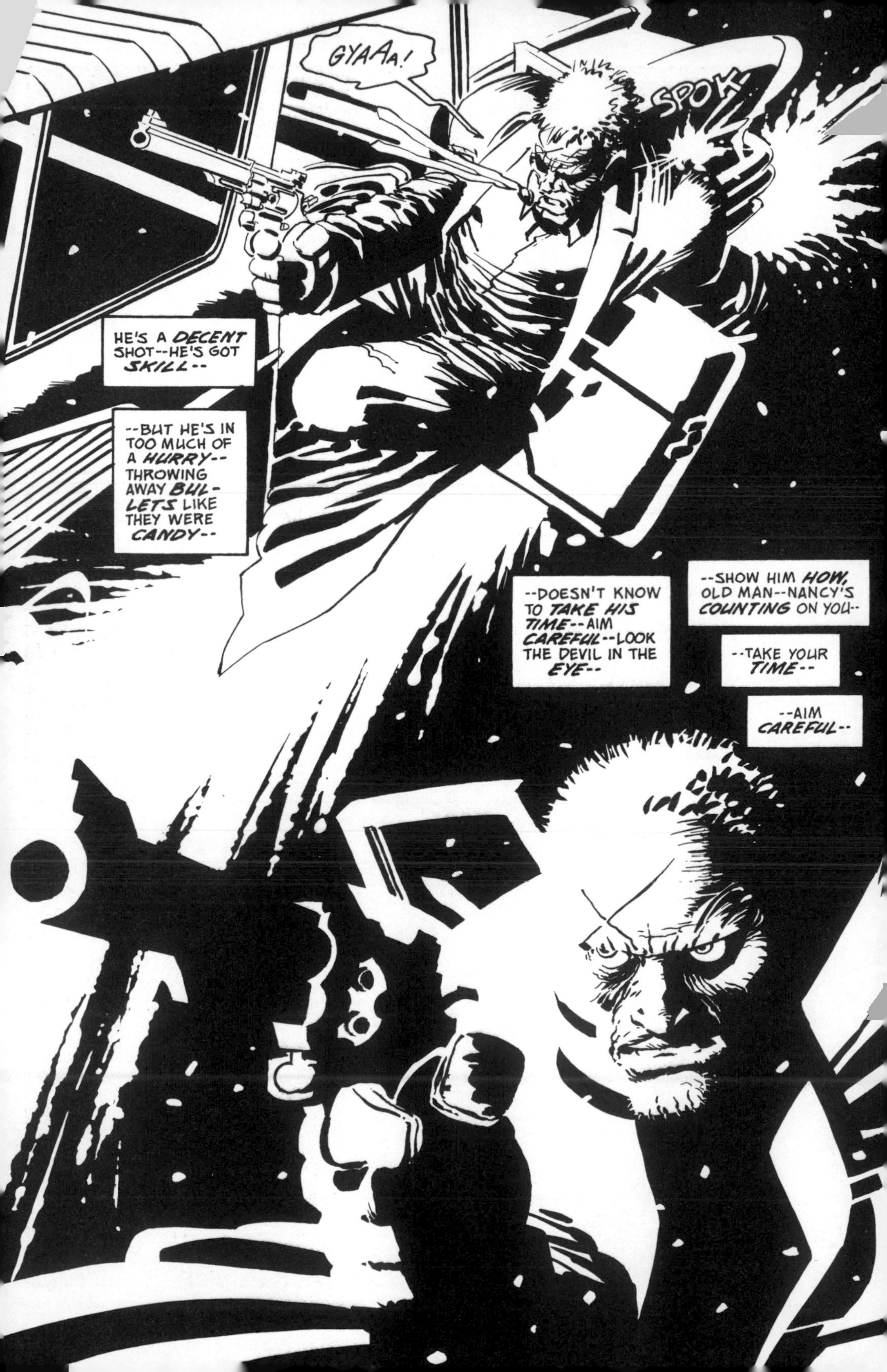
GYAAA!
SPOK
HE'S A DECENT SHOT--HE'S GOT SKILL--
--BUT HE'S IN TOO MUCH OF A HURRY--THROWING AWAY BUL-LETS LIKE THEY WERE CANDY--
--DOESN'T KNOW TO TAKE HIS TIME--AIM CAREFUL--LOOK THE DEVIL IN THE EYE--
--SHOW HIM HOW, OLD MAN--NANCY'S COUNTING ON YOU--
--TAKE YOUR TIME--
--AIM CAREFUL--

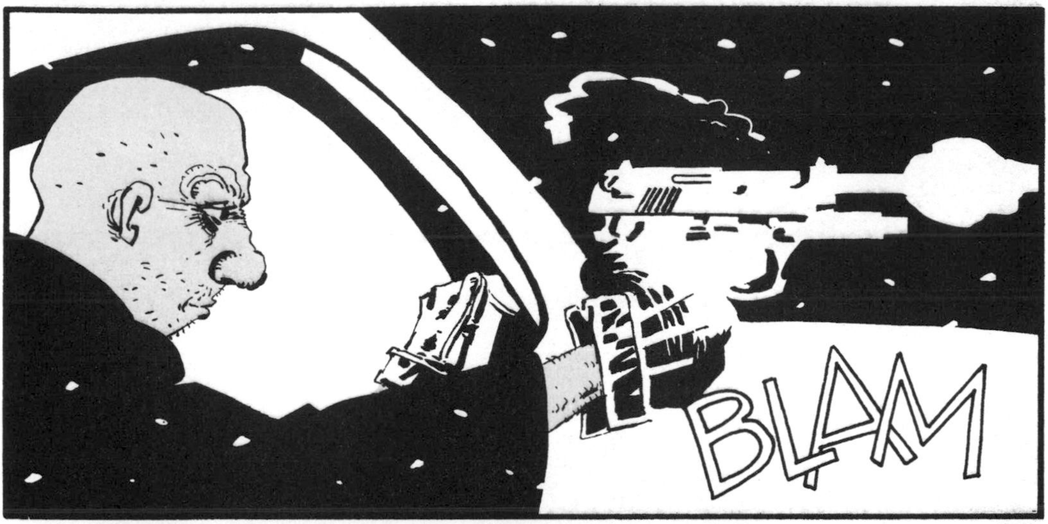
BLAM
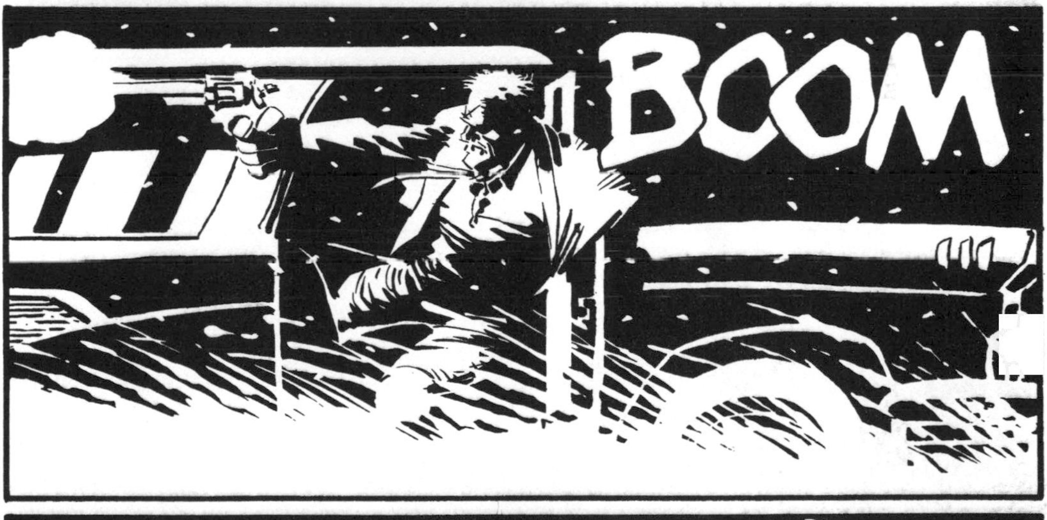
BOOM
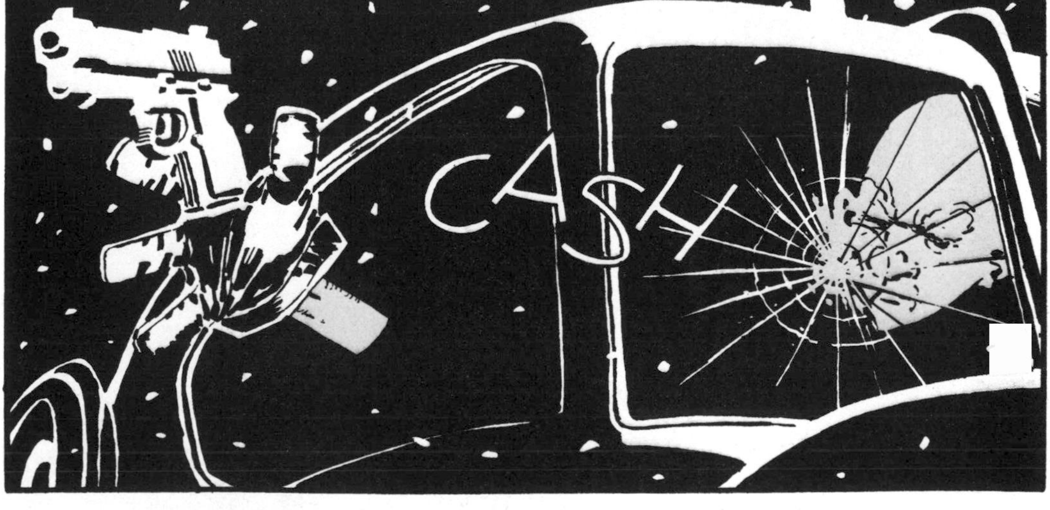
CASH

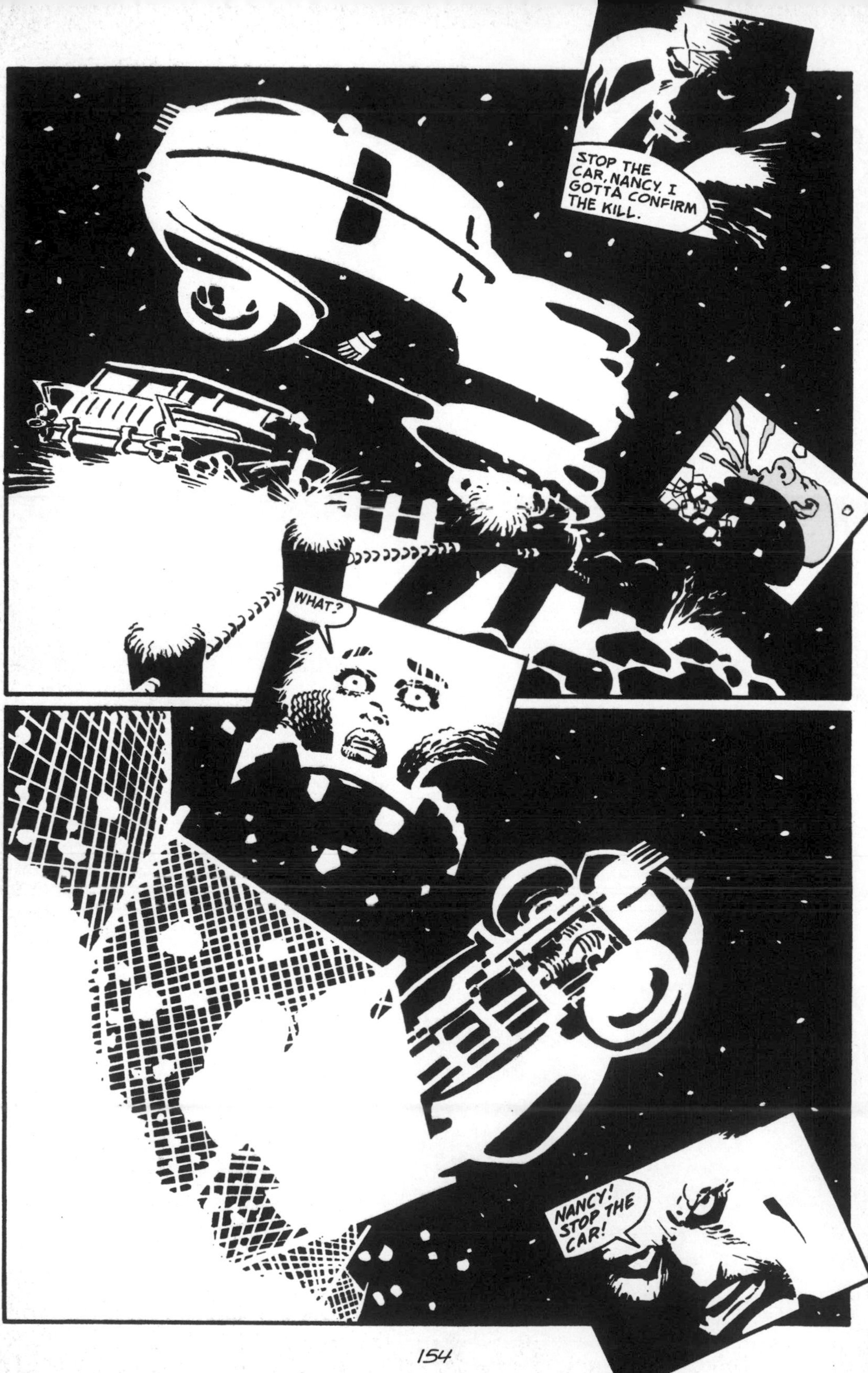
STOP THE CAR, NANCY. I GOTTA CONFIRM THE KILL.
WHAT?
NANCY! STOP THE CAR!

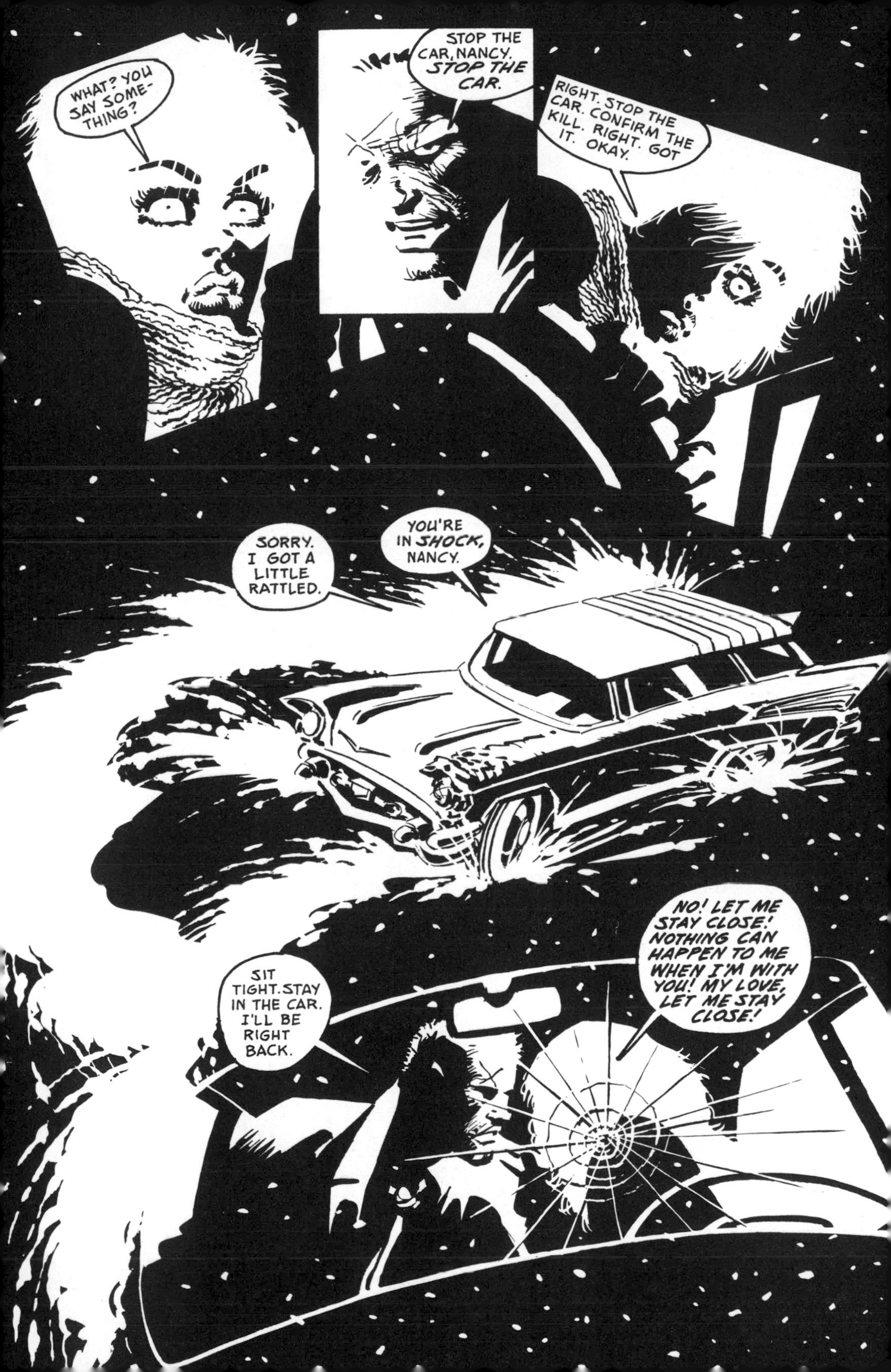
WHAT? YOU SAY SOME-THING?
STOP THE CAR, NANCY. STOP THE CAR.
RIGHT. STOP THE CAR. CONFIRM THE KILL. RIGHT. GOT IT. OKAY.
SORRY. I GOT A LITTLE RATTLED.
YOU'RE IN SHOCK, NANCY.
SIT TIGHT. STAY IN THE CAR. I'LL BE RIGHT BACK.
NO! LET ME STAY CLOSE! NOTHING CAN HAPPEN TO ME WHEN I'M WITH YOU! MY LOVE, LET ME STAY CLOSE!

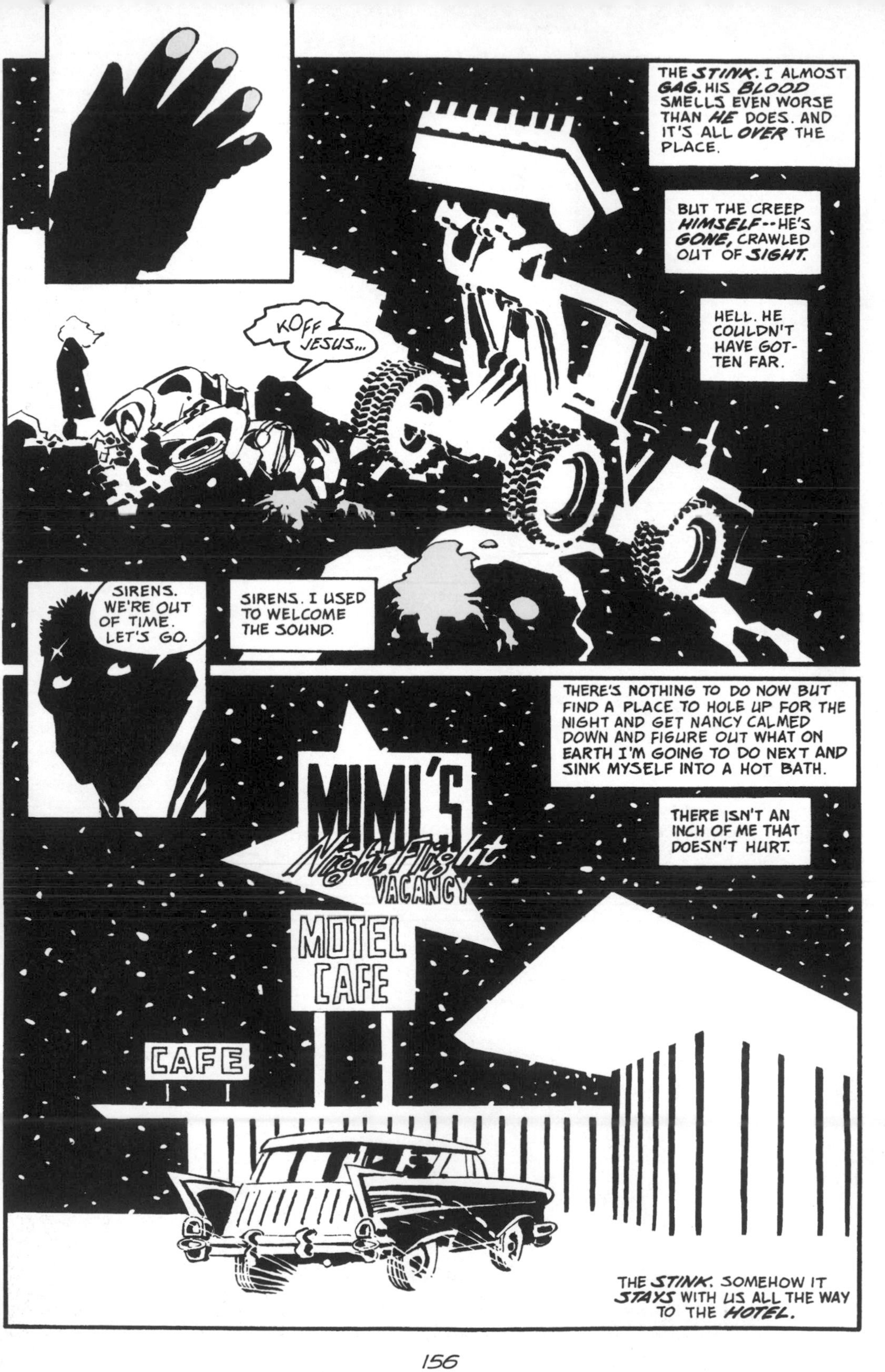
THE STINK. I ALMOST GAG. HIS BLOOD SMELLS EVEN WORSE THAN HE DOES. AND IT'S ALL OVER THE PLACE.
BUT THE CREEP HIMSELF--HE'S GONE, CRAWLED OUT OF SIGHT.
KOFF JESUS...
HELL. HE COULDN'T HAVE GOTTEN FAR.
SIRENS. WE'RE OUT OF TIME. LET'S GO.
SIRENS. I USED TO WELCOME THE SOUND.
THERE'S NOTHING TO DO NOW BUT FIND A PLACE TO HOLE UP FOR THE NIGHT AND GET NANCY CALMED DOWN AND FIGURE OUT WHAT ON EARTH I'M GOING TO DO NEXT AND SINK MYSELF INTO A HOT BATH.
THERE ISN'T AN INCH OF ME THAT DOESN'T HURT.
MIMI'S
Night Flight
VACANCY
MOTEL
CAFE
CAFE
THE STINK. SOMEHOW IT STAYS WITH US ALL THE WAY TO THE HOTEL.

ALL THOSE YEARS. IT'S LIKE THEY NEVER HAPPENED. I'M SUCH AN ASSHOLE. I SWORE IF I EVER SAW YOU AGAIN I'D SHOW YOU I GREW UP STRONG. BUT THERE I WAS, JUST LIKE BEFORE. SCARED. HELPLESS.

ASSHOLE! ASSHOLE! ASSHOLE!

STOP THAT. SETTLE DOWN.

NANCY--I WENT TO YOUR APARTMENT. YOUR WINDOW WAS THROWN WIDE OPEN. YOUR ROOMS WERE ALMOST EMPTY. THAT'S WHY I WAS SO SURE YOU'D BEEN KIDNAPPED.

I'VE NEVER BEEN ALL THAT GOOD WITH PEOPLE. MY EX-WIFE COULD TESTIFY TO THAT.

WHEN IT COMES TO REASSURING A TRAUMATIZED NINETEEN-YEAR-OLD, I'M AS EXPERT AS A PALSY VICTIM DOING BRAIN SURGERY WITH A PIPE WRENCH.

MY WINDOW?... OH, GOD--I'VE BEEN ROBBED AGAIN! THAT'S THE THIRD TIME THIS YEAR!

YOU NEED TO SIT DOWN, NANCY. YOU'LL FEEL A LITTLE BETTER IF YOU SIT DOWN.

=KHEFF=

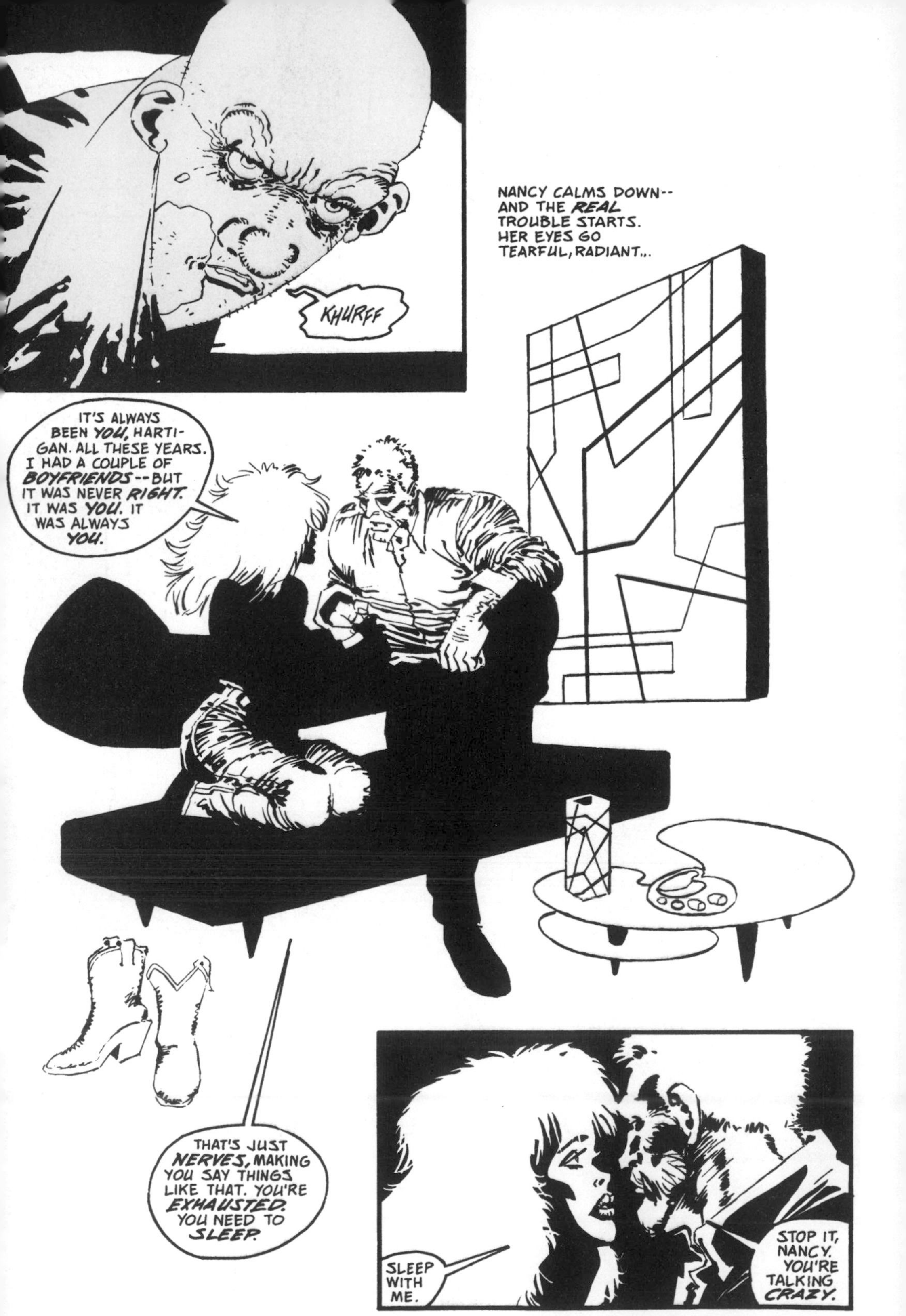

NANCY CALMS DOWN-- AND THE REAL TROUBLE STARTS. HER EYES GO TEARFUL, RADIANT...
KHURFF
IT'S ALWAYS BEEN YOU, HARTIGAN. ALL THESE YEARS. I HAD A COUPLE OF BOYFRIENDS--BUT IT WAS NEVER RIGHT. IT WAS YOU. IT WAS ALWAYS YOU.
THAT'S JUST NERVES, MAKING YOU SAY THINGS LIKE THAT. YOU'RE EXHAUSTED. YOU NEED TO SLEEP.
SLEEP WITH ME.
STOP IT, NANCY. YOU'RE TALKING CRAZY.

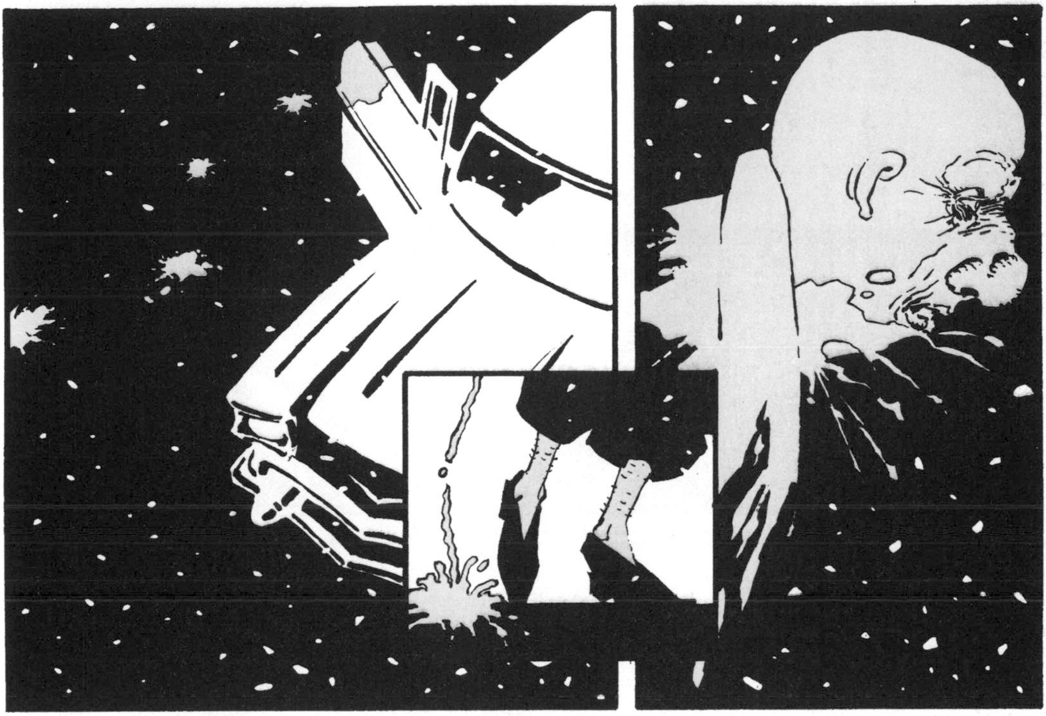

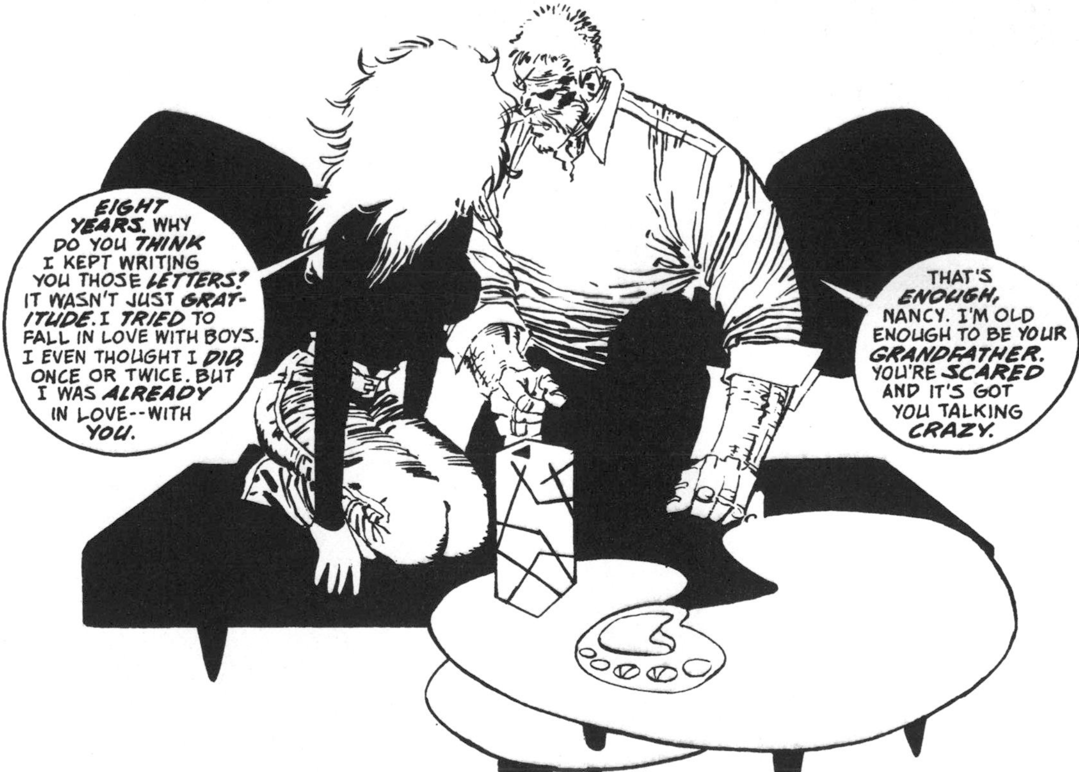
EIGHT YEARS. WHY DO YOU THINK I KEPT WRITING YOU THOSE LETTERS? IT WASN'T JUST GRAT-ITUDE. I TRIED TO FALL IN LOVE WITH BOYS. I EVEN THOUGHT I DID, ONCE OR TWICE. BUT I WAS ALREADY IN LOVE--WITH YOU.
THAT'S ENOUGH, NANCY. I'M OLD ENOUGH TO BE YOUR GRANDFATHER. YOU'RE SCARED AND IT'S GOT YOU TALKING CRAZY.

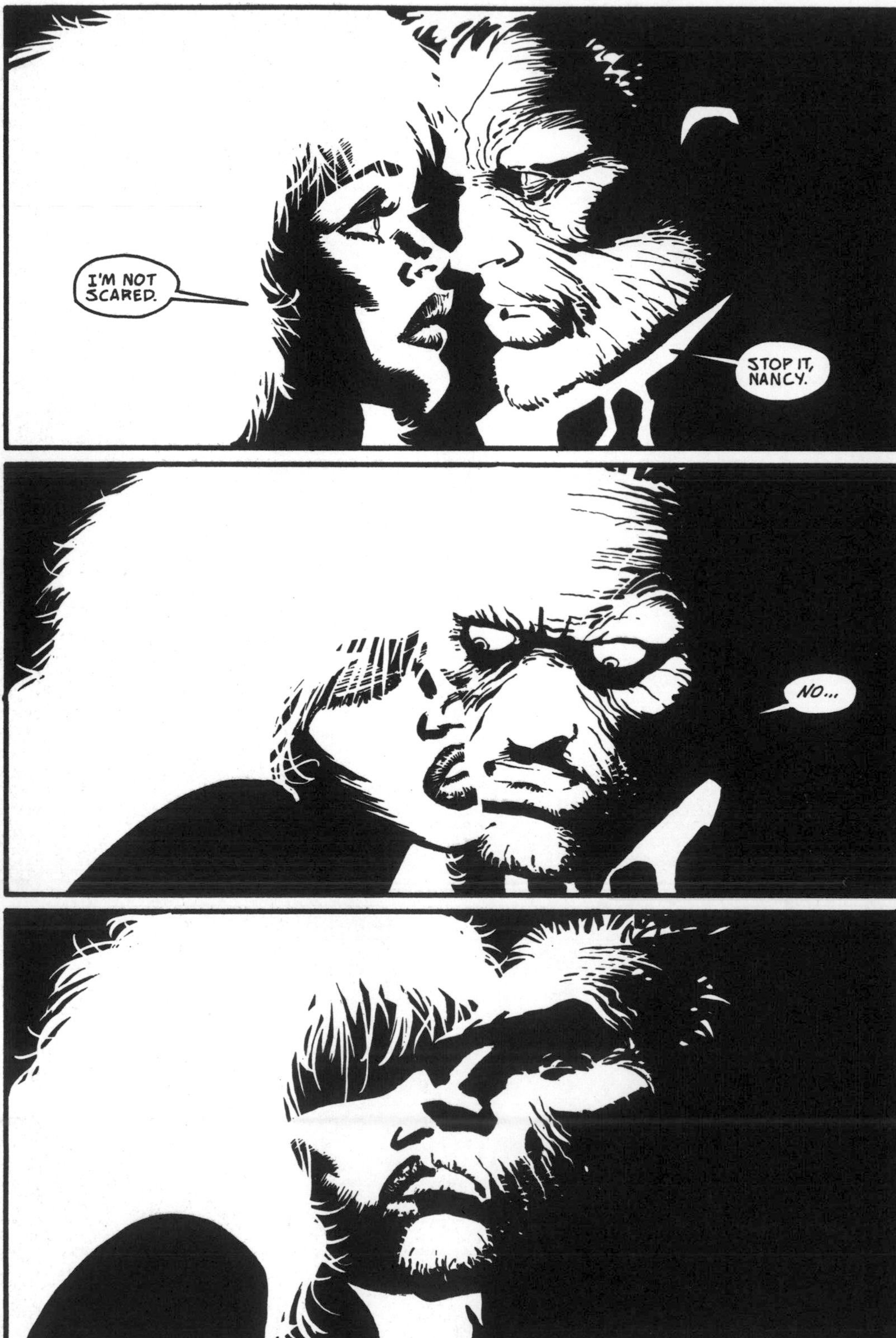
I'M NOT SCARED.
STOP IT, NANCY.
NO...

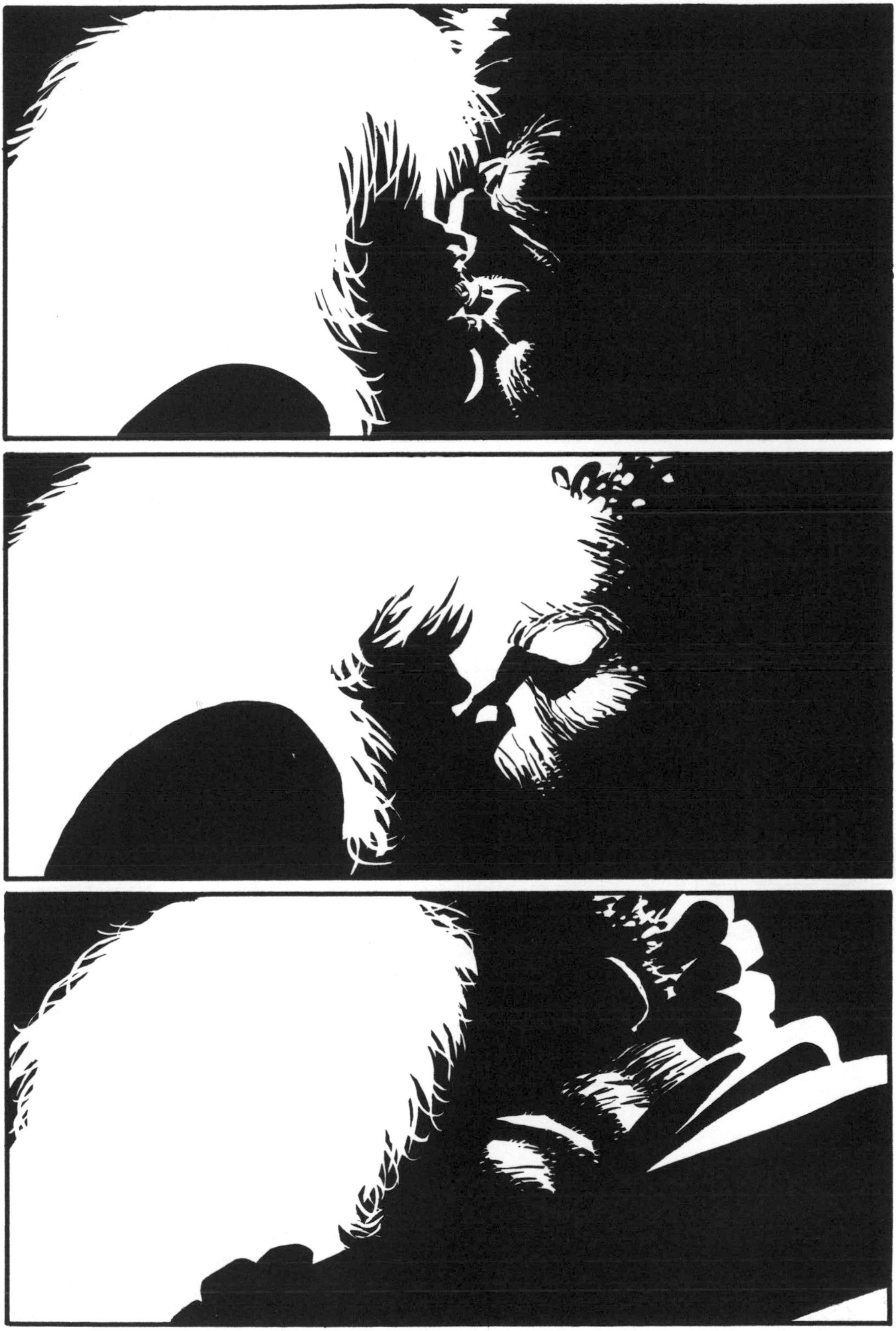

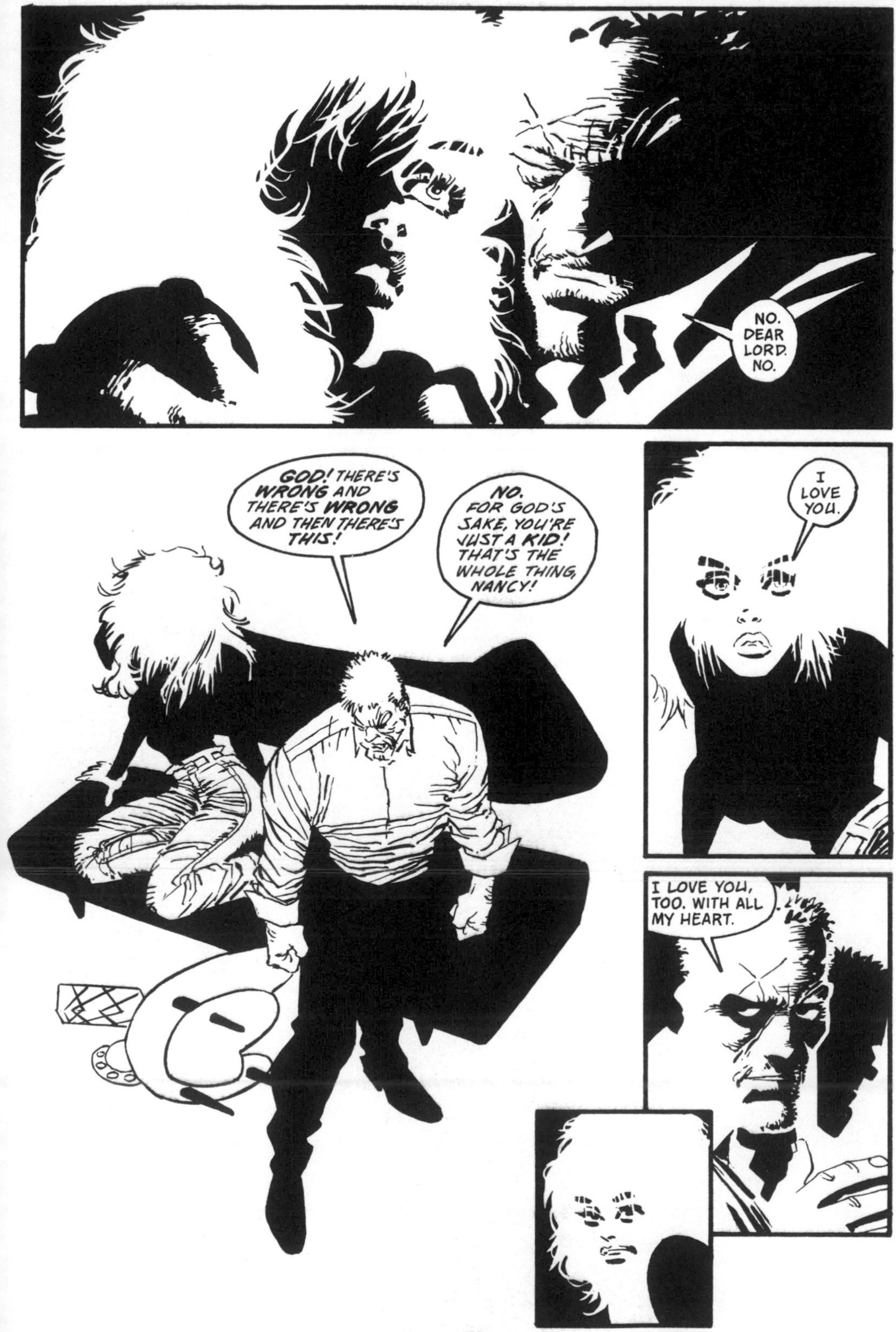
NO. DEAR LORD. NO.
GOD! THERE'S WRONG AND THERE'S WRONG AND THEN THERE'S THIS!
NO. FOR GOD'S SAKE, YOU'RE JUST A KID! THAT'S THE WHOLE THING, NANCY!
I LOVE YOU.
I LOVE YOU, TOO. WITH ALL MY HEART.

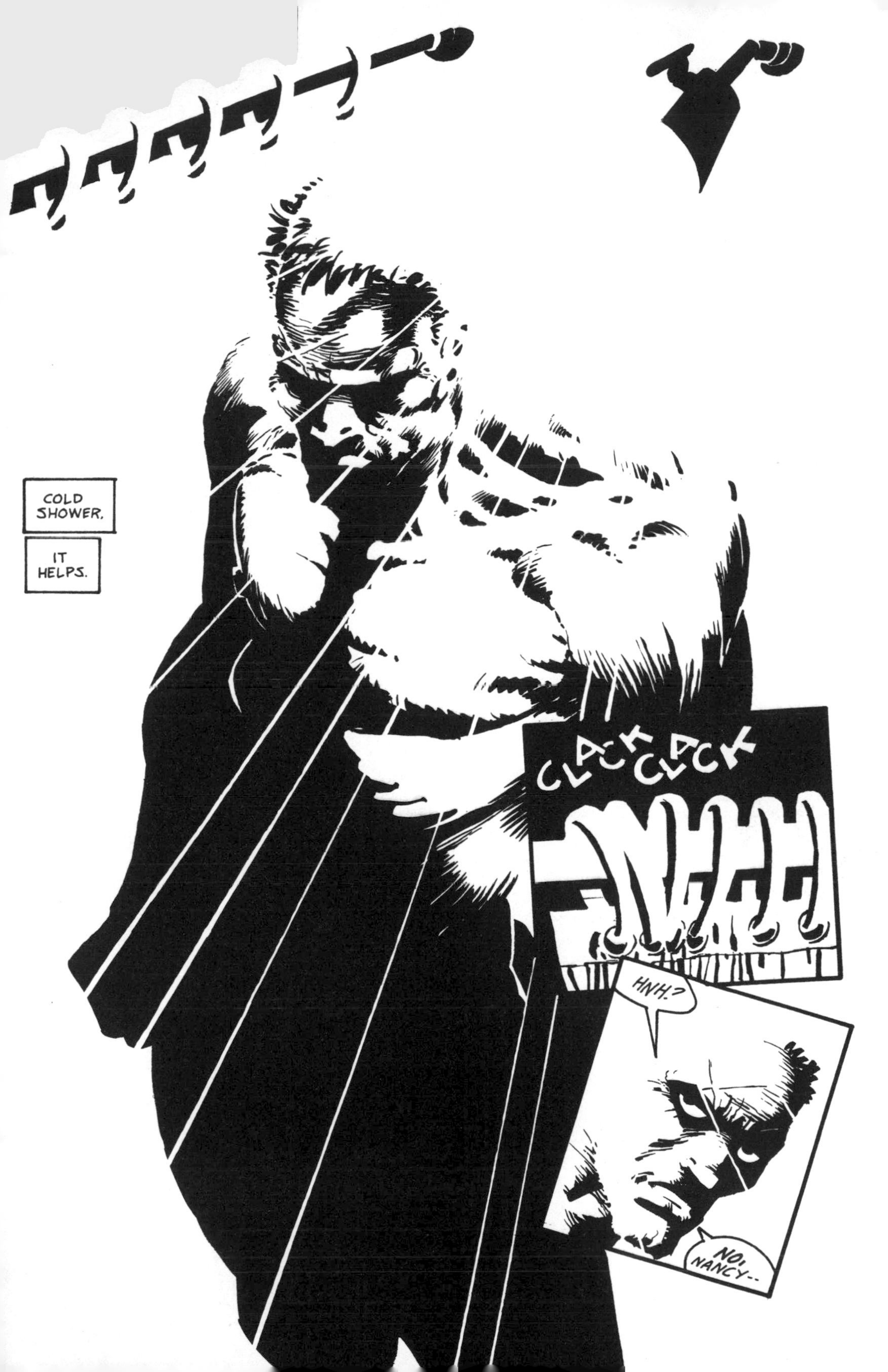
COLD SHOWER.
IT HELPS.
CLACK CLACK
HNH?
NO! NANCY--

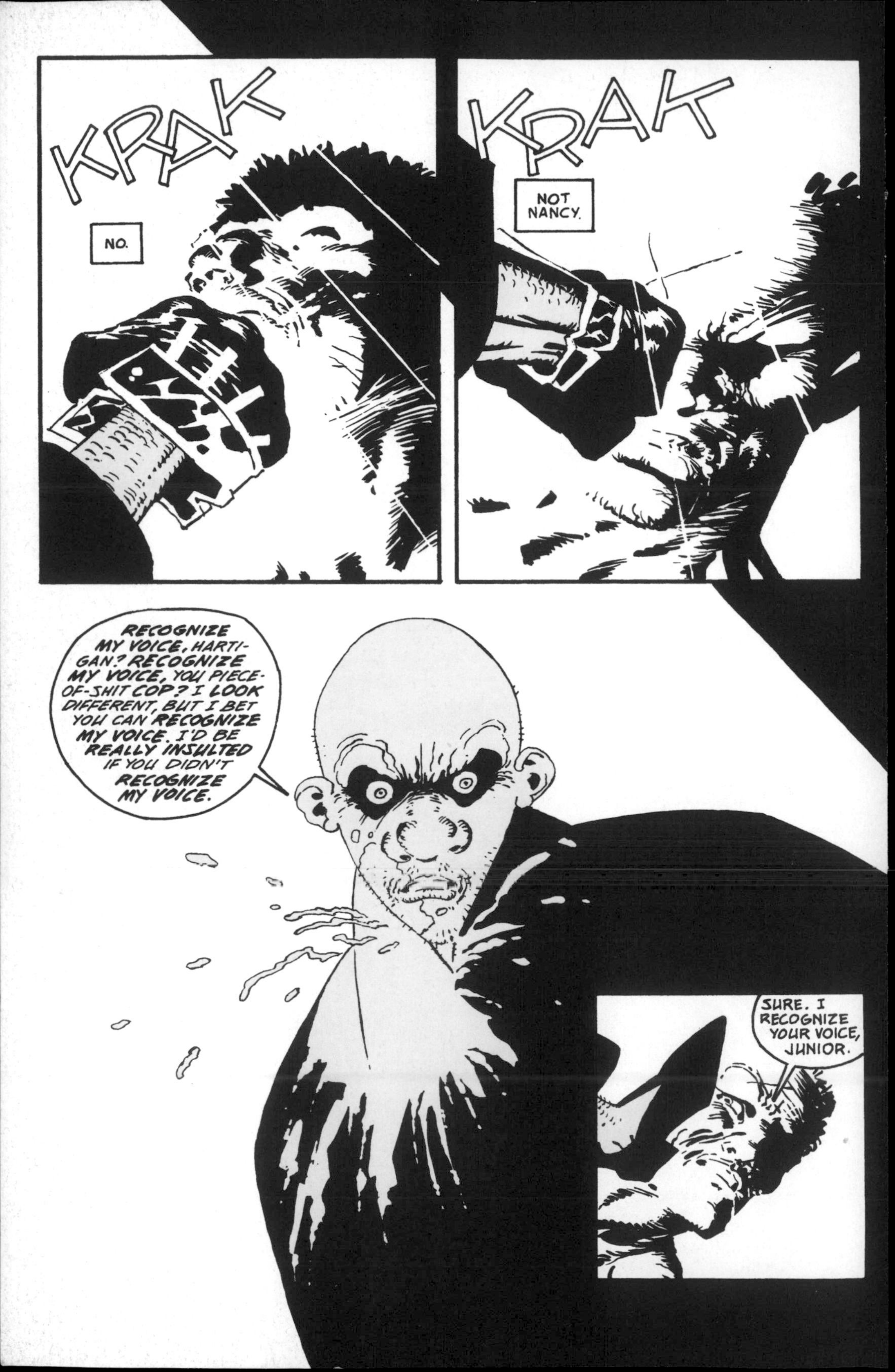
KRAK
NO.
KRAK
NOT NANCY.
RECOGNIZE MY VOICE, HARTIGAN? RECOGNIZE MY VOICE, YOU PIECE-OF-SHIT COP? I LOOK DIFFERENT, BUT I BET YOU CAN RECOGNIZE MY VOICE. I'D BE REALLY INSULTED IF YOU DIDN'T RECOGNIZE MY VOICE.
SURE. I RECOGNIZE YOUR VOICE, JUNIOR.

CHAPTER SIX

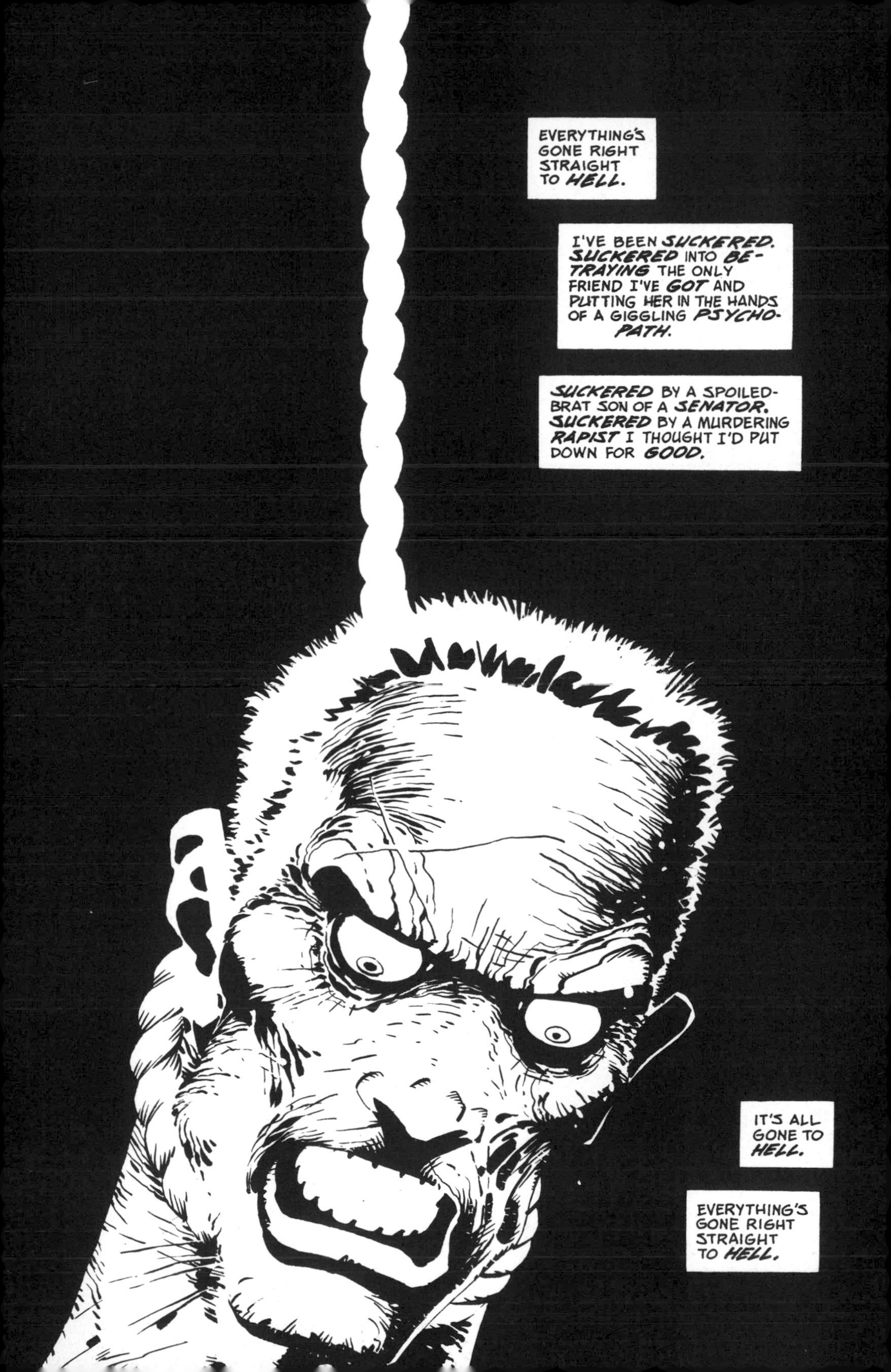
EVERYTHING'S GONE RIGHT STRAIGHT TO HELL.
I'VE BEEN SUCKERED. SUCKERED INTO BETRAYING THE ONLY FRIEND I'VE GOT AND PUTTING HER IN THE HANDS OF A GIGGLING PSYCHOPATH.
SUCKERED BY A SPOILED-BRAT SON OF A SENATOR. SUCKERED BY A MURDERING RAPIST I THOUGHT I'D PUT DOWN FOR GOOD.
IT'S ALL GONE TO HELL.
EVERYTHING'S GONE RIGHT STRAIGHT TO HELL.

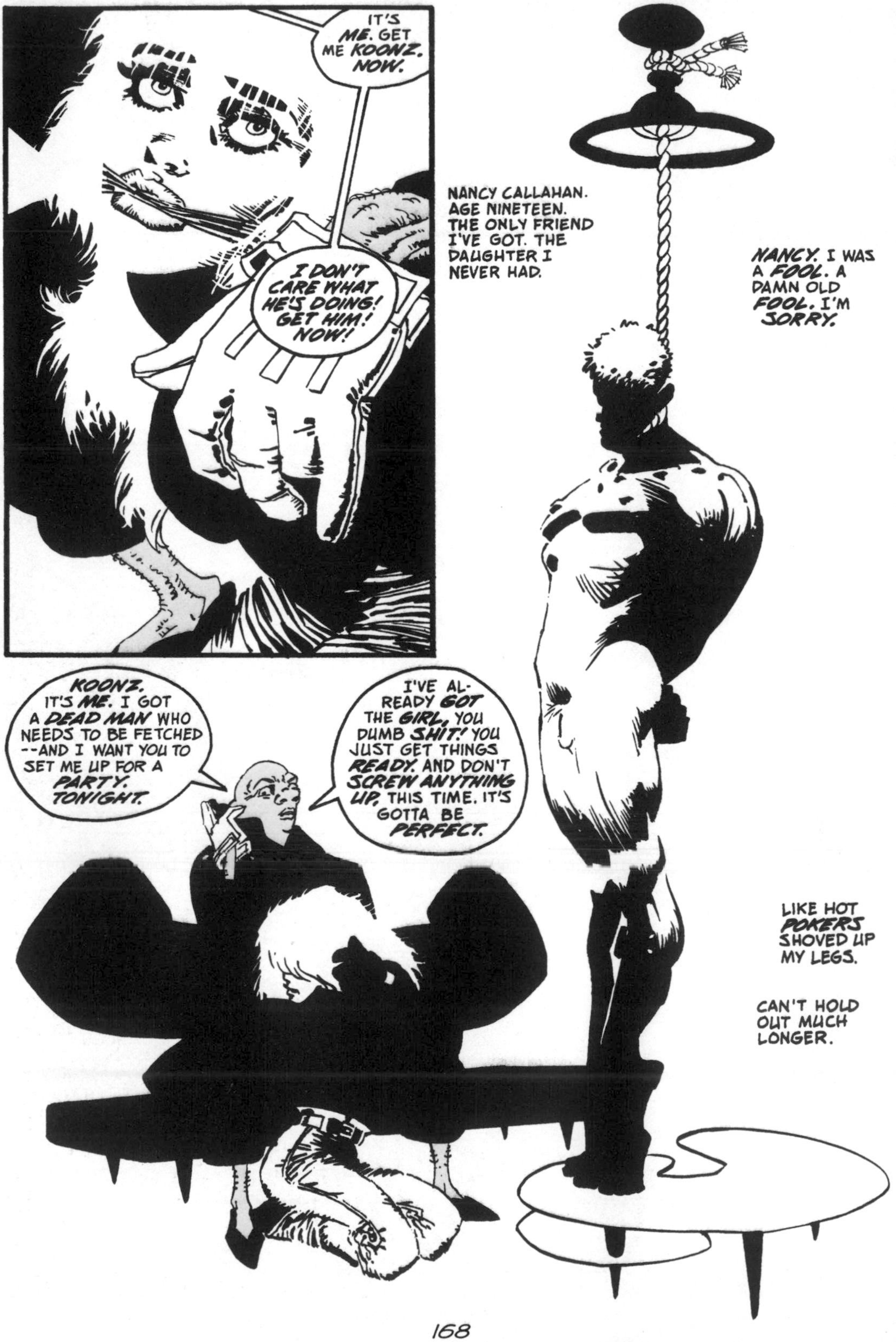
IT'S ME. GET ME KOONZ. NOW.
I DON'T CARE WHAT HE'S DOING! GET HIM! NOW!
NANCY CALLAHAN. AGE NINETEEN. THE ONLY FRIEND I'VE GOT. THE DAUGHTER I NEVER HAD.
NANCY. I WAS A FOOL. A DAMN OLD FOOL. I'M SORRY.
KOONZ. IT'S ME. I GOT A DEAD MAN WHO NEEDS TO BE FETCHED --AND I WANT YOU TO SET ME UP FOR A PARTY. TONIGHT.
I'VE ALREADY GOT THE GIRL, YOU DUMB SHIT! YOU JUST GET THINGS READY. AND DON'T SCREW ANYTHING UP, THIS TIME. IT'S GOTTA BE PERFECT.
LIKE HOT POKERS SHOVED UP MY LEGS.
CAN'T HOLD OUT MUCH LONGER.

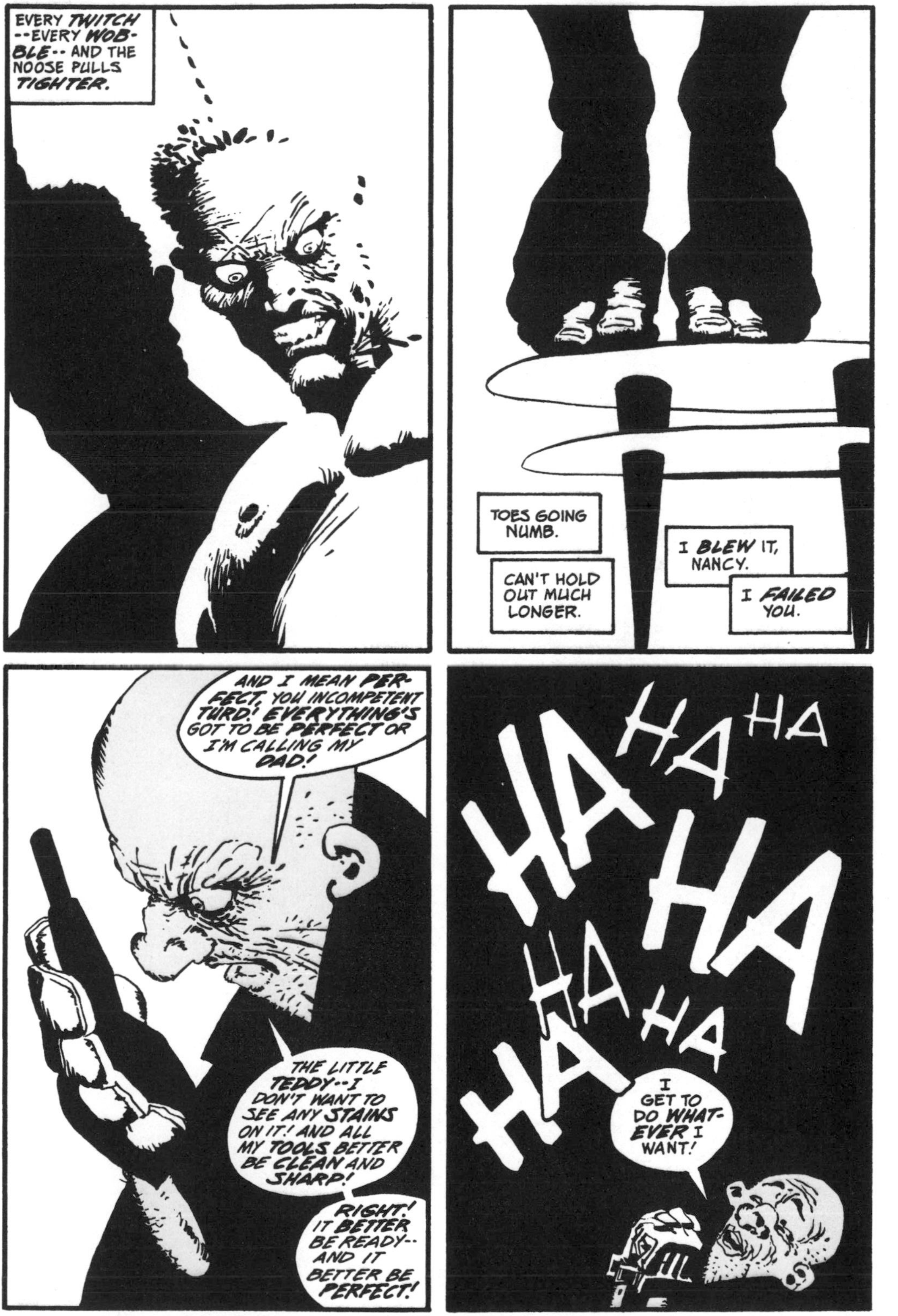
EVERY TWITCH --EVERY WOBBLE-- AND THE NOOSE PULLS TIGHTER.
TOES GOING NUMB.
CAN'T HOLD OUT MUCH LONGER.
I BLEW IT, NANCY.
I FAILED YOU.
AND I MEAN PERFECT, YOU INCOMPETENT TURD! EVERYTHING'S GOT TO BE PERFECT OR I'M CALLING MY DAD!
THE LITTLE TEDDY-- I DON'T WANT TO SEE ANY STAINS ON IT! AND ALL MY TOOLS BETTER BE CLEAN AND SHARP!
RIGHT! IT BETTER BE READY-- AND IT BETTER BE PERFECT!
HA HA HA HA HA HA HA HA
I GET TO DO WHATEVER I WANT!

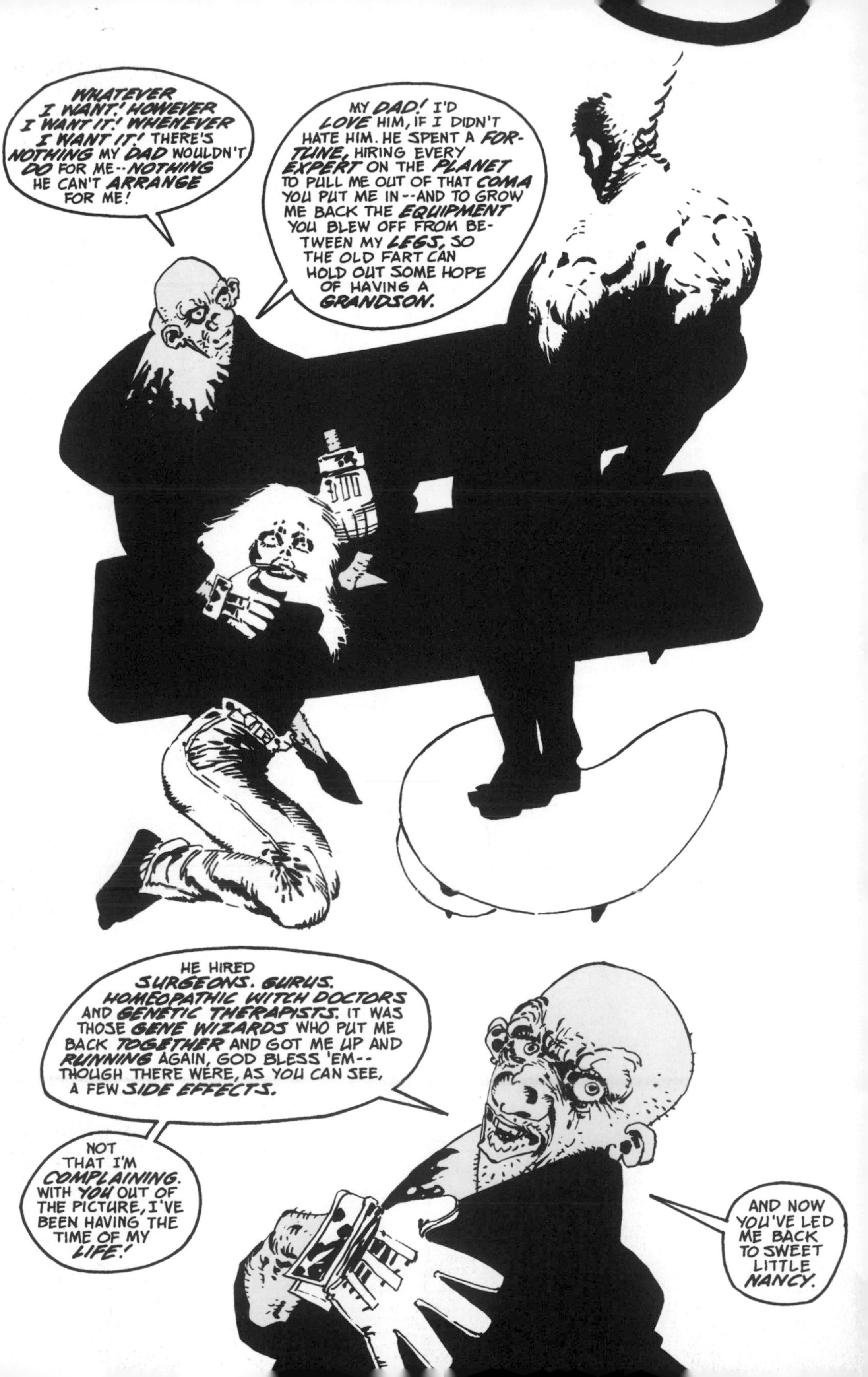
WHATEVER I WANT! HOWEVER I WANT IT! WHENEVER I WANT IT! THERE'S NOTHING MY DAD WOULDN'T DO FOR ME--NOTHING HE CAN'T ARRANGE FOR ME!
MY DAD! I'D LOVE HIM, IF I DIDN'T HATE HIM. HE SPENT A FORTUNE, HIRING EVERY EXPERT ON THE PLANET TO PULL ME OUT OF THAT COMA YOU PUT ME IN--AND TO GROW ME BACK THE EQUIPMENT YOU BLEW OFF FROM BETWEEN MY LEGS, SO THE OLD FART CAN HOLD OUT SOME HOPE OF HAVING A GRANDSON.
HE HIRED SURGEONS. GURUS. HOMEOPATHIC WITCH DOCTORS AND GENETIC THERAPISTS. IT WAS THOSE GENE WIZARDS WHO PUT ME BACK TOGETHER AND GOT ME UP AND RUNNING AGAIN, GOD BLESS 'EM--THOUGH THERE WERE, AS YOU CAN SEE, A FEW SIDE EFFECTS.
NOT THAT I'M COMPLAINING. WITH YOU OUT OF THE PICTURE, I'VE BEEN HAVING THE TIME OF MY LIFE!
AND NOW YOU'VE LED ME BACK TO SWEET LITTLE NANCY.

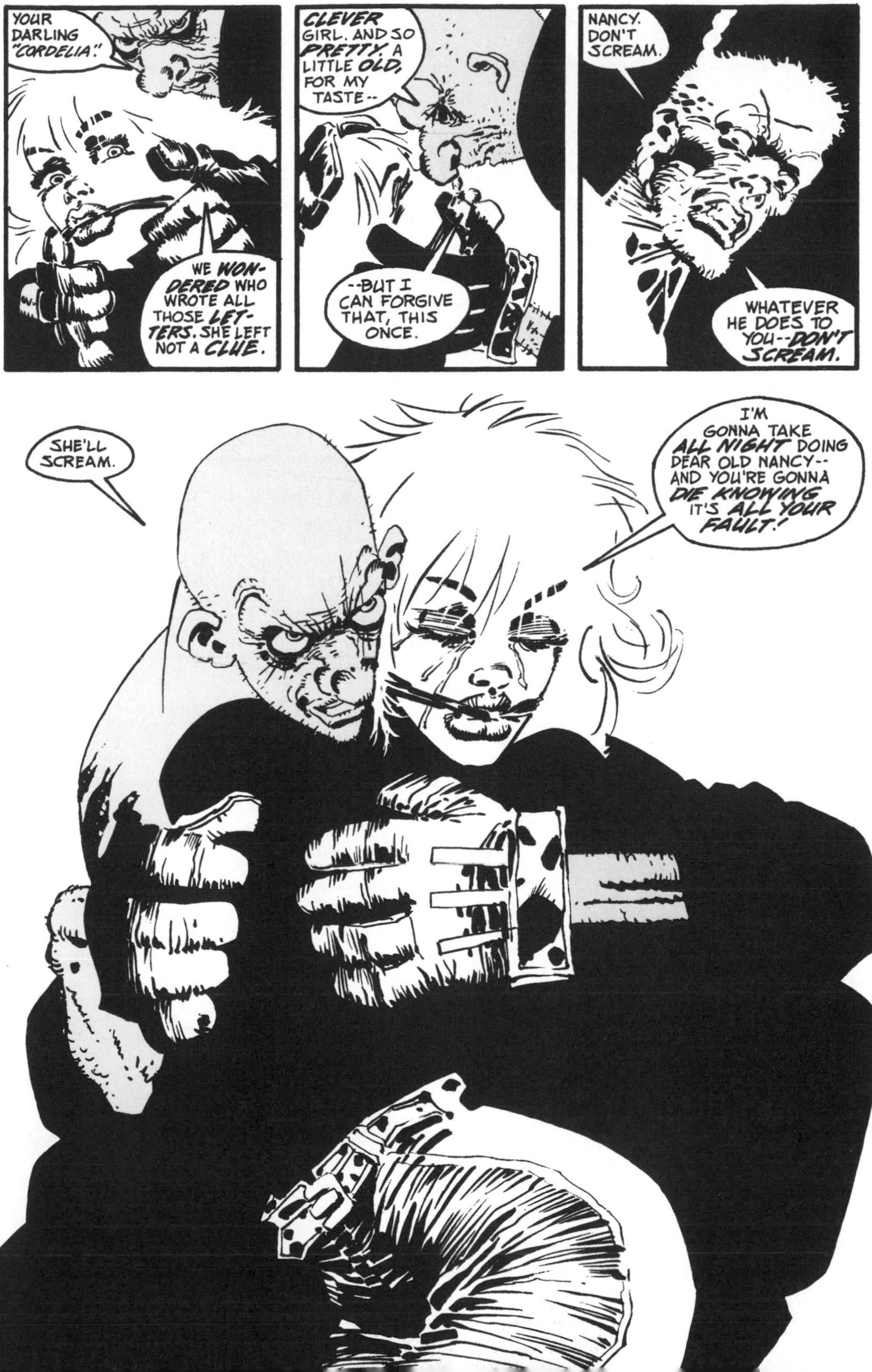
YOUR DARLING "CORDELIA."
WE WONDERED WHO WROTE ALL THOSE LETTERS. SHE LEFT NOT A CLUE.
CLEVER GIRL. AND SO PRETTY. A LITTLE OLD, FOR MY TASTE--
--BUT I CAN FORGIVE THAT, THIS ONCE.
NANCY. DON'T SCREAM.
WHATEVER HE DOES TO YOU--DON'T SCREAM.
SHE'LL SCREAM.
I'M GONNA TAKE ALL NIGHT DOING DEAR OLD NANCY-- AND YOU'RE GONNA DIE KNOWING IT'S ALL YOUR FAULT!

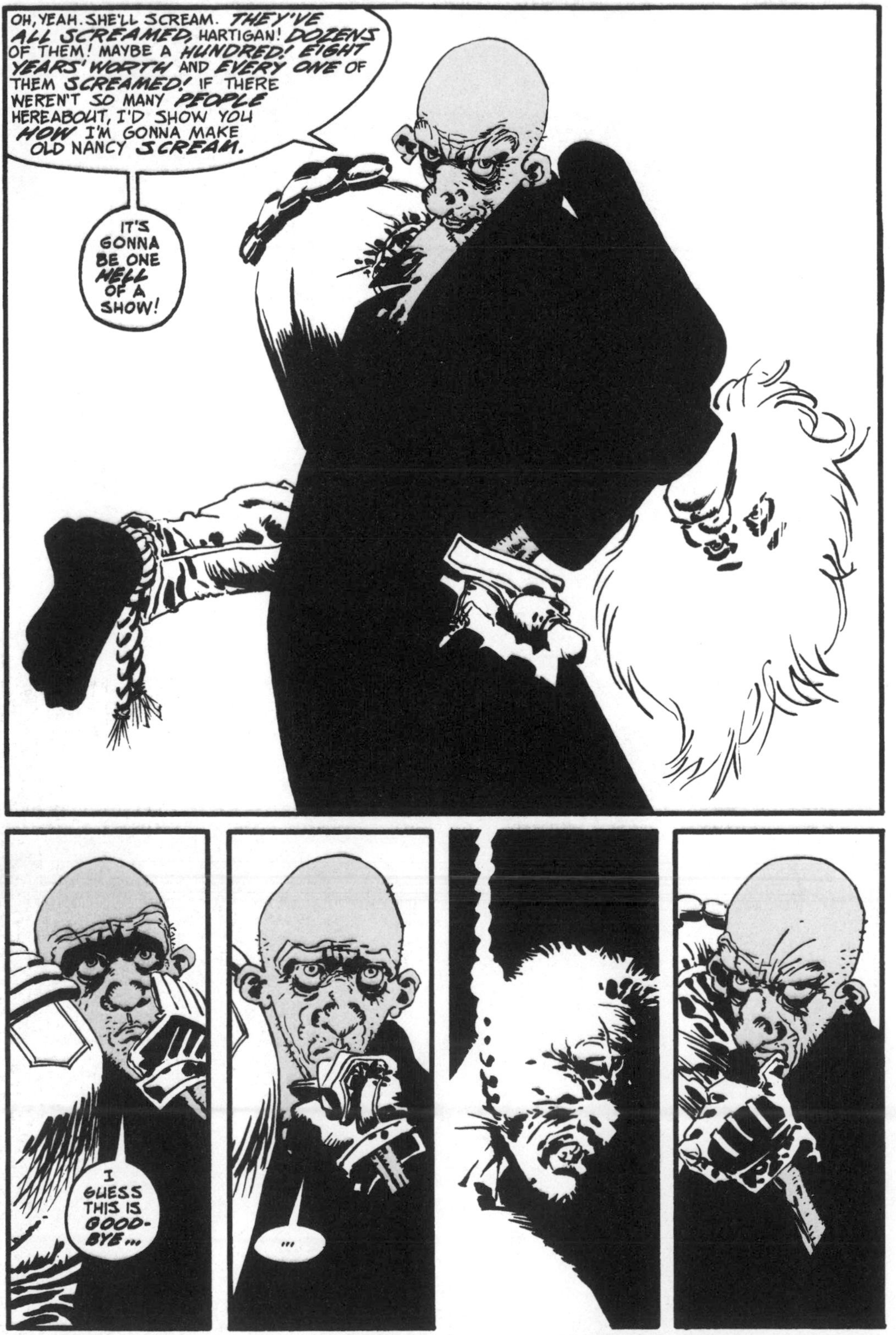
OH, YEAH. SHE'LL SCREAM. THEY'VE ALL SCREAMED, HARTIGAN! DOZENS OF THEM! MAYBE A HUNDRED! EIGHT YEARS' WORTH AND EVERY ONE OF THEM SCREAMED! IF THERE WEREN'T SO MANY PEOPLE HEREABOUT, I'D SHOW YOU HOW I'M GONNA MAKE OLD NANCY SCREAM.
IT'S GONNA BE ONE HELL OF A SHOW!
I GUESS THIS IS GOOD-BYE...
...

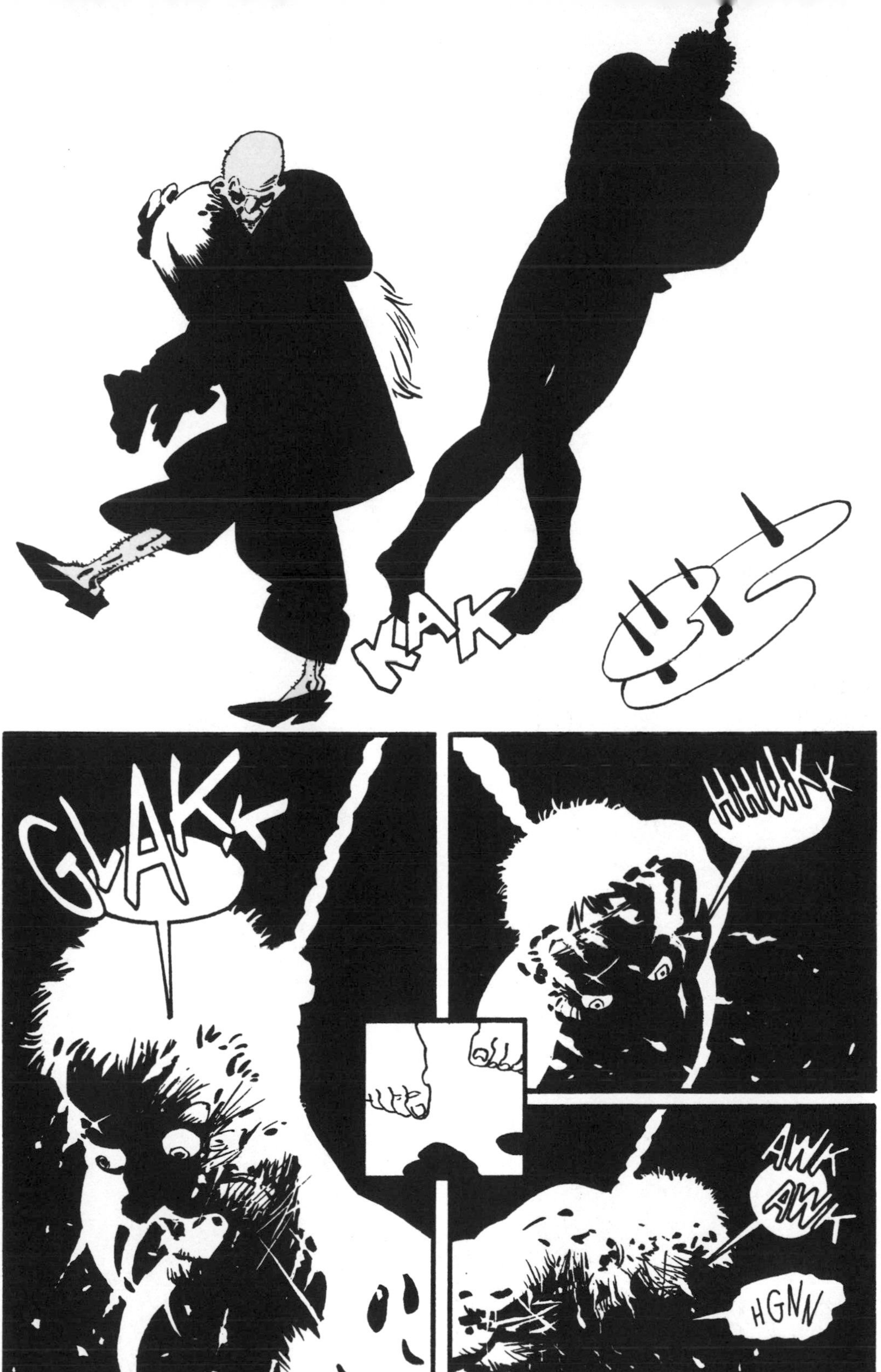
KAK
GLAK
HNK
AWK
AWK
HGNN

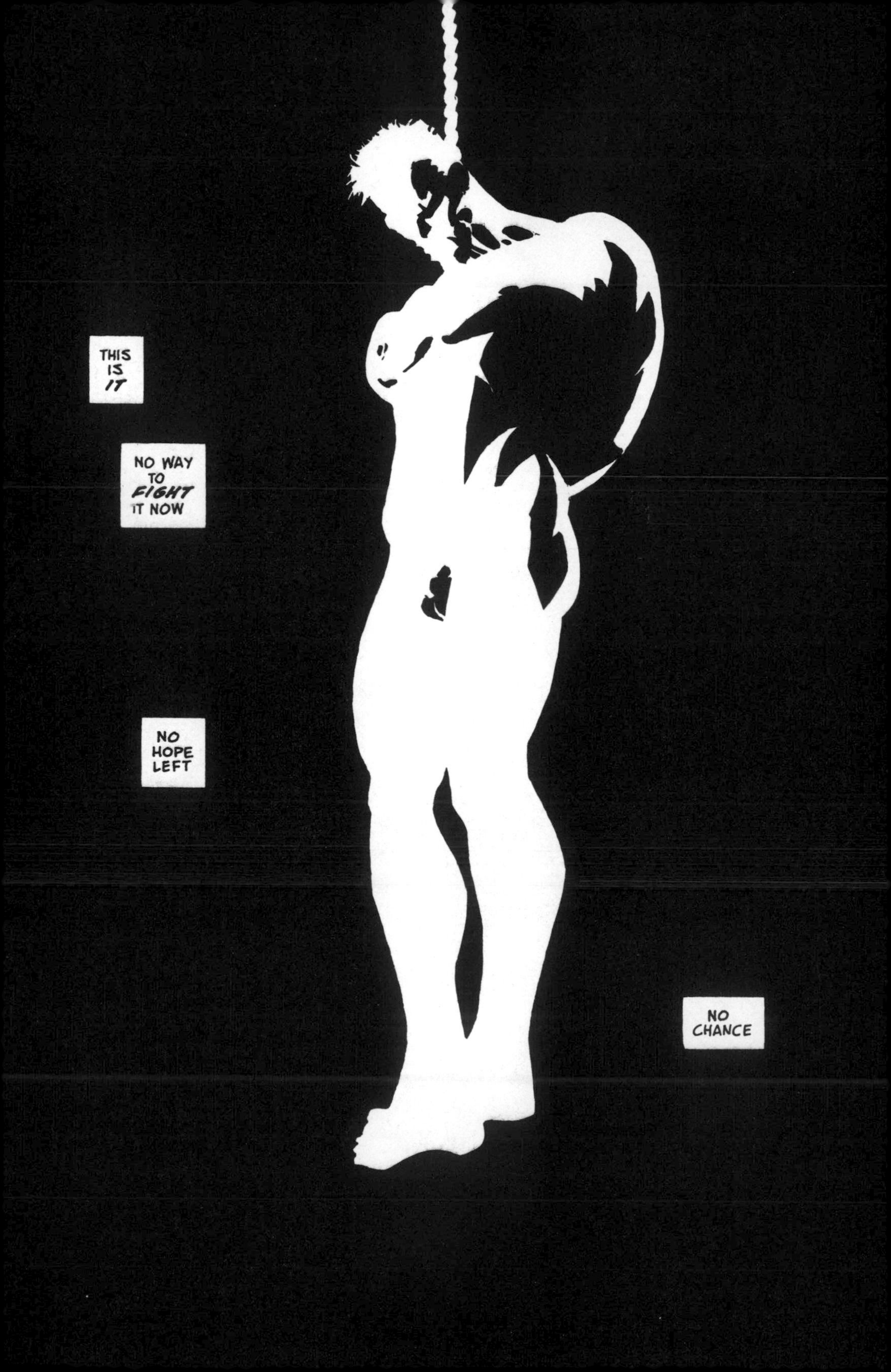
THIS IS *IT*
NO WAY TO *FIGHT* IT NOW
NO HOPE LEFT
NO CHANCE

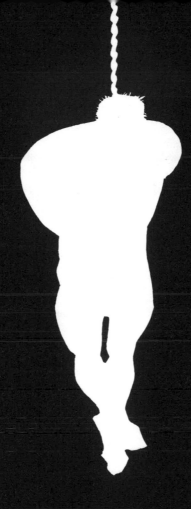

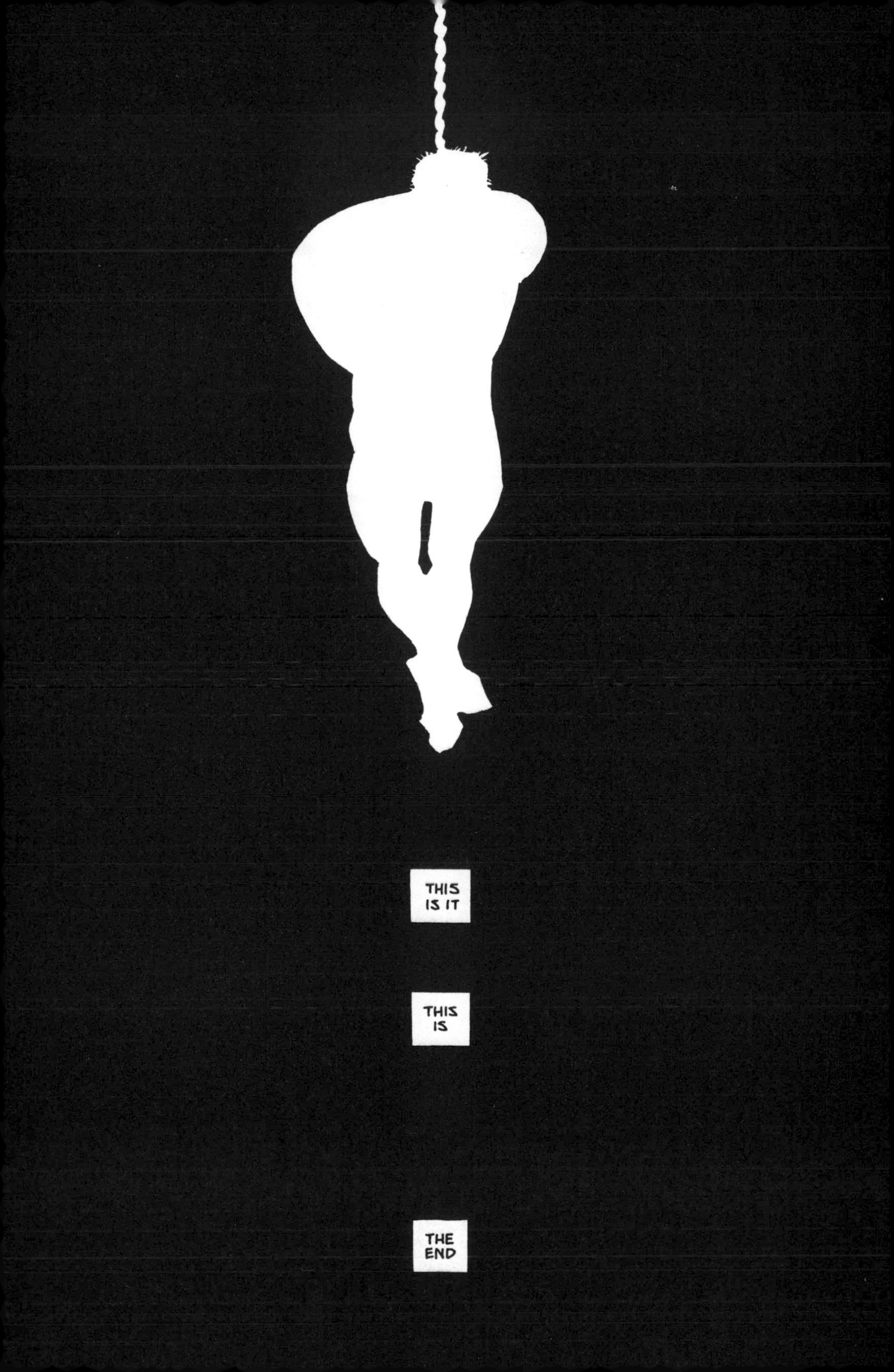

THIS
IS IT

THIS
IS

THE
END

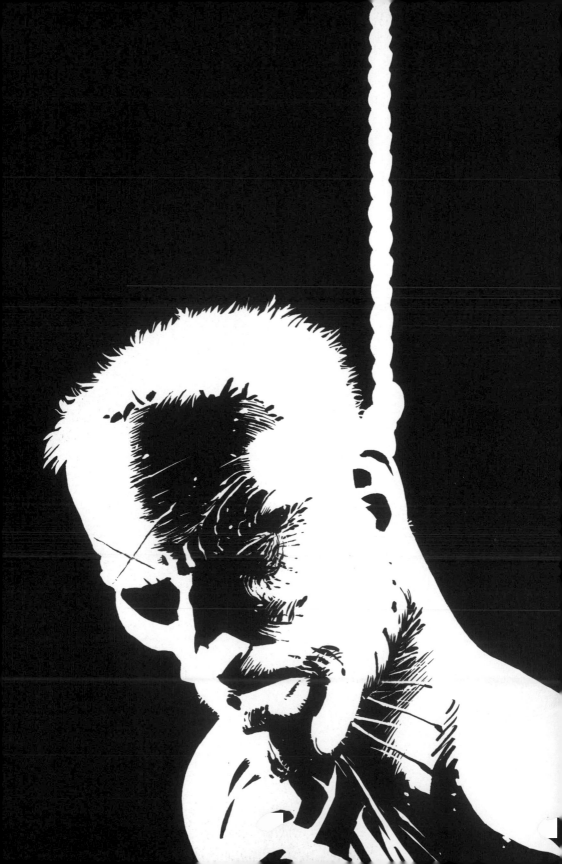

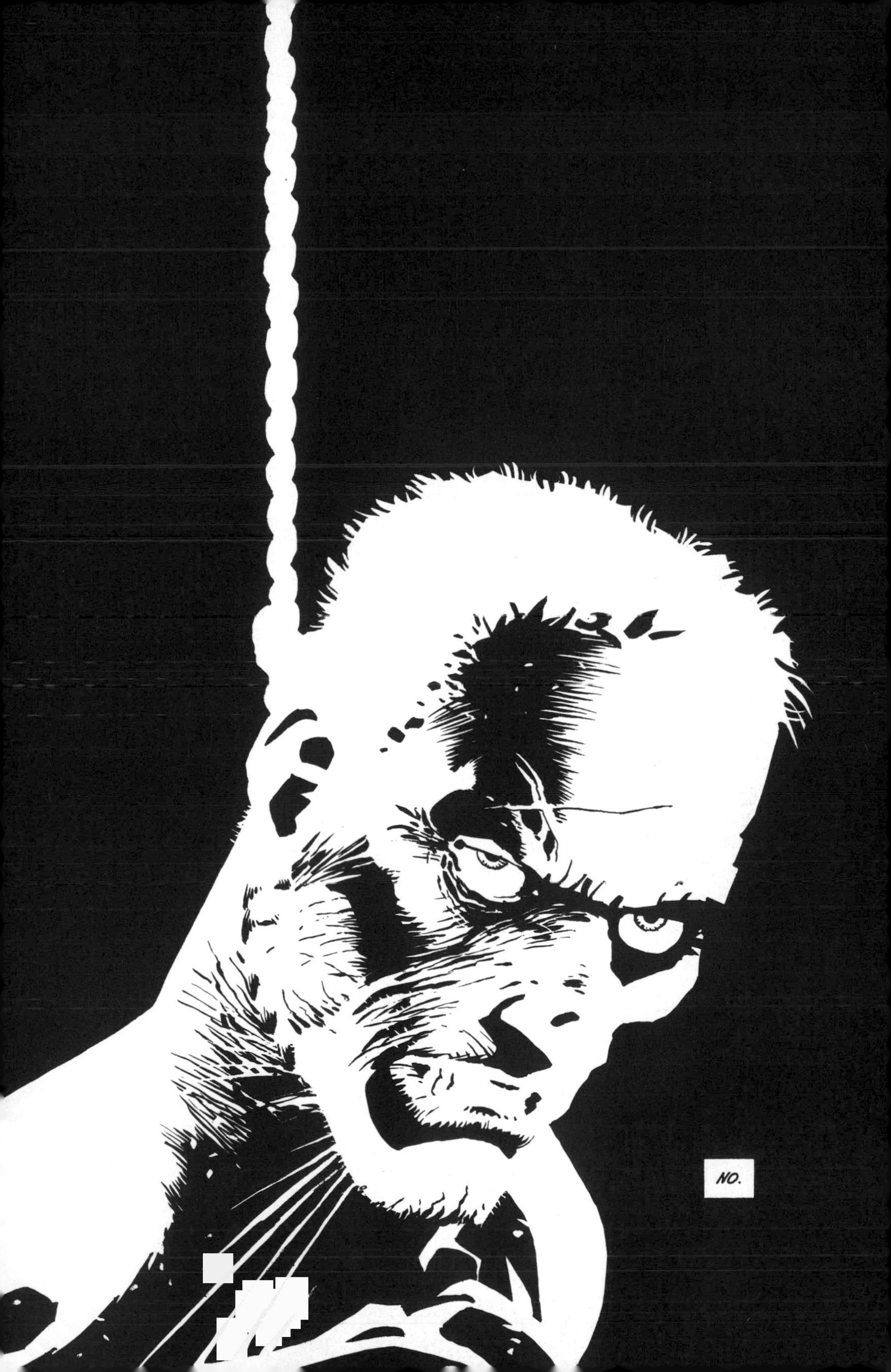
NO.

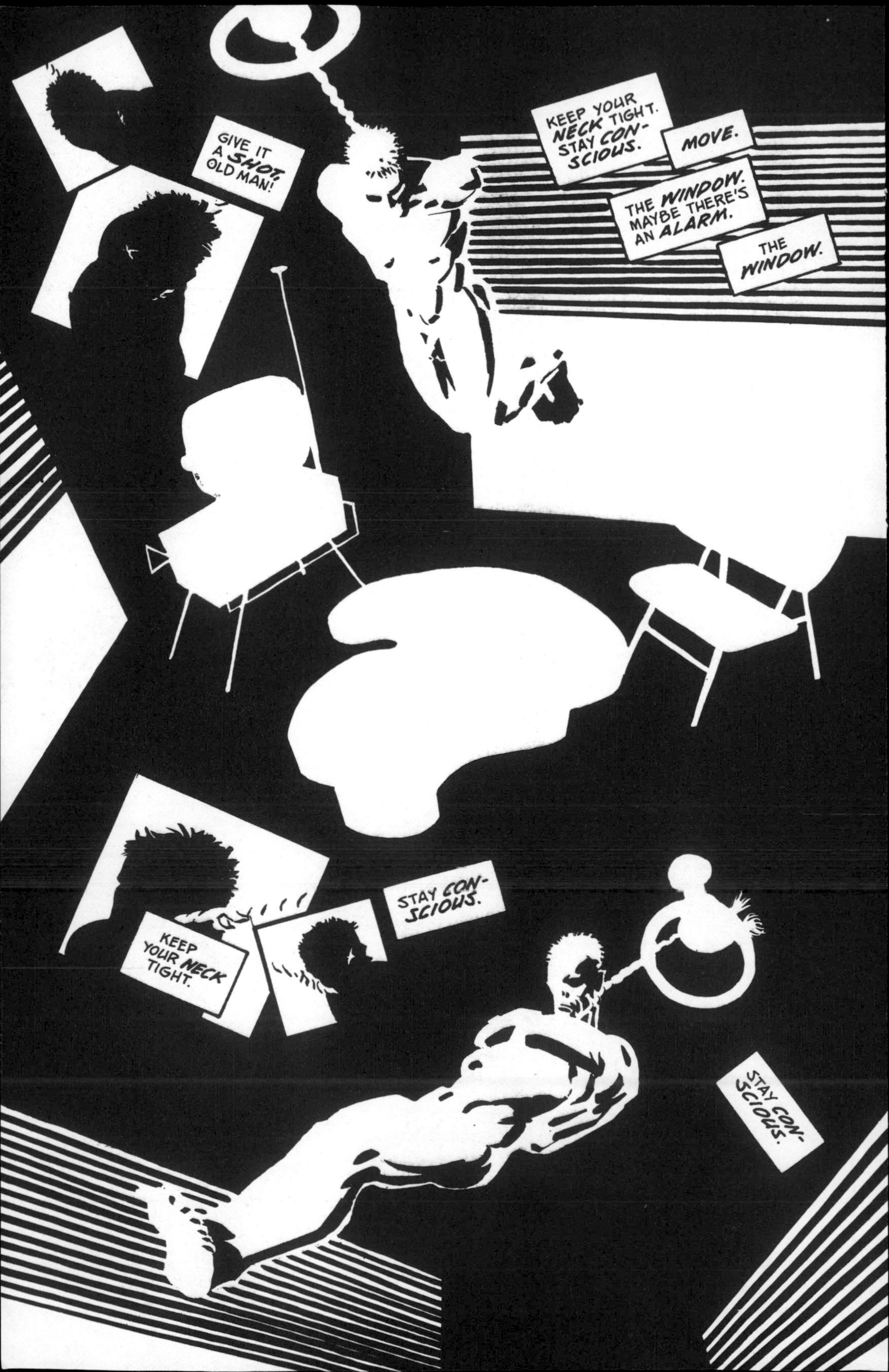
GIVE IT A SHOT, OLD MAN!
KEEP YOUR NECK TIGHT. STAY CON-SCIOUS.
MOVE.
THE WINDOW. MAYBE THERE'S AN ALARM.
THE WINDOW.
KEEP YOUR NECK TIGHT.
STAY CON-SCIOUS.
STAY CON-SCIOUS.

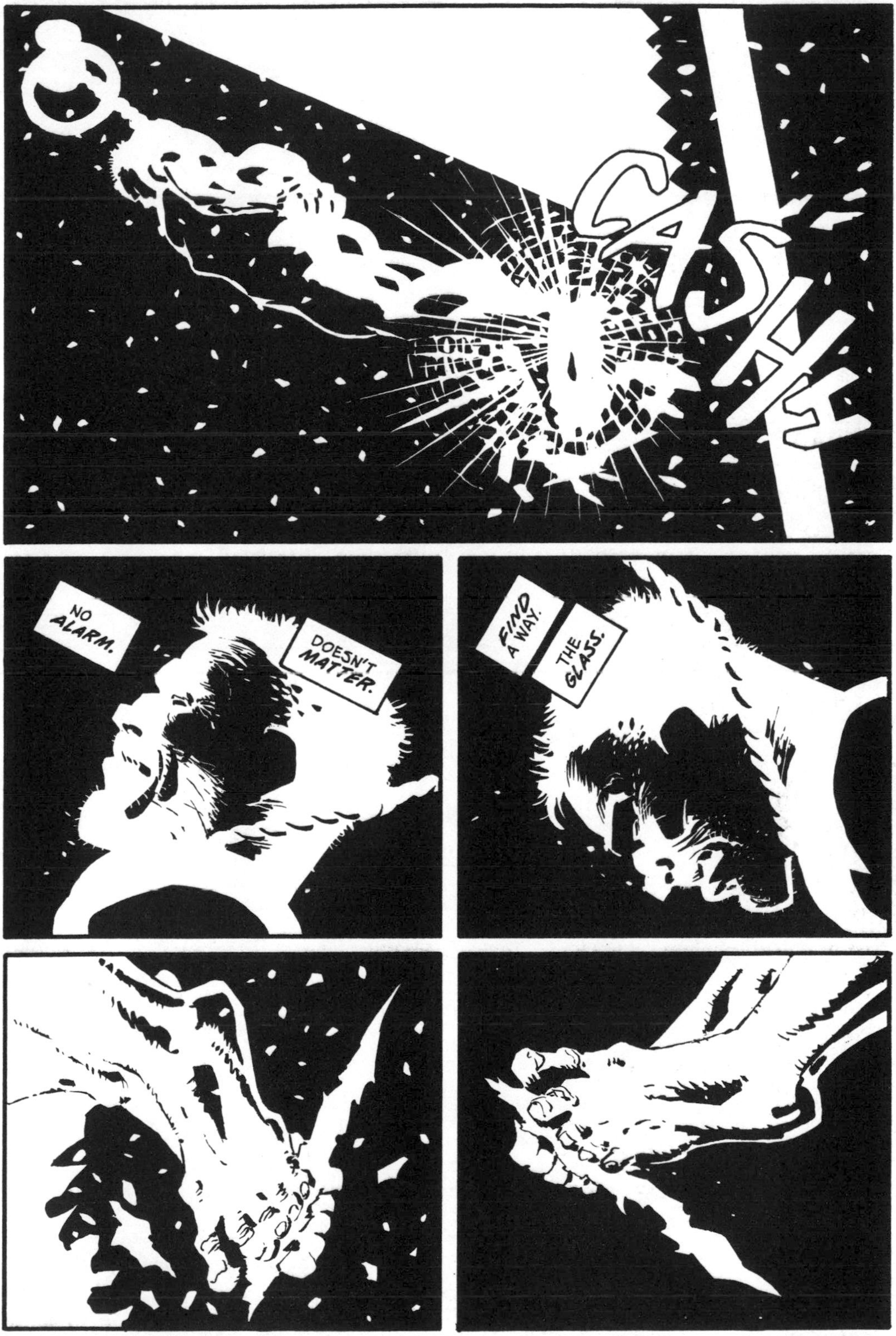
CASHH
NO ALARM.
DOESN'T MATTER.
FIND A WAY.
THE GLASS.

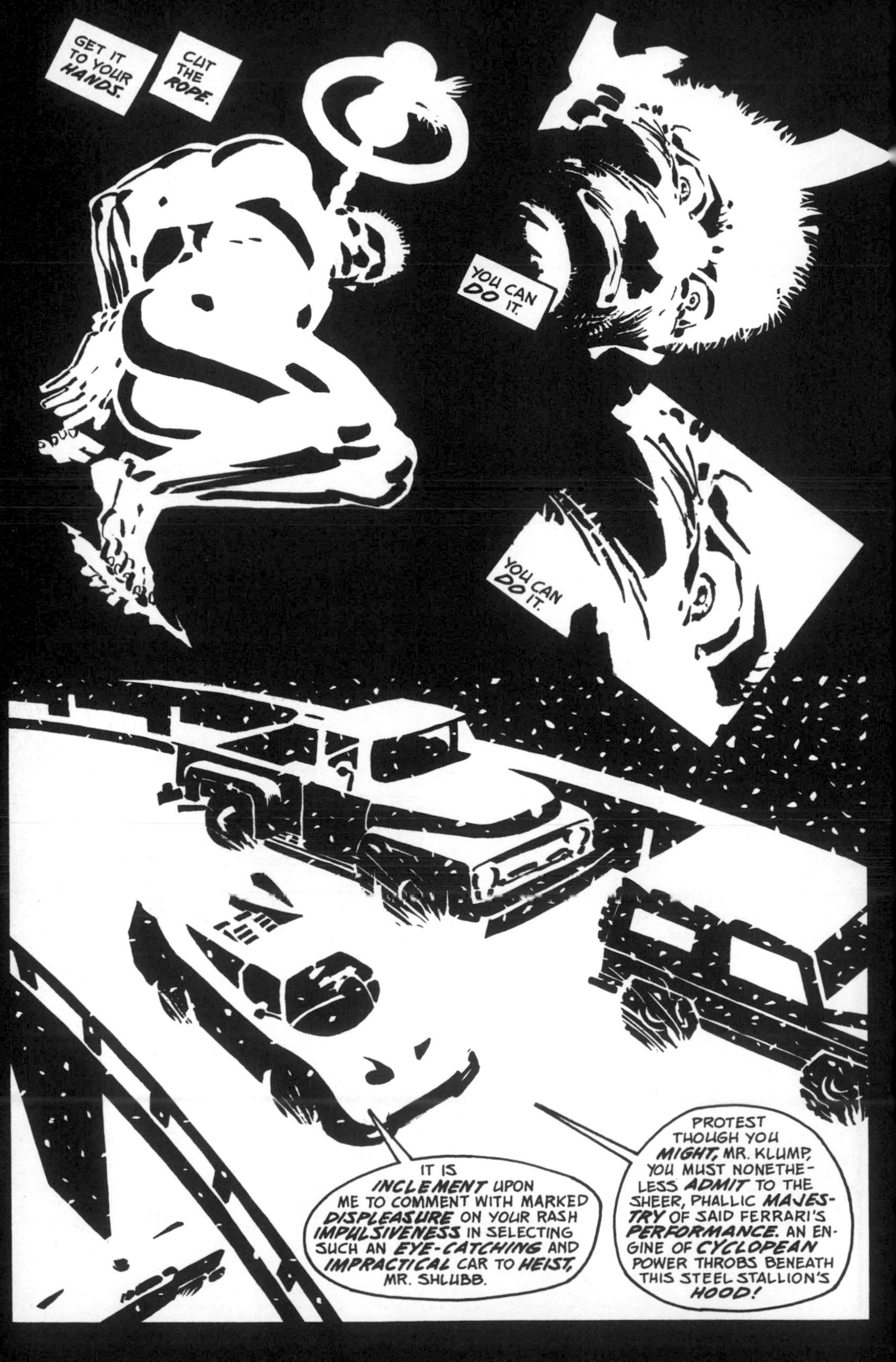
GET IT TO YOUR HANDS.
CUT THE ROPE.
YOU CAN DO IT.
YOU CAN DO IT.
IT IS INCLEMENT UPON ME TO COMMENT WITH MARKED DISPLEASURE ON YOUR RASH IMPULSIVENESS IN SELECTING SUCH AN EYE-CATCHING AND IMPRACTICAL CAR TO HEIST, MR. SHLUBB.
PROTEST THOUGH YOU MIGHT, MR. KLUMP, YOU MUST NONETHE-LESS ADMIT TO THE SHEER, PHALLIC MAJES-TRY OF SAID FERRARI'S PERFORMANCE. AN EN-GINE OF CYCLOPEAN POWER THROBS BENEATH THIS STEEL STALLION'S HOOD!

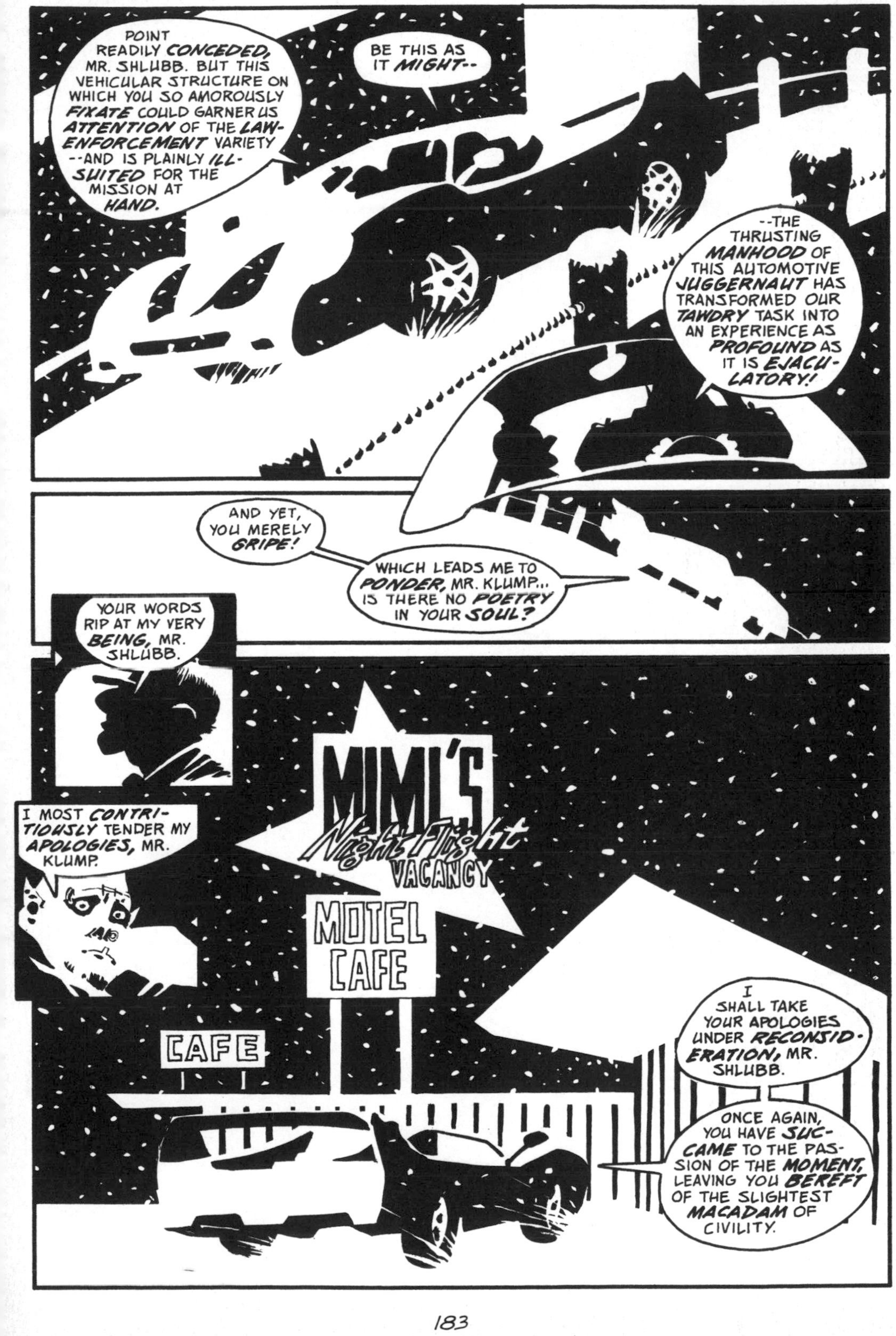
POINT READILY CONCEDED, MR. SHLUBB. BUT THIS VEHICULAR STRUCTURE ON WHICH YOU SO AMOROUSLY FIXATE COULD GARNER US ATTENTION OF THE LAW-ENFORCEMENT VARIETY --AND IS PLAINLY ILL-SUITED FOR THE MISSION AT HAND.
BE THIS AS IT MIGHT--
--THE THRUSTING MANHOOD OF THIS AUTOMOTIVE JUGGERNAUT HAS TRANSFORMED OUR TAWDRY TASK INTO AN EXPERIENCE AS PROFOUND AS IT IS EJACULATORY!
AND YET, YOU MERELY GRIPE!
WHICH LEADS ME TO PONDER, MR. KLUMP... IS THERE NO POETRY IN YOUR SOUL?
YOUR WORDS RIP AT MY VERY BEING, MR. SHLUBB.
I MOST CONTRITIOUSLY TENDER MY APOLOGIES, MR. KLUMP.
MIMI'S
Night Flight
VACANCY
MOTEL
CAFE
CAFE
I SHALL TAKE YOUR APOLOGIES UNDER RECONSIDERATION, MR. SHLUBB.
ONCE AGAIN, YOU HAVE SUCCAME TO THE PASSION OF THE MOMENT, LEAVING YOU BEREFT OF THE SLIGHTEST MACADAM OF CIVILITY.

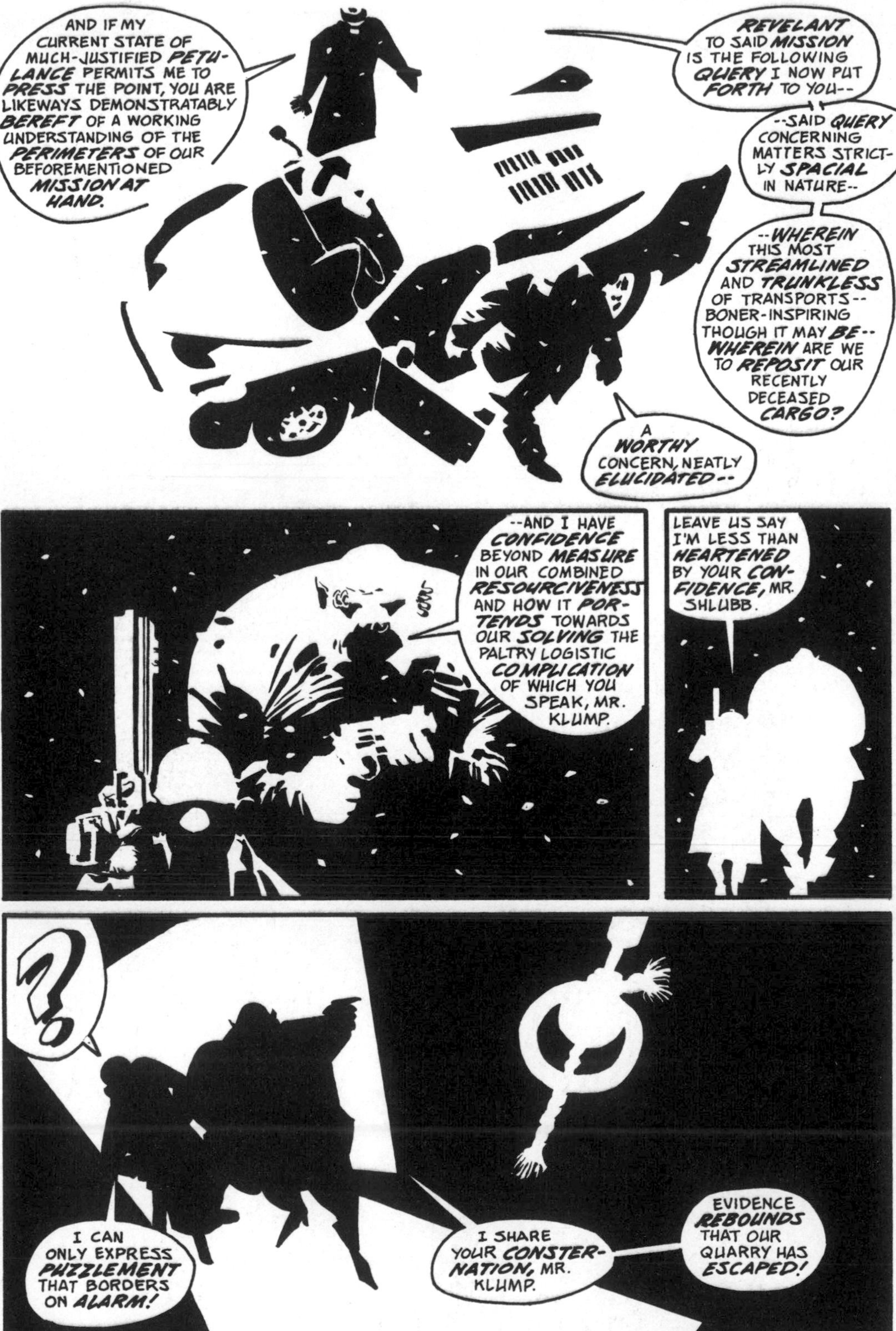
AND IF MY CURRENT STATE OF MUCH-JUSTIFIED PETULANCE PERMITS ME TO PRESS THE POINT, YOU ARE LIKEWAYS DEMONSTRATABLY BEREFT OF A WORKING UNDERSTANDING OF THE PERIMETERS OF OUR BEFOREMENTIONED MISSION AT HAND.
REVELANT TO SAID MISSION IS THE FOLLOWING QUERY I NOW PUT FORTH TO YOU--
--SAID QUERY CONCERNING MATTERS STRICTLY SPACIAL IN NATURE--
--WHEREIN THIS MOST STREAMLINED AND TRUNKLESS OF TRANSPORTS--BONER-INSPIRING THOUGH IT MAY BE--WHEREIN ARE WE TO REPOSIT OUR RECENTLY DECEASED CARGO?
A WORTHY CONCERN, NEATLY ELUCIDATED--
--AND I HAVE CONFIDENCE BEYOND MEASURE IN OUR COMBINED RESOURCIVENESS AND HOW IT PORTENDS TOWARDS OUR SOLVING THE PALTRY LOGISTIC COMPLICATION OF WHICH YOU SPEAK, MR. KLUMP.
LEAVE US SAY I'M LESS THAN HEARTENED BY YOUR CONFIDENCE, MR. SHLUBB.
?
I CAN ONLY EXPRESS PUZZLEMENT THAT BORDERS ON ALARM!
I SHARE YOUR CONSTERNATION, MR. KLUMP.
EVIDENCE REBOUNDS THAT OUR QUARRY HAS ESCAPED!

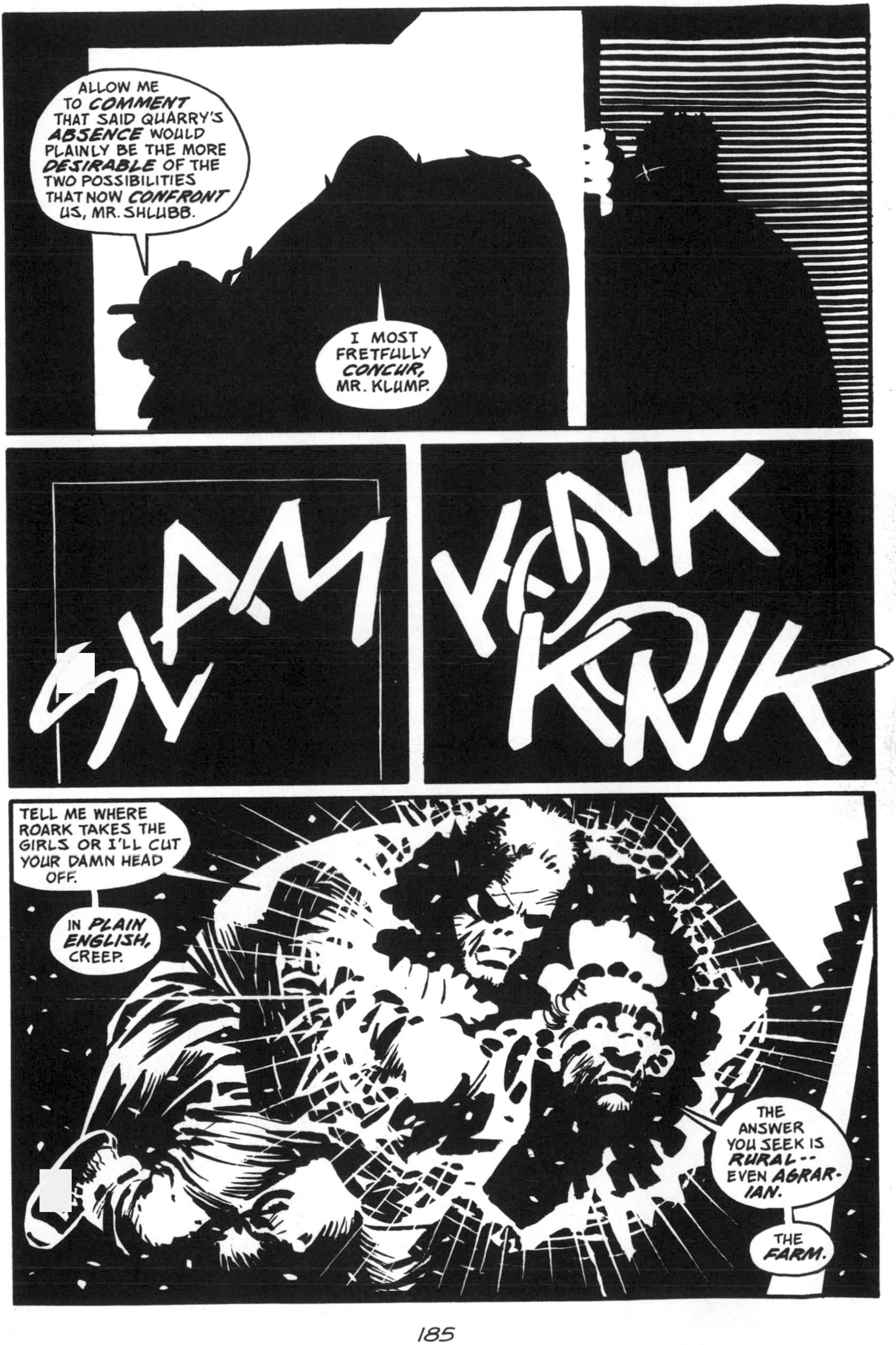

ALLOW ME TO COMMENT THAT SAID QUARRY'S ABSENCE WOULD PLAINLY BE THE MORE DESIRABLE OF THE TWO POSSIBILITIES THAT NOW CONFRONT US, MR. SHLUBB.
I MOST FRETFULLY CONCUR, MR. KLUMP.
SLAM
KONK
KONK
TELL ME WHERE ROARK TAKES THE GIRLS OR I'LL CUT YOUR DAMN HEAD OFF.
IN PLAIN ENGLISH, CREEP.
THE ANSWER YOU SEEK IS RURAL -- EVEN AGRARIAN.
THE FARM.

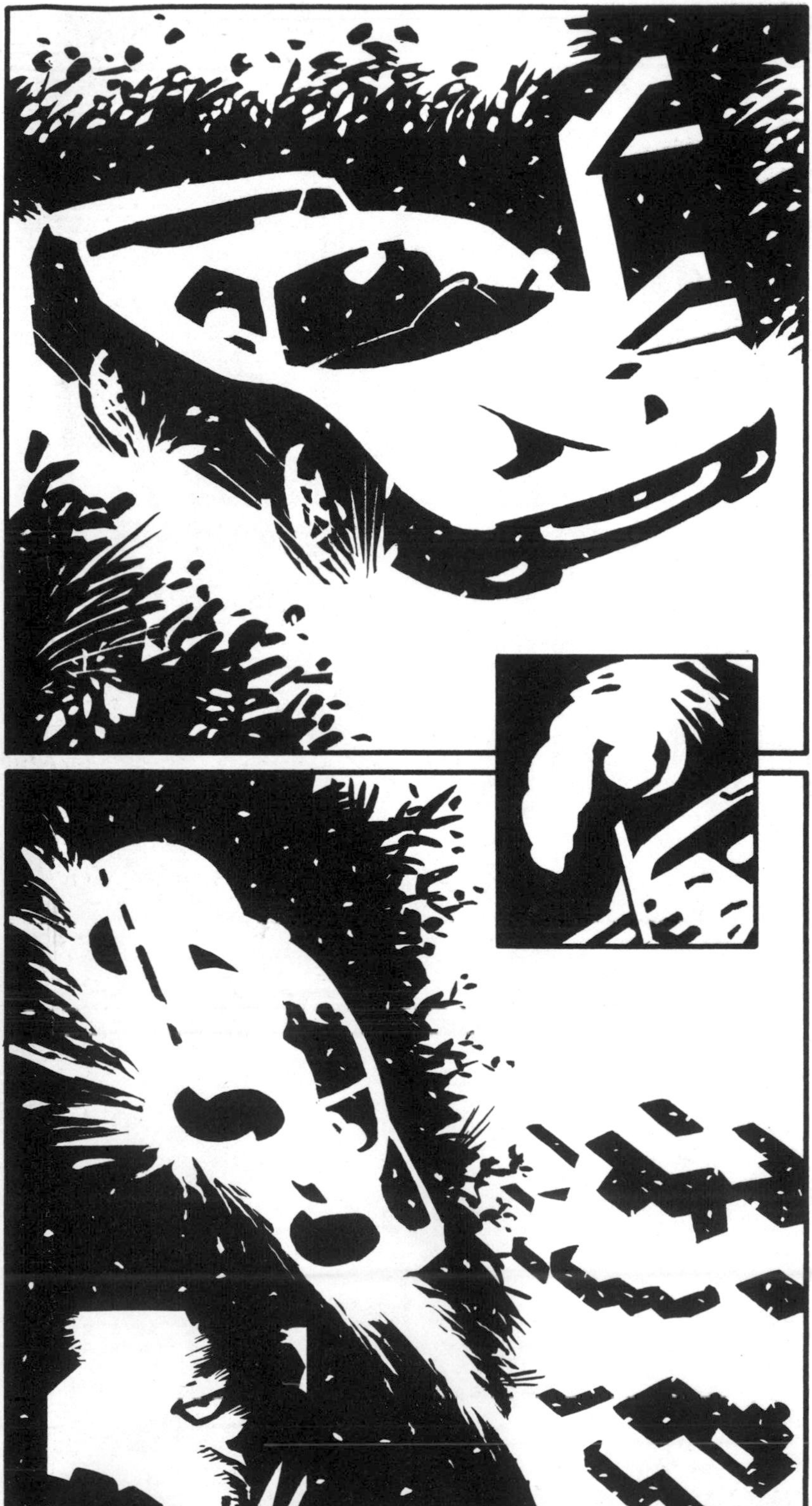

THE *FARM*. THAT'S ALL I NEED TO HEAR. EVERY COP ON THE *FORCE* KNOWS ABOUT THE ROARK FAMILY'S *FARM* -- AND TO STAY *AWAY* FROM IT.

I STICK TO THE SIDE ROADS, LIKE ANY EX-CON DRIVING A STOLEN CAR WOULD.

NO WONDER SO MANY OLD MEN GO FOR SPORTS CARS. THE FERRARI HANDLES LIKE A GIFT FROM HEAVEN. MAKES ME FEEL LIKE I'M TWENTY YEARS OLD.

TWENTY WAS ALMOST FIFTY YEARS AGO, YOU SENILE OLD JERK. DON'T FORGET THAT. KNOW YOUR LIMITATIONS. DON'T GO CHARGING IN PLAYING GALAHAD. PLAY IT AS SMART AS YOU CAN AND PLAY IT MEAN.

SIN CITY SHRINKS IN THE REARVIEW MIRROR, AS CRANKY AND WEARY AS A TIRED WHORE WAITING FOR DAWN AND SOLITUDE.

I CHECK THE CLOCK ON THE DASH. THERE'S JUST ENOUGH LEFT OF THE NIGHT TO PROVIDE COVER OF DARKNESS ONCE I GET THERE. THAT COUNTS FOR SOMETHING. LORD KNOWS I'LL BE NEEDING EVERY ADVANTAGE I CAN GET.

THAT'S IF THERE'S ANY POINT IN ALL OF THIS.

FOR ALL I KNOW SHE'S DEAD ALREADY.

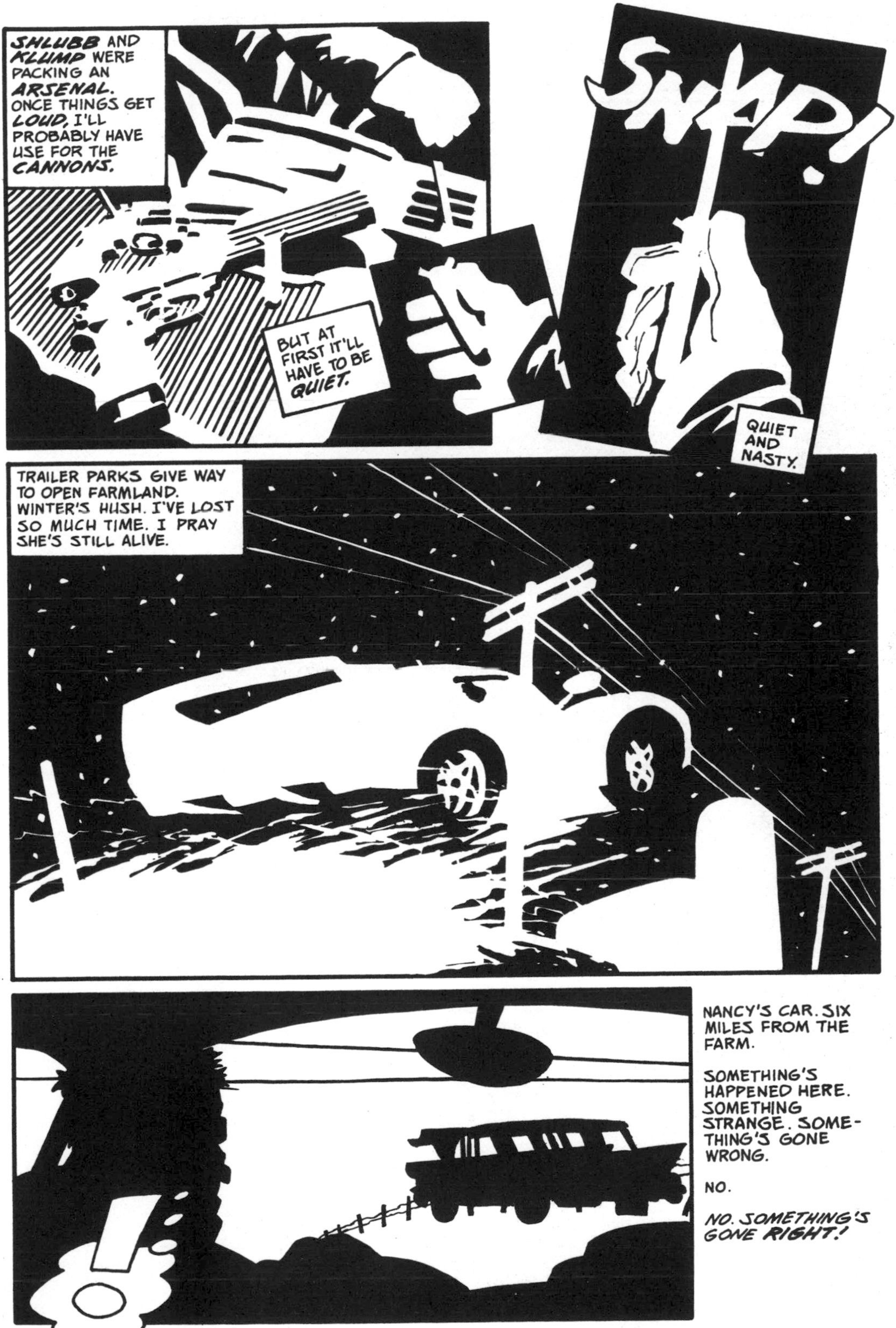
SHLUBB AND KLUMP WERE PACKING AN ARSENAL. ONCE THINGS GET LOUD, I'LL PROBABLY HAVE USE FOR THE CANNONS.
BUT AT FIRST IT'LL HAVE TO BE QUIET.
SNAP!
QUIET AND NASTY.
TRAILER PARKS GIVE WAY TO OPEN FARMLAND. WINTER'S HUSH. I'VE LOST SO MUCH TIME. I PRAY SHE'S STILL ALIVE.
NANCY'S CAR. SIX MILES FROM THE FARM.
SOMETHING'S HAPPENED HERE. SOMETHING STRANGE. SOMETHING'S GONE WRONG.
NO.
NO. SOMETHING'S GONE RIGHT!

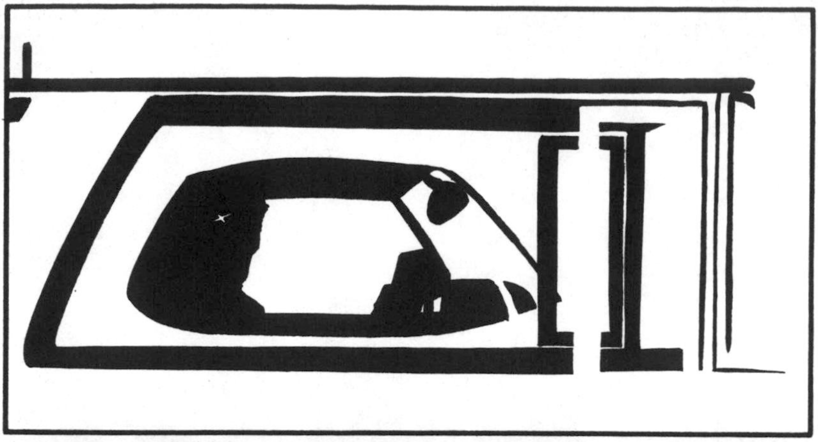

"NOBODY BUT ME CAN KEEP THIS HEAP RUNNING," SHE TOLD ME.

GOOD GIRL. THE CAR STALLED OUT ON THAT YELLOW BASTARD AND YOU DIDN'T TELL HIM HOW TO START IT UP AGAIN. YOU KEPT YOUR MOUTH SHUT.

YOU KEPT YOUR MOUTH SHUT. I'LL BET THAT TOOK GUTS, NANCY. I'LL BET JUNIOR WAS FURIOUS.

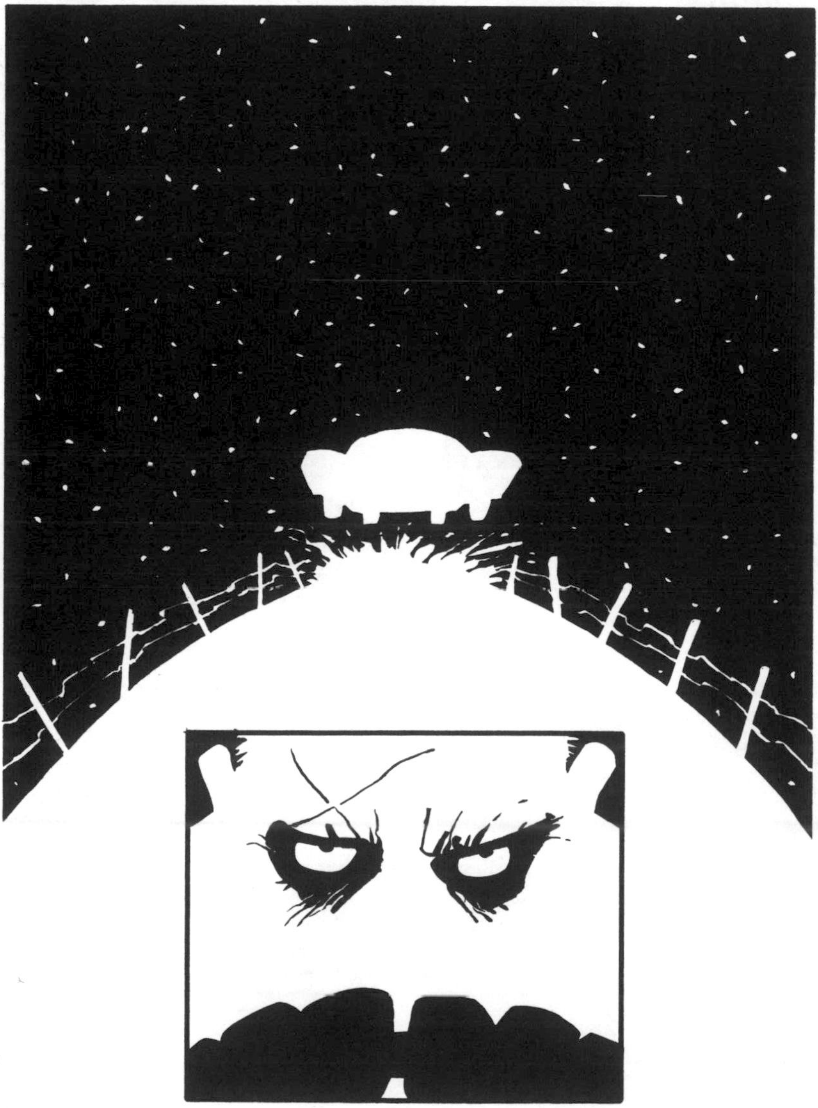

I'LL BET HE SQUEALED THAT SPOILED-BRAT SQUEAL OF HIS. I'LL BET HE SLAPPED YOU AROUND SOMETHING FIERCE. BUT YOU STAYED STRONG. YOU KEPT YOUR MOUTH SHUT. HE HAD TO CALL FOR A RIDE.

HE HAD TO CALL FOR A RIDE AND HE HAD TO WAIT FOR IT. THAT COST HIM TIME. PRECIOUS TIME.

GOOD GIRL. YOU BOUGHT A FEW EXTRA MINUTES. THERE'S STILL A CHANCE.

YOU KEEP ON STAYING STRONG, MY BELOVED. DON'T LET HIM MAKE YOU SCREAM.

WHATEVER HE'S DOING TO YOU, DON'T SCREAM.

DON'T SCREAM.

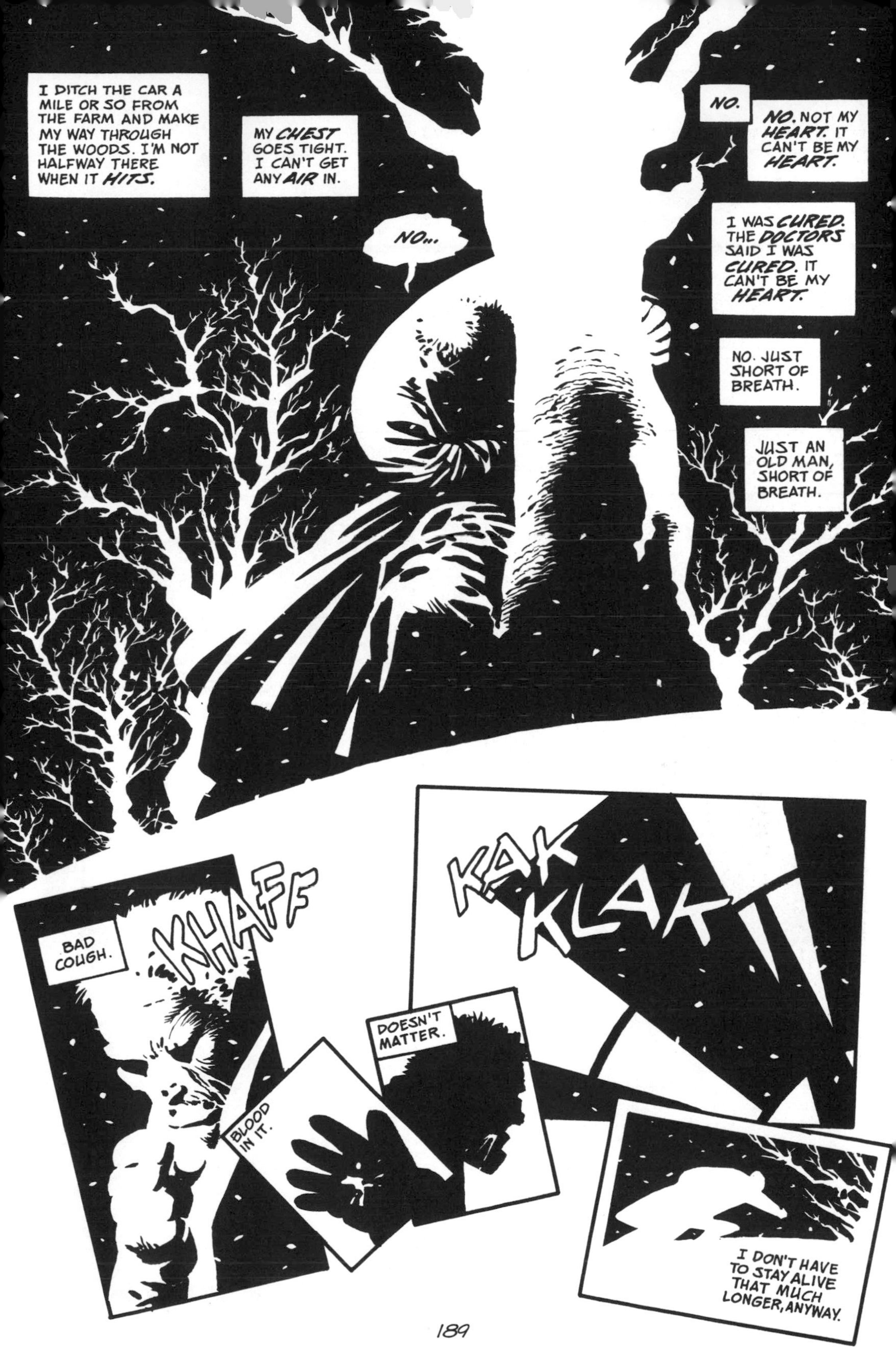
I DITCH THE CAR A MILE OR SO FROM THE FARM AND MAKE MY WAY THROUGH THE WOODS. I'M NOT HALFWAY THERE WHEN IT HITS.
MY CHEST GOES TIGHT. I CAN'T GET ANY AIR IN.
NO...
NO.
NO. NOT MY HEART. IT CAN'T BE MY HEART.
I WAS CURED. THE DOCTORS SAID I WAS CURED. IT CAN'T BE MY HEART.
NO. JUST SHORT OF BREATH.
JUST AN OLD MAN, SHORT OF BREATH.
BAD COUGH.
KHAFF
BLOOD IN IT.
DOESN'T MATTER.
KAK KLAK
I DON'T HAVE TO STAY ALIVE THAT MUCH LONGER, ANYWAY.

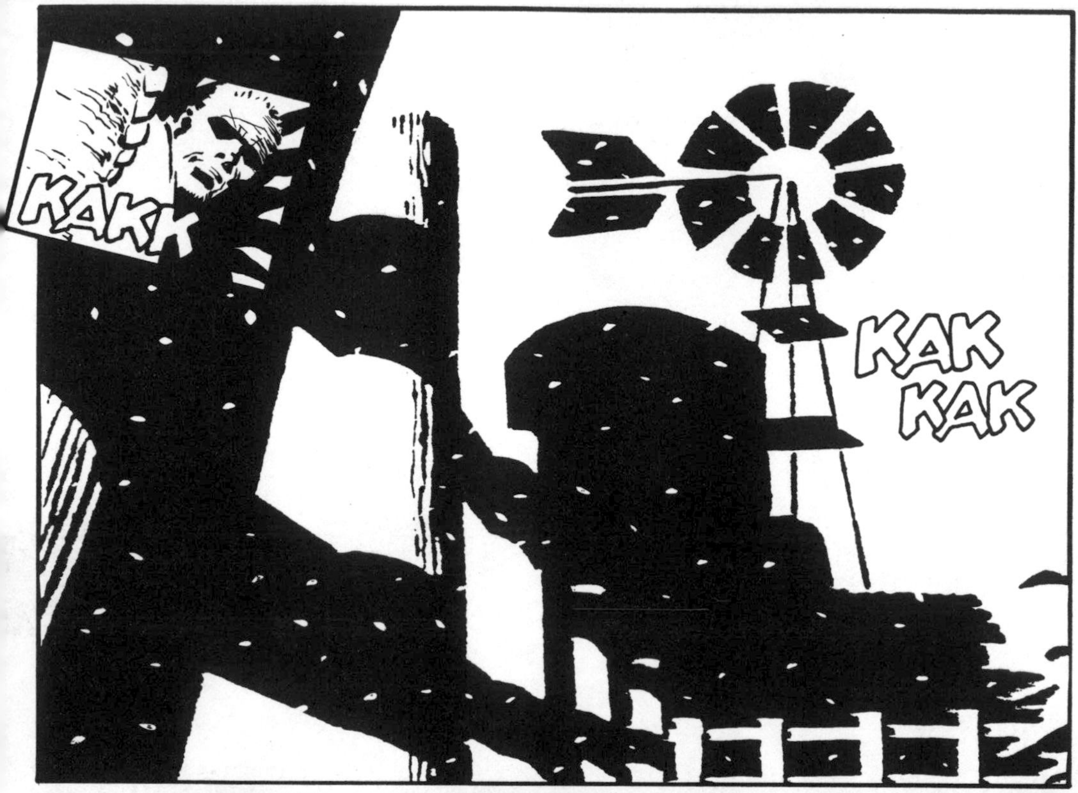
KAKK
KAK KAK

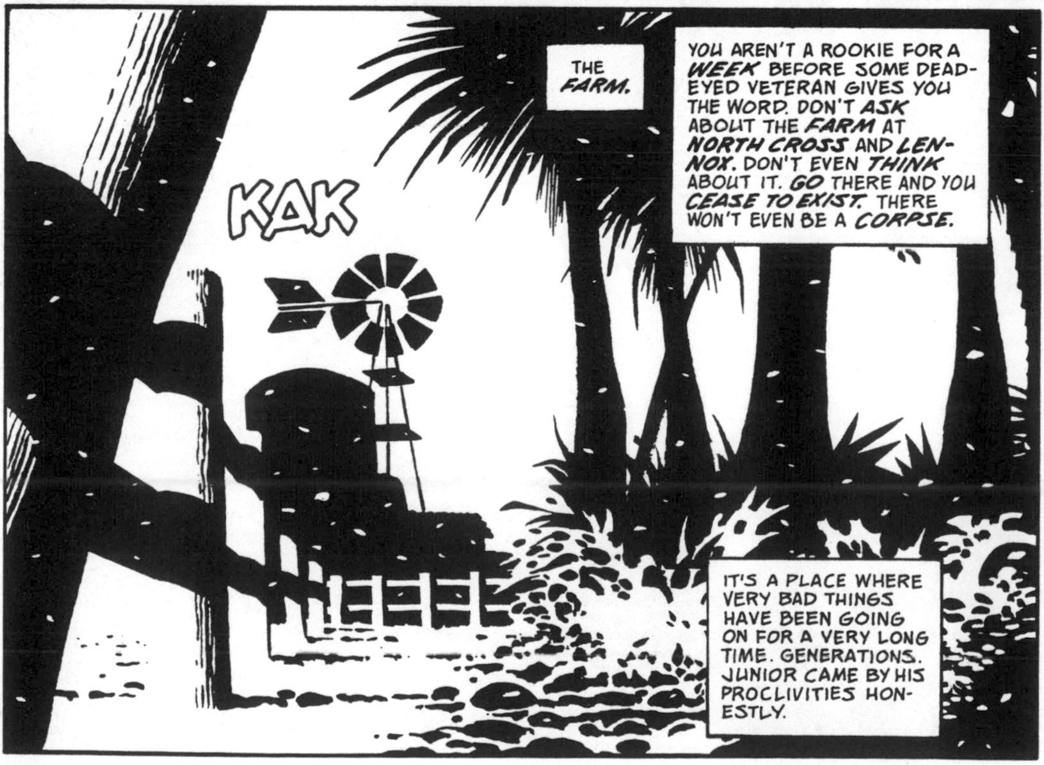
KAK
THE FARM.
YOU AREN'T A ROOKIE FOR A WEEK BEFORE SOME DEAD-EYED VETERAN GIVES YOU THE WORD. DON'T ASK ABOUT THE FARM AT NORTH CROSS AND LEN-NOX. DON'T EVEN THINK ABOUT IT. GO THERE AND YOU CEASE TO EXIST. THERE WON'T EVEN BE A CORPSE.
IT'S A PLACE WHERE VERY BAD THINGS HAVE BEEN GOING ON FOR A VERY LONG TIME. GENERATIONS. JUNIOR CAME BY HIS PROCLIVITIES HON-ESTLY.

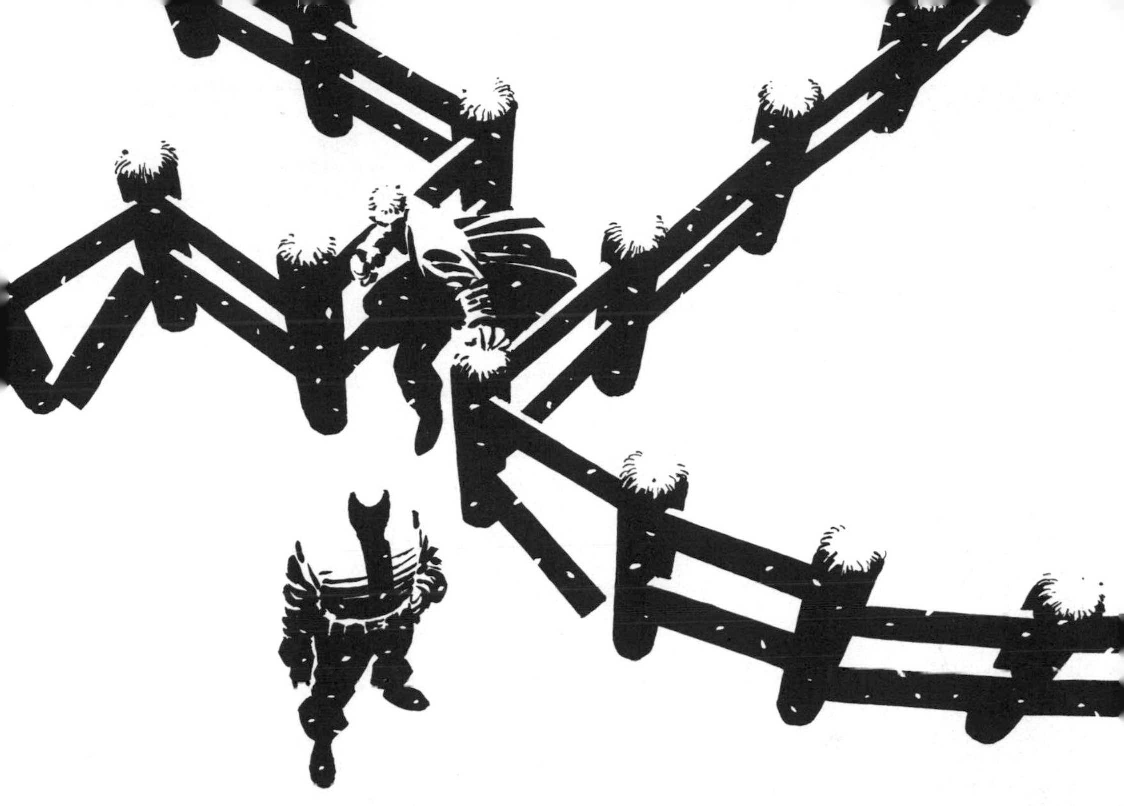

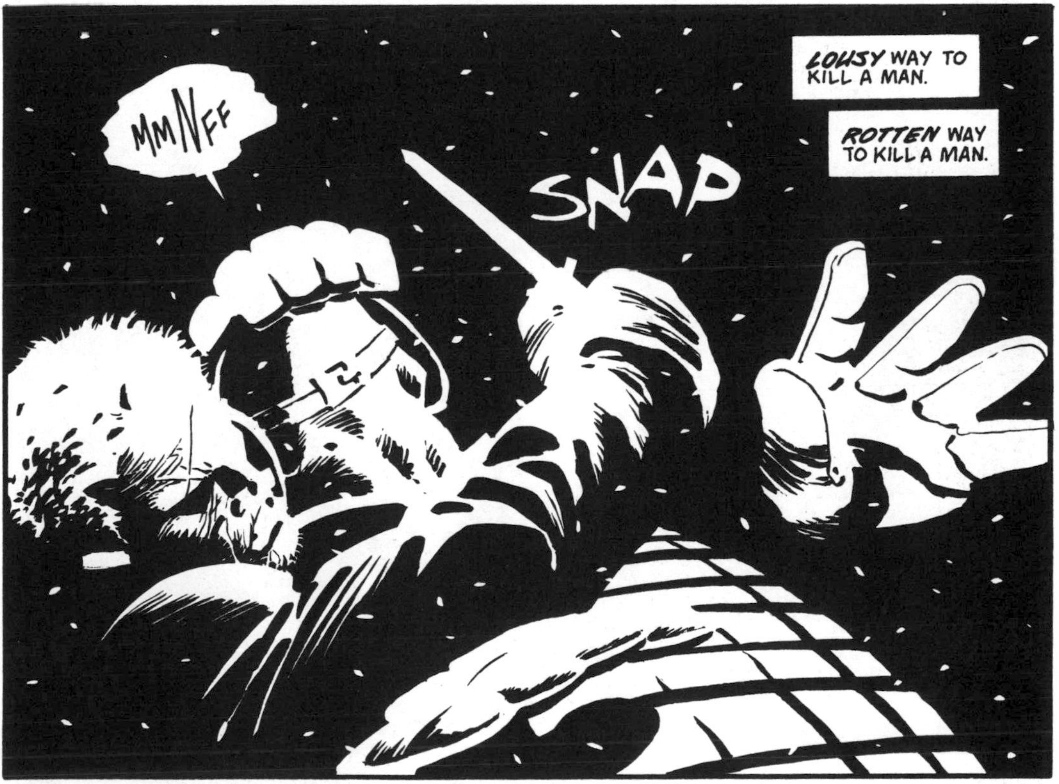
LOUSY WAY TO KILL A MAN.
ROTTEN WAY TO KILL A MAN.
MMNFF
SNAP

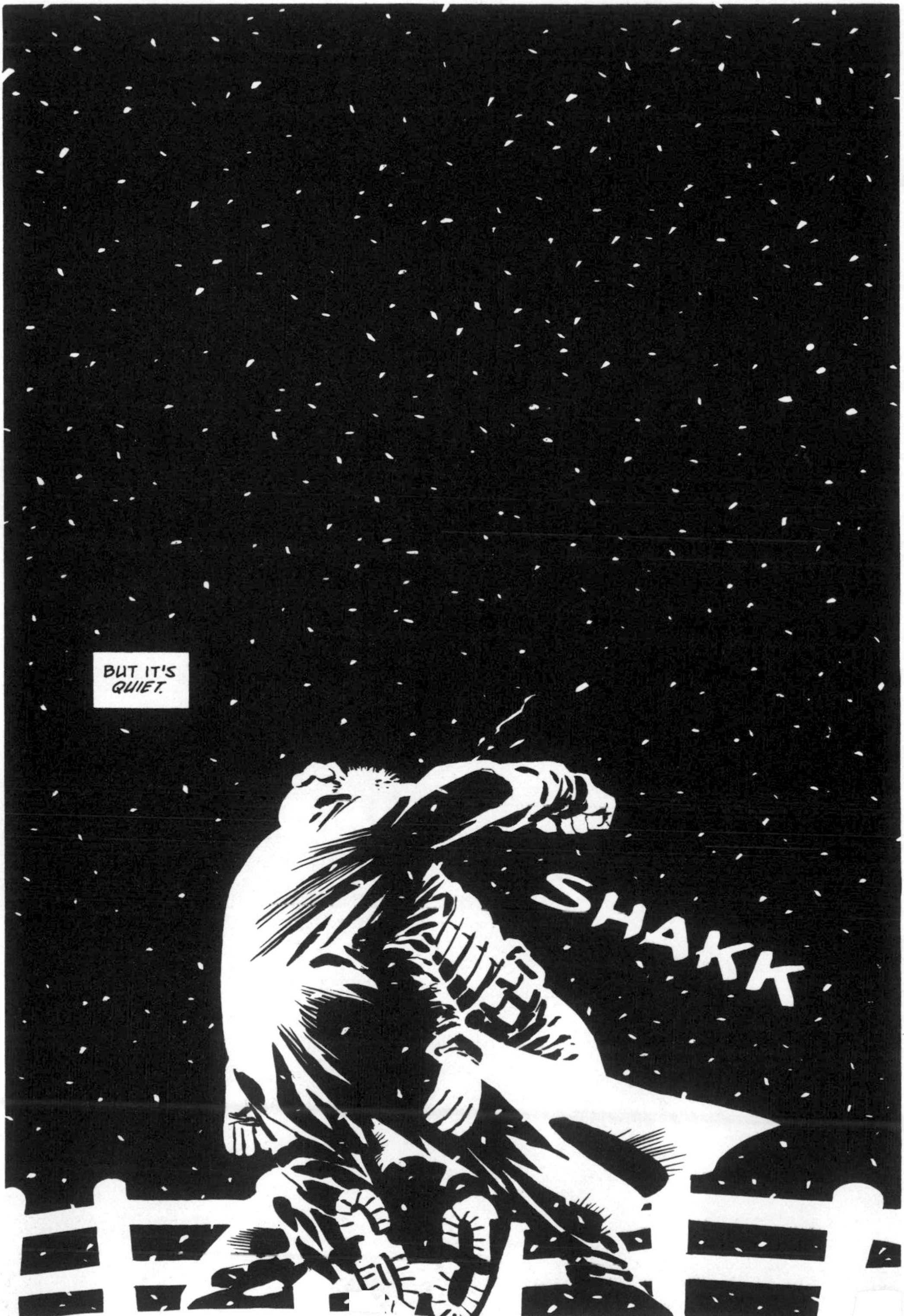
BUT IT'S QUIET.
SHAKK

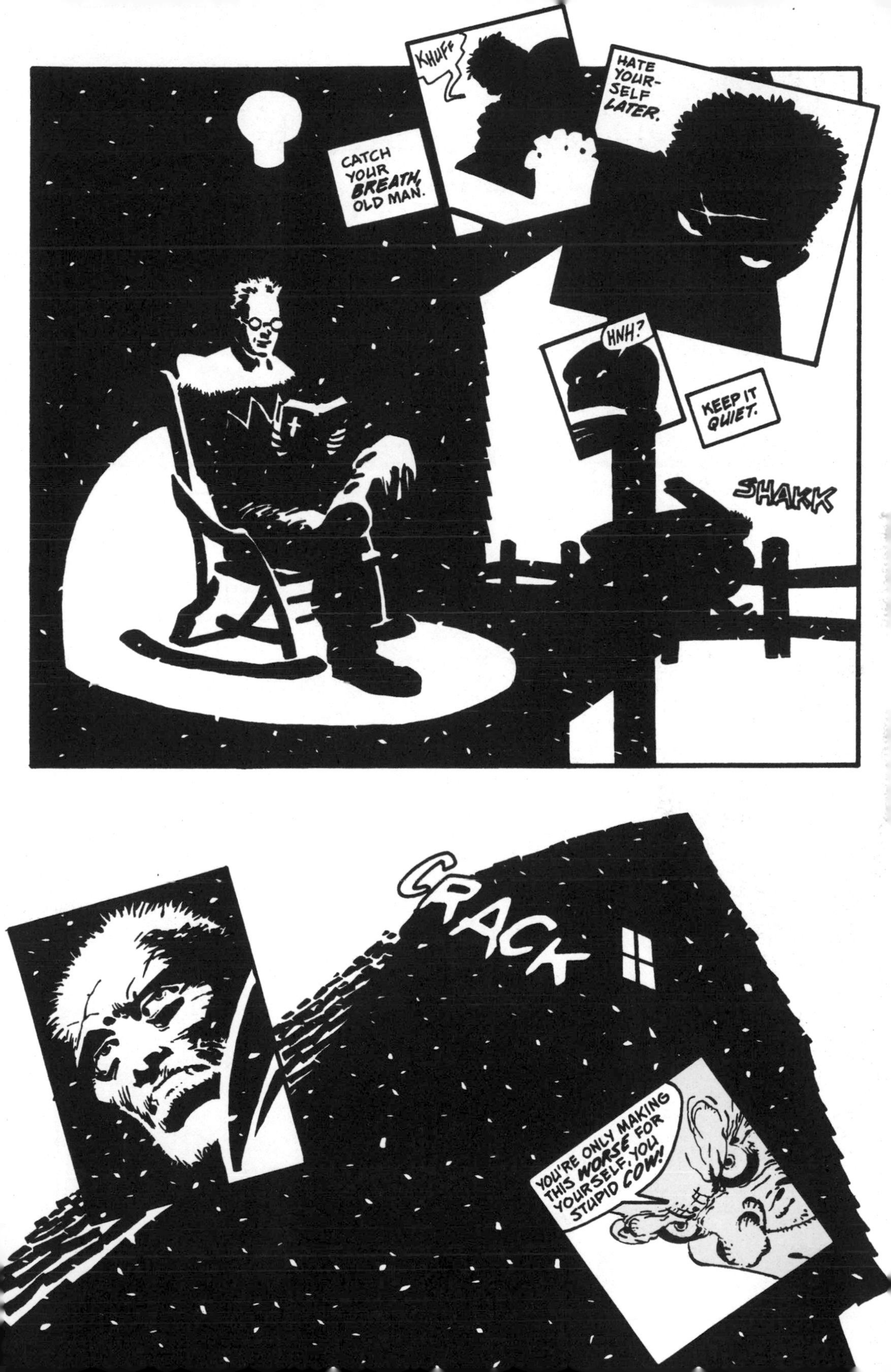

CATCH YOUR BREATH, OLD MAN.
KHUFF
HATE YOURSELF LATER.
HNH?
KEEP IT QUIET.
SHAKK
CRACK
YOU'RE ONLY MAKING THIS WORSE FOR YOURSELF, YOU STUPID COW!

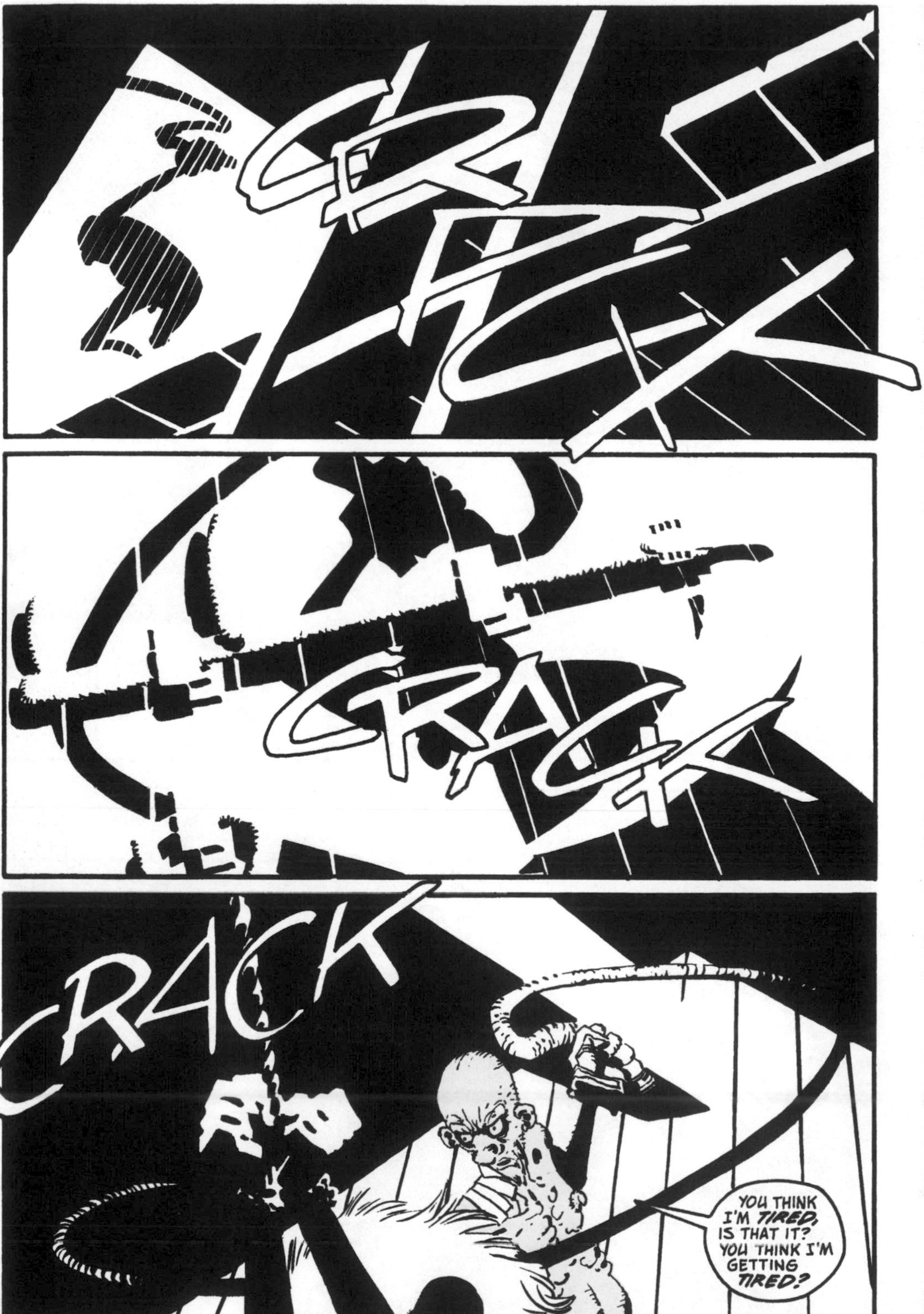
CRACK
CRACK
CRACK
YOU THINK I'M TIRED, IS THAT IT? YOU THINK I'M GETTING TIRED?

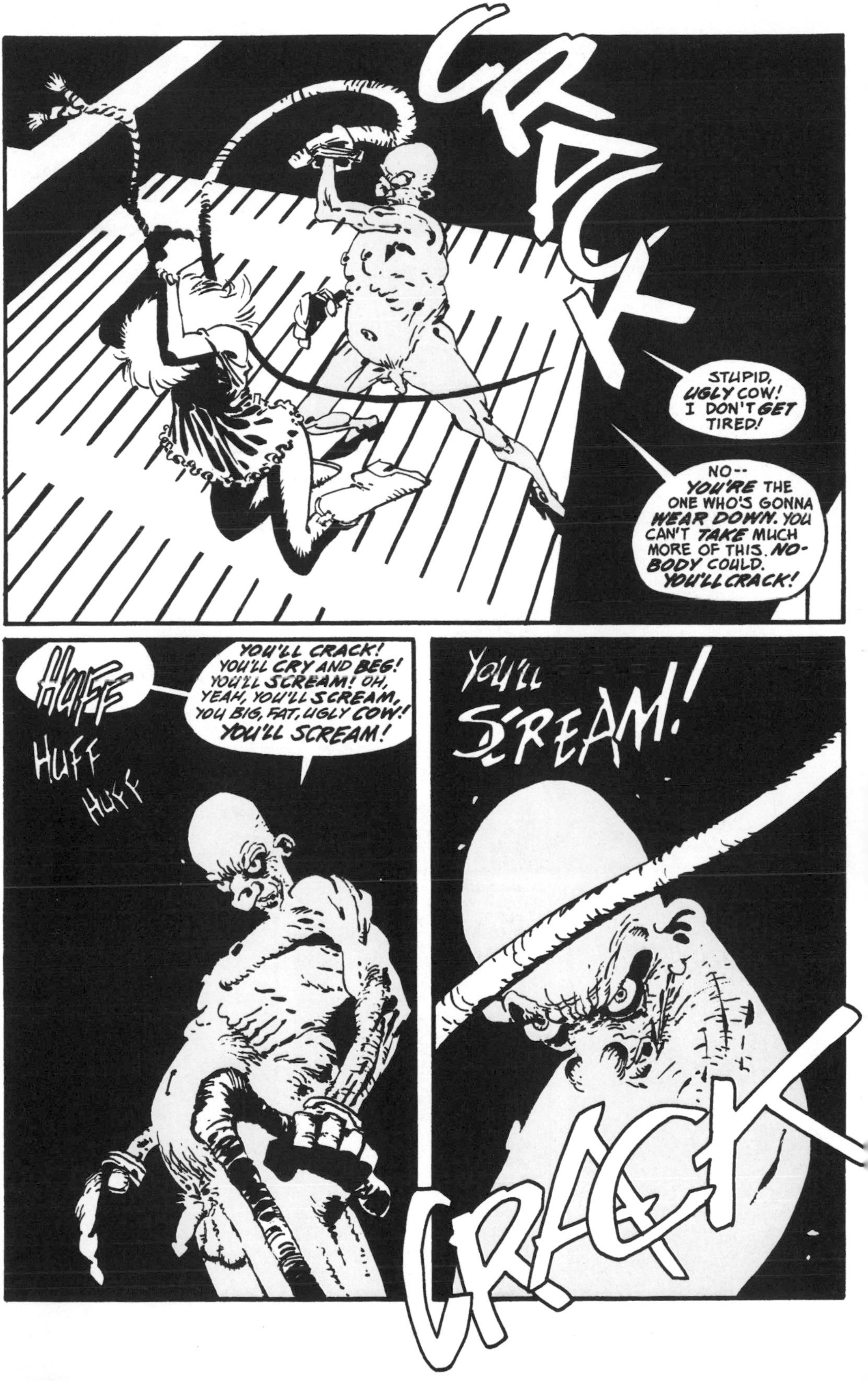
CRACK
STUPID, UGLY COW! I DON'T GET TIRED!
NO-- YOU'RE THE ONE WHO'S GONNA WEAR DOWN. YOU CAN'T TAKE MUCH MORE OF THIS. NO-BODY COULD. YOU'LL CRACK!
HUFF HUFF
YOU'LL CRACK! YOU'LL CRY AND BEG! YOU'LL SCREAM! OH, YEAH, YOU'LL SCREAM, YOU BIG, FAT, UGLY COW! YOU'LL SCREAM!
YOU'LL SCREAM!
CRACK

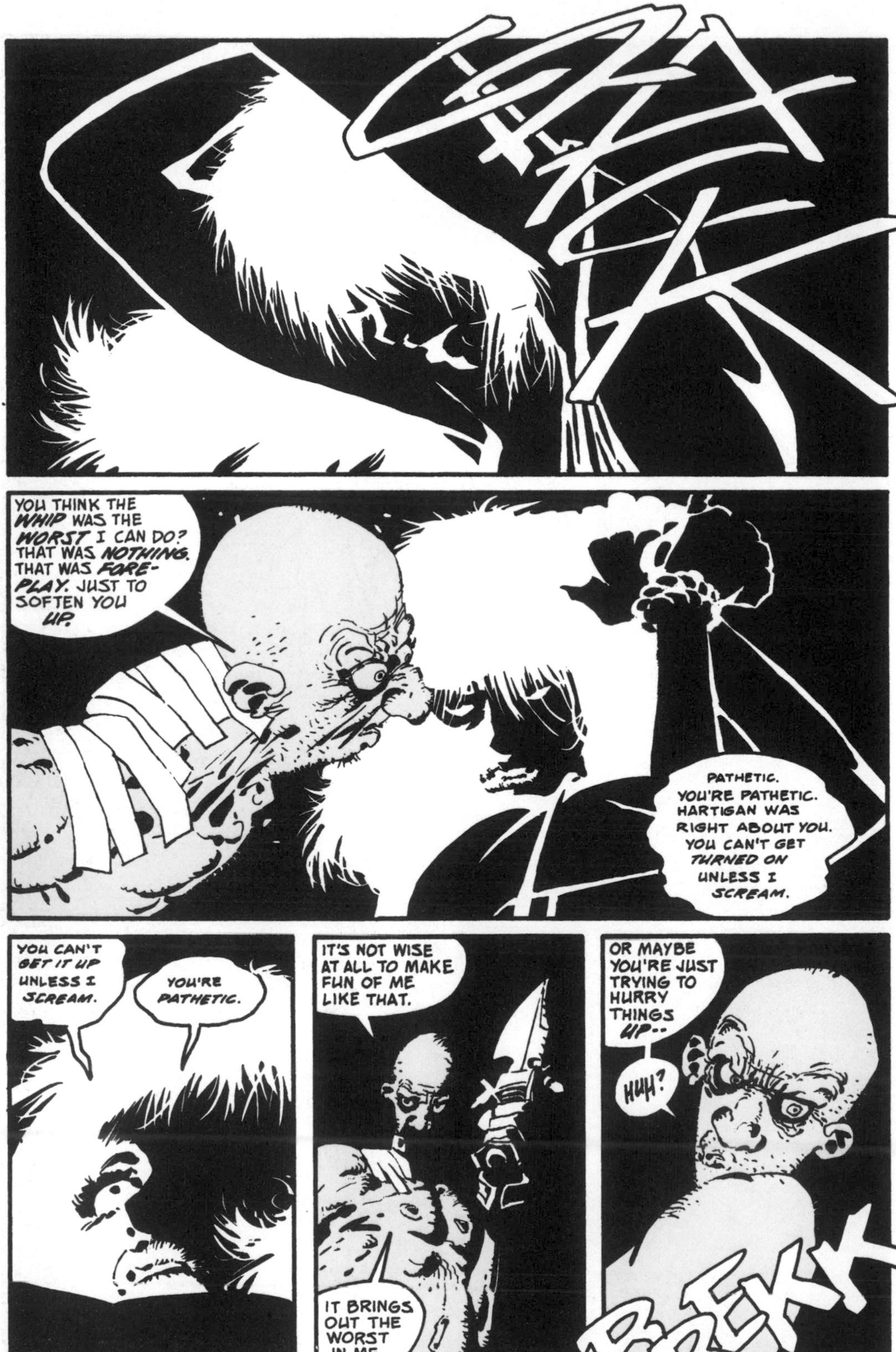
YOU THINK THE WHIP WAS THE WORST I CAN DO? THAT WAS NOTHING. THAT WAS FORE-PLAY. JUST TO SOFTEN YOU UP.
PATHETIC. YOU'RE PATHETIC. HARTIGAN WAS RIGHT ABOUT YOU. YOU CAN'T GET TURNED ON UNLESS I SCREAM.
YOU CAN'T GET IT UP UNLESS I SCREAM.
YOU'RE PATHETIC.
IT'S NOT WISE AT ALL TO MAKE FUN OF ME LIKE THAT.
IT BRINGS OUT THE WORST IN ME.
OR MAYBE YOU'RE JUST TRYING TO HURRY THINGS UP..
HUH?
BREKK

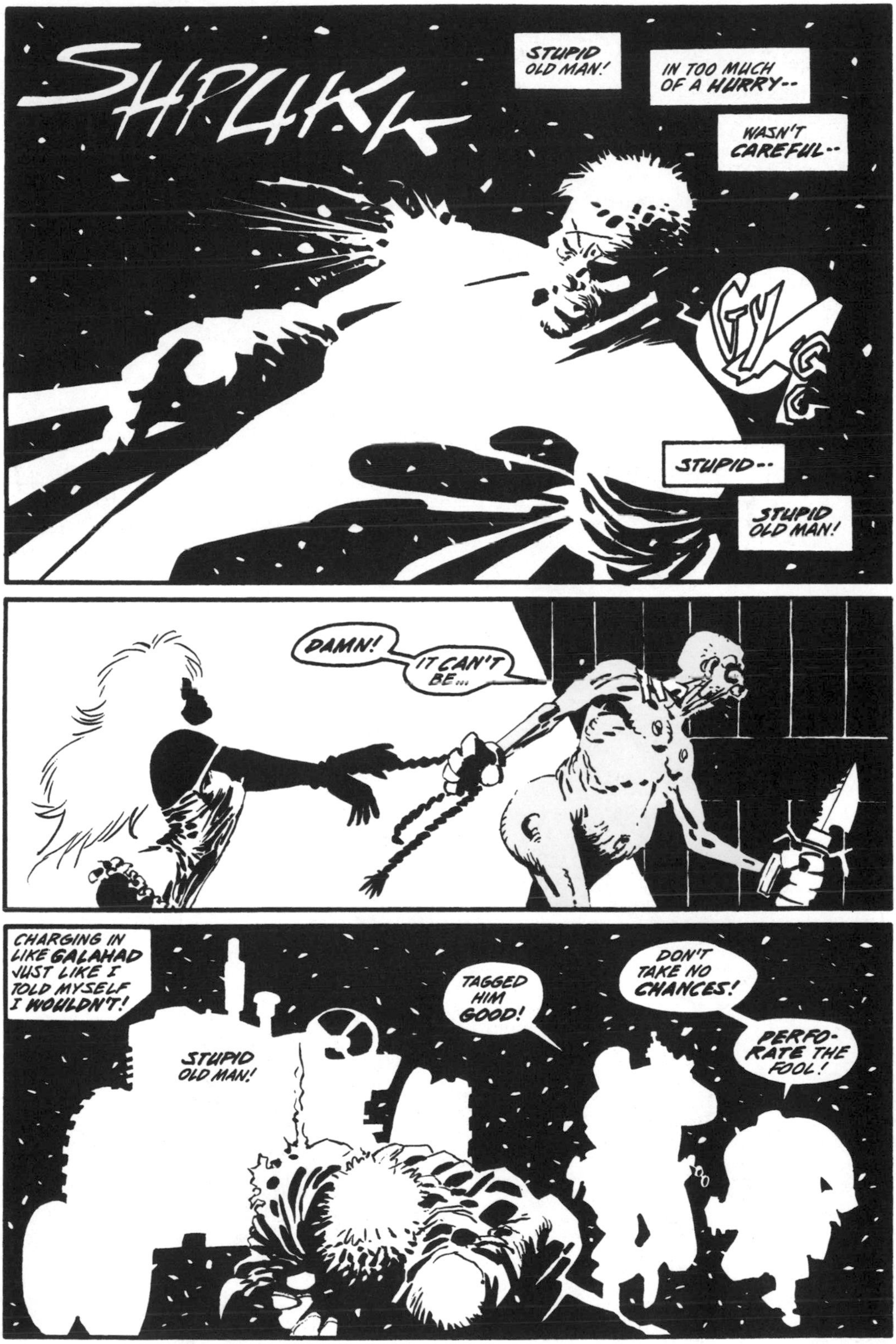
SHPUKK
STUPID OLD MAN!
IN TOO MUCH OF A HURRY--
WASN'T CAREFUL--
STUPID--
STUPID OLD MAN!
DAMN!
IT CAN'T BE...
CHARGING IN LIKE GALAHAD JUST LIKE I TOLD MYSELF I WOULDN'T!
STUPID OLD MAN!
TAGGED HIM GOOD!
DON'T TAKE NO CHANCES!
PERFO-RATE THE FOOL!

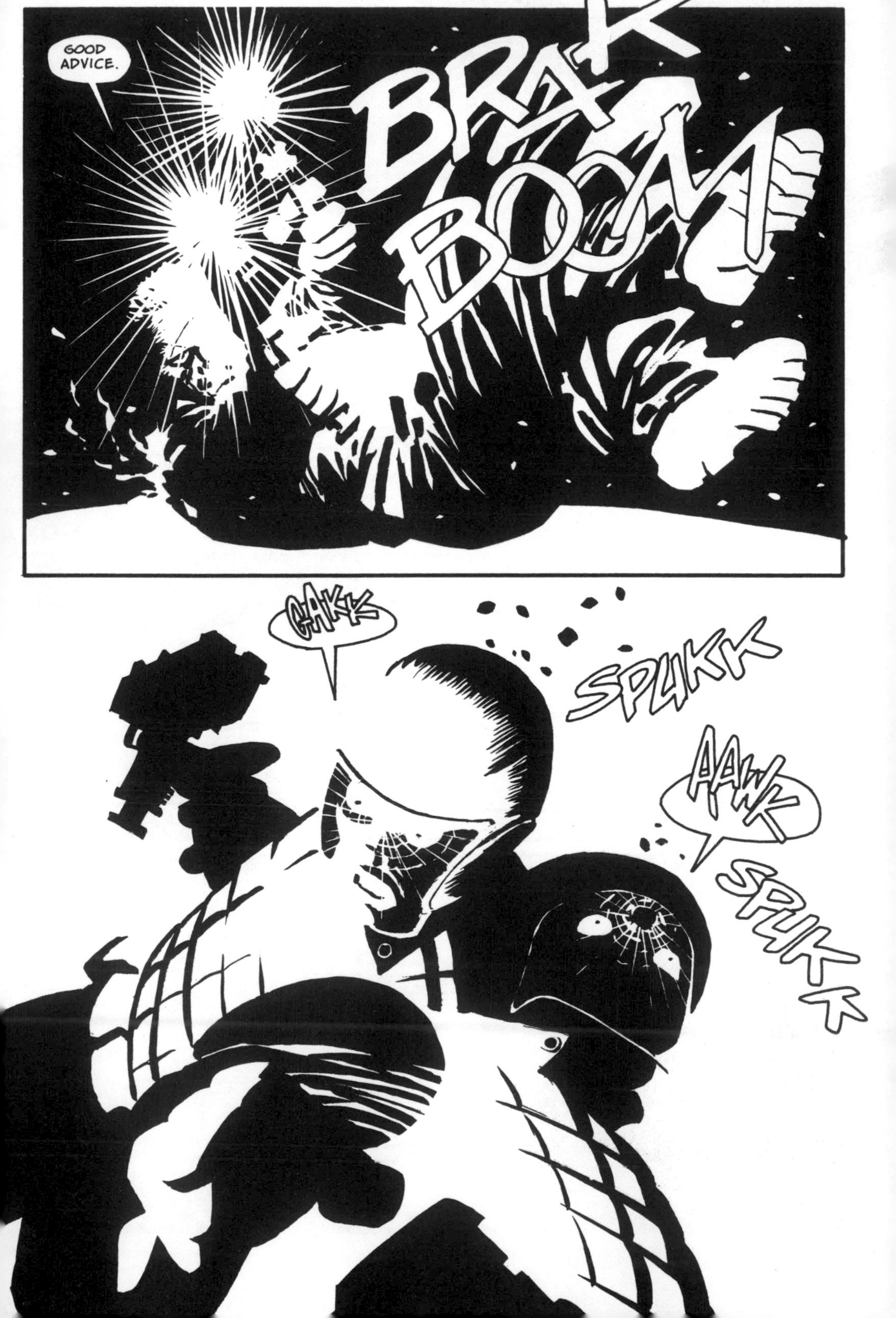
GOOD ADVICE.
BRAK
BOOM
GAKK
SPLKK
AAWK
SPLKK

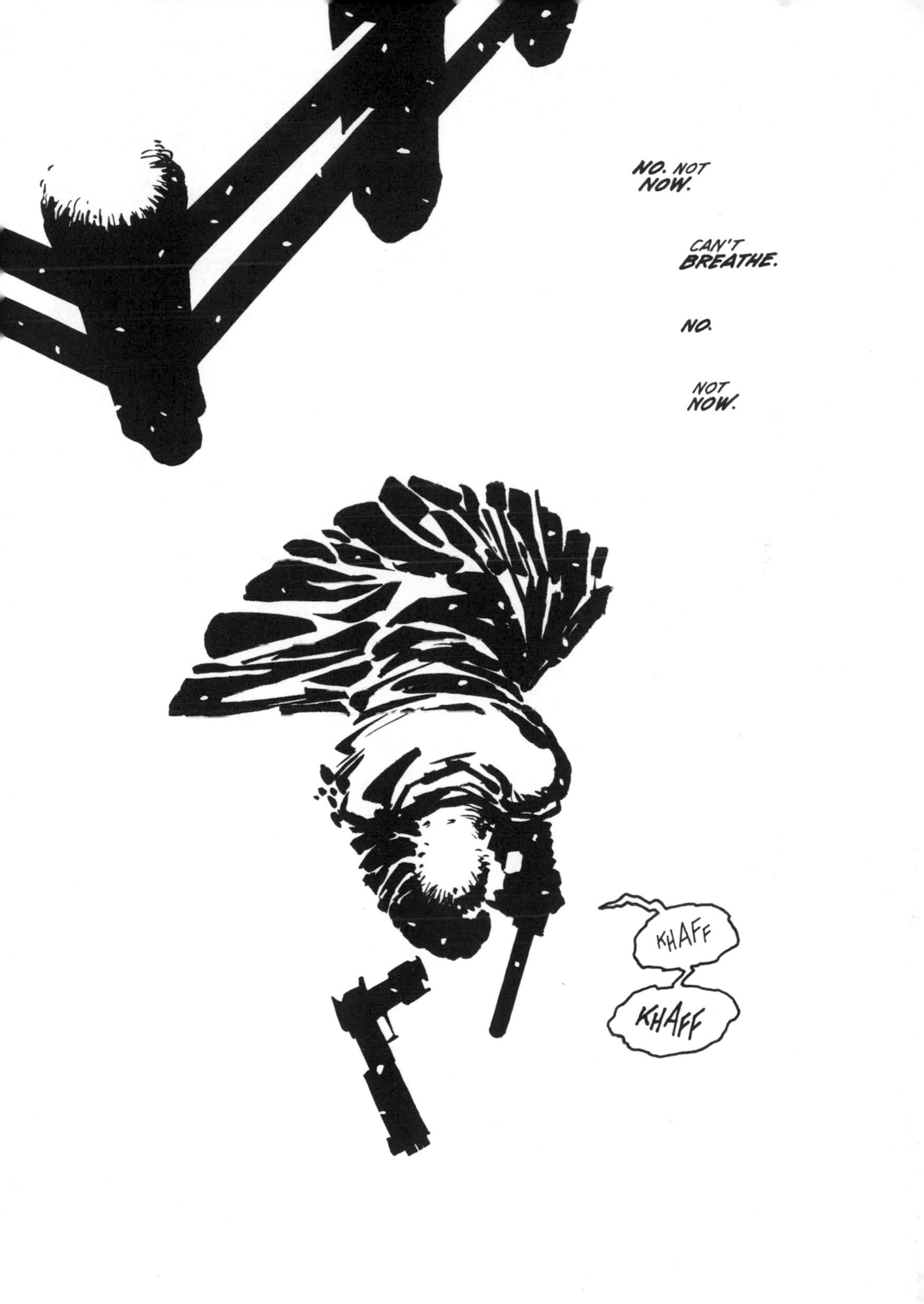
NO. NOT NOW.
CAN'T BREATHE.
NO.
NOT NOW.
KHAFF
KHAFF

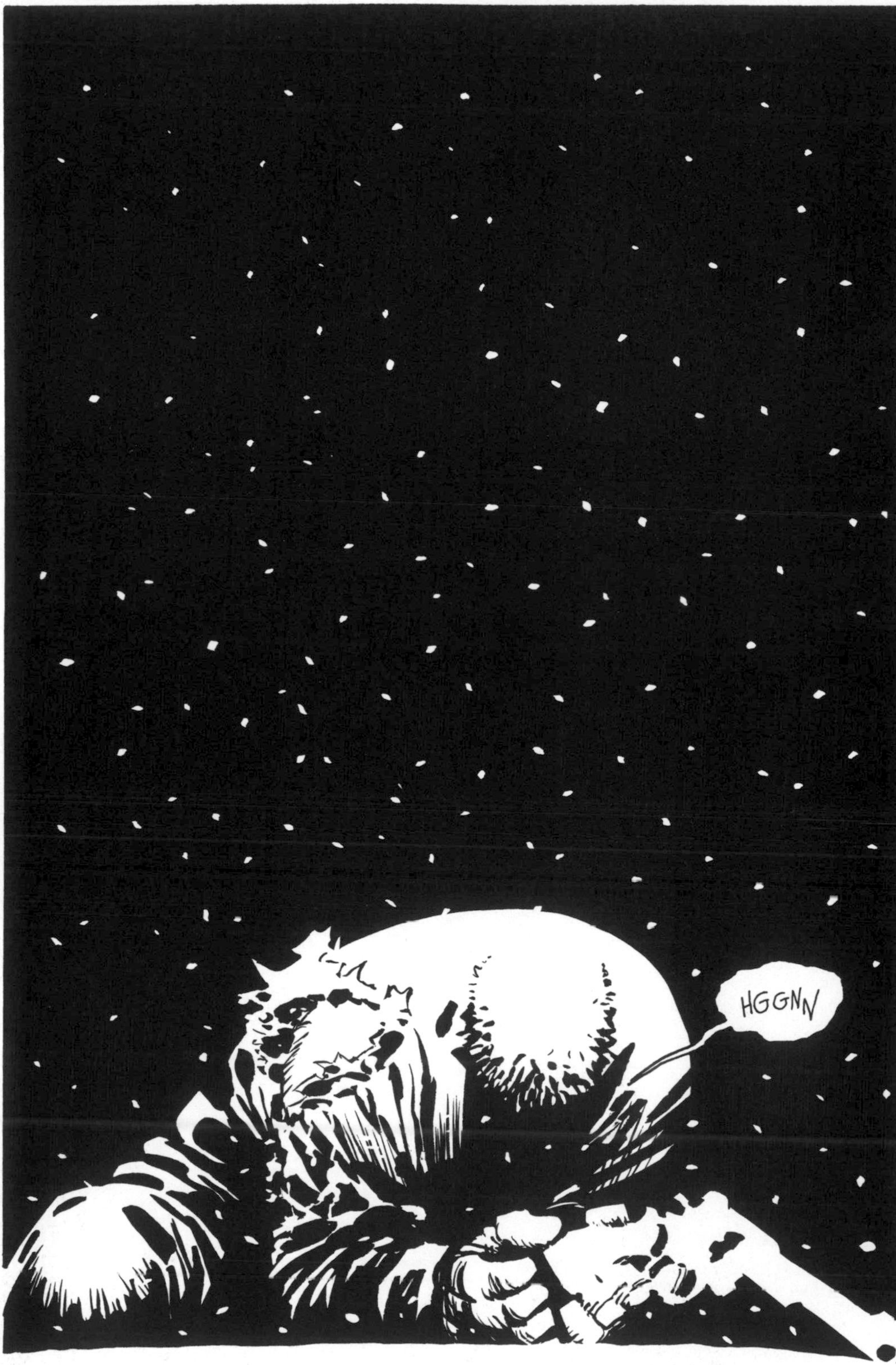
HGGNN

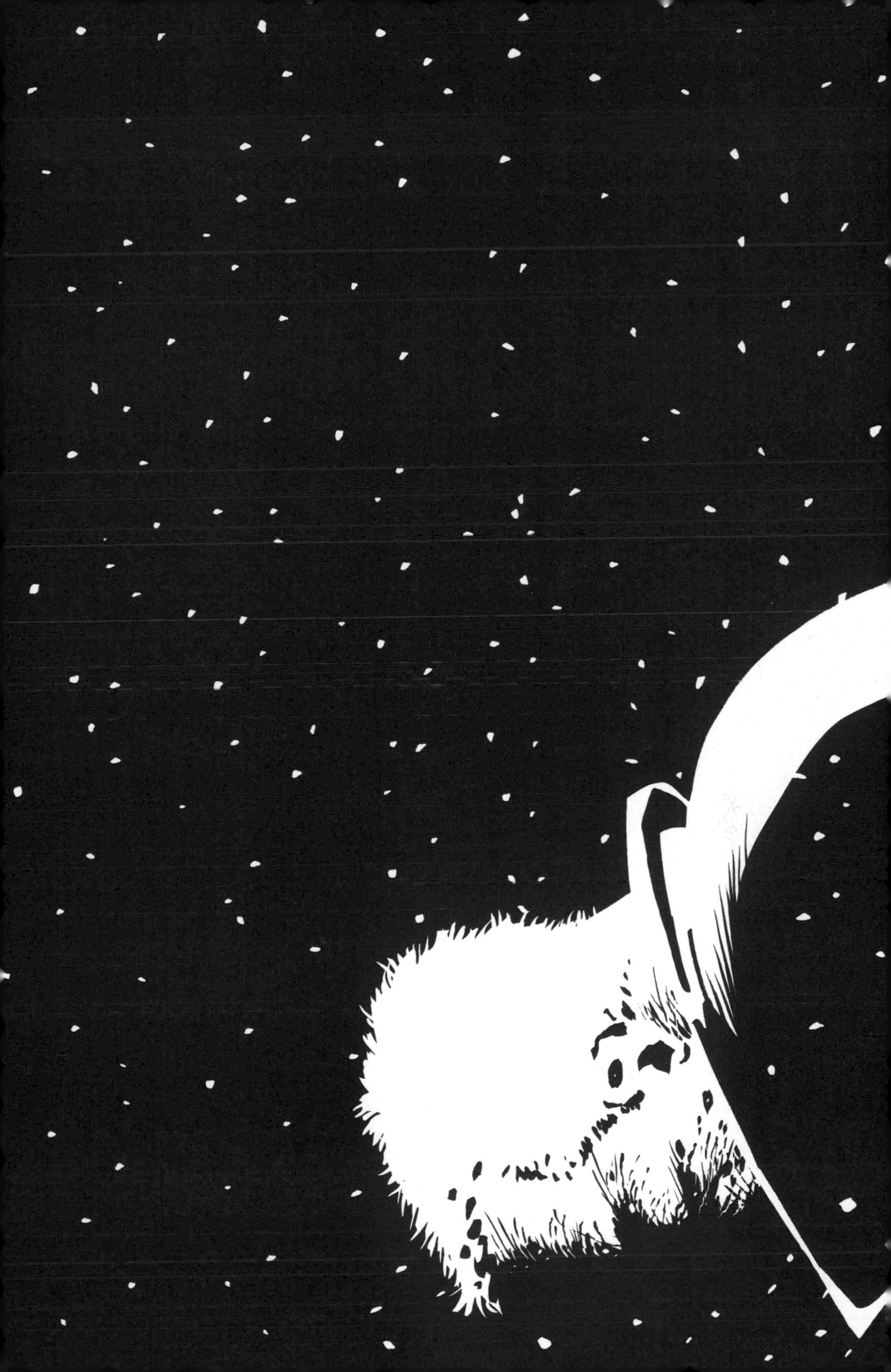

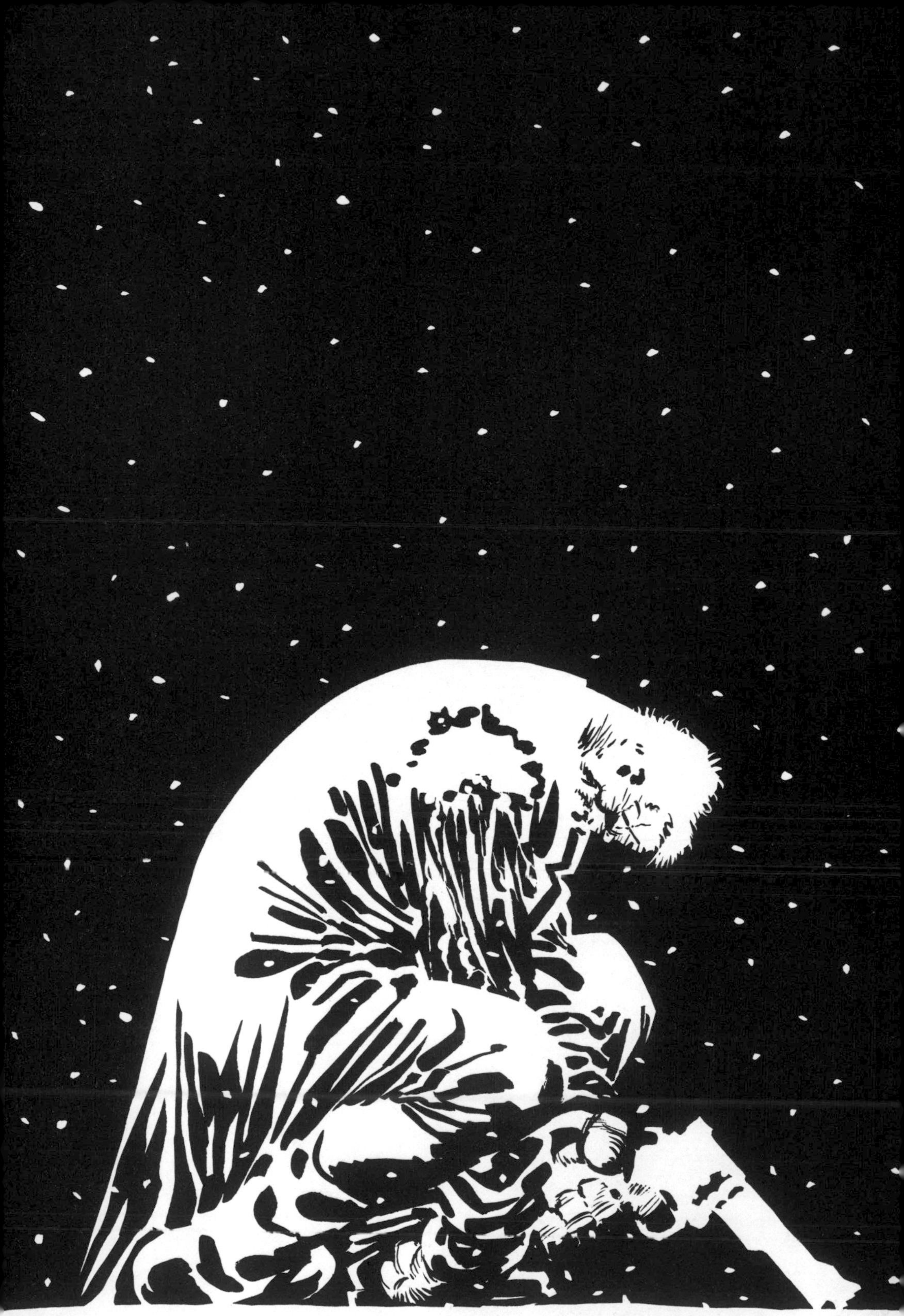

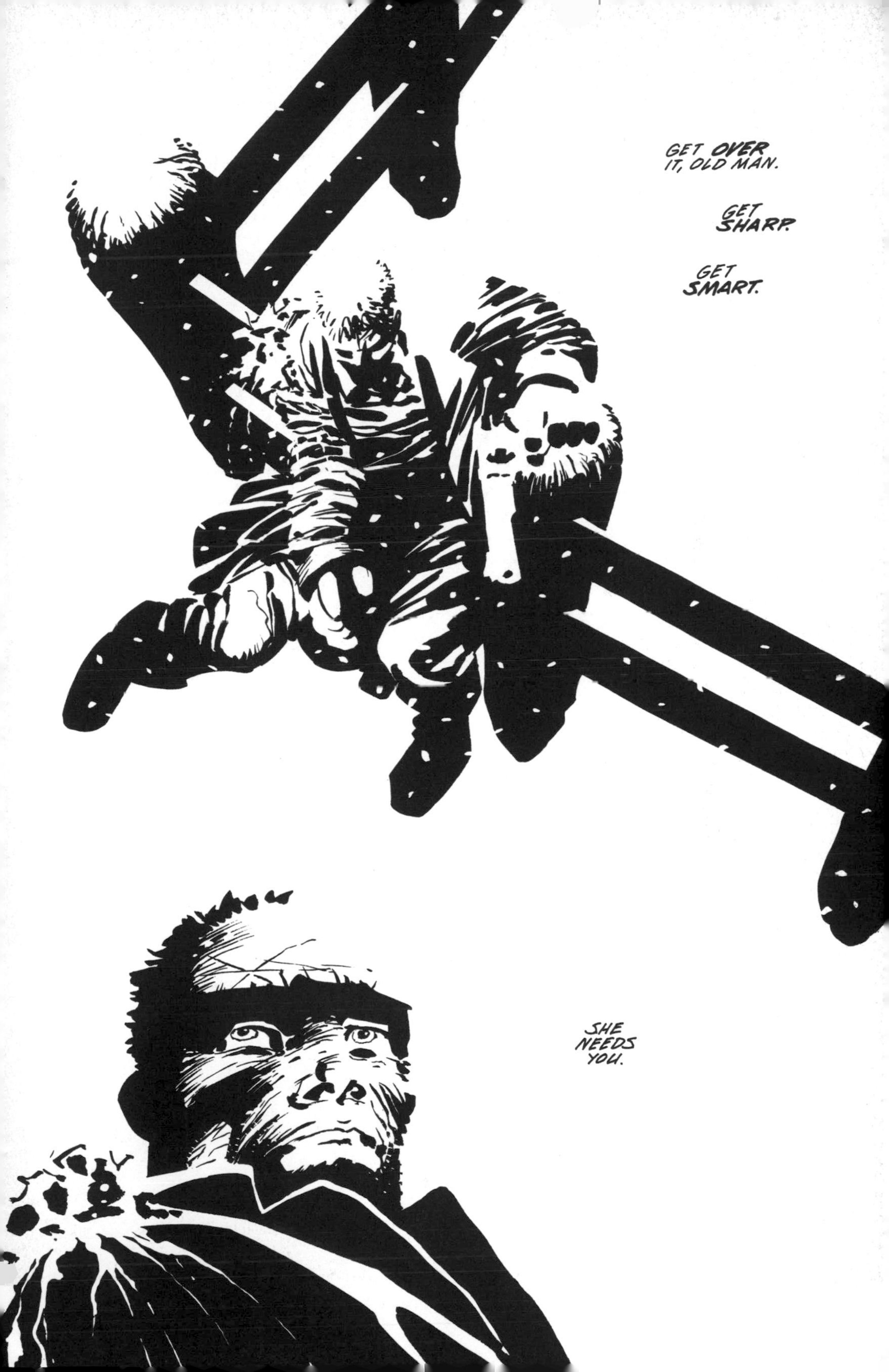
GET OVER IT, OLD MAN.
GET SHARP.
GET SMART.
SHE NEEDS YOU.

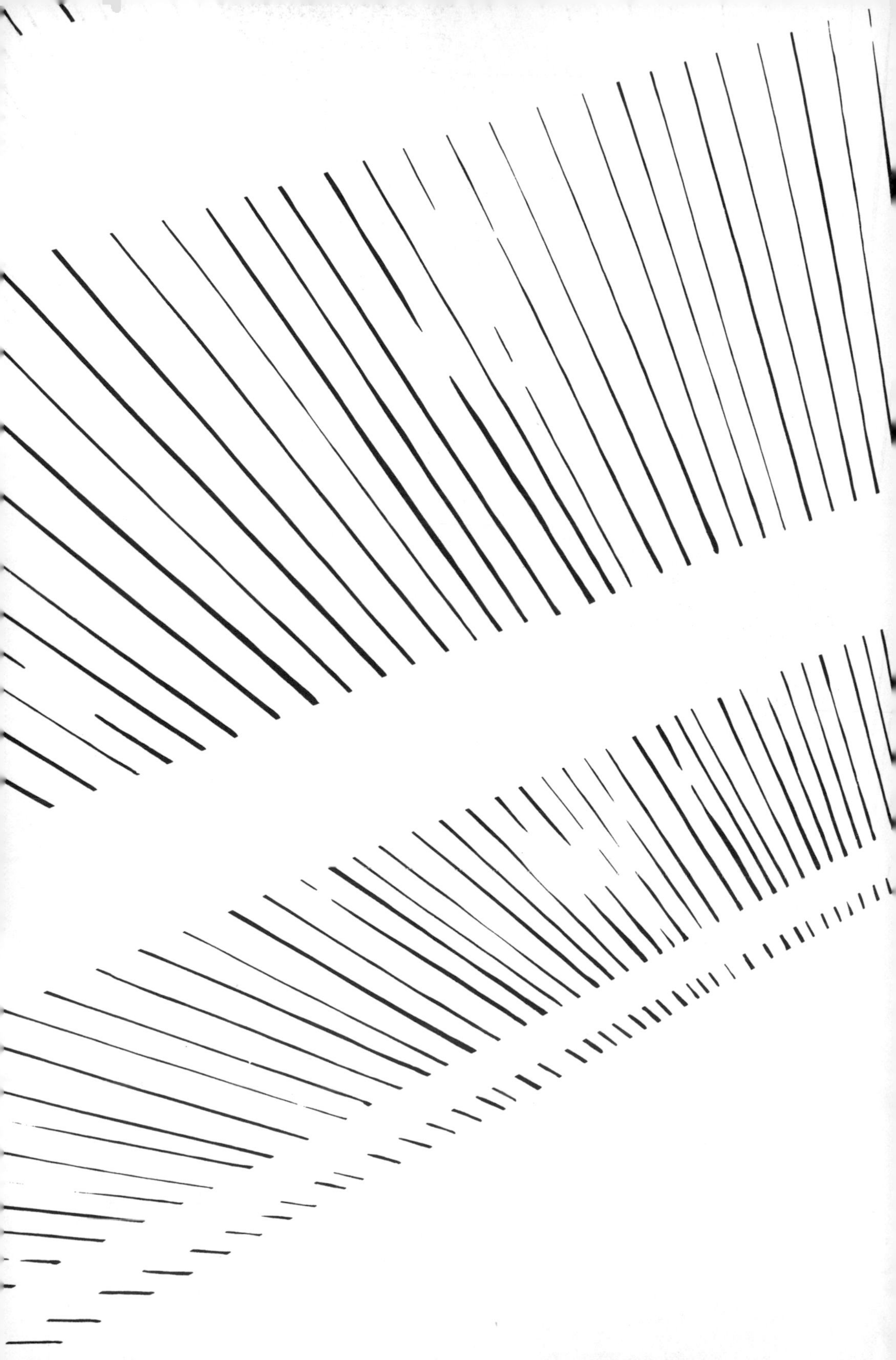

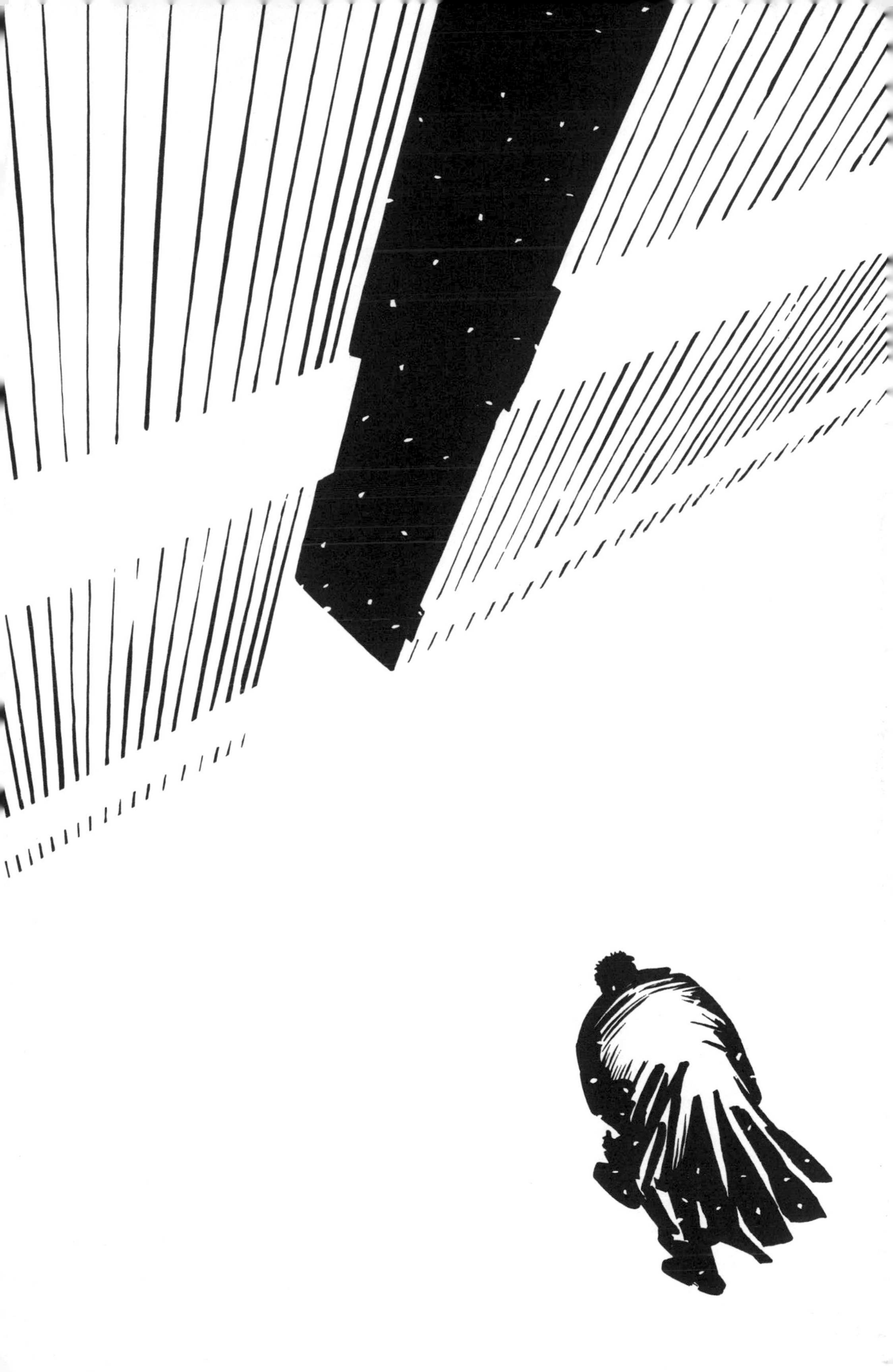

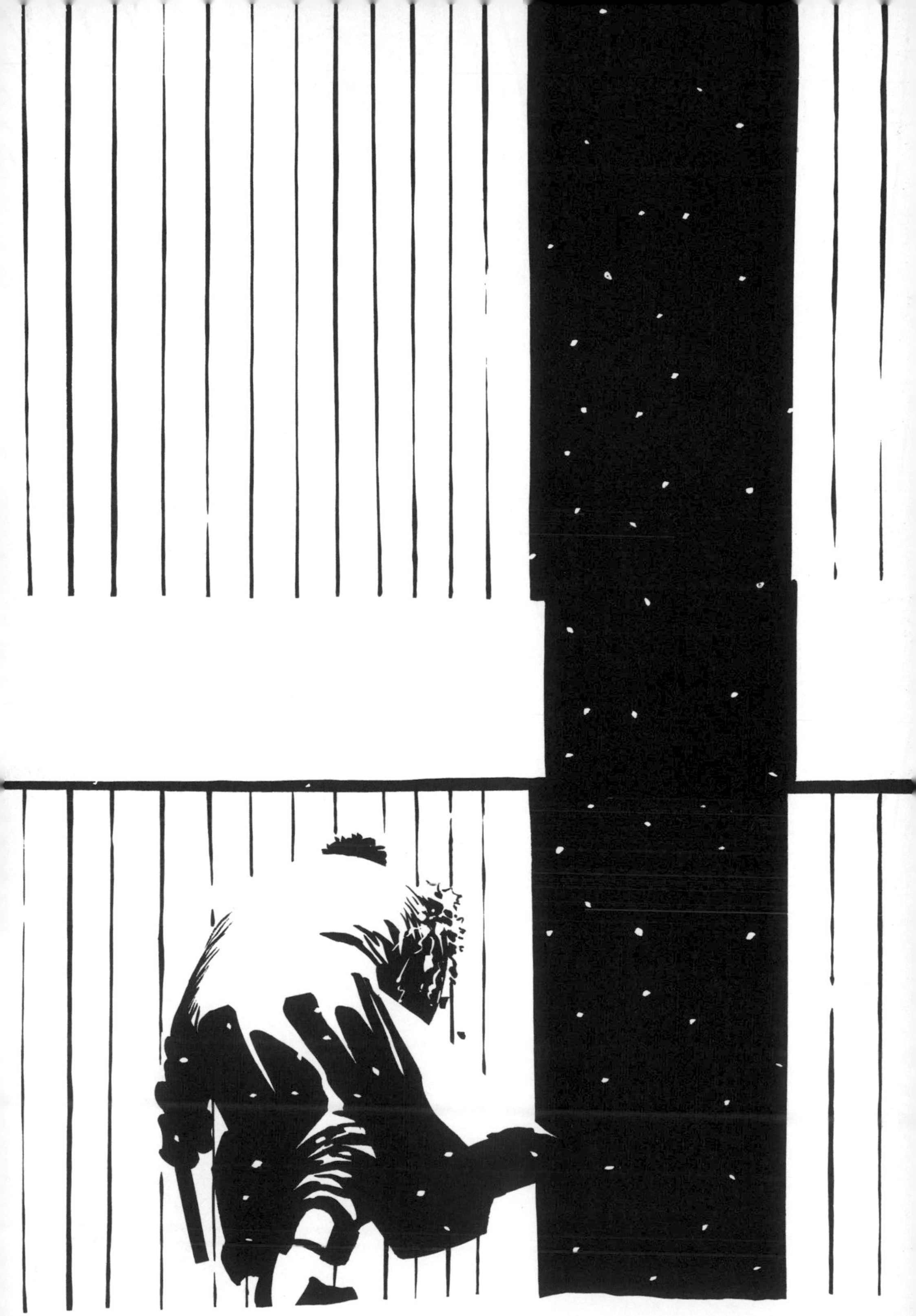

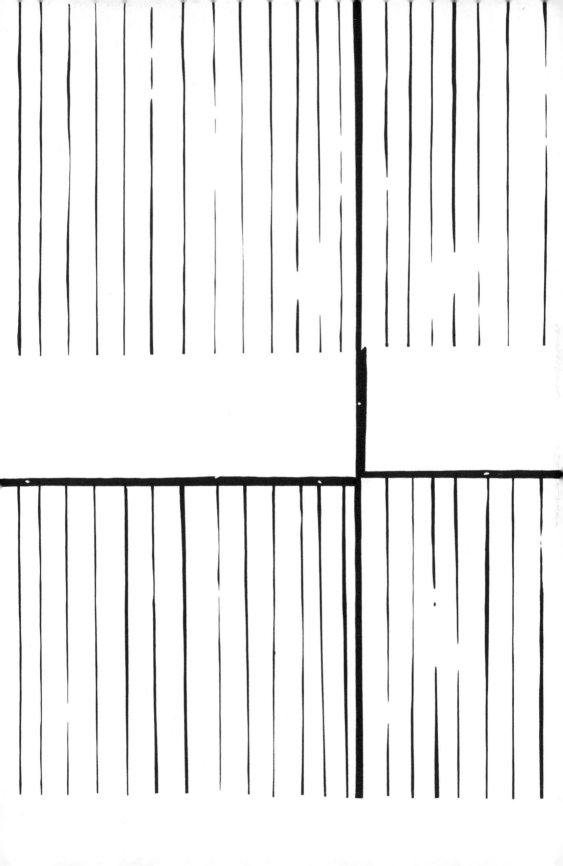

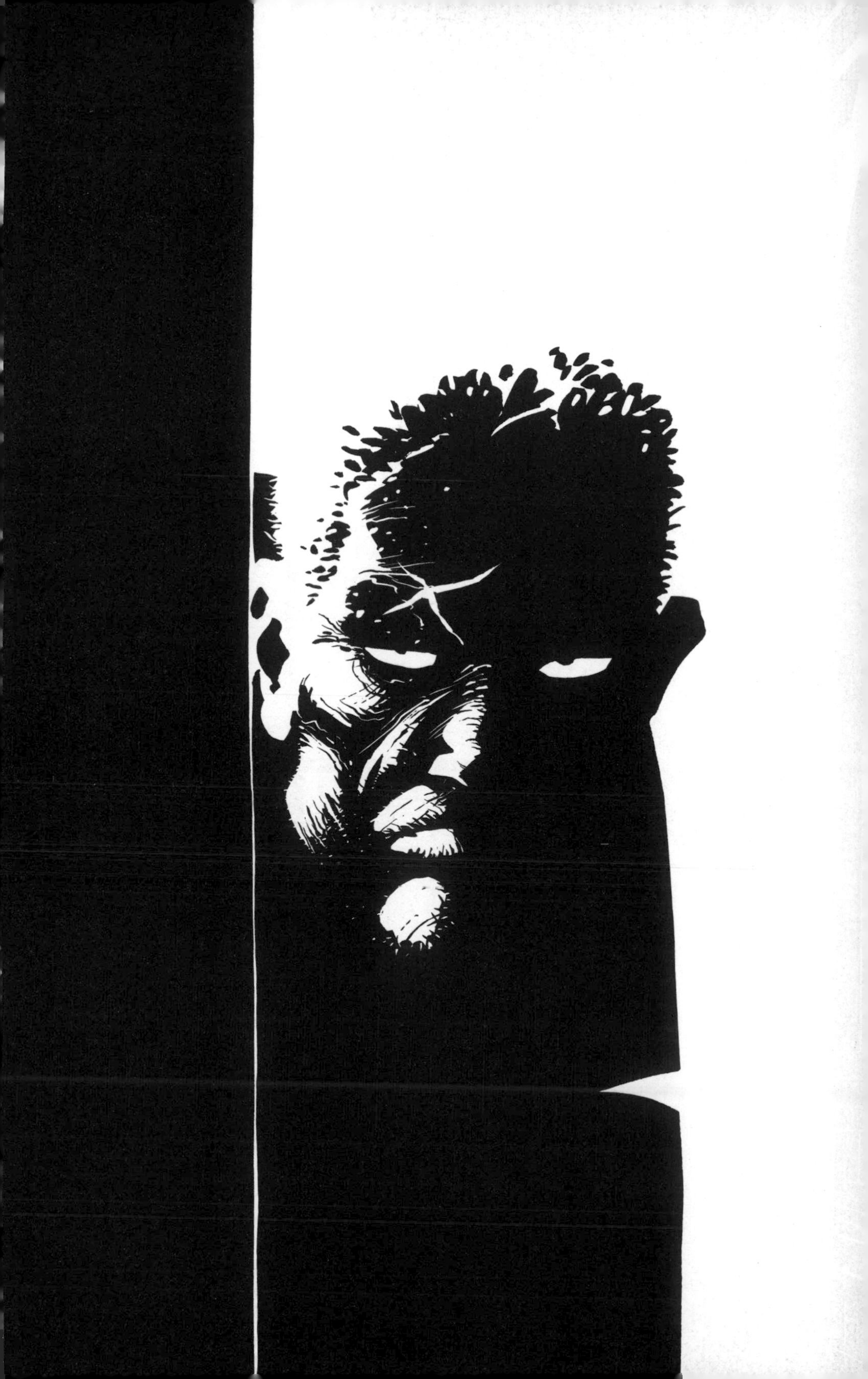

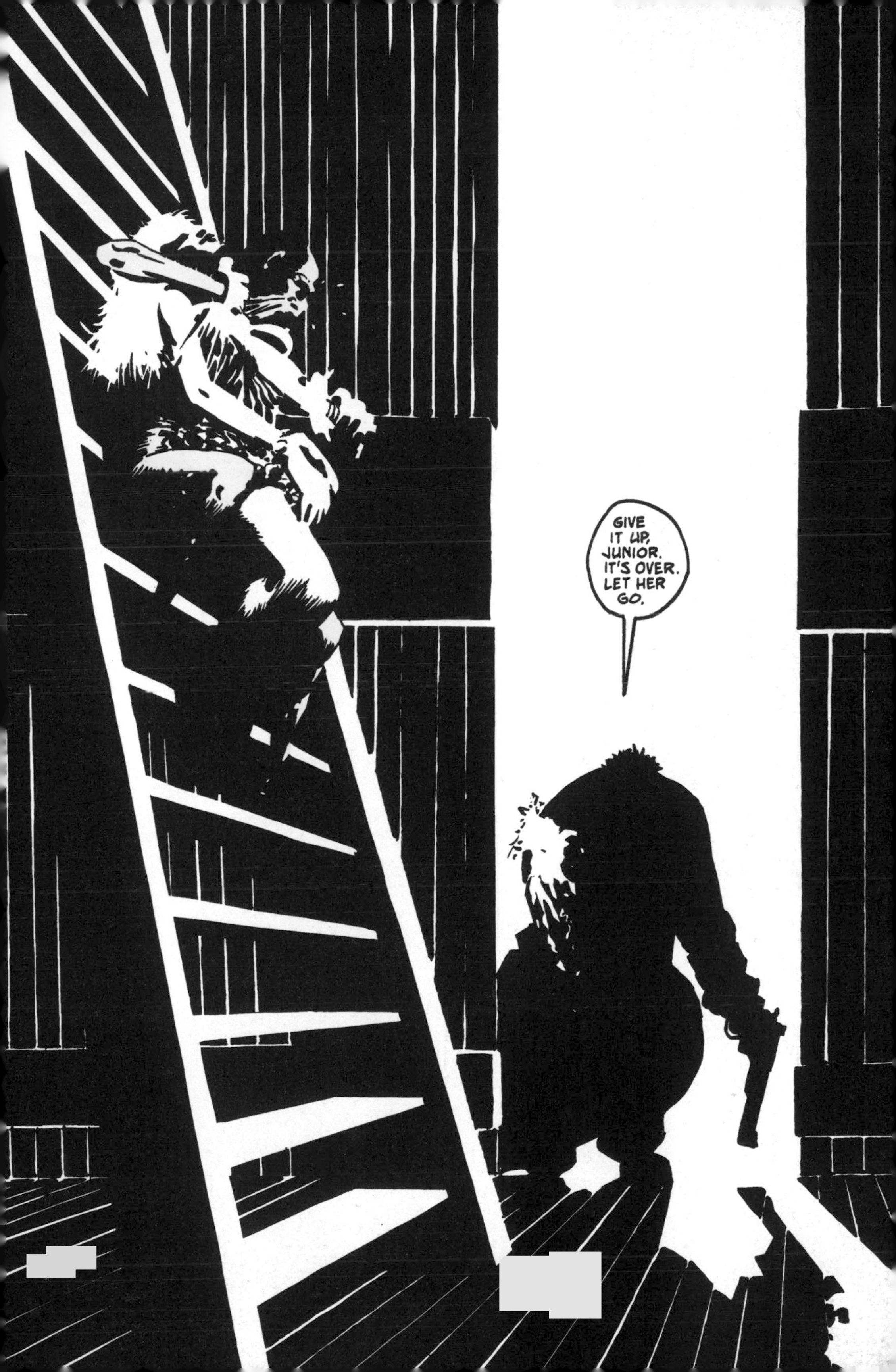
GIVE IT UP, JUNIOR. IT'S OVER. LET HER GO.

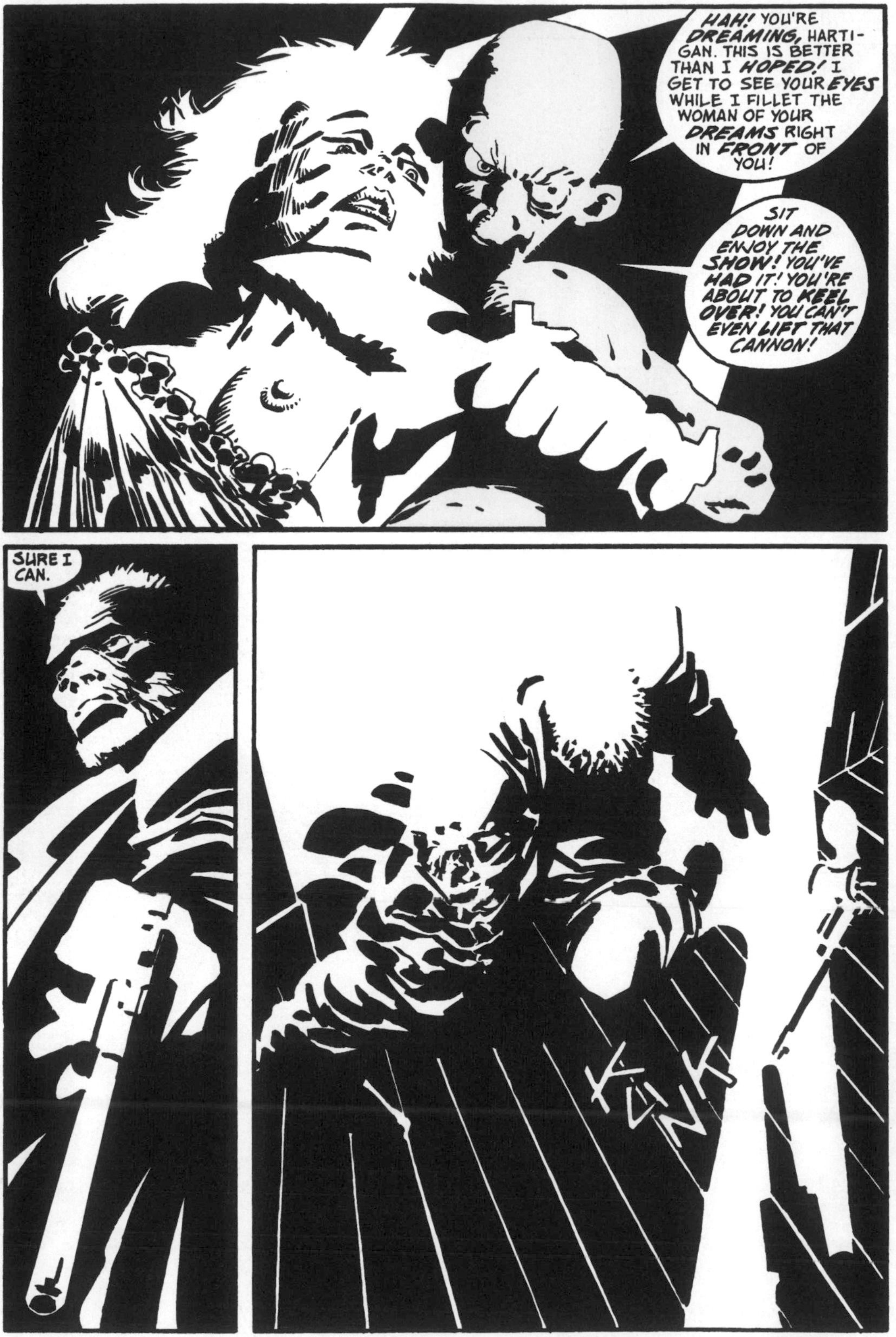
HAH! YOU'RE DREAMING, HARTIGAN. THIS IS BETTER THAN I HOPED! I GET TO SEE YOUR EYES WHILE I FILLET THE WOMAN OF YOUR DREAMS RIGHT IN FRONT OF YOU!
SIT DOWN AND ENJOY THE SHOW! YOU'VE HAD IT! YOU'RE ABOUT TO KEEL OVER! YOU CAN'T EVEN LIFT THAT CANNON!
SURE I CAN.
KLUNK

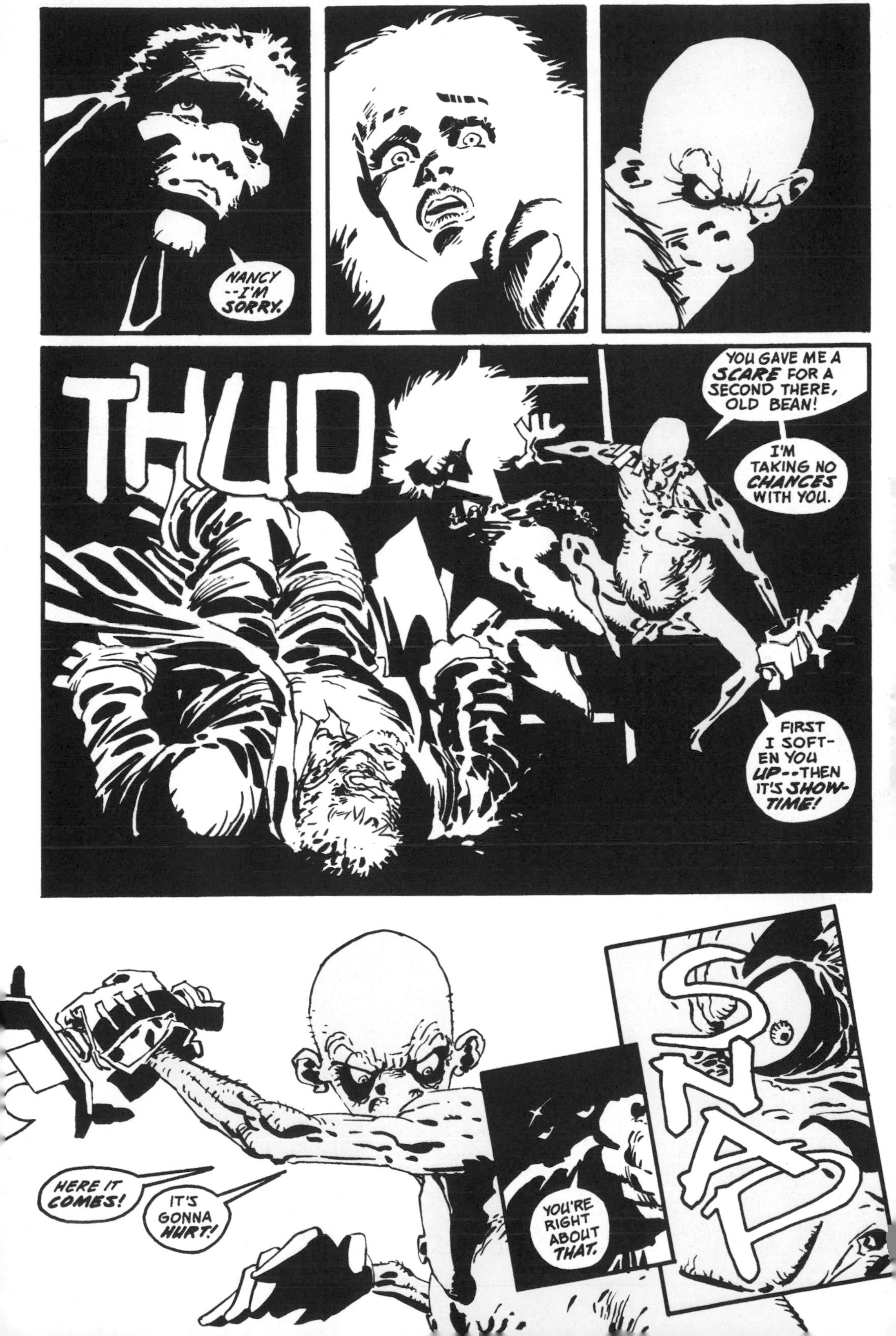

NANCY --I'M SORRY.
THUD
YOU GAVE ME A SCARE FOR A SECOND THERE, OLD BEAN!
I'M TAKING NO CHANCES WITH YOU.
FIRST I SOFT-EN YOU UP--THEN IT'S SHOW-TIME!
HERE IT COMES!
IT'S GONNA HURT!
YOU'RE RIGHT ABOUT THAT.
SNAP

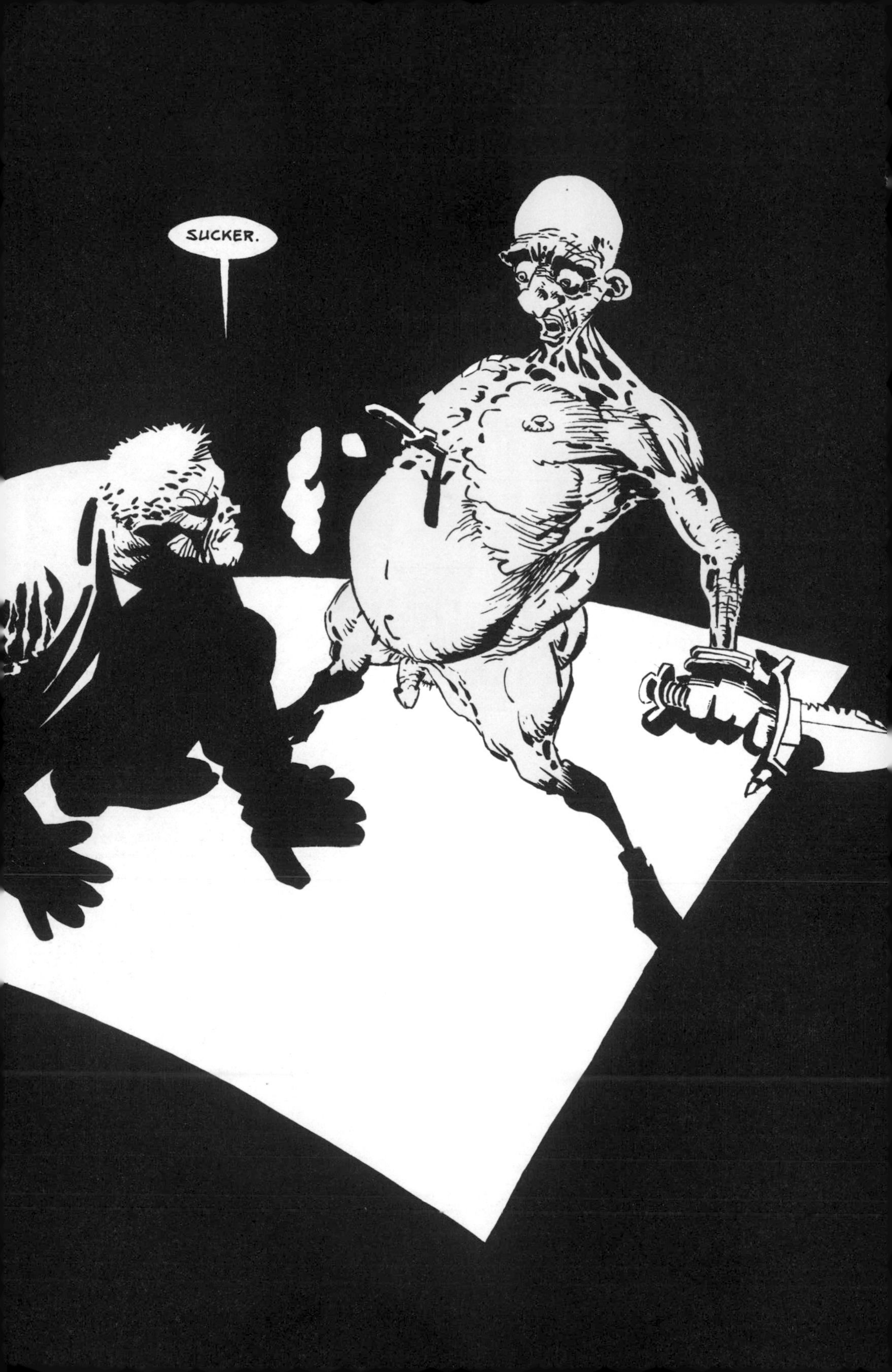
SUCKER.

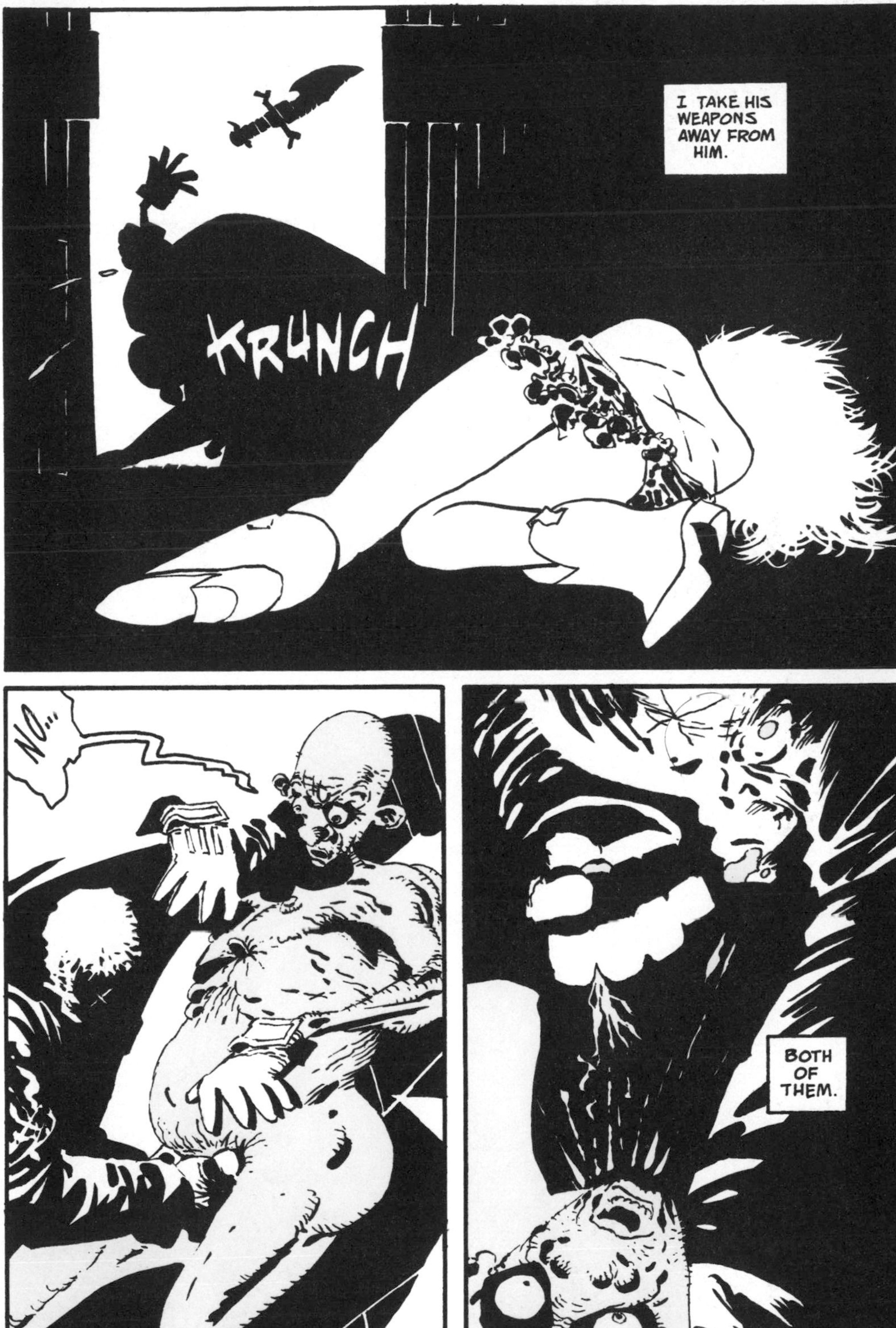
I TAKE HIS WEAPONS AWAY FROM HIM.
KRUNCH
NO...
BOTH OF THEM.

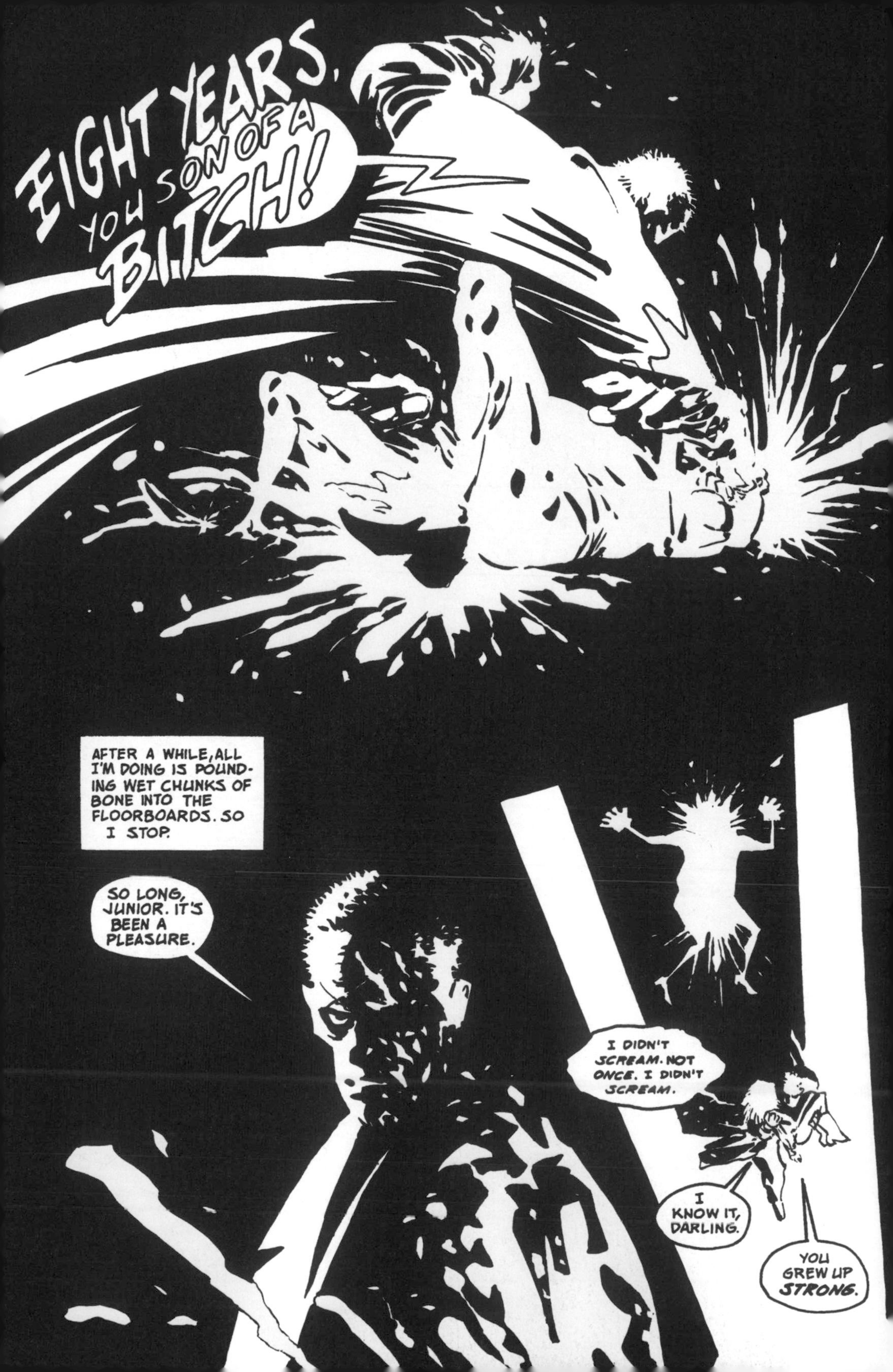
EIGHT YEARS, YOU SON OF A BITCH!
AFTER A WHILE, ALL I'M DOING IS POUNDING WET CHUNKS OF BONE INTO THE FLOORBOARDS. SO I STOP.
SO LONG, JUNIOR. IT'S BEEN A PLEASURE.
I DIDN'T *SCREAM*. NOT ONCE. I DIDN'T *SCREAM*.
I KNOW IT, DARLING.
YOU GREW UP ***STRONG***.

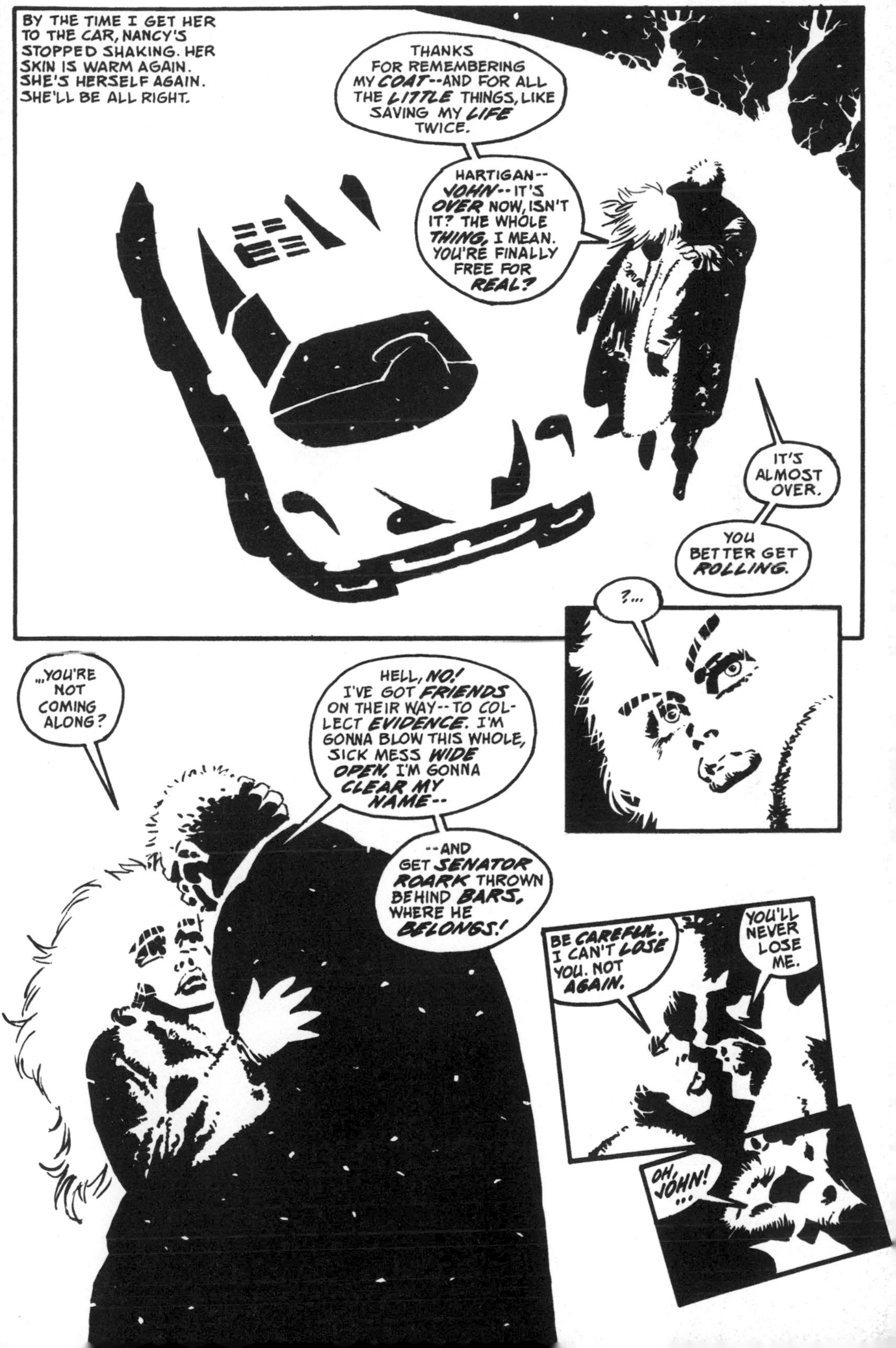

BY THE TIME I GET HER TO THE CAR, NANCY'S STOPPED SHAKING. HER SKIN IS WARM AGAIN. SHE'S HERSELF AGAIN. SHE'LL BE ALL RIGHT.
THANKS FOR REMEMBERING MY COAT--AND FOR ALL THE LITTLE THINGS, LIKE SAVING MY LIFE TWICE.
HARTIGAN-- JOHN--IT'S OVER NOW, ISN'T IT? THE WHOLE THING, I MEAN. YOU'RE FINALLY FREE FOR REAL?
IT'S ALMOST OVER.
YOU BETTER GET ROLLING.
?...
...YOU'RE NOT COMING ALONG?
HELL, NO! I'VE GOT FRIENDS ON THEIR WAY--TO COLLECT EVIDENCE. I'M GONNA BLOW THIS WHOLE, SICK MESS WIDE OPEN. I'M GONNA CLEAR MY NAME--
--AND GET SENATOR ROARK THROWN BEHIND BARS, WHERE HE BELONGS!
BE CAREFUL. I CAN'T LOSE YOU. NOT AGAIN.
YOU'LL NEVER LOSE ME.
OH, JOHN! ...

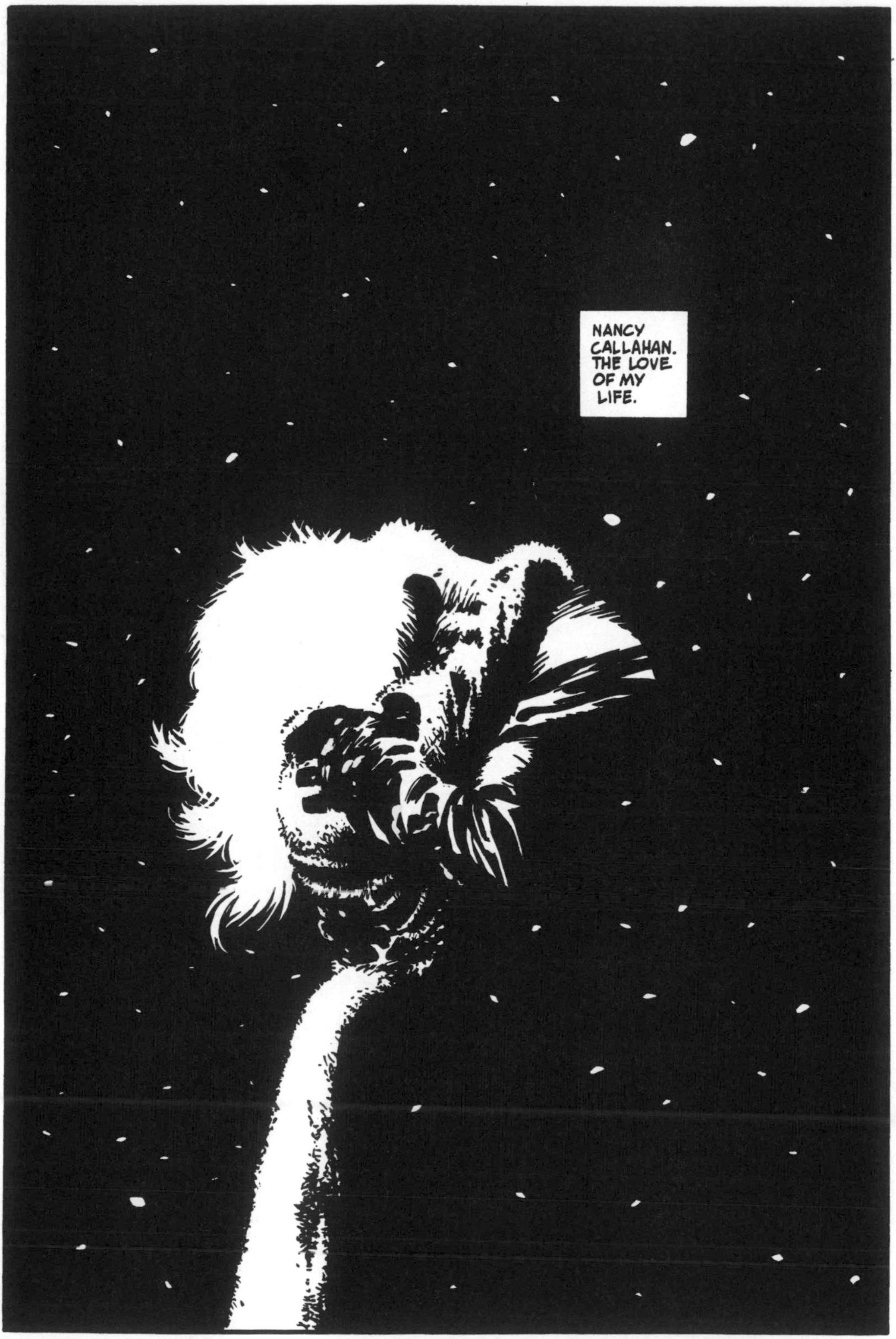
NANCY CALLAHAN. THE LOVE OF MY LIFE.

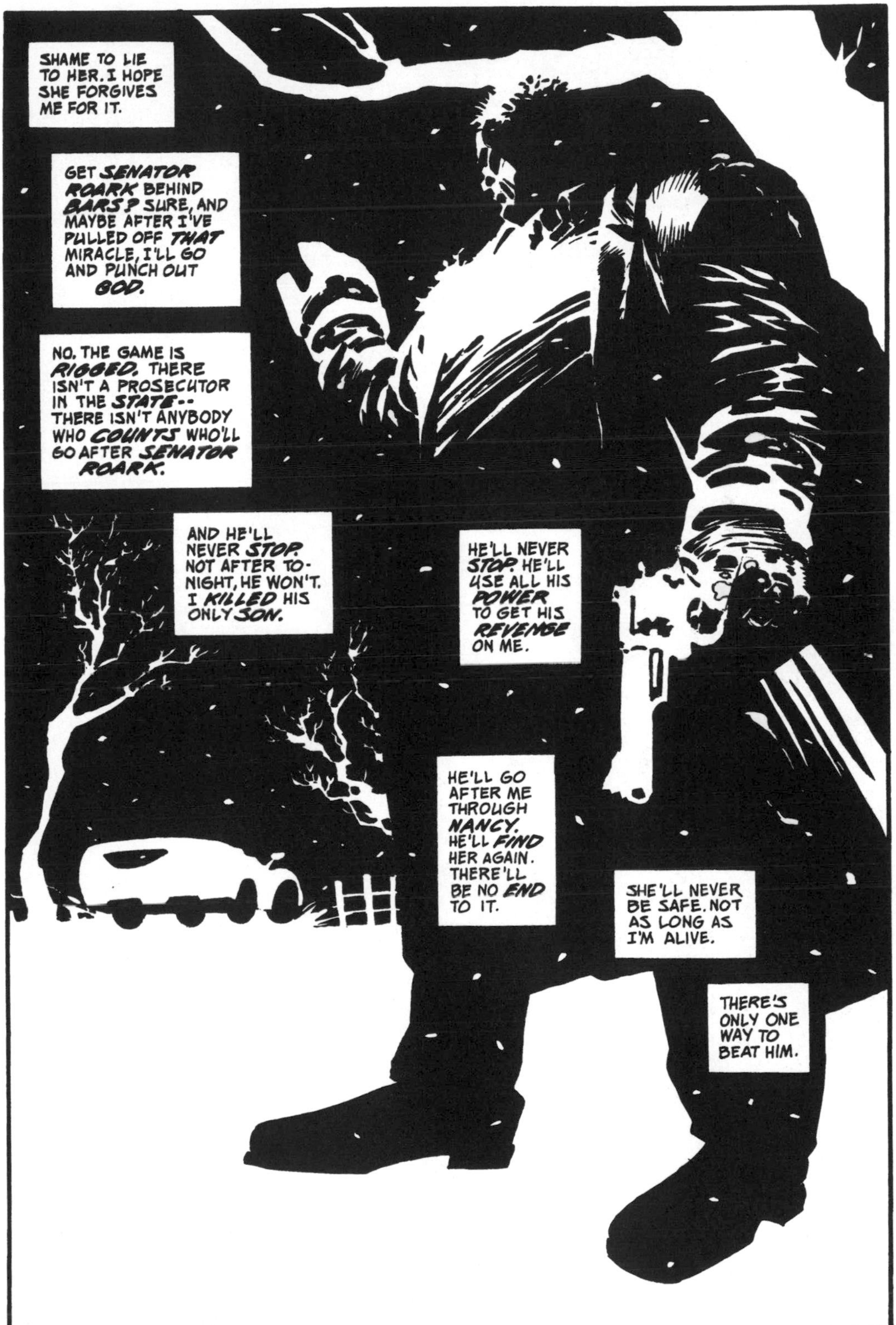
SHAME TO LIE TO HER. I HOPE SHE FORGIVES ME FOR IT.
GET SENATOR ROARK BEHIND BARS? SURE, AND MAYBE AFTER I'VE PULLED OFF THAT MIRACLE, I'LL GO AND PUNCH OUT GOD.
NO. THE GAME IS RIGGED. THERE ISN'T A PROSECUTOR IN THE STATE-- THERE ISN'T ANYBODY WHO COUNTS WHO'LL GO AFTER SENATOR ROARK.
AND HE'LL NEVER STOP. NOT AFTER TO-NIGHT, HE WON'T. I KILLED HIS ONLY SON.
HE'LL NEVER STOP. HE'LL USE ALL HIS POWER TO GET HIS REVENGE ON ME.
HE'LL GO AFTER ME THROUGH NANCY. HE'LL FIND HER AGAIN. THERE'LL BE NO END TO IT.
SHE'LL NEVER BE SAFE. NOT AS LONG AS I'M ALIVE.
THERE'S ONLY ONE WAY TO BEAT HIM.

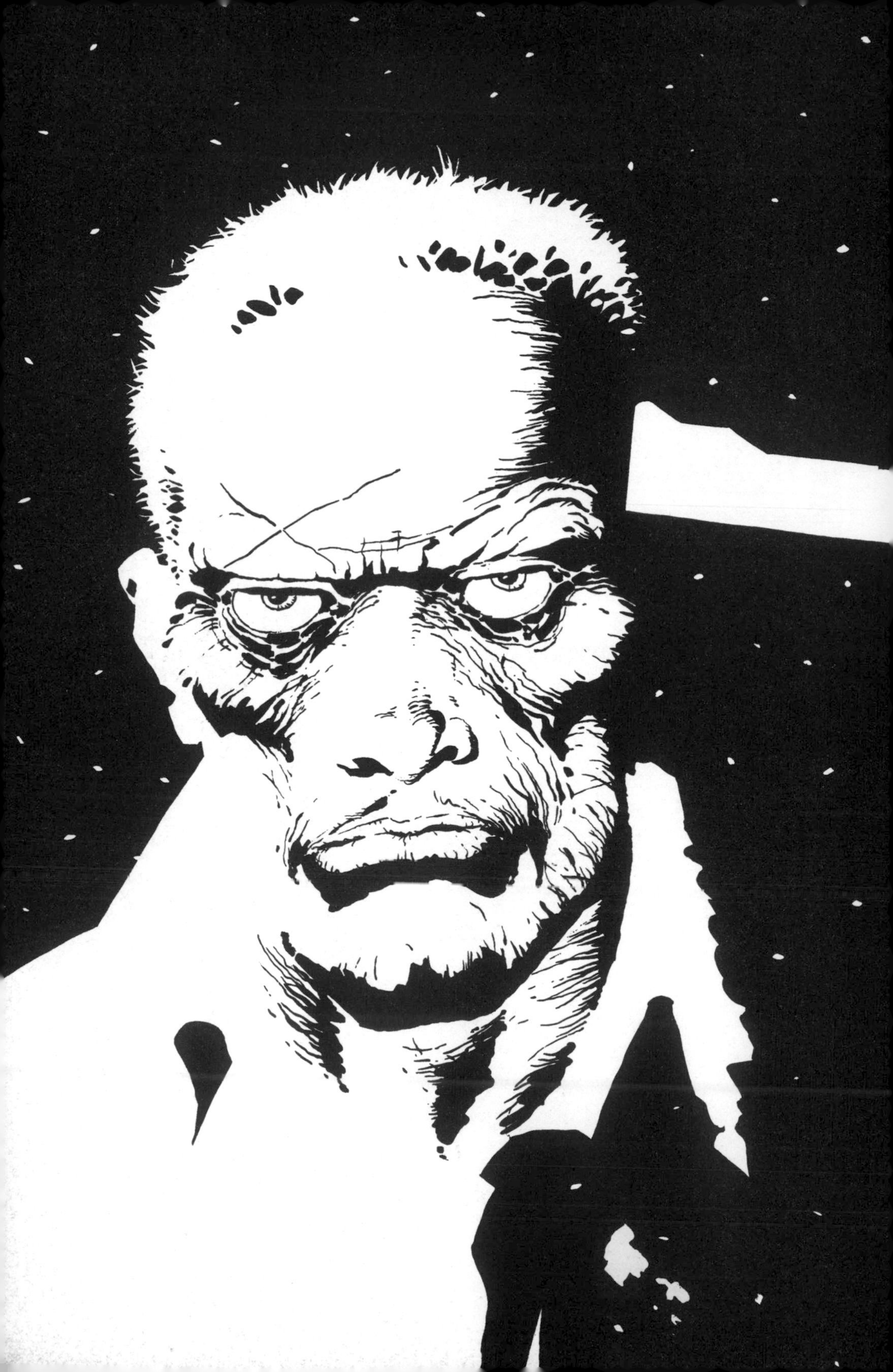

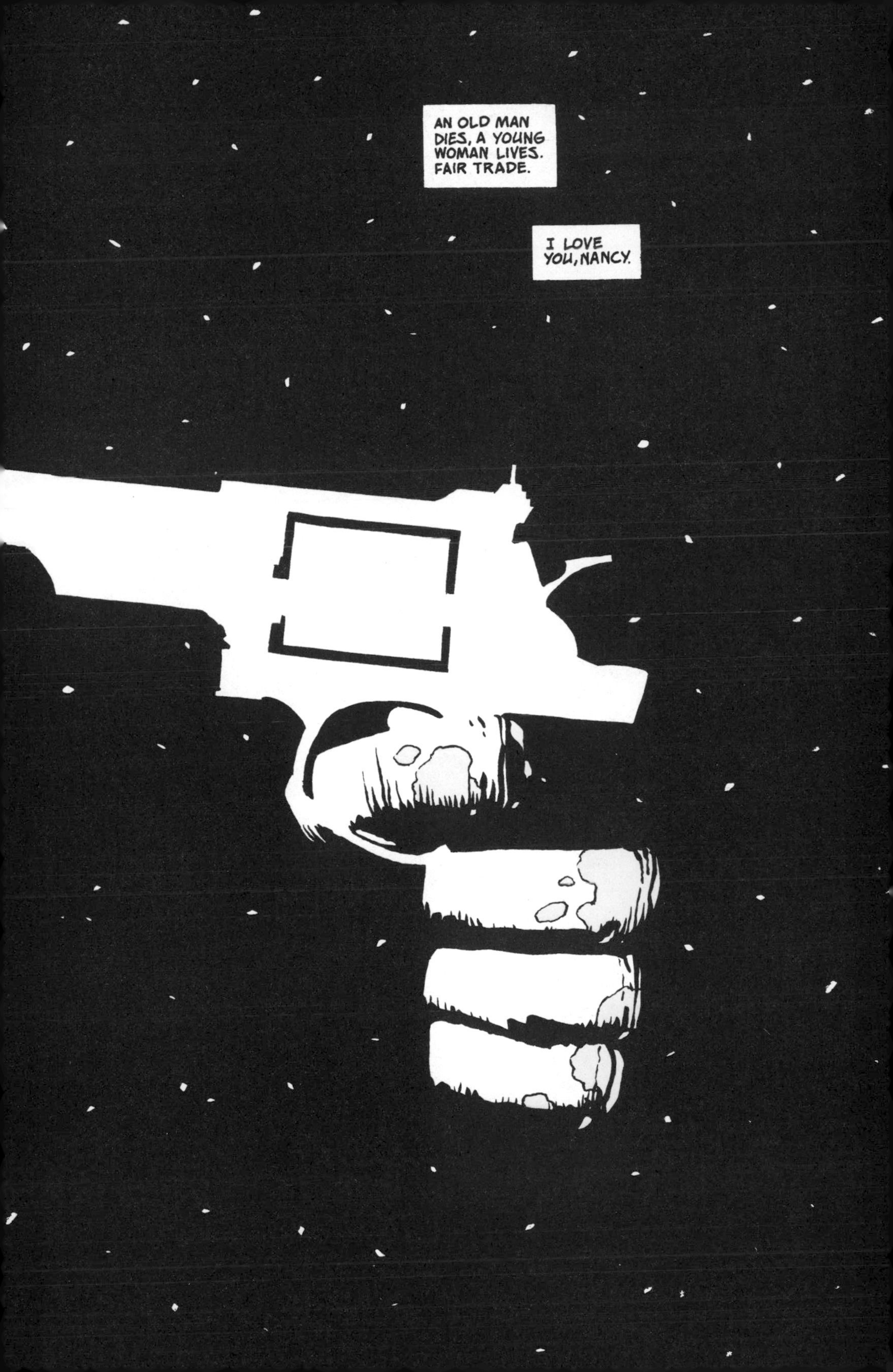
AN OLD MAN DIES, A YOUNG WOMAN LIVES. FAIR TRADE.
I LOVE YOU, NANCY.

BO

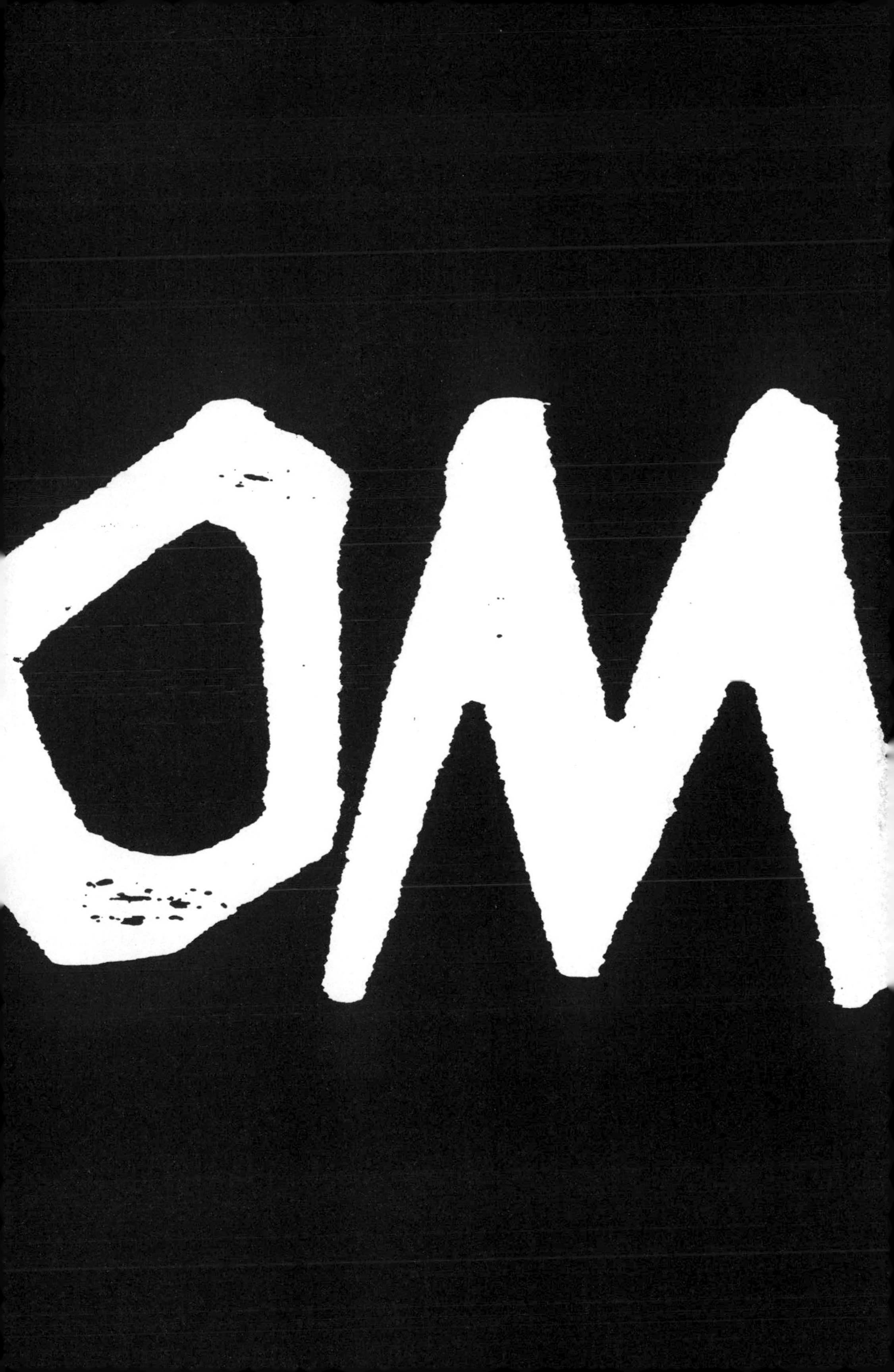
OM

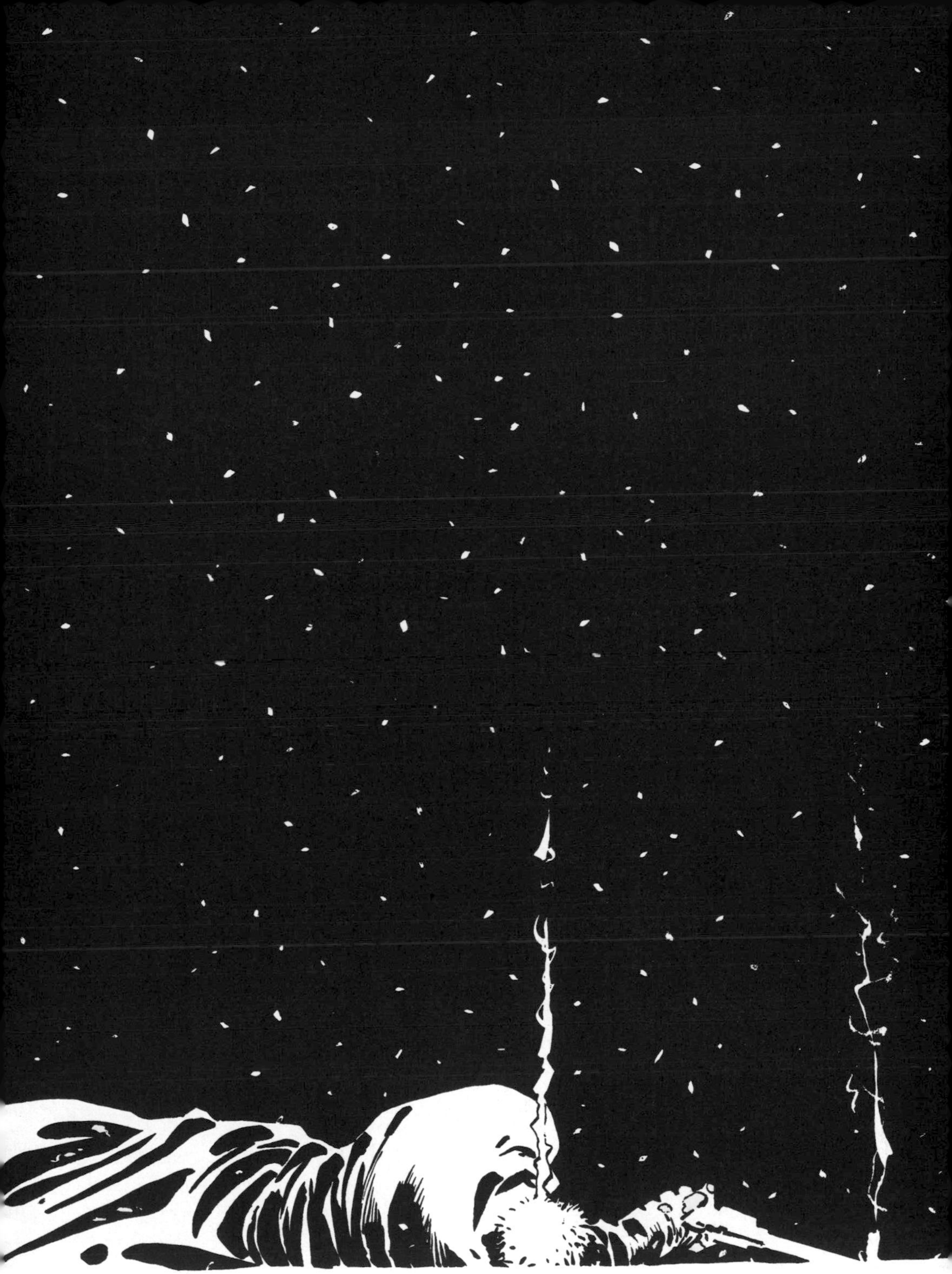

THE END

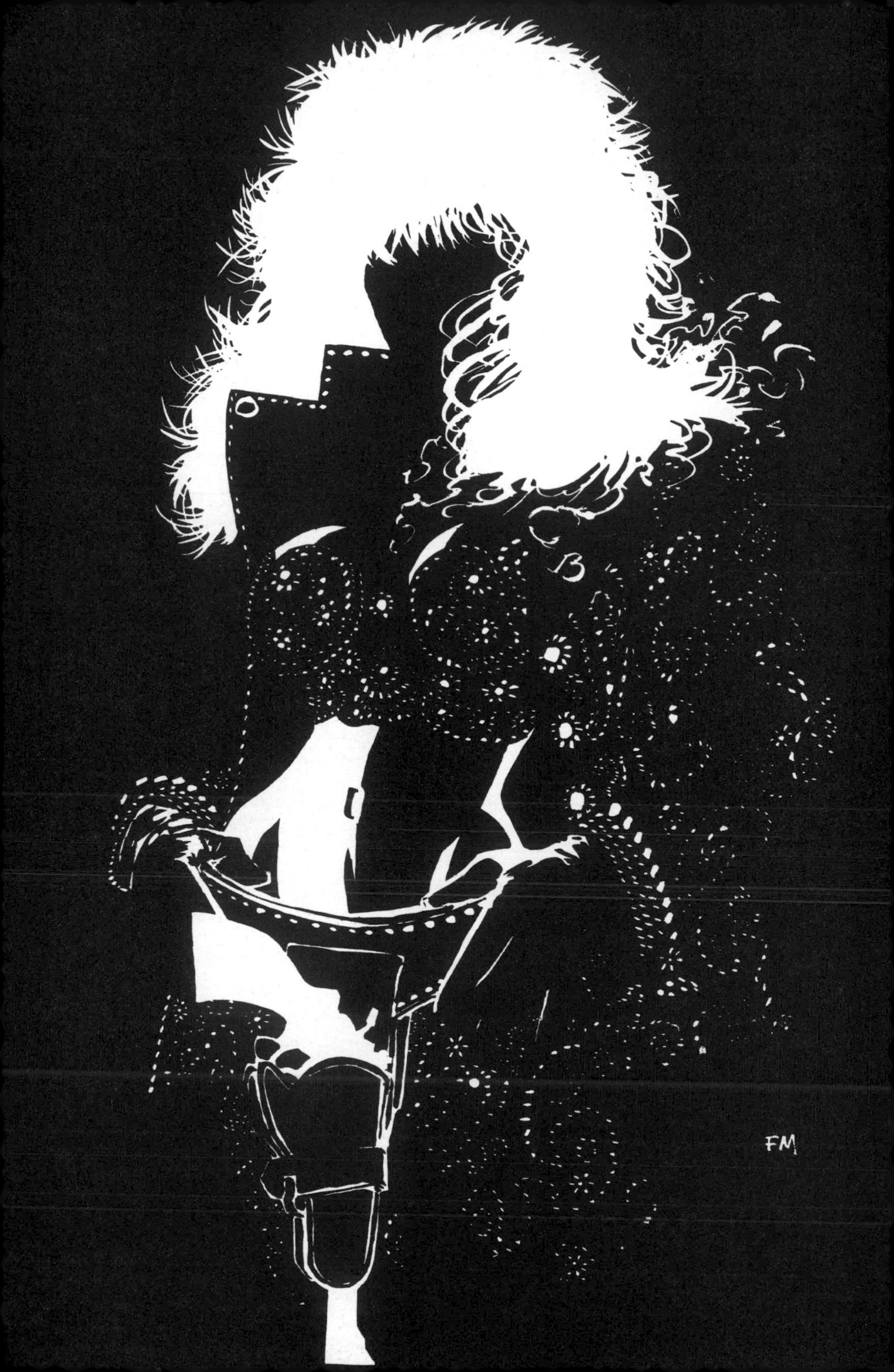
FM

DEDICATED TO
ROBERT PHILIP MILLER

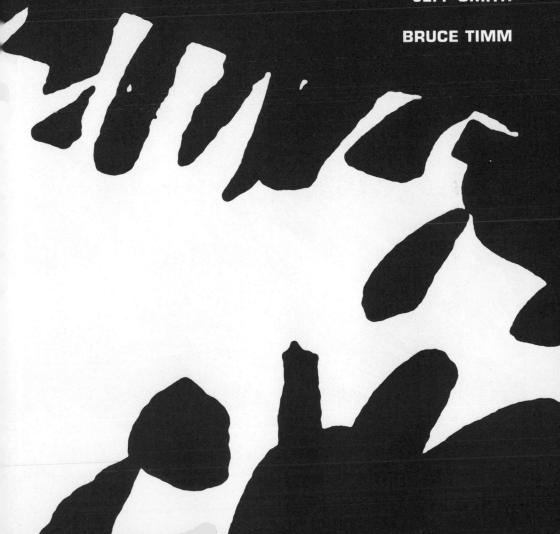

PINUP GALLERY

MIKE ALLRED

KYLE BAKER

JEFF SMITH

BRUCE TIMM

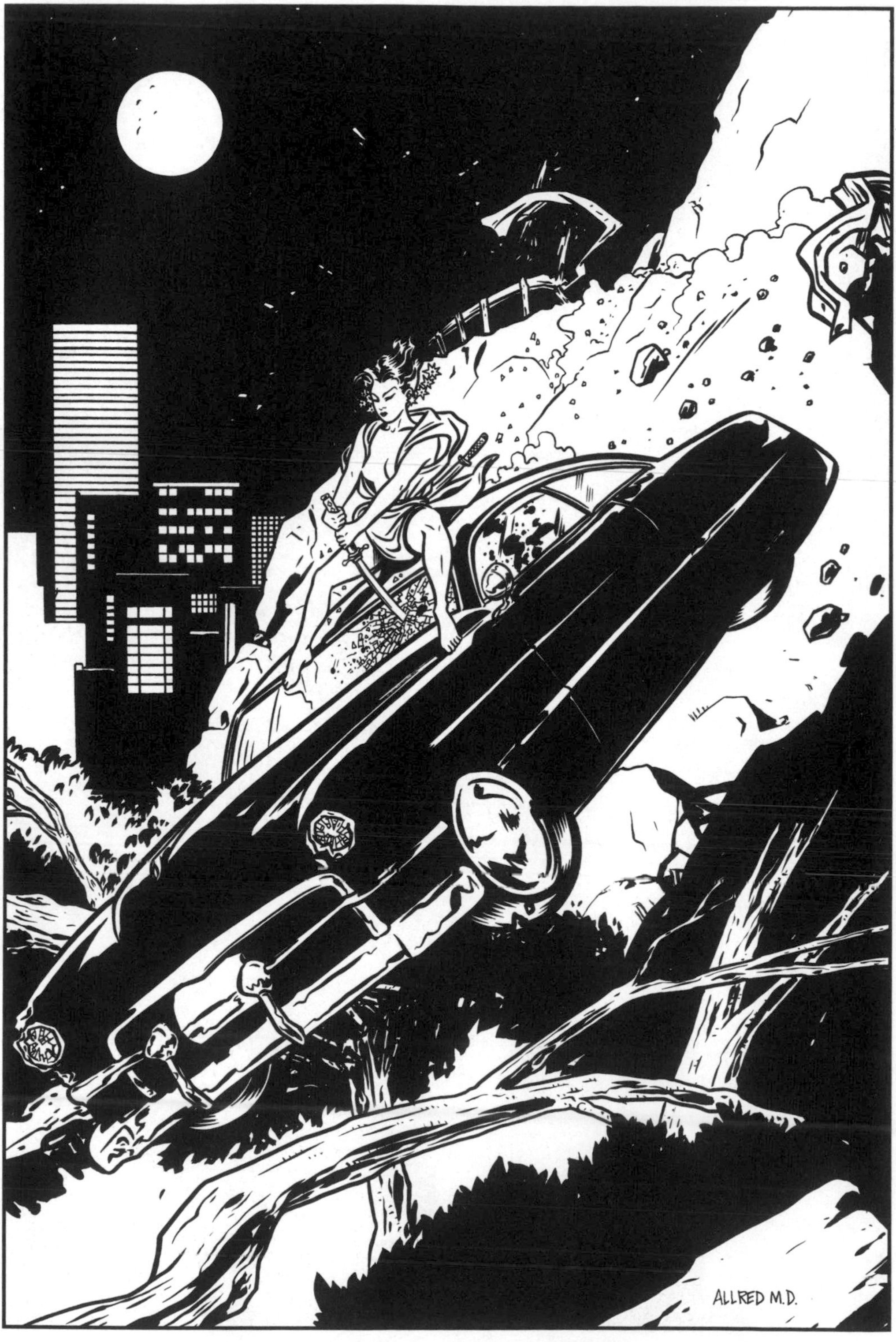
ALLRED M.D.

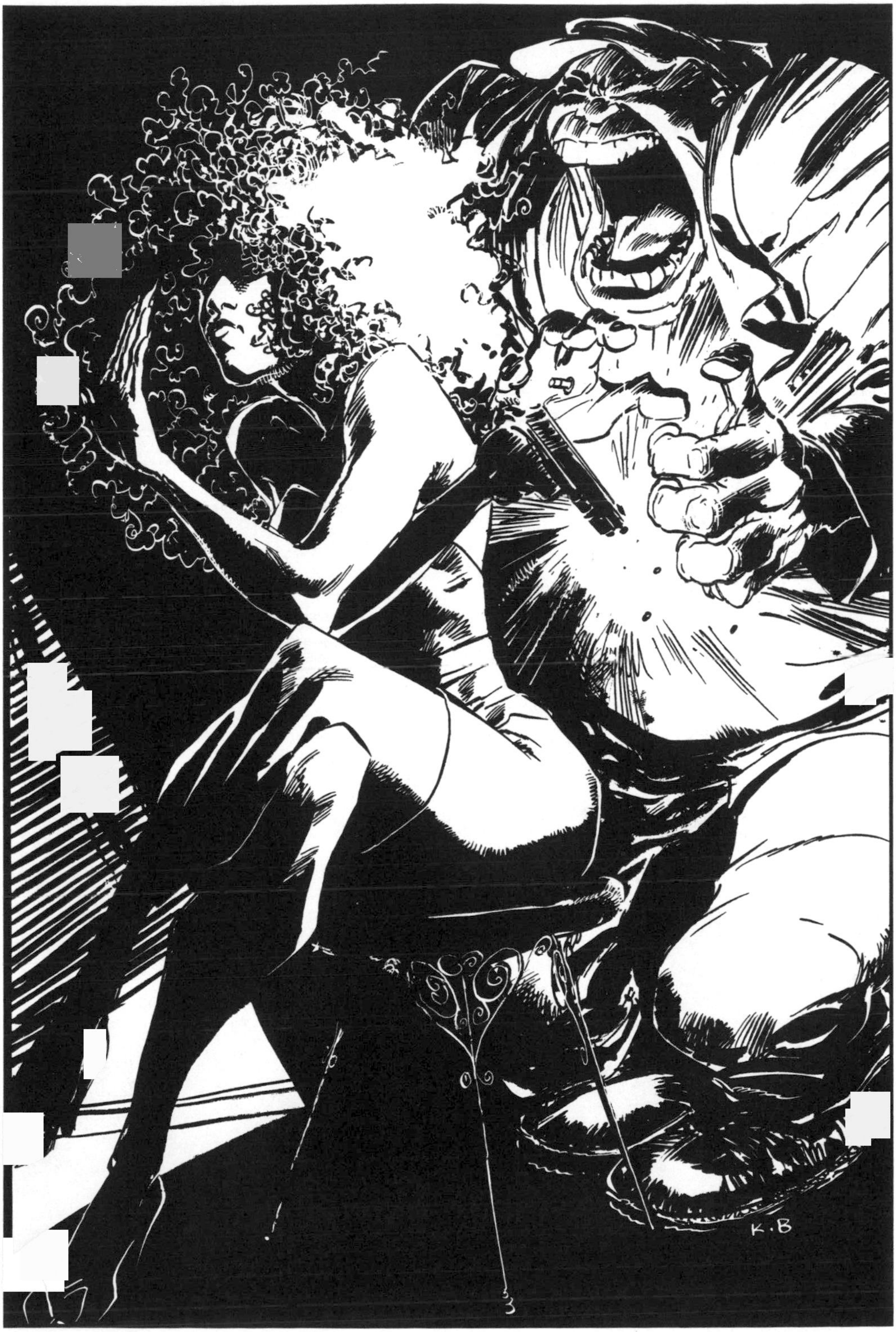
K.B

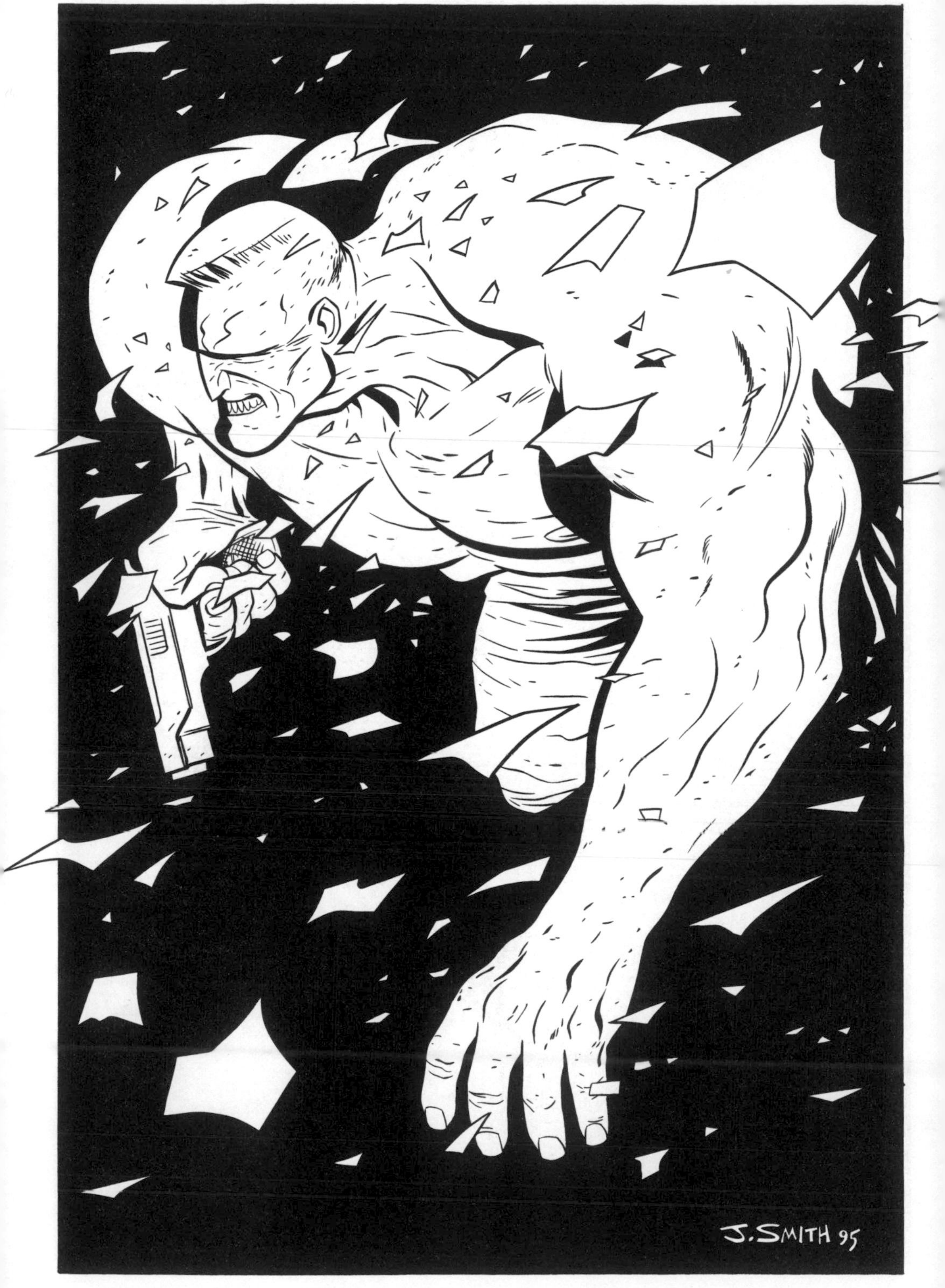
J. SMITH 95

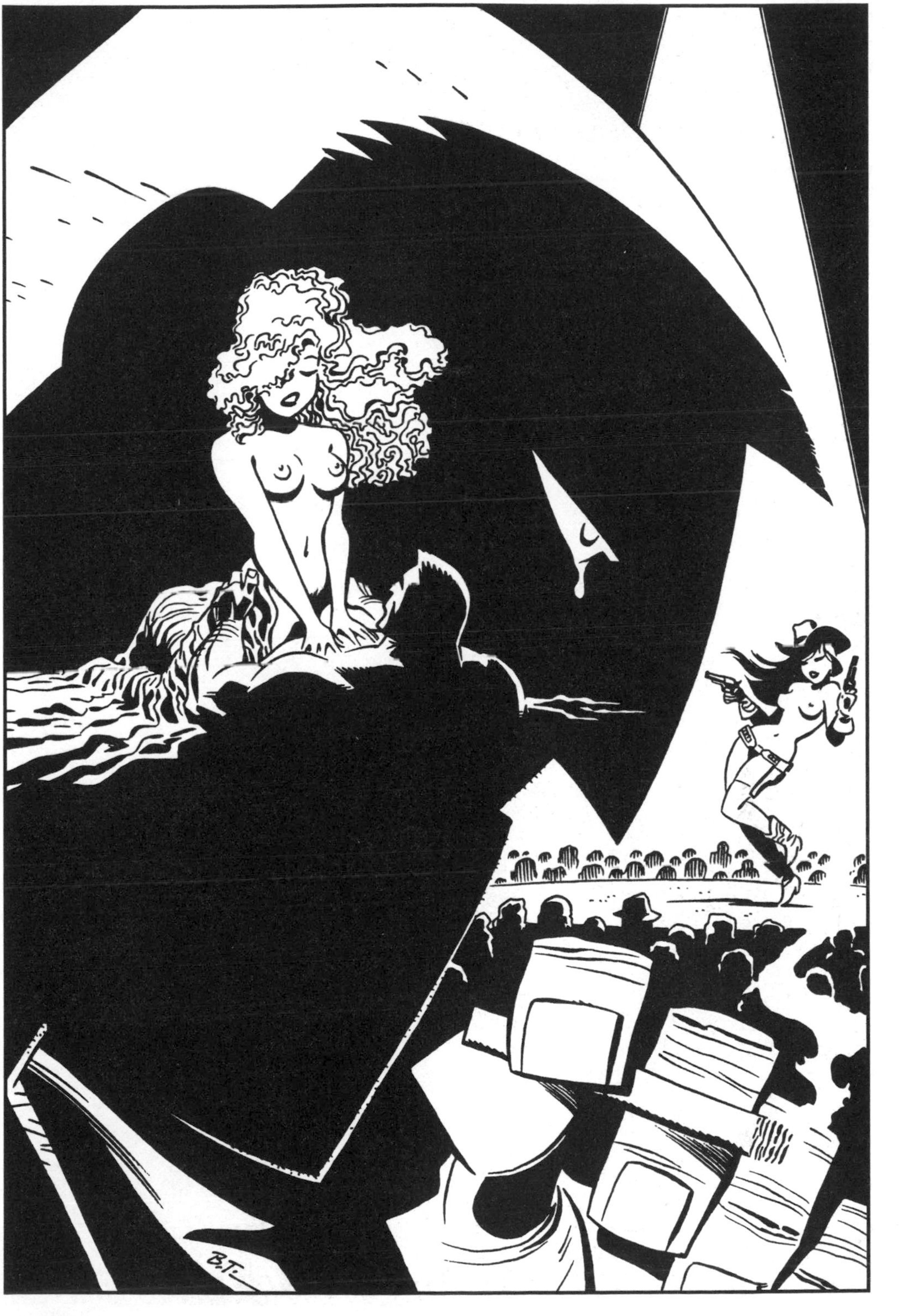
B.T.

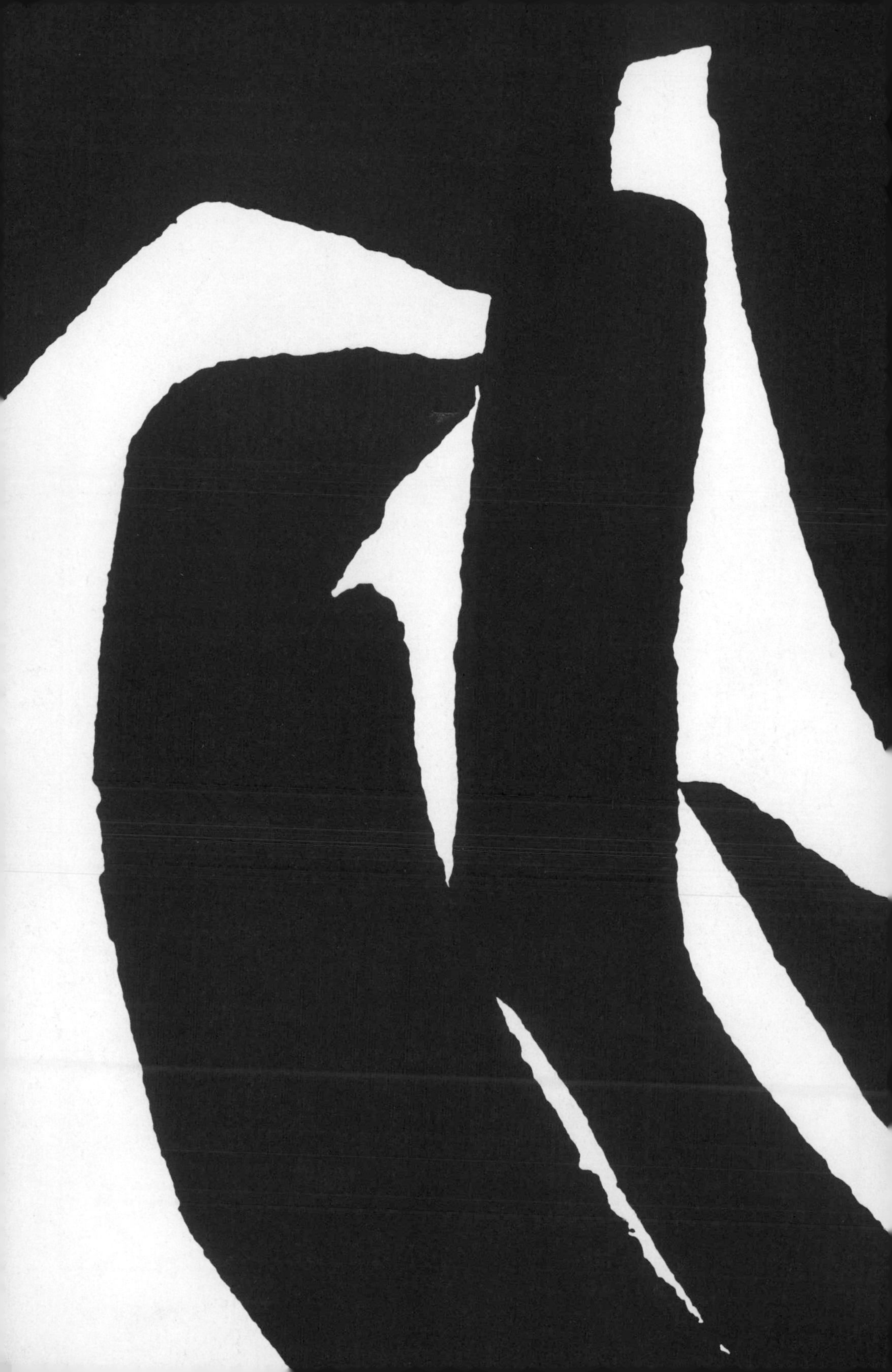

COVER
GALLERY

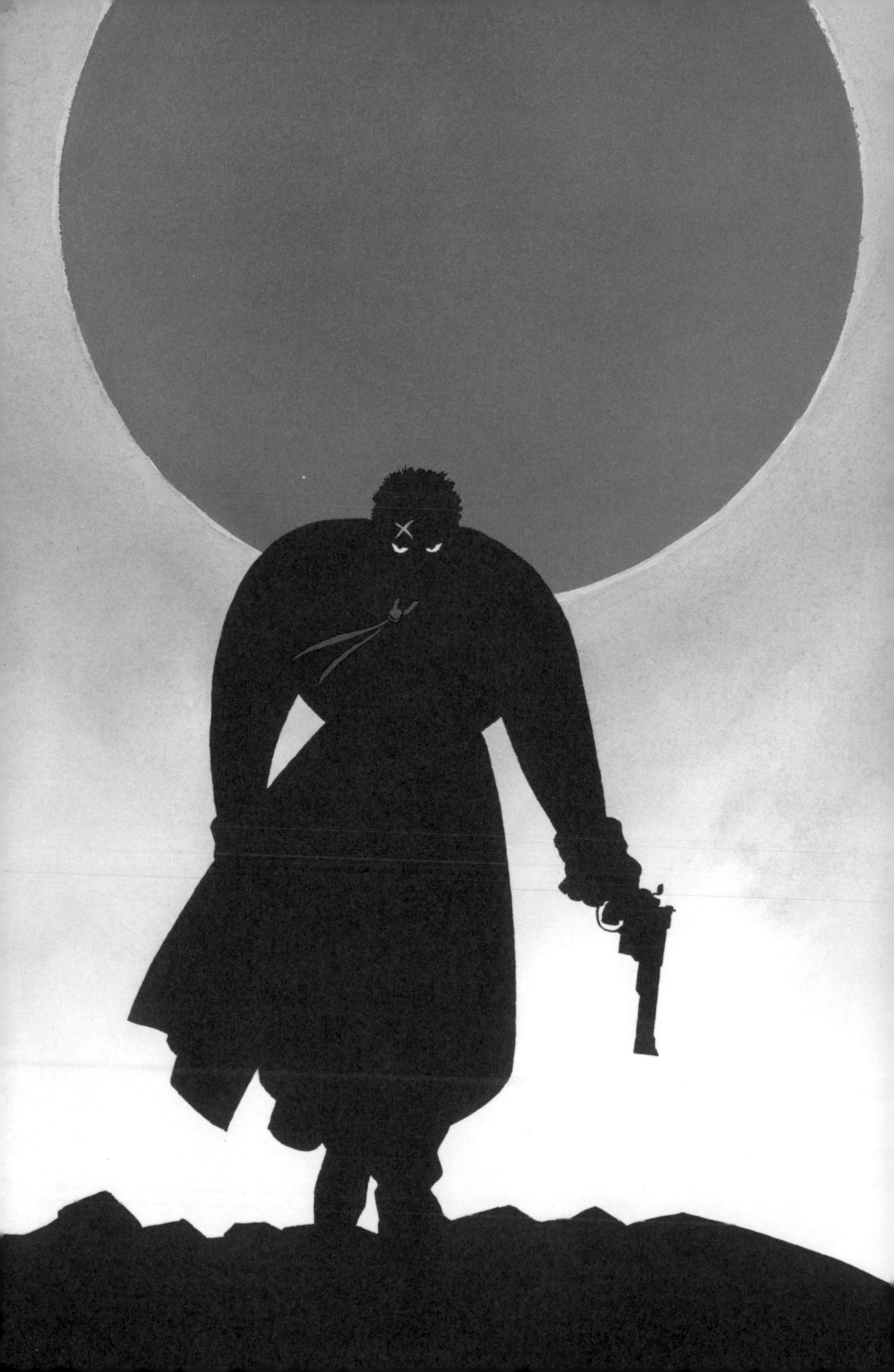

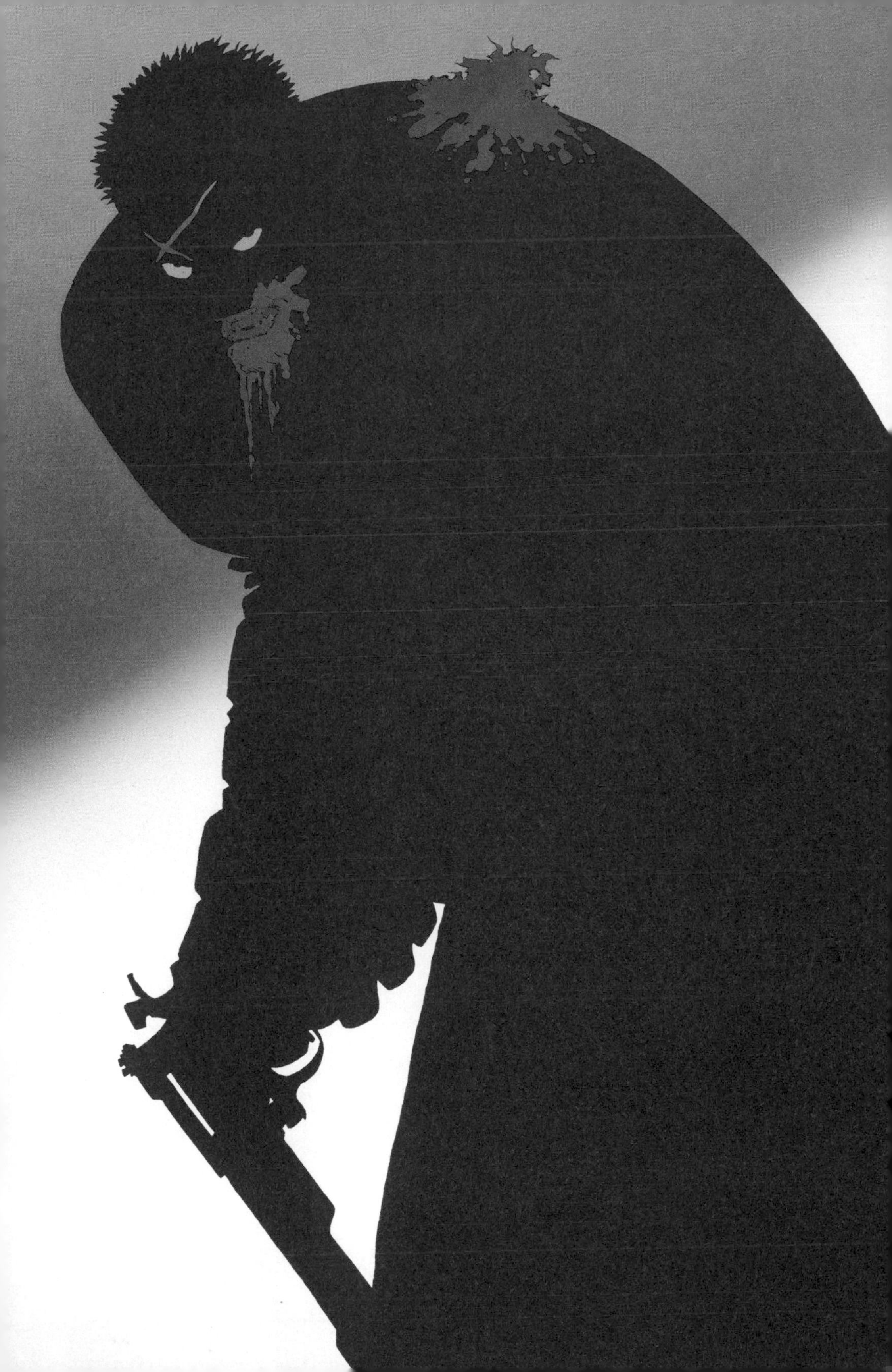

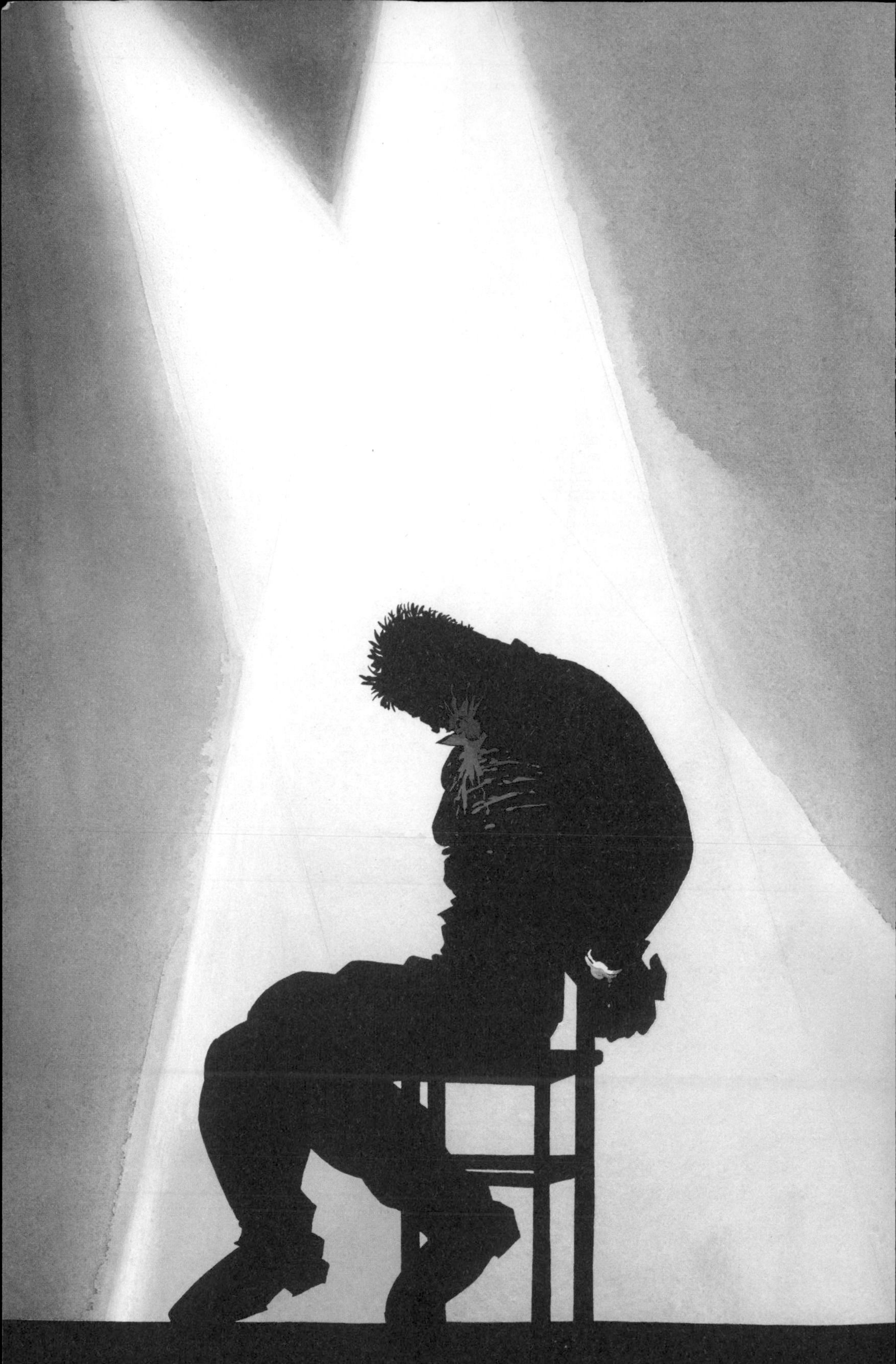

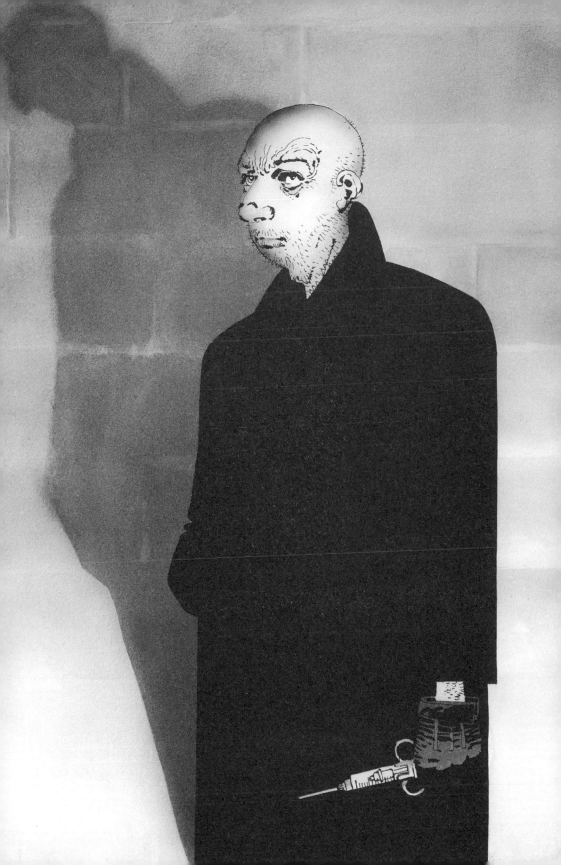

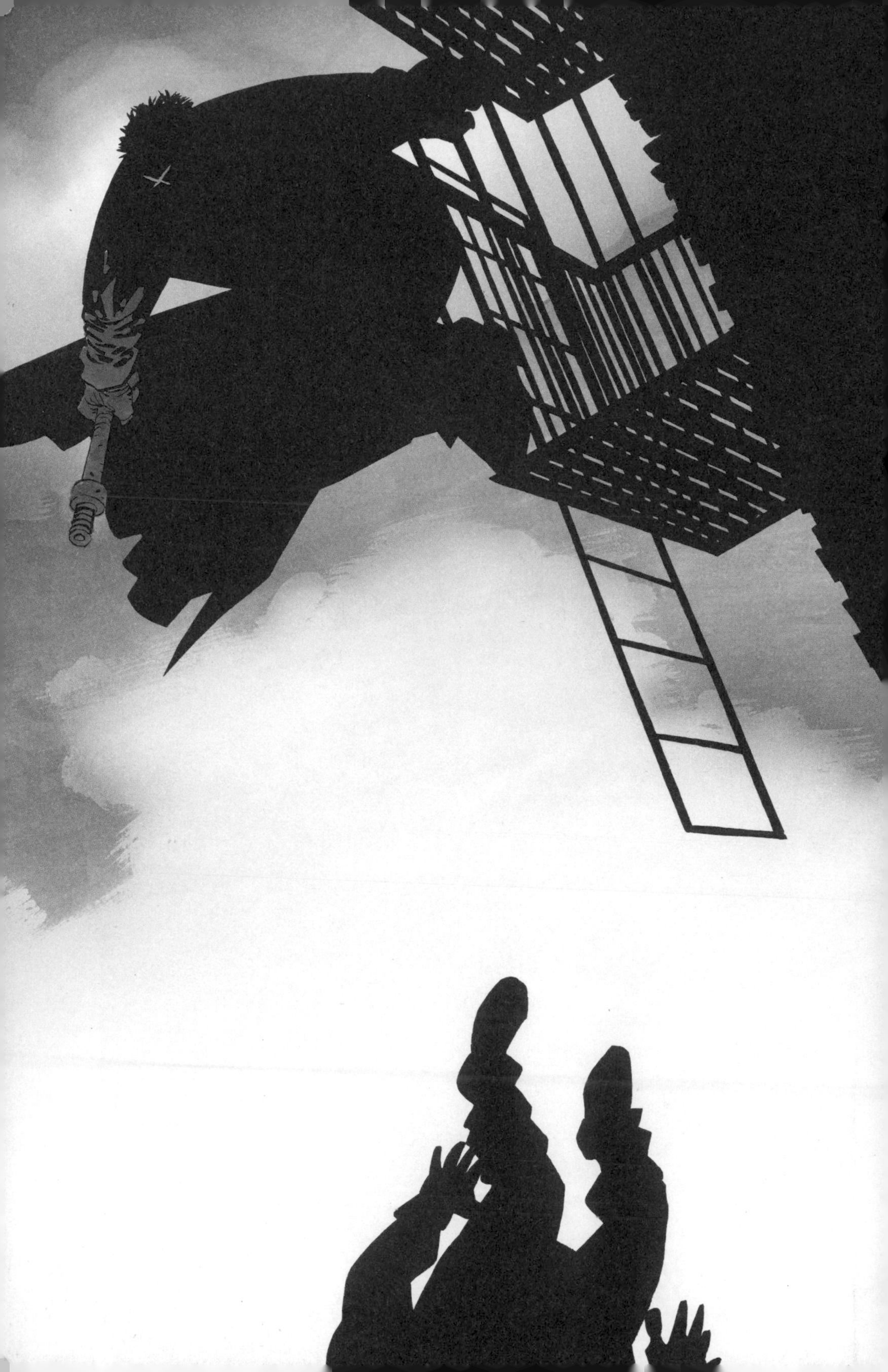